KAUTILYAN ARTHASASTRA

KAUTILYAN ARTHASASTRA

M.B. CHANDE

Published by

ATLANTIC

PUBLISHERS & DISTRIBUTORS (P) LTD

7/22, Ansari Road, Darya Ganj, New Delhi-110002
Phones : +91-11-40775252, 23273880, 23275880, 23280451
Fax : +91-11-23285873
Web : www.atlanticbooks.com
E-mail : orders@atlanticbooks.com
Branch Office
5, Nallathambi Street, Wallajah Road, Chennai-600002
Phones : +91-44-64611085
E-mail : chennai@atlanticbooks.com

Printed in India at Nice Printing Press, A-33/3A, Site-IV, Industrial Area, Sahibabad, Ghaziabad, U.P.

Dedicated to

My late Parents, and
Shri Gopal Damodar Tamaskar and
Martyrs of the Country

Prin. Yoganand Kale
Pro. Vice-Chancellor
Ravindranath Tagore Marg,
Nagpur - 440 001.

RAMNAVMI
Dated 16-4-97

Athah to Granth Jidnyasa

Shri M.B. Chande, a retired Police Officer and a student even at the age of 78 years, has written the book, 'Kautilyan Arthasastra' which is an exhaustive and erudite treatise encompassing Kautilyan administrative system, incorporating dimensional parameters of police, defence, espionage, counter-espionage, punishments, judicial process, both criminal and civil, finance, economy, trade, intelligence, and the entire gamut of home and foreign affairs, including the executive machinery/ methods *inter alia*, the King, ruler of the state, and its subjects, and the methods of ensuring their sustained beneficence, well-being and protection. Marked by depth of understanding, clarity and erudition, the book stands out as an outstanding and significant contribution to the existing source material.

The book has been composed into two parts. The part one describes a broad outline of *Kautilyan Arthasastra*. The part two deals with the English translation of fifteen books originally written in Sanskrit by Arya Chanakya (Kautilya). The author, Shri M.B. Chande, tried to correlate the writings of Kautilya to the present-day environment. He has been successful in bringing out the importance and relevance of Kautilyan philosophy. Uptil now, there has been very little analysis of this nature.

The preface of this book is worth reading. Successful application of some of the methods, propagated by Kautilya, during the career of the author as the police officer has given a practical touch. In fact, Shri Chande has followed the dictum, 'Practice before you preach'. These methods, according to the author, were found to be very useful, result-oriented and fructuous.

The part one of the book consists of eleven chapters: Arthasastra its scope and origin, the relation of Arthasastra to Dharmasastra, the concept, form and source of Kautilya Arthasastra, the author (Kautilya), the date of Arthasastra, the State in Arthasastra, society and social life, state economy, state administration, law and administration of justice, internal security and defence and external affairs. Each of these chapters is a lucid commentary on the topic.

Kautilyan Arthasastra is generally misconstrued as the science of economics. The gamut of economics is only a limited part of the Kautilyan philosophy explained in the Arthasastra. The *Kautilyan Arthasastra* has two aims:

1. It seeks to show that the ruler should protect his territory through proper administration of the state; and
2. It denotes how the territory should be conquered, provided with benevolent and wholesome administration for the general benefit of the inhabitants.

A cursory glance at these aims clearly shows that Arya Chanakya's philosophy in the Kautilyan Arthasastra touches almost every aspect under the jurisdiction of the state. The author of the book, Shri M.B. Chande, has been extremely successful in explaining the different concepts, contents and their relevance to the present day environment of the various topics of the eleven chapters comprising the part one of the book.

The part two of the book deals with the English translation of the fifteen books written by Kautilya in Sanskrit. The part two consists of eighteen chapters. Out of these, the Book Two (the activities of the Heads of the Departments) is very well elaborated (there are three chapters devoted to this aspect). The Fifteen Books translated into English cover the topics ranging from education to the measures of foreign policy. A perusal of the list of topics and their depth, covered in the Fifteen Books, simply makes one wonderstruck and also leads to think about Arya Chanakya with reverence. Knowledge appears to be personified in the form of Kautilya. The author, Shri M.B. Chande, has been successful in explaining the topics covered in these Fifteen Books. Kudos to him!

Kautilyan Arthasastra represents the beautiful flower of the Indian Thought (Bharatiya Vichar Sadhana). It is a treatise on the art of benevolent governance with efficiency by a monarch in the era of 330 B.C. The comprehensive treatment of the topics is unmatched, unparalleled and simply amazing. Even in the today's set up, the relevance of Kautilya's preaching cannot be belittled. Shri K.R. Malkani, the Member of the Rajya Sabha and the ex-editor of the weekly, 'The Organiser' has recently written an article in the *Indian Express* which clearly brings out the worsening conditions of our administration. Read in the context of this article, this scholarly work by Shri M.B. Chande assumes a greater significance.

I congratulate Shri M.B. Chande for accomplishing a feat *par excellence* and wish him every success.

PRIN. YOGANAND KALE
Pro. Vice-Chancellor

Preface

I retired in 1976, after 39 years of Police Service in all its branches, including the Central Bureau of Investigation (CBI) and the security of VVIPs. From my early youth I was infatuated by Chandragupta Maurya and his preceptor Acharya Chanakya—commonly known as Kautilya. My study of Indian History from the ancient period enabled me to author, Shree Ram Janamabhoomi in 1992; A Concise Encyclopaedia of Indian History in 1995; and the Police in India in 1995-96.

Throughout my Police Service I have used some of the methods propounded by Kautilya in his treatise 'Arthasastra' and I found them very useful, result-oriented and fructuous. The Arthasastra was quoted by me in my book: "The Police in India" with significant elaboration. What painfully astounded me was that many people, including professionals with high educational qualifications, have a very scant notion or idea about Arthasastra and its author Kautilya. Surprisingly, many of them construe the Arthasastra to be dealing only with trade, economics, commerce and finance, whereas to another section, Kautilya was knave as he had advocated and used impious or unethical means to achieve his objective. More stunning and abominable, are their dislike and fading recognition of Kautilya and his Arthasastra.

Kautilya had canonized an exhaustive system of policing and laid down several grades of bureaucracy, and the traditions set by him were followed throughout the history world over. Though the Police had functioned in a rudimentary fashion since the Vedic period, the credit of creating a separate agency of Police with specific powers of administration, implementation and enforcement of laws and regulations, and for the prevention of crimes, their investigation, prosecution of criminals in the antiquity of 330 B.C. goes to Arthasastra of Kautilya. From law enforcing agency, a complicated espionage and counter-espionage system, control of border traffic, smuggling and immigration, custom and revenue investigations, effective vigilance, including political and military intelligence, war stratagems and the battle tactics and strategies, including various battle arrays, Kautilya had not left anything to chance. Besides, he had written authoritatively on forensic science and criminology, almost of the modern standard.

Therefore, to commemorate Kautilya in particular, and the various authors, in general, I ventured to compose the present book. I have fully drawn on the contributions made by various early scholars and authors. This will ever remain my unredeemable debt. Although I am aware this exercise is not without diffidence, or shortcoming, in all humility, I place before the readers my modest efforts in the form of this book, tendering an advance apology for any mistake that might have cropped inadvertently.

I am grateful to Mr. Mangesh Deshpande and Miss Jagruti Taikar of M/s Phenix Computers, Dharampeth, Nagpur for correctly processing my manuscript and the printer and publisher for publishing this book in a short time.

My wife, Radha's immeasurable assistance is beyond redemption. Equally, I am grateful to my brother, Keshao Chande (Retired Director, Agriculture, M.P. Indore); and my daughters-in law Dr. Mrudul, D.G.O. W/o Dr. Anil, M.D. and Suneeta, M. Com, B.Ed. W/o Colonel Harish and daughter Anuradha B.Sc. W/o Colonel (Retd.) Anant Dhodapker, B.E.M.B.A. for scouring out the relative references used in the compilation of this book.

In reverence, I dedicate this book to my late parents and Mr. Gopal Damodhar Tamaskar, as also the martyrs of the country. Late Mr. G.D. Tamaskar had authored from 1920 to 1950 over 50 books and 500 articles, mostly on the subjects of Political Science, History, Administration, and various others related to social problems of his time. Most of his books are out of print and they are not extant. His 'Kautilya Arthasastra Mimonsa' in Hindi was published in 1926, when the British Government was adopting all possible atrocious methods to nip in the bud the 'Non-cooperation Movement' launched by the Indian National Congress under the stewardship of Mahatma Gandhi and this Hindi translation was his sterling patriotic achievement in that era of ruthless suppression by the British of Indian patriotism.

I thank prof. V.M. Jha, Director of Centre of Advanced Studies in Sanskrit (CASS) University of Pune for making available to me the summaries of the papers presented by various learned persons at the Seminar sponsored by the Sahitya Akademy during 1995-96. They were useful to me in the composition of this book. I am equally grateful to Professor B.G. Tamaskar of Pune for supplying to me the necessary material and proper guidance for writing this book.

The *Kautilyan Arthasastra* has been composed by me in two parts.

Part one seeks to present a broad outline of Kautilyan teaching on the following connected topics: (1) Scope and origin. (2) The relation of Arthasastra with Dharmasastra. (3) Contents, form and source. (4) Author Kautilya. (5) State in Arthasastra. (6) Society and social life. (7) State economy. (8) State administrative machinery. (9) Law and administration of Justice. (10) Internal Security. (11) Defence and external affairs.

Part two is the English translation of Fifteen Books written by Kautilya in Sanskrit around 330 B.C. This is the basic Arthasastra. The translation of Arthasastra was made in English by Prof. R.P. Kangale and several other writers. Its Hindi translation was made in 1926, by the late literary giant G.D. Tamaskar. Its Marathi translations were made by Shri H.A. Bhave and Mr. and Mrs. Hardas. I abundantly relayed their version in my book.

I have made my own observations about the political situation *vis-a-vis* the state and its administration in India from the Vedic period to date, as also the condition of the subjects; for, I feel that though the Arthasastra was expounded in about 330 B.C. by Kautilya, it is still relevant and capable to arrest the rapidly worsening condition of people on account of their depleted moral values, *inter alia*, mal-governance, mal-administration, and all pervading corruption, both in the administration and society. The means and measures suggested in it can thoroughly clean the augean stable prevalent these days.

The waning regard of Kautilyan Arthasastra by many of the Indian elites is most probably ascribed to the impact on them of the European hegemony of Political Philosophy propounded by Plato, Aristotle, Machiavelli, Bismarck, Hobbes, Engel, Marx and others in the wake of demorcratic set up of governance. This ingratitude of our people towards such a great patriot and a distinguished philosopher and author is something unpalatable and that actuated me to write the present book.

The Western Political Philosophy tried to discover such a state of administrative set up as would be able to render the best kind of life for the common man through ethical means, as they believe that these high ideals were intended to be realised by man, here on this earth, in his lifetime, and the state was intended to make their realisation possible. This has reflected in their political thinking and paying much more attention to the form of the state organisation, and citizens' place in it. Diversely, Arthasastra of Kautilya is not concerned with the problem of the highest good of man as it was beyond the pale of this treatise, because traditionally it was the domain of Dharmasastra, which enunciated spiritual edicts about morality, or pious or righteous behaviour. The king was the head of the state, and was duty bound, as per the ancient traditions, to respect, protect, preserve, and ensure their compliance; and at the same time he had no jurisdiction to modify, correct, or annul any of them. Therefore, Kautilya had paid all his attention to the practical aspect of state organisation and the government for the well-being and the protection of the state along with its subjects. Moreover, he took measures of public welfare and prosperity through the administrative machinery, and his political tenets permeated with the spirit of national unity.

As no political theory can be detached from history and its environs, it has to be basically formed, moulded and tuned in consonance with the socio-political expediencies and exigencies. Aristotle was the senior contemporary of Kautilya and died around 322 B.C. His coveted pupil was Alexander, whose blatant and avaricious invasion and depredations of Indian territory, killing thousands of innocent people, razing to ground of several cities, outraging women, taking them and their children as slaves and other depravities undoubtedly exhibited callous consideration to the righteous teaching of his preceptor. That was the period when Indian sovereignty was in great and imminent jeopardy, and in order to stop the triumphant march of Alexander and drive him away 'lock, stock and barrel' together with his Greek forces from the Indian soil, Kautilya sublimely expoused and expounded this science in his Arthasastra, which incorporated multi-dimensional parameters of defence, protection, punishment, judicial process—both criminal and civil, economy, the entire gamut of home and foreign affairs, administrative machinery, *inter alia*, the king of the state and its subjects. In this context, what Kautilya did not know was no knowledge.

Today as a result of democratic set up in the country, the administrative machinery is largely different. A number of departments visualized in Arthasastra has no place in the present pattern. On the other hand, a number of departments has come into being which the Arthasastra had little conception at that period of time. Nevertheless, what it has to say on some matters, is not without relevance even in the present-day conditions. Its views about the state employees, their qualification and appointment, their despicable corruptibility, disparaging attitude and apathy towards public interest and their lawful needs, and ways of keeping them in check are not quite irrelevant when scandalous scams like sugar, telecommunication, allotment of houses, animal husbandry, urea imports, and several others, big or small, by high government officials, former governors, chief ministers, etc., made the country suffer unprecedented and fabulous losses running into several thousand crores of rupees. On the top of it, these leaders had indulged in fabrication of evidence to defend themselves. The Central Bureau of Investigation (C.B.I.) tried to bale out some of them. The High Court and the Supreme Court were compelled to monitor the investigations of the aberrant police functionaries. Corruption escalated to new height when some of the Members of Parliament were purchased by the head of the Congress Party in order to manoeuvre the majority in the Parliament. For all such acts of treason, the Arthasastra has prescribed the ultimate punishment of death with torture. In this context the Arthasastra of Kautilya is as relevant today as it was during the Kautilyan period.

Its recommendations about the secret service for keeping a watch over state employees, or political activities, or for the purpose of criminal investigation, espionage and counter-espionage etc. positively have a bearing even today. The law, which it embodied, is same law, which coming down the generations through the Smritis, has been in force through all these centuries and has now been replaced, or modified by a code applicable to the whole of India. The very liberal views expressed in this treatise on many matters could well be of interest even to modern legislators.

The strict control of economic life by the state that is visualised in this treatise is something not dissimilar to what is being actually practised today all over the world. The reservation of certain spheres for public sector and the regulation of private enterprise are features characteristic of the economic policy being followed at present in India. In essence, the Arthasastra recommends a similar vibrant policy, and there lies Kautilya's comprehensive visionary capabilities before over two thousand years, when the concept of socialistic pattern of government *vis-a-vis* society was not even dreamt, as monarchy was the order of the day throughout the world and supported by spiritual edicts. Its modest, yet essential aim, was the welfare of the subjects, together with the advancement of the state and it is cognate in today's administrative set up, although in the sphere of foreign policy the *SASTRA* has lost some of its validity. Even then, what it had enumerated about foreign policy is still largely true, when one has the same distrust of one nation by another, the same pursuit of its own interest by every nation tempered only by consideration of exigency, the same efforts to secure alliance with the same cynical disregard of them in self-interest, the same kind of intelligence service maintained by one nation in the territory of another, which we find referred to in the Arthasastra. The present-day cold war tactics are not essentially different from what the text recommends to the *vijigisu* when placed in similar situations.

Now with the unlimited devastative power of atomic weaponry, the danger arising from fanaticism or insensate hatred has become so great that an abhorable race to acquire more and more nuclear strength has started in various countries of the world, and in consequence, the essential wherewithals meant for the benefit of the subjects are being diverted for the purchase and maintenance of these weapons. They cumulatively threaten the very existence of humanity. Our relation with Pakistan and China for the last five decades should be taken into consideration in this context.

However, the advent of the nuclear age installed the United Nations Organisation (UNO) which failed to strengthen its hold on its constituents and maintain peace and tranquillity among the belligerent states. Even the UNO could not check the rising tide of genocide in various countries of the world. The big powers have made the UNO impotent and infructuous. Such types of *vijigisu*, who fail to ameliorate the living condition of millions of people, was never contemplated by Kautilya in his Arthasastra; but contrarily he prescribed severe punishment to such enemies of human race.

Although a new factor—'world opinion' has emerged in recent times as a check on blatantly selfish policies, it is difficult to see how rivalry and the struggle for supremacy between the nations can be avoided and the teaching of the Arthasastra, which is based on the very realities, rendered altogether superfluous, until some sort of world government, or an effective supra-national authority is established. But until that happens, which is the remotest possibility, the preaching of Arthasastra would, in actual practice, be followed by the nations of the world, though it may be unknown to them, or it may be openly criticized or condemned by some elites mentioned earlier. And this immemorability has crowned perennial and sublime glory on 'ARTHASASTRA AND ITS PROGENITOR KAUTILAYA, THE GREAT'

MADHAO BALWANT CHANDE

Contents

1

Arthasastra: Its Scope and Origin

Erroneously the Arthasastra of Kautilya is generally construed to be the science of economics and particularly dealing with finances *vis-a-vis* income and expenditure. Even prior to the days of Kautilya, the Indian population largely depended for their livelihood and sustenance on agriculture, cattle rearing and trade. Since the earliest time, *Arth* has been regarded as one of the *Trivarga*, or three goals of human existence, the other two being, *Dharma* and *Kama*. In this connection, *Artha* is traditionally understood to stand for the material well-being, as well as, the means for securing such wealth for a healthy social order. Like the other two goals, *Artha* also has primarily all pervading concern with life of an individual from the pre-conception to post-death phase. It is the individual who has to pursue wealth-*Artha* as one of the goals of his life, and this can not be achieved without security to life and livelihood-*VRTTIH*. Therefore, *Artha* is the sustenance of men who inhabit the mother earth; and for their overall well-being material and its means are closely associated and interdependent and hence essential, in order to obtain their livelihood, protect and sustain it; and insure their existence by providing proper security.

State Responsibility

The well-being of the people in general was to be pursued and preserved, and as an individual person could not do it by himself without the assistance of the administration of the state, he delegated this vital task to the state, *vis-a-vis* its administration. In consequence, this aspect has become the most essential function of the state and its statecraft. As contemplated by the tenets of 'Arthasastra', in addition to the protection of the earth and its inhabitants, the acquisition of territory and the concomitant protection of the population of the acquired territory became its ardent and sacred duty. Thus, this composite science of 'Arthasastra' encompasses and pervades multifaceted and multidimensional state functions cumulatively responsible for the well-being of the people, which was entirely the state responsibility.

Aims of Arthasastra

This implies that Arthasastra has two-fold aims. First, it seeks to show that the ruler should protect his territory through proper administration of the state, and secondly, it denotes how the territory should be conquered, provided with benevolent and wholesome administration for the general benefit of the inhabitants. Both these aims were as altruistic as mandatory. These precepts were necessarily concerned with the internal as well as external policies of the state and, therefore, the Arthasastra had extensively dealt with them along with politics, sociology, administration and justice system, both civil and criminal and the attendant penalties/punishment to the aberrant citizen. Abreast these topics, there necessarily followed methods of defence, offence and warfare strategies, including espionage and counterespionage. However, conquest of territories outside the territorial and then known geographical borders of India was deprecated. Arrian, the Greek historian had written 'on the one hand, the sense of justice prevented any Indian king from attempting to conquest beyond the limits of India'. This explains why Indian kings did not invade other countries as was done by the Muslims and Christians.

Origin of Arthasastra

This title of the science of Arthasastra appears to be as queer as unusual and antiquated. It has its origin in Mahabharata, where it has been mentioned at two places. In (12.161.9) Arjuna is described as expert in Arthasastra and in 12.290.104, Arthasastra was observed and followed by best and benevolent kings. However, in later times this name does not appear to be in common use, as later writers preferred to name this science. '*NITISASTRA*', which stood either for '*DANDA NITISASTRA*' or '*RAJNITISASTRA*'. This is explicit by the works of *NITISARA* of KAMANDAKA; the *NITIVAKYAMRTA* of SOMDEVA; the *NITIPRAKASIKA* of *VAISAMPAYNA* and so on. However, the nomenclature 'DANDANITI' is the oldest name for this science. The Mahabharata in (12.59.78) has given the name of DANDANITI to the composition by BRAMHADEVA at the beginning of creation with the ardent and ulterior object of protecting the earth and its inhabitants, and as such its study was considered necessary and essential by a prince, who in due course of time, would ascend the throne, and eventually guide him in the administration of the state and its statecraft. *DANDANITI* literally means the use or employment of the rod, and obviously it refers to the earliest methods of punishment on wrongdoers by the state. *DANDA*, as the sceptre held by the monarch, has everywhere been the symbol for state authority. All topics connected with the working of the state, including justice administration come within the purview of this science since early days.

Some authors like U.N. Ghoshal has expressed the view that Arthasastra is comprehensive and composite science of which *DANDANITI*, is only a branch. Since *NITISASTRA* is concerned with the protection of one's own territory, and also of that acquired from others, it has the same full scope of ARTHASASTRA. That KAMANDAKA himself makes no distinction between ARTHASASTRA and NITISASTRA appears evident from the fact that in the initial verses of his work, he paid homage to Kautilya (VISHNUGUPTA) to the effect that Kautilya had taken out the nector of *NITISASTRA* from the ocean of ARTHSASTRA; and as such both of them had prominently the same objective and scope.

The origin of the SASTRA is obscure. Although it is hyperbolic, it is a parable. An account of this supposed origin is found in chapter 50: SHANTIPARVAN, of the Mahabharata. Though this account is mythical, interestingly it throws some light on this question. It has been stated that at the beginning of creation, in the '*KRTAYUGA*'; men were righteous and acted according to *DHARMA*, although there was no ruler, nor punishment, but as in course of time people were overcome by delusion, greed, love of pleasures, and other base passions eventuating in anarchy everywhere (like the present-day condition in India). The gods apprehensively requested BRAMHADEVA to set things right. In consequence, BRAMHADEVA composed a treatise containing hundred thousand edicts dealing with *TRIVARGA*, that is *DHARMA*, *ARTHA* and *KAMA* in order that an orderly and peaceful existence free of audacity and depravity may be attained and ensured for the inhabitants of the earth. These commandments were germane to the *NITISASTRA* and prevented people from deviating from the *ARYAPATH* (equivalent to good behaviour) as described in NITISASTRA (Mahabharat 12.59. 74). In the following stanza-78 this treatise is definitely given the title of *DANDANITI*. In continuity, it has been stated that God *SANKARA* reduced this *NITISASTRA* to ten thousand edicts having regard to the decreasing longevity in the succeeding years (Mahabharata 12.59.86-7). This abridged text was known as *VAISALAKSA*. Indra, later reduced this text to five thousand edicts in his work *BAHUDANTAKA*. The process of reduction of the text continued to three thousand by *BRAHASPATYA* in his work *BRAHASPATYA*; and finally to one thousand edicts by KAVYA (USANAS) in his work *AUSANASA* by USANAS who is also called BHARGAVA. All these texts were related to *NITI* or *DANDANITI* (Mahabharata 12.59.80-92).

This account of the origin of the *NITISASTRA* is no doubt fanciful, but shows the ardent concern of the political-religious leaders to check and punish the religious, social, and political aberrations of people prone to tend antiethical, immoral, antisocial and antinational. The teachings of USANAS alias BHARGAVA and BRAHASPATI have been extensively quoted in the entire chapter 12 of Mahabharata. USANAS is otherwise known SUKRA. The traditions of SUKRA and BRAHASPATI were the founders of this *SASTRA*-science and, in fact they were quite old. It would not be unreasonable to suppose that these two sages were the real persons who served as Purohitas to some king and instructed them in art of governance. That, these schools of *NITISASTRA*, claimed to have been followed by these two Purohitas, is also evident from the ARTHASASTRA of Kautilya, even if the historicity of these two may be regarded open to question.

Unfortunately, all early works on this science are lost. The beginnings of this science must have preceded the composition of Kautilya Arthasastra by few centuries. The opinion of K.P. Jaiswal that Arthasastra as a science originated prior to 600 B.C. does not appear to be wide of the mark (D.R. Bhandarkar — *Some Aspects of Ancient Hindu Polity*). Territorial kingdoms had been in existence since the day of Mahabharata war (about 3000 B.C.) A number of these had attained prominence at the time of the rise of Buddhism in 560 B.C. such as Kosala, Vatsa, Avanti, Magadha, etc. (*Political History of Ancient India* — Rai Choudhary; *Age of Imperial Unity* — R.C. Mujumdar). In 494 B.C. King AJATHASTRU of Magadha succeeded in overthrowing the powerful VIJJIS (VRJIS) by contriving dissensions effectively purused by his scheming minister VASSA KARA. (*The Wonder that was India* — A.L. Basham). It is obvious that long before the period which witnessed the growth of the power of Magadha at the expense of its neighbours, the problem of internal administration and relation of neighbouring states must have been tackled by seeking recourse to the principles of this science. The Kautilya Arthasastra is the earliest work on it that has come down to us, although it clearly marks the culmination of a long period of speculation on the subject matter of this science. Moreover, this science has undoubtedly its genesis in the thoughts and precepts of several generations of ablest and practical administrators and it stood the test of the times and secured the well-being of the society in all its aspects and spheres.

Position of Purohitas

The fact that BRAHASPATI and USANAS were Purohitas is very significant. In the early days, as the *RGVEDA* points out, the Purohita was always there by the side of the King to advise, guide and help him in all the spheres of his activity; and as a state functionary, the Purohita was next in importance only to the king. In due course of time separate ministers or *mantrins*, or *ammatyas*, came to be appointed only gradually as and by the secular task of the state multiplied and the functions of the Purohitas were more and more confined to religious spheres, but at the same time their pre-eminent position was still maintained in the teaching of the SASTRA, because the first among the state dignatories to whose appointment Kautilya refers is the Purohita. The Purohita was expected to be present in the camp and even on the battlefield in those days (10.1.6. and 10.3.32). Here it may be keenly noted that Purohitas and Brahmans are synonymous and they relate to the wisdom and scholarship of this kind of teachers. It may be aluded that the Mahabharata mentions seven such Purohitas as the promulgators of the science of rulership. They are : (1) BRAHASPATI (2) VISALAKSA, (3) KAVYA (USANAS), (4) MAHENDRA (Indra), (5) PRACETA MANU, (6) BHARADVAJA, and (7) GAURASIRAS. The work of PRACETA MANU cannot be identified with MANUSMRITI which is claimed to be the work of SVAYAMBHUVA MANU, to whom Kautilya refers to in his Arthasastra. The work of PRACETA MANU is now non-existent. Although the Purohitas were the founder of this science-*SASTRA*, it was naturally the ministers or the *mantrins* who, in due course of time, became more and more concerned with the study and propagation of this science which was formulated and developed very early for the guidance of the kings on matters of administration and state policy at home and abroad.

2

The Relation of Arthasastra to Dharmasastra

As the *sastra* (Science) originated with Purohitas, it has few distinctive features. As it is intended to teach a ruler how he should conduct himself in the various situations that were likely to arise in the course of his regime, it was particularly instructional in character. That was keeping with the role of the Purohitas, who, as the king's preceptors, could lay down rules for the king to follow, telling him what he should do and what he should avoid diplomatically. As a result of this, again, this science is pre-eminently practical in its aims and objectives. By '*DHARMA*' it should always be unequivocally and pertinently meant righteous behaviour and duties and propounded edicts to check the ambivalence of human nature which tend to break the most elementary rules designed to protect their fellow citizen's life and property, person and to maintain order in the society.

DHARMASASTRA has far better claims to a high antiquity than *ARTHASASTRA*, which in turn is older than *KAMSASTRA*, as these sciences on *TRIVARGA* had followed one another in time, as well as in rank and value. It was only when special schools for each separate branch of learning replaced the ancient vedic school, that schools of *ARTHASASTRA* could take their rise and become impetuous in passing years resulting in its general acceptance as a branch of *DHARMASASTRA* first, and then as an independent branch of study (Introduction to the Punjab edition of Kautilya Arthasastra, p. 20). *ARTHASASTRA* is thus regarded as only offshoot of *DHARMASASTRA*; and in particular, the Kautilian Arthasastra is believed to be indebted to works on *DHARMASASTRA* for its teaching. It may also be noted that the word

DHARMA in these texts refer primarily to duties of the four *varnas* or *ashramas* according to *APASTAMBA DHARMASASTRA* etc. Although the word *DHARMA* inclusively sometime means 'Law,' it has created the impression that the *DHARMASASTRAS* are primarily works on law, but they are nothing of the kind. They, no doubt, contain a few rules which fall within the ambit of law, but these happen to be included only incidentally, as in any case the formulation of legal rules was not the primary concern of the vedic schools.

Moreover, the standpoint of the *DHARMASASTRA* is not that of a law-giver, but that of a moral preceptor who lays down duties and regards deviation from them as sin to be expiated by the individual himself rather than crimes to be punished by the state. The *DHARMASASTRA* propounds that an individual has to atone himself his sins with which no law-giver can be seriously concerned. The general tendency of Arthasastra is thoroughly realistic, mundane or worldly, as opposed to the strictly ideal religious principles; some of them may be of special importance to one and the same may appear secondary to the others and even be passed over. The fact that the essence of the difference lies in the circumstances that '*DHARMASASTRA*' is in its origin addressed to ordinary individual and is concerned with the strict observance of his duties by him, while '*ARTHASASTRA*' is primarily concerned with the administration of a state by its ruler. The points of contact between the two *Sastras* arise from the fact that *DHARMASASTRA* also contemplated of dealing with 'duties' of the king and referring to certain matters related with the sphere of law proper.

We find that, it is gradually that works on *DHARMASASTRA* came to devote more and more attention to questions of law and administration, as it is evident that while *APSTAMBA* has only 139 *SUTRAS* (stanzas) dealing with these topics out of a total of 1372 *SUTRAS*; and *BAUDHAYANA* has 147 in a total of 1,248 *SUTRAS*; VASISTHA devoted 189 out of 1,039 and GUATAMA has 212 out of 1,000 *SUTRAS* similarly complied. The *SMRITIS* of MANU and YAJNAVALKAYA, which admittedly belong to the second phase in growth of *DHARMASASTRA*, and these topics cover roughly one-third of the entire work and receive for the first time a fulness of treatment that was conspicuously lacking in earlier *DHARMASASTRAS*. Obviously, MANU is the first *DHARMASASTRA* writer to treat law in a more or less systematic and codified manner, and he was conscious of his role of moral preceptor even in these sections. It is YAJNAVALKYA who had treated law very systematically and without an admixture of moral exhortation in his chapter on law — *VYAVAHARA*.

By implication, it could be stated that the source for the topics of law and administration sketchily dealt with in *DHARMASASTRA* was derived by the various authors from *NITISASTRA* or '*ARTHASASTRA*;' which appear to be treated as symbolically synonymous, for duties of the king — *RAJDHARMAS i.e.* rules regarding the governance of a state form the legitimate subject matter of this *SASTRA*; nay they are the special province of this *SASTRA* alone. Various authors including Jolly, Buhler, Kangle and others support this view.

But what is true of *RAJDHARMAS* is equally true of law. There seems to be a general impression that *NITI* or *ARTHASASTRA* was originally not concerned with law. But as stated above, it seems *NITISASTRA*, which in its origin, was DANDA*NITISASTRA*, must have been concerned with law, the violation of which warranted *DANDA* or punishment or some kind of punitive action. Moreover, in early work of this *SASTRA* conflicting opinion on questions of punishment for perjury robbery, hereditary shares, desertion of wife, contractual payments, scuffle, gambling etc., have been expressed. Therefore, undoubtedly *NITISASTRA* was concerned with law from the earliest days. As a corollary *DHARMASASTRAS* have incorporated the needed law from the *NITISASTRA*. On the same analogy, the Mahabharata derived its material from early treatises on this *SASTRA* as many pieces of Mahabharata appear as small or succinct *NITISASTRAS*, or abstracts thereof. While agreeing with JACOBI that politics and law were interrelated like different threads of fabric, there are sufficient grounds found in these *SASTRAS* that *NITISASTRA* and *ARTHASASTRA* were importantly concerned with both law and politics since the inception of the science.

Some critics, like Balakrishna Ghosh has questioned the existence of independent work on forensic law to which the *SMRITIS* could be indebted. They contend that Hindu law (not Hindu Code Bill) was never systematised and the administration of justice depended to some extent on the whims and caprices of the particular individual who was entrusted with this sacred duty of justice deliverance. One may perhaps, grant the operation of whims and caprices in a few cases, but they were few and far in between, as an individual's predilection can nowhere always be kept out in the administration of justice. Human nature, now and in the past, had always been the same and, therefore, the 'Rule of common law' has been envisaged and brought into practice to contain within the legal and social restrictions the ambivalence and vagrancy of aberrant citizens. Even in the present democratic condition of India, the whims and caprices of a certain political party in power or its representative head are apparent resulting in the irretrievable sufferance of this country. Therefore, it is not only improper but also maleficent and malevolent to assume that the administration of justice in ancient India was without the guidance of any recognised law.

Apart from *DESADHARMAS, KULADHARMAS, JATIDHARMAS* and so on, which no administrator could dare to ignore, there must have been in existence a body of civil and criminal law to which an appeal could be made in court of law, as expounded in *SMRITI*. The *MANUSMRITI* refers to king's duty to try the cases of litigants in accordance with the procedure laid down in the *SASTRA*. Again it refers to punishment for false testimony.

One cannot, therefore, reasonably deny the existence of clearly formulated law on the ground that the texts containing law have not come down to us, because the verses must have originally formed part of a body of teaching handed down from generation to generation by the ancient method of oral transmission. Most of the earlier teaching, as transmitted in different schools, is no longer extant. The incorporation of all that teaching in the Kautilya Arthasastra is apparently responsible for its disappearance in later times; and likewise it is also ascribed to *SMRITIS* which appropriated this law from those texts.

3

The Content, Form and Source of Kautilya Arthasastra

Content and Form

The Kautilya Arthasastra contains Fifteen Books (*ADHIKARNAS*). Of these the first five deal with what is called *TANTRA*, which is akin to the internal administration of the state. The next eight, deal with *DAVPA* and they relate to the relationship of the state with the neighbouring states. And finally, the last two are miscellaneous in character.

BOOK ONE deals with the equipment of the king for the performance of his duties as a ruler. It discusses such topics as the training of the king, the appointment of ministers and other officers of the state, the daily routine to be normally followed by the ruler and so on. BOOK TWO principally describes the details of the various executive officers of the state. It gives a comprehensive account of the state activities in various fields, including a discourse on such questions as settlement on unoccupied land, building a fort laying out the capital and so on. BOOK THREE, which is concerned with law and order and its administration, reproduces a complete code of law. BOOK FOUR deals with suppression of crime. It shows how to trace, track and punish thieves, murderers, dacoits, and other criminals. BOOK FIVE deals with miscellaneous aspects such as measures that may be necessary in emergencies, and steps to be taken against seditious persons. It also lays down scales of salaries for different categories of state servants. It also explains how a candidate for a high office should endeavour to secure and retain it. Finally, it gives advice to chief minister on ensuring continuity of rule on the demise of the ruling monarch.

BOOK SIX enumerates the qualities necessary to make each of the seven *PRAKRATIS* or constituents of the state ideal. It also describes *RAJMANDALA* or circle of kings as a preliminary to a discussion on the states' relations with its neighbours. BOOK SEVEN contains elaborate discussion on the way in which each of the six *GUNAS* on measures of foreign policy may be used in the various situations that are prone to arise, the ultimate goal set before the ruler is conquest of the world. Here various ways in which rivals can be outwitted by stratagems and devises overcome by force have been mentioned. BOOK EIGHT is concerned with *VYASANAS*, that is, calamities, shortcomings or weaknesses affecting the various *PRAKRATIS*. It is necessary to overcome the calamity before any aggressive activity can be undertaken. BOOK NINE deals with preparation for war and describes the kinds of troops that could be mobilised for an expedition, *inter alia*, the proper season for the start of the expedition, the precaution to be taken and inherent dangers to be guarded against, before starting the expedition etc. BOOK TEN is essentially concerned with fighting and the various methods of warfare. It also describes the battle array and even petty matters relating to camping ground, and such allied topics. BOOK ELEVEN has only one chapter explaining how the would-be conqueror (*VIJIGISU*) should subjugate *SAMGHAS* or independent oligarchial principalities. BOOK TWELVE shows a weak king, when threatened by a strong king, should frustrate the latter's designs and ultimately overcome him. BOOK THIRTEEN is mainly concerned with the conquest of the enemies' fortified capital by subterfuges or fighting. It also describes how the conquered territory should be ruled by the conqueror — the *VIJIGISU*.

BOOK FOURTEEN describes various secret remedies and occult practices useful for getting rid of enemies or traitors or people prone to indulge in committing or adopting treachery or treason. Finally, BOOK FIFTEEN describes and illustrates from the text itself the thirtytwo *TANTRAYUKTIS* or methods of treating a subject.

It is the peculiar characteristic of the ARTHASASTRA that it went into full details or even the minutest point connected with its subject matter, and at times it appears prolix or even prosaic. The impression of prolixity that is sometimes created is due to the author's endeavour to speculate, imagine and foresee every possible eventuality and the related details in any particular situation. It does not show any difference in style, both of versification and prose i.e. *BHASYA*. This style of writing is not queer as the tendency in ancient India to versify the teaching in many branches of learning, particularly if they had a practical use or application, is well-known, as versification is useful for memorizing. Prose style has been used because it is intended as an abstract of the entire earlier teaching on the subject. The style of ARTHASASTRA continuously exhibits that mixture of prose and verse which is so common in *SUTRA* works. Its tenseness is not that of the philosophical or other similar *SUTRAS*. The text, on many occasions, is found difficult, because of the technical nature of its contents and the many technical words used therein. On the whole, it can be claimed that it is easy to understand and grasp the text provided the technical nature of its contents is borne in mind. The *SUTRAS* are simple in construction and free from obscurity caused by long compounds or involved expressions. The *SLOKAS* — stanzas or verses — are characterised by extreme simplicity. It is true that at some places one is not quite sure of the meaning of many words and expressions used in the text. Therefore, the interpretation of many passages in the text has remained uncertain. It is the vocabulary and language of ARTHASASTRA show striking peculiarities. There are numerous technical terms. Many of them are defined in the ARTHASASTRA itself, but there are others that are not defined; and they are to be construed either by inference or implication. Nevertheless, after all allowances have been made, it can be maintained that the text is not difficult in style and comprehension.

Source

The first *SUTRA* of ARTHASASTRA contains the statement that it was composed mostly by bringing together all treatises on this science written by earlier teachers. The work is thus declared to be the compilation made from earlier works on this *SASTRA*. This pragmatic science, though intricate it is, to some may not appear intricate. For, there is no doubt that it is based on earlier sources and is not original work in the sense that the author had thought out everything contained in it independently. The very nature of its contents, which required a thorough knowledge of many diverse subjects, makes it unlikely that any single author, however gifted, could have produced this work by relying on his own intellectual capabilities alone. The existence of earlier science is clearly indicated in other places in the text itself, and the relative importance of earlier tradition handed down by generation has been maintained. The fact that this work is based on earlier work is alone borne out by another consideration, as the text reveals that material from different sources has been used in its preparation. We find differences in terminology in some cases and in very rare instances contradictory statements. Moreover, the text refers to a number of earlier authorities and mentioned what are apparently opinions held by them. There are in all 112 places in the text where such opinions have been mentioned. In 25 of the cases, the opinions are attributed to school of the *SASTRA*, namely the BARHASPATIYAS (in six places); the AUSANASAS (in seven places); the MANAVAS (in five places); the PARASARAS (In six places), and AMBHIYAS (in one place). In 28 places the opinions are ascribed to individual teachers like, BHARADVAJA (7); VISALAKSA (6), PISUNA (5), KAUNAPADANTA (4), VATAVAYADHI (5), and BAHUDANTIPUTRA (1). In the remaining fiftynine cases the opinions are attributed to predecessor teacher — ACARYAH. However, it is to be importantly noted that Kautilya himself is represented as adopting an entirely reasonable stand and such preachings as would suit to and control the then existing socio-political and religious conditions and thwart or prevent the ethical aberration, and hold the disintegrated Indian polity together and prepare it to face effectively the Greek invasion of India.

The principle topics on which there are such controversial opinions are: (1) the manner in which the punishment should be inflicted by the ruler (1.4.5.10); (2) the use of secret text for finding out if an officer is upright or loyal or not (1.10.16.20); (3) the person to whom the *KSETRAJA* son belongs (3.7.1.3-6); (4) the types of enemies against whom it is more advantageous to march (7.5.3-8, 12-15); (5) the type of ally whom it would be more advantageous to secure (7.9-9.34); (6) the kind of state undertaking which should be preferred in newly acquired territories (7.11.13-16-7.12.9-24); (7) the choice between diplomatic moves and actual war (7.18.29-33); (8) relative merits of different types of rulership (8.2, 5-25); (9) the relative seriousness of the various calamities of a divine or human origin (8.4, 2-43); and (10) occasion suitable for marching against an enemy (9.1, 12-44). Although there is an element of artificiality in the manner in which the opinions of Kautilya's predecessor teachers have been presented in the text, it should be always remembered that the MAHABHARATA tradition shows acquaintance not only with the names of the ancient teachers, but also with their teaching, with which, obviously, such an erudite scholar like Kautilya, must have been not only acquainted, but also fully conversant. It seems plausible that the opinions of earlier learned authorities were worked up and schemingly arranged by Kautilya, which creates the impression of artificiality in some places, but that was ardently done with a desire to present all the pros and cons of a question rather than an attempt to convert a genuinely held opinion in the prevalent circumstances. ARTHASASTRA is essentially a practical science, its declared aim is to teach the ruler how to govern his kingdom, and what general principles it enunciated are all concerned with practical affairs.

In the days of Kautilya this science of statecraft had become a tangled maze of divergent ideas. The credit goes to Kautilya alone for the virtual reconstruction of this science after he overhauled it. It is undoubtedly clear that where Kautilya is represented as differing from the earlier teachers, his is generally the same and moderate standpoint as compared with many extreme, often one-sided, sometimes irrational and redundant veiwpoint of the predecessors. The ARTHASASTRA composed by Kautilya is more sober, more rational and inevitably more advanced than was the case in the earlier writings. There is no doubt that his superior political acumen and insight and practical wisdom have no parallel in the annals of the posterior history of this country; as even today these precepts are followed all over the world in order to safeguard the interest of the state and its population.

4

The Author and Date of Arthasastra

The Author

The question of authorship and the date of the treatise has been the subject of a rather heated controversy. The traditional view in this matter is that KAUTILYA, also known as CANAKYA or VISHNUGUPTA, who destroyed the power of the NANDAS and placed CANDRAGUPTA MAURYA (CHANDRAGUPTA as spelt generally) on the throne of MAGADHA, is the author of this work. And as CANDRAGUPTA is historically known to have been installed to the throne in 321 B.C., or thereabout, the date of this composition is assumed to be the end of the third century B.C. This traditional view is reinforced by the fact that a statement about the authorship of the work is found in the first chapter, where towards the end, it is stated that the *SASTRA* was composed by Kautilya avoiding all prolixity etc. At the end of the work it is stated that this *SASTRA* was composed by that person who, in resentment, rescued the earth from the NANDA king and so on. There is also the fact that the work is called KAUTILYA ARTHASASTRA : *i.e.* the ARTHASASTRA of KAUTILYA and composed by KAUTILYA in the colophons at the end of various *ADHIKARANAS* or Books in the text. Finally, there are those numerous places in the text where we find criticism of the opinion of earlier teachers, followed by the assertion of *KAUTILYA's* own opinions. In all these cases *KAUTILYA's* opinion has been stated last, indicating that the statement of the controversies proceeds from him. This establishes the fact that the rest of the work is also composed by him.

The tradition that KAUTILYA is the author of this *SASTRA* has been generally accepted since fairly ancient time. The *NITISASTRA* of KAMANDAKA asserts that the wise VISHNUGUPTA, who had destroyed the NANDAS by his magic lore had given the earth to CANDRAGUPTA and extracted the nector of *NITISASTRA* from the ocean of ARTHASASTRA. Similarly, there can be no doubt that DANDIN has this work in mind when he referred to the DANDANITI composed by ACARYAH (ACHARYA) VISHNUGUPTA — for the sake of Maurya king. It is true that DANDIN mentions, VISHNUGUPTA or CANAKYA as the name of the author and does not refer to the name of KAUTILYA. But there can be little doubt that in the ancient tradition all the three names belong to the same individual. The drama — MUDRARAKSASA written by VISAKHADATTA — clearly shows that *KAUTILYA* is the alias name for CANAKYA, who is the central figure of that play of political intrigues. Similarly, in various contemporaneous works, *KAUTILYA* or CANAYKA or VISHNUGUPTA has been mentioned to be the person, who was instrumental in overthrowing the Nandas and placing Candragupta Maurya on the throne. It is found that at least from the 5th to 6th century A.D. onwards this work is undoubtedly believed to have been composed by Kautilya.

It is unfortunate that the comparison of such a genuinely, gemmy and sterling work of *ARTHASASTRA* by its author Kautilya should be made by scholars, both Indian and foreign, with the works and personality of BISMARCK, MACHIAVELLI or GARIBALDI etc. when there is basic difference in their works. The composition of KAUTILYA is not memoirs, but an all pervading treatise on a branch of the study composed in the traditional manner and based mainly on the earlier teaching on that subject during the period in which there was no existence either of the three European authors or their composition. Many arguments have been advanced by various authors for rejecting the authorship of Kautilya for this work. To start with, the very existence of such a person as Kautilya at the time of Candragupta Maurya is regarded as doubtful, becuase in the ARTHASASTRA Kautilya does not refer to CANDRAGUPTA or his empire, PATLIPUTRA, the capital of the empire, and allied details have been passed over in absolute silence by this alleged ancient statesman meditating in the days of his retirement on the maxims of policy. Obviously, such reasoning has been based on a misunderstanding of the nature of his work. One has a right to expect a reference to contemporary personalities, events, situation and so on in a work of the kind of Bismarck's Memoirs, but it seems hardly fair to expect the same in a work which is altogether of different kind and which deals with general principles of statecraft etc.; and moreover, in the ancient

Indian references to contemporary events in works of any kind are, as a rule, hard to find. And in the case of scientific works in particular, which often claimed to be based on the teaching of some mythical sage, if not of the Creator himself, a reference to any contemporary event or person would appear to be almost inconceivable.

It is argued that Kautilya could not have written this work which deals only with the problems of a moderate-sized state. It is true that the text is primarily addressed to the ruler of a comparatively small state, normally a member of a circle of twelve, more or less similar states. But such has been the basis of this theory of this *SASTRA* and the author did not contemplate to materially depart from the tradition. Besides, it must not be forgotten that, the text sets before such a ruler the ideal of *VIJIGISU* — the would-be conqueror, who is to try to establish suzerainty over the whole world — an ideal which is no invention of Kautilya as it was there in the *SASTRAS* taught before him (Beniprasad: *The State in Ancient India*, p. 252).

To disprove the authorship of Kautilya for this work it is further argued by yet another set of critics that it is not the work of a practical statesman at all, but the composition of a pedantic pandit, filled as it is with endless and pedantic classifications and definitions' (Winternitz: *Some Problems of Indian Literature*, p. 97). There are innumerable instances in the Indian history of all the periods of learned men or pandit being successful ministers, the most conspicuous instances being those of HEMADRI at the court of YADAVA kings and of SAYANA and MADHAVA at the court of Vijayanagara kings [D.R Bhandarkar: *ABORI*, VII (1926) p. 73]. Moreover, in the ancient days the association of pandit with administration was inevitable, for, ministers were for the most part drawn from the class of Brahmins, meaning learned men, a tradition followed during the Maratha regime. Analogous to this practice, there were ministerial kazis during the Muslim rule and clergies during the Christian rule, wherever they ruled throughout the world. It is also true that the work is filled with classifications and definitions, because an indepth study of a particular theme or point was made by the author and that shows his wisdom, erudition, and sagacity in handling the intricate, all permeating and pervading, and yet ticklish issues of political science, which ARTHASASTRA obviously is. Such arguments are not only puerile but also baseless, for, men fully conversant with realistic running of a state and the administration of its foreign policies were alone capable to compose such a treatise.

O. Stein, a German scholar, after laborious investigation found that the *ARTHASASTRA* does not reflect the same condtions of state, polity, public life etc. that are revealed in the account of Megasthenes. Jolly, Keinth and Winternitz, more or less, tagged the same arguments. The presumption of these critics is hypothetically incorrect and misleading as the text does not process to be a document describing the actual condition in any one or particular kingdom. It is a theoretical treatise intended for the guidance of rulers in general, and it claims to be based mainly on earlier treatises of the same kind; and as such the actual condition prevalent in the kingdom of Candragupta Maurya did not deserve and warrant any mention. Moreover, Megasthene's work, though earlier in date, has been found to be far inferior in intrinsic value to the itineraries of the Chinese pilgrims and to the great Arabian work a Alberuni on India; and in consequence, there are impressive doubts and reservation about the accuracy of these statements, which obviously have been made to browbeat the Indian philosophy in an attempt to establish the inconceivable propagation by foreigners that all that was Indian were inferior to them, and that they stemmed from the fact that they ruled the country for several years. But even after Independence such a trend of thinking should be allowed to be continued is a serious matter and thought-provoking, whether the posterity should be allowed to inherit this wrong impression about the greatest political pandit of the post-Mahabharata Period. Actually, it is confidently asserted that the evidence of Megasthenes, which is very sketchy and skeleton like is against the authenticity of ARTHASASTRA, as he had seen significantly little of Indian's land, its people and their living conditions, the various states *vis-a-vis* their administration methods. All the Alexander's historians had attempted to show that the Indian forces and their strategies were too far inferior to those of the Greek forces, but this contrived lie has been exposed by the conquest of Candragupta all the territories acquired by Alexander prior to his forced departure from India in about 317 B.C. For this premiere and pre-eminent historical occasion PLINY had described that Candragupta Maurya had mobilised a vast army consisting of 600,000 infantry, 30,000 cavalry, 9,000 elephants and about 8,000 chariots, all on daily pay. This would hardly have been possible without material resources more powerful and supple than the few taxes mentioned by Megasthenes (Jolly).

Date of Arthasastra

It is argued by critics that HARAHURA and KAPISA, as they lay beyond the North-West Frontier of India, were not known to Indians from the third century B.C. This belief is entirely erroneous, as there is ample and justifiable proof of commerce between India and Babylonia, and between India, Iran and Egypt long before the fourth century B.C. SENNACHERIB, the ASSYRIAN king of about 700 B.C. had planted among other things, cotton of Indian origin. North-Western India was conquered by DARIUS I about 518 B.C. and incorporated in the ACHAEMENIAN Empire to form the twentieth satrapy. Moreover, an Indian contingent consisting of infantry, cavalry and chariots was included in the army of XERXES that invaded Greece as HERODOTUS tells us (*Cambridge History of India*, Vol. 1, pp. 334-5 by A.V. Williams-Jackson.) There is evidence to show that even during the still earlier ELAMITE rule in Iran there was undisturbed commerce between capital Susa and India; and that Indian vessels were cruising and coasting along GEDROSIA to Arabia ORMUZ and Persian Gulf before the time of Alexander (W.W. Tarn : *The Greeks in Bactria and India*, p. 367). *Ipso-facto*, it is proved that the North-West Regions of India were thoroughly known to Indians since about 700 B.C.

Although Greek influences are to be found in India in the sphere of art, astronomy, coinage and so on, the ARTHASASTRA is singularly free from them and exhibits original knowledge that belongs definitely to an earlier age or period. In the fourth century B.C. in the age of Plato and Aristotle, political thought in Greece was at its zenith, but the Indian political thinking was not affected by it and it was intrinsically and entirely independent and original as found in the ARTHASASTRA, which deals with a number of topics which have formed the subject matter of other independent work; foremost among these is the topic of law and suppression of crime. In the matter of the various prevalent sciences, inclusive of art and crafts, the ARTHASASTRA represents a different tradition altogether. Without weighty ground, this overwhelming evidence of unanimous Indian tradition cannot be pushed aside; else one practises scepticism, not criticism.

It is quite clear that the ARTHASASTRA was composed before VASTSYAYANA wrote the KAMSUTRA, as he is usually assigned to fourth century A.D. YAJNAVALKAYA-SMRITI and MANU SMRITI presuppose the existence of ARTHASASTRA. Various Buddhist works like LANKAVATARA SUTRA also mentions ARTHASASTRA. In 3.20.16 of ARTHASASTRA occurs a rule laying down punishment for feeding SAKYA, AJIVAKA and other heretical monks, at rites in honour of the gods and manes, but the same rule has excluded NIRGRANTHAS or Jains. Sakyas and Ajivakas were Buddhist, and the punishment indicated here was in keeping with the state of things as they prevailed in the age of Maurya Emperor, who had adopted Vedic culture. Besides, there is the more important evidence of the inscription in the caves of the BARABAR hills, near Gaya (Bihar) which records the grant of the caves to the AJIVAKAS by king Asoka, (PIYADASI). Similarly, the nearby three hills of NAGARJUNI were dedicated to AJIVAKAS by DASRATH, a successor and grandson of Asoka. (A.L. Basham: *History and Doctrines of the Ajivakas*). In the Seventy Pillars Edict on the DELHI-TOPRA pillar Ajivaka has been mentioned. As after Maurya period Ajivakas or Ajivikas disappeared more or less completely from the history after that period. In 11.1.4-5 are enumerated a number of small rulers (SAMGHAS) or what may be called oligarchies belonging to KAMBOJA, SURASTRA, LICCHIVI, VRJI, MALLA, MADRA, KUKURA, KURU, PANCALA, most of which had disappeared after the Mauryan period. These SAMGHAS could not have been in existence after the third century B.C. From this it is manifest that the *ARTHASASTRA* was composed not later than the 3rd century B.C.

Some critics doubt the authorship of *ARTHASASTRA* by Kautilya, because the text refers to Kautilya in the third person and states his opinions in the same manner as it does those of other teachers, and, therefore, it was not the normal practice of writing in those days. Nevertheless the text of Kautilya is peculiar in several ways. There is no mere juxtaposition of the views of different authorities, including the one claiming to be the author of the entire work, but almost invariably a resolute and unequivocal assertion, though in a controversial tone, of Kautilya's opinion against those of others, which are rejected by Kautilya as unacceptable and that too on rational grounds. This was the impatient temperament of Kautilya, who in his intolerance of injustice and wrong had destroyed the mighty NANDA dynasty and placed his own protege CANDRAGUPTA on the throne in its place.

Some critics such as BRELOER, while admitting that ARTHASASTRA was a document rich in administrative law, a sketch of a *magna carta*, considered it to be a book for the Emperor Candragupta; and found an exact parallel with what was done by TRIBONIAN at the instance of Eastern Roman Emperor, JUSTINIAN by collecting old sources in order to create a new law. To belittle Kautilya it has also been said by such critics that old codes of law were collected and formed by a school of learned men into a modern work under the guidance of Kautilya. The critics often forget that there is nothing in the whole of ARTHASASTRA to show that it was composed at the behest of any ruler and that it was intended to serve as a guide to any particular ruler of a specific kingdom.

Throughout, the text is addressed to the 'King' or the 'rulers' in general, and nowhere it has been addressed to Candragupta, thereby negating the belief that Kautilya had purposely and specifically composed this work for the guidance of Candragupta. It is also forgotten that, as for law, the situation in ancient India was entirely different from what it was in the contemporary Roman Empire. The Roman law was always state made. The earliest code of law, the TWELVE TABLES, was passed by the Senate and set up in the Forum. From time to time edicts were issued by the various Emperors. There was, besides the common law, embodied in a number of Treatises by lawyers. The result was that by the time of Justinian, who ruled at BYZANTIUM over the Eastern part of the Roman Empire nearly a thousand years after the publication of the TWELVE TABLES in Rome, it was impossible to know that which part of a statute was in operation and which had been suppressed by some imperial decree. It was necessary to create order in this maze of legal literature. It should be importantly noted that a committee of ten learned jurists appointed by Justinian took eight years to produce the JUSTINIAN CODE, which they did by abridgement and consolidation, cutting out repetitions and contradictions. Like was never the case in ancient India. Moreover, BRELOER himself admits that in India the king or the state was not the law-giver. On the Roman pattern no Indian state had promulgated a particular law code for its justice deliverance. Apart from some local or other customary law, law was regarded sacred and held to be universally valid. In spite of some difference among the learned on points of law, there was never confusion or chaos. Moreover, nobody of learned men was necessary to put together the ancient law as this was continuously studied in the various schools. Kautilya must have consulted works older than his but he *de facto* remained the sole composer of this text.

The temptation to consider the *ARTHASASTRA* to have been composed specifically for the guidance of Candragupta should be resisted, as the existence of the Empire of Candragupta is completely ignored in this work. In fact, no event that can be regarded as contemporaneous with the author is directly referred to in it, because Kautilya preferred to stick to the method of the SASTRA which was intended for the guidance and use of rulers in general and not, repeat not, of any particular ruler; though it appears strange that an author writing a work on politics should so completely keep out all references to contemporary events, particularly when he had taken an active part in shaping the political destiny of Magadha and Candragupta Maurya. However, it appears feasible that the desire to avenge the insult meted out to him by the Nanda king, as the tradition spells about it, Kautilya might have composed the ARTHASASTRA of his own; and possibly it was after that he became associated with Candragupta in the joint adventure to overthrow the Nanda dynasty.

Despite the various prevalent legends about Kautilya, information about him that can be regarded as absolutely reliable is meagre. All sources, Brahminical, Buddhist, and Jain, are, however, agreed on one point that Kautilya was responsible for the destruction of the Nanda rule in Magadha and the establishment of Candragupta Maurya on that throne. There has been a difference of opinion about the correct form of the name of the author of ARTHASASTRA, some preferring the form 'KAUTALYA'; other 'KAUTILYA'. Foreign writers like Jolly expressed the opinion that the author was nicknamed 'KAUTALYA, because of his association with crookedness and knavery. Indian authors like P. V. Kane has expressed, similar opinion. Practically all the earlier works refer to him as 'KAUTILYA'. The VISHNU PURANA has mentioned KAUTILYA twice in IV, 24.6-7; the VAYU PURANA also twice in 37.324-325 and MATSYA PURANA once in 227.22. 'KUTILA' is the only name from which 'KAUTILYA' has been derived as a result of secondary sankritization. The Third NIDHANPUR PLATE of BHASKARAVARMAN of KAMRUPA has in line 5 of the First Side the word, "KAUTILYO" followed by seven brahmins belonging to the GOTRA KAUTILYA (*Epigraphia India*, Vol. XIX-1927-1928, pp. 245-250). Even today many families belong to KAUTILYA *GOTRA*. 'Gotra' names in the families are supposed to be transmitted from generation to generation without any change of form or corruption.

CANAKYA, the other name of the ARTHASASTRA author, apprears to be patrimonic. CANAKYA and KAUTILYA have been so unequivocally identified with the tradition of MUDRARAKSASA that their identity must have been taken for granted long before the play was written as CANAKYA is found in PRAKRIT works, where it got corrupted and subsequently assimilated and used in parlance. As stated earlier DANDIN refers to CANAKYA. TANTRAKHYAYIKA has among its opening verses a salutation to the 'GREAT CANAKYA' along with other makers of the science of Kingship. The name VISHNUGUPTA appears to be the personal name of the author.

Jolly arguing that this is the work of a Pandit, not of a political statesman, suggested that this Pandit was a Southerner and he could not have been connected with Candragupta's Empire in the North. According to 2.20.37-38 in the text, the largest day of the year has a duration of

18 *MUHURTAS*. This length of the day, at the summer solstice, which comes to 14 hours 24 minutes is possible only in the North India. Any conclusion concerning the home of the author from this indication would be suspect, as it may be argued that Kautilya most probably had taken over this information from earlier sources. Similarly, in 2.20.41, it had been mentioned that the sun sets no shadow at mid-day in the month of ASADHA. This means that the sun is vertically overhead at noon at the time of summer solstice. This is possible only at a place with a latitude of about 22½ degrees North, *i.e.* a place to the north a VYNDHYAS. Again the text in 2.24-5 mentions certain region in connection with the amount of rainfall such as, ASMAKA. AVANTI, APARANTA and the HAIMANYA most of them belonging to the North or North-West. Similarly, in connection with defamation, he refers to PRAJJUNA and GANDHARA (3.18.8), region that are definitely in the North-westernly direction. In 11.1.4-5 a number of oligarchies (SAMGHAS) are enumerated and they are KAMBOJA, SURASTRA, LICCHIVI, VRJI and so on and they are all situated in the North, North-West and West; and none in the South. The overall impression concluded by the study of ARTHASASTRA is that it described principally conditions then prevalent in Northern India, whatever may have been the place of birth of Kautilya. In some books it has been mentioned that CANAKYA (CHANAKYA as generally spelt) has adopted this name as he belonged to a place named CHANAK, but no other corroboration to this presumption could be traced in ARTHASASTRA or other contemporary literature (KAUTILYAN ARTHASASTRA—H.A. Bhave, p. 23.) However, according to Buddhist source, which followed immediately Kautilya Arthasastra, like the TIKA on the MAHAVAMSA, CANAKYA, that is KAUTILYA or VISNUGUPTA was an inhabitant of TAKSASILA, and this appears to be not unlikely in the absence of any cogent evidence to contradict this inference. Consequent upon the partition of the Indian sub-continent on 15 August, 1947, TAKSASILA, the then international seat of learning, has been ceded to Pakistan.

5

The State in Arthasastra

The Arthasastra is not a theoretical treatise on political science, nor does it directly concern itself with the question of the origin of the state, its nature or its functions. It does not inquire how some men come to rule over others and how the majority of men are content to be governed by few. It also does not refer to the various forms that the state organization is found to take and discuss their relative advantage and disadvantages, or merits and demerits. Whatever it says on such questions is only incidental. All the same, it primarily concerns with matters of practical administration of the state with an intensive study of all aspects of good governance and of relation with other state.

As was then the established tradition, monarchy is assumed to be the normal form of government. The entire teaching of the SASTRA is addressed to the king, who was considered to be the single ruler of the state. Concerning the origin of monarchy, the text incidentally refers to the circumstances in which it may be supposed to have been originated. In 1.13.5-7 it is mentioned that when people were oppressed by the law of the fishes, 'bigger fish swallowing the smaller one', they made MANU, the son of VIVASVAT, the king, fixing one-sixth part of grain, and one-tenth part of the goods and money as his share as the contractual price for ensuring their security and their well-being. This appears to be the original contract for the establishment of monarchy, where alone the might of the king was right. However, it may be noted that this is not the theory of social contract as is envisaged in the work of HOBBES or ROUSSEAU several centuries later. The first king ever, according to the passage, was Manu referred to above, who is evidently the supposed founder of the Solar Dynasty of kings, for VIVASVAT is the Sun, who is considered to be descended from god. This does not appear to be the fully developed theory of the 'divine origin of king', which idea was more completely developed in the MANU SMRITI, where in 7.3.8 it is asserted that the king was created out of the essences of eight divinities — INDRA, ANILA, YAMA, ARKA and others and as such he is endowed with their various powers and declared to be the incarnation of god or a great divinity in human form. There is no such categorical declaration in the ARTHASASTRA, where in Book Four there are frequent references to the King's obligations to the subjects, who gave him the authority to ensure their security and well-being, and protection from anti-social elements, like deceiptful artisans and traders, thieves, dacoits and murderers etc. as well as their protection from natural calamities, such as fire, floods etc. This is their *YOGAKSEMA*, which implies much more than mere protection of person and property; and *inter alia* includes prosperity and happiness etc. as in the text it has been asserted that the happiness of the subject lies in the happiness of the king and in what is beneficial to the subject his own benefit (1.19.34). Foreign critics like W. RUBEN, in sarcasm while branding this theory to be 'pious sentiments' became oblivious of the natural corollary that follows from this thesis that if the subjects are not happy and contented they become dissatisfied towards the ruler; and that might be the end of his rule, as was manifest during the French Revolution, and the disintegration of the mighty Union of Socialist Soviet Republic (U.S.S.R.). According to the Arthasastra the ruler is dependent on the suffrage of the ruled.

In Chapter two the king has been asked to pursue such activities as are beneficial to the subjects. These prescribed activities are: settlement on virgin land, building of dams, tanks, and other irrigational works, providing pastures for cattle, opening trade routes and ensuring safety on them, working of mines and so on. Besides, in all discussions on matters of foreign relations, these state activities are intended to be always kept in view by the ruler as objectives to be achieved. In fact the king is advised even to enter into a treaty with his natural enemy, pertaining to such undertakings as are meant to further the well-being of his subjects, in order that he may be able to outwit the latter, and achieve the ulterior objective. The ruler has to allow the interest of the subject to prevail over those of the state as stated in the context of the sale of commodities, whether indigenous or imported (2.16.4-6). The ruler has been asked to take care of the subjects like a father when a natural calamity occurs (4.3.43). This idea that the king should be as a father to his subjects is referred to elsewhere (2.1.18). In essence, the ideal set before the ruler is that of paternalistic rule, which preserves the memory of the very ancient times when the head of the tribe or clan was in actual fact the paterfamilies of the entire group. The ideal persisted, though the structure of social and state organization had materially changed and even in a democracy the paternalistic ideal not only continued but it also made the people sovereign. Actually, Kautilya propounded the theory of a 'welfare state' by stating that the state has the necessary and unavoidable duty to maintain minors, aged persons and those in distress when they have no one to look after them. (1.12.1 and 2.1.26)

There is another aspect of the protection which is laid down as the ruler's duty: and that is the protection of the social order founded on the system of *VARNAS* and *ASRAMAS*, for which the ruler is directed to see that every one carries out the duties so ordained and assigned to him (1.3.4, 16-17). This kind of social order is regarded as sacrosanct and having behind it the sanction of Vedas. Any disturbance of this order is not to be tolerated as that would lead to *SAMKARA* or a confusion of the *VARNAS* and their respective duties, which might result in the destruction of the society along with the state itself. Although reservation of the Vedic social order was one of the primary duties of the ruler, it was never the case that Vedic religion was the state religion, and a theological state is thought of in this work. No organised theological body was there to intervene in affairs of the state to safeguard religious interest or to enforce religious sanctions.

With the help of *DANDA* the ruler was supposed to prevent might from proving right and to enable the weak to hold their own against the strong, as in the absence of *DANDA*-punishment, the strong would swallow up the weak and there would be anarchy everywhere. (1.4., 13-15). It is, of course, obvious that the *DANDA* represent the coercive power of the state, reminding the maxim, 'spare the rod and spoil the child'. What one encounters today is nothing short of anarchy, because the Indian state failed to be abided by this all pervading rule— the use of *DANDA*. At the same time Kautilya has cautioned the ruler that only a just use of *DANDA* secures the protection of the people, while at the same time it ensures happiness for the ruler. An unjust, careless, or improper use of this power by the ruler might lead to serious consequences, the most serious being a revolt (*KOPA*) of the subject against the ruler (1.4.,12). The Arthasastra enumerates a very large number of acts on the part of the ruler which are likely to make the subject dissatisfied with his rule and the threat of a revolt of the people is expected to check on the wanton use of this coercive power by the ruler (7.5.27). In the final analysis, the ruler's authority and continuation in office depended on the contentment of the subjects, who may have no voice in the choice of the ruler; but it is they who have ultimately the power to allow him to continue or to remove him depending on how he behaves. The SASTRA has nothing against regicide if the ruler is unjustly behaved or fails to protect the subjects. The guillotine used during French Revolution in Europe has also shown that a malevolent and unjust ruler had to be done away with for his failure to protect the general interest and well-being of his subjects. In a democratic set up of our country it could be done by suffrage, before people take recourse to anarchial steps which subsequently may eventuate into bloodshed.

The size of the state contemplated by Kautilya, for the regulation of which the SASTRA was formulated, is one of a moderate size. Its entire teaching on the foreign relation of a state is based on the theory of the *MANDALA*, which presupposes the simultaneous existence of at least a dozen states within the borders of India; and it can be supposed that the state visualised by the SASTRA is by any reckoning as large as a modern state of present-day India. Unlike the later work like *MANU SMRITI* the text does not use the word 'RASHTRA — Nation' for this purpose. Now a *JANPADA* in its origin appears to have been a territory on which a particular people or tribe or clan was settled, such as the PANCALA JANAPADA; KOSALA JANAPADA and so on. At the time of the rise of the Buddhism in about 300 B.C. there has been the reference to the well-known sixteen *MAHA JANAPADAS* in Buddhist literature presumably in existence; and all these were situated in the north and north-east India. In chapter 5.3 scales of salaries have been laid down and for superior services they are as high as 48,000 *PANAS* per years. *PANA* being a silver coin, the total salaries recommended for the various grades of servants would appear to be possible only in a state with large resources at its command. Kautilya did not leave anything to chance, as when he first formulated the SASTRA, it was primarily concerned with a state of a comparatively small size; but in view of his recommendation to expand the territory by conquest, he took note of such development. The position of the monarch during the Vedic age considerably changed, and monarch had assumed more or less absolute control over the state machinery. One need not suppose that it was the SASTRA that brought such absolute monarchies into being; more likely, it nearly took note of the prevalent facts and framed its rules accordingly for regulating the state administration. Kautilya had pointed out that foreign ruler, having no interest in the welfare of the conquered state, is likely to deplete its men and resources, or to sell it for money to a third party and leave the people to their fate.

K.P. Jaiswal has attempted to show that *VAIRAJYA* is a kind of kingless constitution, apparently meaning thereby something akin to anarchy, wherein the aim of political organism is rejected, and in consequence, people behave indifferently and irresponsibly; on the other hand for similar state K. Deb meant it to be aristocracy. Kautilya has advocated the administration by '*SAMGHA*' which is a sort of oligarchy, in which origin it seems to have been a confederation of clans, each clan maintaining its chief: all the kings together forming the ruling council of the *SAMGHA*. It is stated that to *VIJIGISU*, the conqueror king's friendship with a *SAMGHA* was very advantageous, as the constitution of the *SAMGHA* was able to instill a feeling of solidarity among the confederating units. The presence of a number of chiefs on the ruling council also prevented any sudden shift of policy, such as is likely to be the case with a single ruler, whose action may be swayed by his personal whims and caprices. At the same time Kautilya cautions against the unity of the confederating members of the *SAMGHA* as it is capable to destabilize the regime by creating dissensions among them. The SASTRA recommends that the chiefs of the *SAMGHAS* should be just and benign in their dealings with other members so that there is no scope for the creation of dissension among them (11.1.55-56). Contrarily, some critics tried to show Kautilya's anxiety to do away with the *SAMGHAS* for the sake of building up an empire; or that he set himself to the task of undermining their power (R.C. Mujumdar : *Corporate Life in Ancient India*).

In chapter 11 it is said that it is better to have a *SAMGHA* on the side of the king as *SAMGHA* is invincible; and that so long as *SAMGHA* is friendly to the ruler, he is advised to make use of it with expedient of SAMA and DANA; and that it is only if a *SAMGHA* proves hostile to the ruler-*VIJIGISU* that ruler is advised to use *BHEDA* or *DANDA* overcome the hostility. This is understandable in view of the ideal of establishing his suzerainty over all states that is set before the *VIJIGISU*, but at the same time it shows no special desire to support or exterminate the *SAMGHAS*. These are almost near English equivalent to the words to *SAMA* — persuasion (in few cases should be cajoling); *DAMA* — threat or frightening. *BHED* — dissension, at times inducement of treachery or treason; and *DANDA* — infliction of punishment.

Whatever the form of government, the presence of certain elements is more than essential to make a state. This is embodied in the well-known doctrine of *PRAKRTIS*. Of these the seven are enumerated:

SVAMIN, the ruler; *AMATYA*, the minister; *JANAPADA*, the territory with people settled on it, *DURGA*, the fortified capital; *KOSA*, the treasury; *DANDA*, the army and *MITRA*, the ally (6.1.1). The last name primarily indicates the state's foreign relations. It is obvious that Kautilya had made this analysis of the elements that make up a state organization from the practical standpoint of administration, and they are enumerated according to their relative importance.

Of the various items of expenditure listed in (2.6.11) only the first four refer to the king's personal expenditure, and all other items refer to the expenditure on matters connected with state activity *vis-a-vis* its administration. Kautilya was more than specific when he stated that every precious item or article or land, that is delivered to the royal family, should be recorded in account books (2.7.2) and by implication it follows that the treasury was not the king's personal property; and the ruler was not permitted to adopt or pursue policy of personal aggrandizement at the cost of the subject's welfare or the general good of the state. At the same time Kautilya refers to three powers that operate in a state — the power of personal energy and drive of the ruler himself, the power of an army and treasury, and the power of counsel and democracy; and all these cumulatively help the king to easily overcome energetic or mighty rivals (9.1.2.-I6).

In chapter 8, Kautilya has enumerated several qualities required of a good king, besides his personal qualities like eloquence, boldness, memory, intelligence etc. A competent ruler is one who is a native of the territory, who follows the teaching of the *SASTRAS*, who is free from disease and is strong and of noble birth. This list of qualities is quite exhaustive and not free from romantic and utopian idealism, of which Kautilya was aware of, as a ruler born with all these qualities must indeed be rare. Therefore, Kautilya laid considerable stress and importance on the training of a ruler in all the spheres of his activities as an administrator of the state. The requirement that the ruler should be trained in Philosophy is not the same thing as Plato's plea that philosopher should be the king; as obviously Kautilya did not like the idea that destiny of India lay only in the hands of voluptuous and indolent tyrants and substituted for it a picture derived from historical example that rulers of India stood on a higher rung of contemporary culture. In addition, a ruler was expected to exercise control over his senses and keep such passions as lust, anger, avarice, pride, ego and so on in check (1.6.1). Seven vices, three arising from wrathful temper and four originating in lust are mentioned and their relative seriousness discussed at length (1.6.1-12). There are instructions as to how the ruler should adjust his conduct in respect of the three goals of *DHARMA*, *ARTHA* and *KAMA*, as he was not expected to lead the life of an ascetic or a saint (1.7; 9); and has a special position and the responsibility to ensure material prosperity not only for himself, but also for the subjects.

It is the king or ruler who sets the tone to the whole administration and his subordinate officers follow him as he is. The supremacy of the conduct of the ruler has been brought out in the clearest possible terms. But no ruler, however, competent or powerful, can run the state single handed, lays down the text. He is to be assisted by ministers in his task and guided by a *PUROHITA*, who, in practice must have wielded great influence over the ruler, and through him over the administration, but he does not seem to occupy any position in the administrative set up. In any case the *PUROHITA* was not a representative of an organized church, claiming an authority superior to that of the secular power. There was in India little scope for a clash between the church and the state such as found in the history of the West. The appointment, punishment and dismissal of a *PUROHITA* by the king have been envisaged in the text (1.10.2; and 9.3.14).

Constitutionally, the state functionary next in importance to the king, is the *AMATYA* or *MANTRIN*; the former stands for all high officers of all departments, whereas the latter seems to be primarily a counsellor because of his training and knowledge, and was required to give expert advise on all the state affairs. Kautilya asserts that a king should appoint three or four counsellors, neither more nor less. It is argued that a single *MANTRIN* would be difficult to control, two might quarrel and ruin the state or conspire against the king. At the same time, a larger number would affect the secrecy of counsel, on which naturally great stress has been laid (1.15.34-40). Three or Four *MANTRINS* form a consultative body and the secret consultation is to be about undertakings that may have to be carried out. An undertaking is to be discussed in its five-fold aspects—(1) ways and means of starting an undertaking, (2) resources in men and material necessary for it, (3) place and time of execution, (4) forestalling obstacles and (5) its successful accomplishment. In addition, there is *MANTRI-PARISAD*, which is a council of heads of departments and its main functions have been declared to be : (1) starting work on a new undertaking, (2) continue an undertaking already begun, (3) improving a work, and (4) implementation of orders issued (1.15.52). It implies that this council of heads of departments is concerned with the execution of decision made by the king. It is also expected to keep a watch on those who may not be loyal to the king (1.15.51). It is stated that the king should follow the course of conduct that is recommended by the majority or that is capable of leading to the achievement of the object (1.15.58-59). The king has the power of vetoing. There is no evidence in the text of a hereditary nobility, resident either in the capital or in the country-side, who may be supposed to belong to upper privileged class. It gives the impression that wisdom and capability were the only yardstick for their being so appointed, in addition to their loyalty to the state.

There is no reason to doubt that there is no constitutional check thought of in this text on the absolute power of the monarch. What checks are thought of are indirect. The *DANDANITI* impressed on the ruler the fact that it is in his own interest to make use of his power with judiciousness. In addition, the constraints imposed by the Vedic way of life as sacred, would also serve to make the ruler behave with moderation.

Of course, the *PUROHITA* would constantly be reminding him of his duty and that would be a sort of check, though the *PUROHITA* has no power to enforce his will on the ruler. Perhaps, the most effective check on the ruler's behaviour is likely to be the fear of losing his throne, an oppressive ruler is bound to lead to discontent among the subjects who might, if unable to bear oppression any more, rise in revolt against him and bring about his downfall. But Indian tradition does not encourage belligerent attitude by subjects, who being fatalistic, would hardly rise in revolt against the oppression as is noticed in other countries of the world.

Monarchy is hereditary, and Kautilya specifically expresses himself in favour of rulership continuing in the same family. In normal circumstances the eldest son, it is said, should succeed to the throne. If the monarch has an only son, and that son is disaffected or dangerous, it is recommended that he may be placed in confinement or sent to exile; and if necessary may be passed over and succession fixed on some suitable son in the family. Great stress is laid on the worthiness of the prince. Only a prince endowed with the requisite qualities is to be crowned, and his proper training is emphasized. After some time, Kautilya considers the partiality of the monarch towards the crowned prince, who may resort to patricide in certain circumstances and forcibly take the reins in his own hand. It is for this reason Kautilya lays great stress on the proper training of the prince. Apart from a refractory prince, the monarch may have to face dangers from other sources. A disgruntled or ambitious minister, or other officers may conspire to oust the ruler and establish himself on the throne. Kautilya comprehensively discussed the problem of conspiracies against the ruler and recommended measures to put them down. It is characteristic of this text that it tenders advise to the likely conspirators as well; and this does not mean that the text recommends conspiracies against the ruler. It only points out how, when a conspiracy is hatched, and those concerned should be careful to safeguard their own interest. All attempts to oust the ruler, whether by conspiring officers or by the subjects rising in rebellion against oppression, imply only the substitution of one ruler by another, and at most a change of dynasty. The form of government would remain the same even after the attempt has succeeded. Sovereignty is not intended to be transferred to a council of noblemen in a sort of aristocracy or to representatives of the people in a kind of democracy.

6

Society and Social Life

The 'Arthasastra' is a text on political science and is not primarily concerned with the society and its organization. Nevertheless, it cannot avoid a reference to the soical order and life prevailing in society; for political life has no existence outside the society. It is obvious that social life has been reflected in this treatise as throwing light on the conditions that actually prevailed when it was composed.

According to the tenets of *BHAGWAD GEETA*, the social order in the country was based on the '*Varnas*' and '*asrama*' system as it is believed throughout the past several generations that it was prescribed in the Vedas, and immaculately followed as divinely ordained and immutable. The state has no hand in its creation, nor has it the right to try to modify it. The duty of the state is only to preseve this order; and not allow it to be disturbed in any way. In this respect the standpoint of 'Arthasastra' in no way differs from that of 'Dharmasastra'.

The text describes the specific duties of the four '*Varnas*—Brahmin, Ksatriya, Vaisya and Sudras'. Brahmins were the repository of knowledge and their main functions were to acquire and impart as much knowledge as possible to the remaining three '*varnas*'. The Ksatriyas formed the fighter class endowed with valour and the duty of the protection of the state and its subjects from external aggression and internal disturbances. Acquisition of territory through bravery was also their job. The 'Vaisya' indulged in agriculture, trade and commerce and the Sudras formed the labour corps, by that they were required to supply labour of any kind as required by the remaining three 'varnas'. Practising of arts and crafts was the privilege of Sudras alone.

During that period troops were recruited from all the four 'varnas', the representatives of which participated in state administration, even at the ministerial level. Still more significant is the fact that the 'Arthasastra' look upon the 'Sudras' as an Arya community, which is distinguished from '*mleccha*' a non-Aryan community. Pledging or sale of a minor belonging to any of the four 'varnas' to work as a slave was forbidden. Kautilya has made special attempts to assimilate the masses in the Aryan fold without any differentiation or discrimination relating to the 'varnas'.

Brahmins have occupied special position in the society and exercised powerful influence over the state — administration and the king in their capacity as advisers. They had a monopoly of imparting education to all and of priestcraft. The religious life of the community was under their control. As a privileged class, Brahmins received less punishment for an offence in comparison with that meted out to persons belonging to other 'varnas' for committing the same offence. They also enjoyed special rules of heritage and exemption from state taxes.

There were numerous communities in the society whose place in the scheme of four 'varnas' could not be easily determined. An attempt has been made in the Arthasastra to bring them into some sort of relation with the 'varna' system. This was done by mixing various 'varnas' through marital bondage, and inter-'varna' marriages were not deprecated, though they were not very common. Concerning the mixed communities it was laid down that each such community should be endogamous and should follow its traditional profession and immemorial custom and the law of inheritance, which may be peculiar to any region or community or 'SAMGHA' or village, should be recognized and upheld. The word used for 'community' is 'jati', which obviously implies membership by birth and which clearly corresponded to caste. Different castes existed and they were named by the profession followed by it.

A highly organized society existed. Monogamy was the general rule, but occasionally polygamy was also practised. Polyandry was almost unknown. The marriage was sacred bond until death. A childless widow was allowed to remarry, because Vedas recognised in full the keen deisire for the performance of funeral rites by the child of the dead. Child marriage was a rarity. Wife was given a place of honour and no ceremony was considered to be effective without her participation. Generally people had a high standard of morality. The unit of a social formation was the family which consisted of several members under a common head. There was no rigid caste system although class system due to vocations existed. There were approximately 50 castes which arose out of the professions followed by the constituents. However, they observed the spiritual edicts prescribed for the four '*varnas*'. This was the need of the prevailing circumstances which enveloped frequent dynastic wars. The caste system was not fully stratified and it was flexible so as to permit one to easily cross from one caste to another depending on his personal achievement in the study of literature and valour in war and ingenuity in trade irrespective of his birth. This system was based on sound economic principles of division of labour which ensured efficiency and excellence and perfection of production. It provided social insurance and promoted social service activities, and was responsible for preserving the purity of blood amongst various groups. The concept of organic unity and inter-dependence ran through the whole caste system, and each unit formed part of the whole. While none was allowed to remain in want, each was under an obligation, as long as he was able to contribute his share of labour, according to his capacity and calling for the benefit of the society. Thus was the ancient tradition preserved, social tranquillity safeguarded, civil and economic welfare secured and individual happiness and contentment provided. It was this mould of the society that enabled the total rout of Alexander and his military might.

People were generally non-vegetarian, and they considered cow to be sacred. Women were respected. Willing prostitution under state control was permitted. There were also state-controlled ale houses. Gambling, as a means of recreation, was allowed. All these vice-dens were under the strict surveillance of the secret agents of the state and they constituted a major source of revenue and information for the benefit of the state.

The extreme rigidity of the social structure proved to be detrimental to the growth of a sense of unity among all the people, as the consciousness of the feeling of separateness in the various social groups had prevented any fusion, however, gradual, between the different groups, which could have created a sense of unity. The tribal groups with their customs and cultures maintained their own separate identity and power in the administration and protection of the state. Loyalty tended to be felt towards the ruler or his dynasty, and not to any such entity as a state, and it was purely on the regional basis. Any conception like the nation state was unknown.

A healthy and beneficial practice of observance of the four '*Asramas*' existed and it represented four different ways of life to be adopted according to one's aptitude and bent of mind, rather than as successive stages in the life of the same individual. These '*asrams*' are : (1) Life of celibacy for perfection in education, (2) married life to fulfil the divine intention of procreation, (3) Retirement, and (4) renunciation in order to attain salvation and redeem the cycle of rebirth. The 'Arthasastra' has extensively dwelt upon the marriage laws, dowry, revocation and inheritance. Rules for the remarriage of a woman were also formulated; and much greater freedom for women was implicit in the rules governing marriage, marital relations and inheritance. Although people belonged to the only religion — Hindu, there was freedom of worship as several temples, in which were installed different deities, were constructed at various places in town, and particularly at the four main gates of a city. These temples were 'Brahmas, Indra, Yamas and Senapati'. There were temples of goddess Kali, Shakti etc. These temples owned large properties and they were considered sacred. Any sacrilegious act was harshly punished. For instance, the theft of a temple bullock was to be dealt with by capital punishment.

Irrespective of jurisdiction, Judges were asked to initiate '*suo moto*' proceedings against any complaint concerning a temple when brought to their notice. The practice of offering virgin maidens to the temple — "Devdasi" — was prevalent. Fairs and festivals were held to honour the temple. Despite sacramental feeling, no scruples about the sanctity of the temple property were allowed to come in the way of state interest, as temple property was allowed to be appropriated for augmenting resources of the state in times of political calamity.

Side by side with the belief in deities and their worship in temples was the belief in malevolent spirits called '*Rakshasas*' and their propitiation. One of the eight divine calamities was evil spirit and closely related to this faith were the beliefs in magical practices; superstition of all kinds and mysticism. Black magic or sorcery was prohibited and penalised, although magical rites for the common benefit were permitted. Practices which were supposed to produce occult manifestation or miraculous effects existed. Kautilya has even propounded their use for the elimination of the enemy and benefit of the state. Several alchemic and chemical recipes as would endanger the life of person or property were prepared by Kautilya, who recommended their use against the enemy, internal as well as external. Most of the Book Fourteen of the 'Arthasastra' has described a number of rites and practices producing evil effects and recommended that the extreme gullibility of people should be used unhasitatingly to the advantage of the state to further its own end. People were habituated to consult the stars and constellations before starting on an expedition or undertaking a work, and Kautilya deprecated this practice. There can be little doubt that this picture of belief in stars, in omens, in miraculous and occult manifestations, in magic with its power for good or evil, in the possession of occult powers is true to life. Superstitiousness and credulity of a high degree had characterised the life of the vast majority of people in that age, and that was in consonance with the belief of many anterior generations.

People wore cotton and woollen clothes, and men and women adorned with gold and silver ornaments and costly jewellery. Proficient craftsmen to produce such goods existed and they had a flourshing market outside India in the contiguous countries. People recreated themselves in various stage performances financed by the community by contribution, and failure to participate in such community social functions was penalised. There were eating, drinking, gambling and dancing houses for the enjoyment of the people, and they were a source of state revenue as the fees paid by the people and the proprietors of these houses were proportionately paid in the state treasury as tax. Taxation system existed in order to pool resources for running the administration, inclusive of welfare means for the subjects. Every possible and just source was tapped to replenish the treasury.

All the evidence points out to a high degree of standardization and organisation implying strong centralisation with full control over production, distribution and a highly efficient system of taxation. In essence the picture is one of the rigid and highly evolved bureaucratic machine, capable of organising and distributing surplus wealth and defending it, but little conducive to political liberty of the individual. The civilisation flourished to its highest glory and perfection, and Kautilya had composed the 'Arthasastra' for the benefit of the subject and the state bearing in mind the prevalent socio-political order and aiming at alround improvement *par excellence.*

7

State Economy

The state was sustained by the revenue it collected from the subject, who followed different vocations to make a living and pay taxes to the state. These principal vocations were agriculture (*Krishi*); cattle tendering (*Pasupalya*), and trade (*Vanijya*). These three together constituted '*Vartta*' largely meaning livelihood, and '*vartta*' was capable to provide the state with money, grains, cattle and various kinds of other products, and above all the labourers required to do these professions and the army enabling the state to hold its own people and the enemy in check. The impact of artisans and craftmen on the state economy was supposed to be comparatively negligible. As there can be no Kingdom without a country or a territory, the state could not have any existence without 'vartta'.

An important state activity, frequently referred to in the 'Arthasastra' is the settlement on unoccupied land (*Sunyanivesa*). This was not the transformation of pastured land into agricultural fields, but the occupation and settlement for the first time of new virgin territory, the relative merits of such land to be reclaimed and settled have been exhaustively described by Kautilya, alongwith the demographic features. The shifting and settlement of population in the neighbouring country was also suggested by him. (This is synonymous to the emigrants of Bangladesh in Indian territory these days.) All the unoccupied land belonged to the king, that is, the state.

Land ready for agriculture was to be given to those who were willing to pay taxes, but the grants were made for life only, implying that the farmers were not full owners, failure to till the fields by the grantees enabled the state to retrieve them and give them to the willing tiller. If the land was made arable by the peasant it was retained by him. The state helped settlers with seeds, cattle and even cash for the reclamation of the land; but these were not subsidies, or free grants, and were treated as loans to be subsequently recovered by the state at the convenience of the peasants. It was suggested by Kautilya that an entirely new country or kingdom could be created in this manner. It was sort of a strategy to acquire territory which formerly did not belong to the state and was an intrusion on foreign land so that once the demographic balance was tilted in favour of the emigrants, the intruded territory was claimed by them. (In World War One 1914-18, Germans had adopted this ruse to claim Poland's territory). The 'Arthasastra' recognises private ownership in lands, though it presupposes at the same time the existence of state owned or crown lands. Rights of alienation were recognised.

All minerals found in earth, inclusive of ores, treasures etc. belonged to the state, likewise was the case with gems and pearls, found beneath the earth or ocean.

The text recommends gift of lands to priests, preceptors and others. Grants to Brahmins were to pass inheritance belonging to the same category. They were devoid of state taxes and not permitted to be sold or mortgaged. In other words they had only usufruct of the land, neither full ownership nor exemption from taxes. These lands were not 'Jahagir' and they could not establish feudal relationship.

Kautilya asserted that best lands should not be dependent on rains, natural resources of water like rivers, lakes etc. should be tapped and irrigation should be developed for improving the agricultural products. Irrigation was mostly looked upon as a state activity, privately owned irrigation tanks were also thought of. Irrigation tax was levied. Various methods have been suggested for the increase in the yield of crops, both qualitatively and quantitatively, and the separate agriculture department was created for that purpose. Methods that could improve the quality of the various seeds of cereals were practically worked out and such seeds were distributed to cultivators through the agriculture department. For labourers on land the wages were fixed by the state and they were on monthly basis. The wages included cash and food grain for themselves and their families. The same scale applied to horticulture. It has also been stated in the 'Arthasastra' that when no prior agreement as to wages was made, the tiller was to get one-tenth of the crops and the herdsman one-tenth of the butter produced from the herd in his charge. The agriculture department closely watched the cultivators and all their agricultural processes so that they should not be cheated while claiming and receiving the state claim by way of taxes at the time of harvest, as agriculture yields were the most important part of the state revenue. There were private and state owned granaries to store foodgrains to be used when the yields were deficient and required replenishment from such hoarded stock. Destruction by pests, insects and animals was also carefully thought of and preventive or remedial measures were suggested. Barren or inferior types of lands were used for forestry and human habitation. Quite a substantial income came to the state from its forest wealth and raw materials produced in the forest which were to be turned into finished articles in factories established for the purpose. These included wood-ware, metal-wares, earthen-wares, cane-wares, ropes etc. from which a large amount of defence material was manufactured. It was expected of the officers in charge of the armoury to be thoroughly conversant with the qualities of such raw materials. The superintendent of cattle was in-charge of cattle and all other animals owned by the state and he looked to their health and care through his veterinary assistants. A separate record or log book was maintained for each animal comprising of all the relevent details. Such meticulous care was propounded by Kautilya. (In the historical period one finds partial simulation by Napoleon and Shivaji of these instructions.) The hides were used for preparation of leather goods including footwares, armours, buckets etc. Killing or maiming of cow was forbiden and guilty for these acts was drastically penalised. Animal herds were not reared for their meat. Special care was taken of bullocks, horses, camels and elephants, belonging to the various units of the army in feeding, training and exercising them; and to keep them battle worthy was the duty of the unit commanders.

Provision of routes for trade and commerce purposes was another important state activity. All trade was under the control of the superintendent of trade who fixed the fair price of the various commodities after taking into consideration such factors as investment of capital, interest charges, duties paid, rent and so on; but they were not competitive prices, and yet they did not include exorbitant profits. A profit of five per cent on indigenous goods and ten per cent on foreign goods was allowed, and heavy fines were prescribed for exceeding these limits. When there was glut of any commodity, the superintendent of trade intervened and centralized the sale of that commodity, so that the price did not slump. It is apparent that the state functioned as the trading corporation for the purchase and sale of goods at fixed price, and a definite attempt to strike a reasonable balance between the interest of the state, the traders and the customers was made. The superintendent of market was another officer who looked after the customers' interest and ensured that the trader and artisans did not cheat them by fraud in weighing and measuring, or by supplying inferior quality of goods or adulterated commodities. He was also to watch and ascertain that the goods sold in the market were not stolen property. The state manufactured a very large variety of commodities and their sale brought it substantial revenue. The state indulged in the import and export of goods, either through state officers or through private agencies; and bartering of goods was generally the practice. Foreign trade was encouraged by giving special incentives and partial tax exemption. The list of dutiable articles included practically everything from flowers, vegetables, fruits etc. on the one hand to diamonds, pearls and other precious stones on the other. Excise and customs tariff varied from one-sixth to one-twentyfifth. Goods required for a marriage or a sacrificial or other sacred rites and goods intended as gifts were not charged any duty. Imports of arms of all kinds as well as jewels, grains and cattle was duty free. It was a general rule that goods having great benefit to the state and seeds of rare kind were allowed to come in duty free. Trade by land and sea was prevalent and sketchy navigation facilities existed. Traders were given necessary protection against marauders. Weights and measures used in trade were manufactured by the state, and it was their monopoly which made it responsible for their standardization. Details about the different weights and measures and the weighing machines had been given. And a large number of balances—'*Tula*'—were also mentioned. From the description given, it appears that these were not the usual pairs of scales, but were rather balances of the steel-yard type, with two unequal arms, and marked with figures from zero to one hundred to indicate the weight in '*palas*' of the article suspended from the other end. The prices of these weighing apparatus were also fixed. A curious feature of this weighing system was that different standard of weights etc. were used for different traders, with the intention to secure double advantage to the state which received payments by larger measure, but paid out with smaller one. (This practice was prevalent in Egypt during the third to fifth Dynasties.) Weights and measures were subjected for inspection every four months and specific fee was prescribed for this state undertaking under a special department and officer for that purpose.

Coins were manufactured by the mint master (*taksana*) who had a separate department under his control. The alloys for metals of gold, silver, copper etc. used in coins were meticulously worked out and the proportion of their ingredients were fixed in such a manner so as to be commensurate with the market value of that particular coin. Gold coin had not been mentioned in the text, though they were minted later during the reign of Asoka and his successors (273-185 B.C.). Two kinds of currency were prevalent, one for use in trade, and the other for receipt in the treasury. Stringent punishment was prescribed either for adulteration or counterfeit of any coin and the inspector of coin was assigned this job; and his delinquency in duties was equally penalised. At the same time merchant guilds were allowed to manufacture their own coins with their mark with the sanction of the state and on payment of the necessary tax to the state for that purpose.

Metallurgy was known. Gold, Silver, Copper, Lead, Tin, Brass, Bronze, Iron etc. were extracted from various mines and their ore-contents in the soil were explained. Mines for precious stones like diamonds, rubies etc. existed, and pearls were fathomed out from oceans. They were exclusively state controlled, so also the manufacture of articles of gold, silver and precious stones. A separate department was created for that purpose. Twelve kinds of income was derived from mines and the state revenue was augmented, and treasury replenished. Textiles formed another flourishing industry and good source of state revenue, for there was considerable market of Indian textiles abroad, particularly Iran, Greece and Egypt. There was a separate department for this purpose. Yarn spun from wool, cotton, jute, bark-fibre, hemp and flax was in use. Silk and linen industries also flourished and added to the state revenue. Women weavers have been mentioned in the Arthasastra. Ropes, tangs and straps for domestic and army use were manufactured.

Chariots, carriages and other sundries of conveyance required by the army were manufactured by the state under a special department for that purpose.

State exercised strict control over the artisans' work and delay or failure in the delivery of the article according to the instruction of the customers was made a punishable offence. A number of legal stipulations have been mentioned in the 'Arthasastra' concerning trade and industry, including debt, interest to be charged, redemption of loan, mortgage, guarantee, use and misuse of pledge, etc. The law of partnership laying down the rules about the honesty, dishonesty and liability of the partners was also formulated.

All in all it is apparent that there was not much scope left for private enterprise in industry, although every expert had his guild. Employer-employee relationship *vis-a-vis* the wage structure, sharing of profit and loss, payment of bonus, incentives etc. were also regulated and any breach was made punishable.

Economic activities ensured substantial benefit to the state treasury which formed the inherent strength of the king in the protection and expansion of his kingdom. The different sources of income were classified under various budgetary heads; as also the items of expenditure. The majority of the items of expenditure concerned the state, its administration and the army. A large part of the state revenue was received in kind and godowns were constructed at various places to store different commodities and creating buffer stocks in order to prevent a wide fluctuation in prices; and these stores exercised a great influence on state economy. Methods of augmenting state revenue during an emergency and calamity, either man-made or natural, were suggested. A well public distribution system was in vogue. With a rigid control of the entire economic life in the state, and unlike in modern planning, emphasis was on control rather than development, as such was the practice prevalent in those days throughout the known countries. The general pattern of economic life had its base in agriculture, cattle-rearing, farming, trade, supplemented by a few small industries. High and comprehensive taxation was necessary for the king for the expansion of his dominion. The taxation policy adopted by Kautilya was not his entire innovation, but a large portion of it was derived from earlier practices/ sources; but at the same time it was his genius to modify and improve it according to the then existing expediencies and accorded the steel frame for its efficient and benign operation, safeguarding the interest, both of the state and its subject.

8

State Administration

This kind of state control over the economy was not possible wihtout an efficient administration, and the following is its epitome.

Foremost amongst the state dignitaries were the '*mantries*' (minister); '*purohita*' (priest-*cum*-preceptor); '*senapati*' (army commander); and *yuvaraja* (crown prince); and they ever always mentioned in that order. Though the same salary was laid down for all the four, the order of enumeration may be regarded as indicative of their protocol rank, and the sequence of authority as it was the warrant of the precedence. Down this grade were the chief of palace attendant and the chief of the king's guard; and any chink in their probity or fidelity made the king vulnerable. It was envisaged by Kautilya that if all these six officers came together, they could overthrow the king, who was, therefore, advised to keep the power of the treasury and the army in his own hands.

Amongst the most important administrative officers was the finance minister *samahartr*. His chief functions were accountancy and budgetary work, for which guidelines were mentioned in order to secure efficiency. In addition, he was in the administrative charge of the entire countryside — *Janpada*; and he proxied the king in the latter's absence from the kingdom. Besides, he maintained an encyclopaedic account concerning all the towns and villages of his charge with the help of the town or village headman — *gopa* or *gramica*. He organised a web of secret service agents for surveillance which helped him in maintaining law and order in the countryside. Under him there were different officers down to the level of village watchmen for investigation and detection of crime; and criminal and political intelligence concerning anti-state activities or propensities of the subjects. Revenue and police duties of these officers were overlapping; and they functioned as such. It appears that the function of the finance minister also included the functions of the modern day home minister and he had to impress on the people the efficiency of the ruler's administration. He may be regarded as a sort of governor or administrator general in the countryside. Protection of a village was the cumulative responsibility of the village; so also was the case with the person and property of its residents. These officers had a range of power, but at the same time a deterrent was imposed by awarding stringent punishment to the aberrants or delinquents. *Nagarica* was the city superintendent having alike powers, but he was not concerned with budgeting and accounts of the city, and he had also to look after civic functions like the modern day municipalities.

Another important officer of about the same status mentioned in the earlier paragraph, was *samnidhatr* who was incharge of the actual revenue and other income received by the state. He had to construct several store-houses or godowns for storing various commodities and ensure their alround security and safety. A prison-house was also under his charge. Apparently, everything that needed to be properly guarded, whether material objects or persons was regarded as the concern of this authority. He was supposed to be the encyclopaedia of all the store-houses and their contents of his charge. He was regarded as one of the most trusted officers of the king as he had to build the secret treasury of the king through condemned prisoners, who were executed after the construction work of the treasury was over.

An office of very great importance situated in the capital was *aksapatsala*. It was a sort of record-*cum*-audit office. The records maintained there pertained to: (1) activity of each state department, (2) working of the state factories and the conditions governing production in them, (3) prices, samples and standards of measuring instruments for various kinds of goods, (4) laws, transactions, customs and regulation in force in different regions, village, castes, families and corporation, (5) salaries and other perquisites of state servants, (6) what is made over to the king or members of the royal family, and (7) payments made to and amounts received from foreign princes, whether allies or foes. Really, a more comprehensive record-house can hardly be thought of under this officer. In addition, he was also to control and regulate the working of each state department and of each state undertaking. It was from this office that officers received their assignments of specific undertakings with instructions about carrying them out. When the year ended or the undertaking completed, it was to this office that they were to bring the accounts and the balances for thorough audit.

Special officers appointed to guard the frontiers were called *antapalas*. Forts were erected in all directions on the frontiers and only through specific Posts/points ingress or egress into or out of the territory was permitted. This officer controlled the entry of men and goods into the kingdom. He issued passes to incoming traders, stamp their goods, and after charging them a cess for the road sent them on to their destination.

Duta or an envoy was appointed by the king when a policy decision was taken after consultation with minister. His appointment was not permanent like an ambassador in the court of a foregin territory, but he was an envoy sent for placing and pleading the case of his state before the foreign king with respect to some specific matter. According to the nature of his mission he was either a plenipotentiary or vested with limited powers of negotiation, and accordingly he was remunerated.

The higher officers of the state were usually referred to *amatyas* of which there were three grades. The appointment of the head of a department was to be made by a royal order. He was known *adhikarana sasanasthah* mentioned in the decree with reference to an officer or department to which he was appointed by the king. *Yukta* was an executive officer who was appointed or employed as head of the department.

Qualities and qualifications of persons to be appointed for state service were also prescribed by Kautilya. The essential qualifications were: spirit, intelligence, proved integrity, honesty, loyalty to the state, incorruptibility, power of command and expression etc. Various tests, were prescribed to find out whether these qualities were possessed by the candidates. The king or queen were not to be brought in for the purposes of these tests. These tests do not appear to be practicable, as they could not be used on the extensive scale that would be necessary when a large number of officers were to be appointed. Some candidates could have failed in some of the tests and passed in some, and therefore, for the appointment to a definite post the passing of a particular test was compulsory. For instance bravery was a necessary qualification for recruitment in the army, whereas piousness and incorruptibility were essential for the profession of judge. Voluptuousness for a magistrate-*cum*-police officer was necessarily considered to be a disqualification; but all the same these tests, though they differed from one appointment to another, were essential to find out the presence or absence of these traits, rendering the incumbent eligible or non-eligible for the appointment. At the same time Kautilya was specific in asserting that one who had squnandered his patrimony, or one who had spent everything as soon as he had earned it, or the miser who amassed wealth by causing hardship to himself and his dependents should be summarily disqualified for any state appointment, or continuity in service. Kautilya had also given advice to the candidates how to acquire the state service.

The most remarkable feature of the Arthasastra is the uninhibited manner in which the organisation of the secret service is recommended to be used for a variety of purposes. Two types of secret service were distinguished. One is *samstha* — the establishment, the members of which were generally stationed; and the other was *samedra* — the rover, the member of which moved from place to place as their services might have required. Further these two categories were subdivided under different names for their functions. These secret service agents worked within the country and also in foreign territory for espionage and counter-espionage. The secret service was highly organised and it lacked any loop-hole. It was counter-productive and inherently secret and in many cases the secret service agents operated incognito and rarely exposed as such when they were indulged in spying and counter-spying. Sufficient care was taken to ensure that the agent did not double-cross. Unethical or immoral methods for the elimination of the treacherous or unrighteous persons were recommended, but at the same time greater care was to be exercised to ensure that no innocent person should be the victim. These agents were also used for the surveillance over state servants in order to generally find out corruption of any kind against the state and particularly against the state property involving fraud, embezzlement, misappropriation, thefts etc. Various means were employed to detect such offenders. Frequent transfers of servants were also ordered. The punishments prescribed for such offences against the state varied from high fine to imprisonment for a long period or on occasions death, traitors were likewise punished. The criss-cross network of secret service agents held the state employees on tenter-hooks and made them always alert, honest and dutiful in the discharge of the assigned functions.

Salaries and wages to be paid to state employees were also prescribed and the scale varied from service to service depending on its importance and state utility, the standard of living to be maintained, and the price index. Normally, one quarter of state revenue was spent on these payments, which included incidental and other expenses for government purpose. Salaries ranged from as high as 48,000 to as low as 60 *panas* (a standard and commonly used silver coin) for the different categories of state employees, and they were for the whole year. *Pana* was a silver coin about three-quarters of a tola in weight. The salaries were fairly on a liberal scale and they ensured efficiency, probity, loyalty, honesty and cumulatively prevented discontentment, which made all the difference in service. This pattern also showed that such high expenditure in administration could only be borne by a comparatively big and flourishing state. Payments to some employees were partly in cash and partly in kind. The salaries were structured in such a fashion that an average family of seven persons could subsist comfortably and honourably and as there was satisfaction generally the servants could not be prone to corruption and apathetic to their duties.

New settlements were thoroughly planned and encouraged by the state by the grant of tax-free land to various categories of the subjects belonging to four *varanas*. Such lands were, however, inalienable. Land in lieu of salary was given, but the grant of a whole village was to be avoided as far as possible.

Should a servant die while in state service, his wife and children became entitled to his wages and food-ration, and state was required to look after minors, aged, or the sick persons in the family of the deceased servant. When there was death, birth or illness in the family of the deceased servant, the state rendered help with money and honour.

Teaching was the monopoly of the Brahmins and the state could not interfere with their work. This is the reason that in the elaborate discussions of the entire administrative set up of the state, Kautilya did not mention anything about education. Knowledge of the various trades and crafts was handed down by one generation to the other, from father to son, or from the practitioner to his apprentice, usually belonging to the same class. Therefore, the state did not concern itself with the imparting of education, either academic or professional.

Public health was also not the concern of the state. There were army doctors, who were to keep themselves in readiness with medicines, instruments and bandages when a fight was about to start. The state took suitable steps when there was an epidemic and prevented any physician lending his indirect support to criminal activities by agreeing to treat patients secretly.

The administrative system described by Kautilya was true to the reality. The Mauryan Empire was administered by dividing it into provinces which were placed in-charge of viceroy, who was often a prince of royal blood, and such an arrangement was natural, for a wholly centralised administration in the far flung Empire from Afghanistan in the north to Narmada valley in the south; and the entire Indus-Gangetic plain spreading across east to west, due to difficulties of communications in those days.

The Arthasastra is theoretical in character and it set forth the ideal scheme of administration in any state after taking into account all aspects of state's possible activity, and accordingly described in fairly minute details the way in which a state should be administered. A well managed state even in the modern days can hardly avoid setting up in actual practice and the system of administration, more or less similar to the one recommended by Kautilya in the text. Various scholars have suggested that there is a common origin in the administrative system prevailing in the Achaemenian Empire to which the Hellenistic states were successors, because North-West India, for some time, before the invasion of Alexander, was included in the Achaemenian Empire (530-330 B.C.). It was also quite natural for the Seleucids, who had inherited the region from Persia to Syria to continue this administrative system. It is also apparent that Kautilya was not its primogenitor, as such a system had existed during the Mahabharata period (3500 B.C.), and perhaps, even earlier to it, according to the spiritual edict of *sastras*. What Kautilya had created is that he made over all improvements in this ancient system and rendered it to the state of his period for the protection of the state and its subjects and its efficient administration, as also the well-being of the people and it was endeared and eulogized for several centuries as the ideal of efficient administration *vis-a-vis* public service.

9

Law and Administration of Justice

This subject had been treated by Kautilya in a special compilation — BOOK THREE, setting forth in detail the law to be administered in the court. The judges are called *dharmasthas*, a name which apparently refers to *dharma*, or law by which they were to be guided in their work. The king was the final arbiter of justice, most probably in an appellate or revisionary capacity. Justice was intended to be made available to the subjects very much nearer their places of residence, and all courts were on the same footing, the final appellate authority being the king, and the judgement pronounced by him was unquestionable. Four judges of the states or *amathya* were to be appointed at: (1) a frontier post, (2) at headquarters of ten villages, (3) at headquarters of 100 villages, and (4) at the chief city among 800 villages, which in effect, was the state capital. These judges were to function independently. However, a bench of three judges was constituted for a person seeking permission to renounce wordly life or, a woman, whose husband strayed away from home for a long period of time, asking for permission to remarry. These judges were supposed to be expert in law.

A list of priorities was laid down for taking up cases for consideration. The affairs of temples, heritages, heretics, Brahmins learned in the Vedas etc. were to be taken first in this order, and then those of minors, old persons, sick persons and so on. However, this rule of priority was susceptible to change in view of certain exigencies. The judges were supposed to look cases arising out of mutual transactions among the subject covering marriage, incurring debt, sale, forcible seizures, trespass with criminal intent, scuffle and so on in which two parties were involved; and the aggrieved party was to take the matter to the court for seeking justice. The nature of the wrong suffered might be monetary, or any other loss, or physical or other injury. There were private suits for redress of wrong or injury.

Valid and invalid transactions were clearly enunciated and each ingredient constituting the transaction was clearly defined. A suit filed on the basis of invalid transaction meant not only the loss of the suit and the usual fine, but also a heavy fine in addition for relying on inadmissible transaction. Even the witnesses cited in support of this suit were to be fined. This was sort of law of contract of the modern time. This method deprecated filing of false, malicious or frivolous, suits and encouraged filing of genuine plaints.

Ordinarily, unless a complaint was lodged by the aggrieved party, the judge could not proceed in the matter. However, in the cases of affairs concerning temples, Brahmin, ascetics, women, minors, aged persons, sick persons and orphans, the judge had to introduce proceedings *suo moto*, if these did not approach the court. In this connection it was laid down that the affairs of these parties could not be dismissed on the plea of absence of jurisdiction or by postponing them or on ground of adverse possession.

It was not necessary that the complaint was to be in writing. When a complaint was brought before a judge, the clerk of the court was required to write down the following details: the time and place of the transaction, the amount of debt, and the name, caste, place of residence etc. of the complainant as well as of the defendant. He was then to record the questions put to both the parties along with their replies. Before, however, the case was proceeded with, the judge was to ask both the parties to furnish competent sureties, which was intended to ensure that the fine would be received by the state, whichever party loses the suit. Law of evidence to try these cases was also prescribed. Filing suit on the same plea was forbidden. Three to seven days' time was allowed to file the reply both of the plaintiff and the defendant and delay in filing reply was fined. Failure to file reply within three fortnights meant the loss of the suit by the defendant. As of today, there was provision for filing reply and counter reply by the contesting parties. Documentary, oral and circumstantial evidence disposed of the case; and more reliance was placed on the primary evidence of eyewitness. Quantum as well as quality of evidence was considered, independent witness had more weightage. Before tendering evidence the witnesses were to be adjured in the presence of Brahmins, a water pitcher and fire to bear witness truthfully, and the form of adjuration varied with the *varna* of the witnesses. A witness, when cited, was bound to give evidence; else he laid himself open to fine. For perjury severe punishment was given. Principles for arriving to a conclusion by the judge and the resultant verdict to be pronounced by him were extensively laid down. The party losing the suit was required to pay a fine to the state out of the decretal amount. If the defendant admitted the claim, this fine was reduced to half.

The necessity for the judges to decide the cases impartially was vividly brought out in the punishments laid down for dereliction of duty by them. A judge erring the procedure was to be suitably punished — from fine to dismissal from service. For fining innocent person, the judge was himself to be fined double the amount of the imposed fine; for making an innocent person suffer a corporal punishment, the judge was to undergo the same punishment. Any loss suffered by a party through the wrong judgement of a judge, the former was compensated eight times over. Procedural law and positive law were mentioned and the latter related to *dharma* by which was meant the *varna* and *asrama* order, and if it was threatened or disturbed by some social upheaval, it was the king who set it right. The king had no legislative power and the *dharma* was prescribed in various spiritual edicts.

Codes of law were not formulated in ancient India by law-givers specially appointed for the purposes like in Greece, nor was law the result of any legislative activity by an assembly of elders or the king. Law, as administered in courts, was regarded as immemorial, and that was true for all time. That was because in its origin it was that body of customs, and practices, common to the Aryan communities, which had been faithfully observed from generation to generation.

In Arthasastra the law was set forth under seventeen different heads: (1) marriage and allied topics, (2) partition or inheritance, (3) property dispute, (4) failure to participate in community affairs, (5) non-payment of debt, (6) concerning deposits, (7) concerning slaves and labourers, (8) undertakings in partnership, (9) revocation of a sale or purchase, (10) non-conveyance of gifts made, (11) sale without ownership, (12) concerning ownership, (13) forcible seizer of an object, (14) verbal injury, (15) physical injury, (16) gambling and challenging, and (17) miscellaneous. All matters arising out of these basic laws have been elaborately mentioned in the Arthasastra together with the nature and quantum of punishment to be inflicted on the offender.

Under the head (17) Miscellaneous, a large collection of offences, arranged in groups, in accordance with the amount of fine to be imposed has been mentioned. Most of the offences were of new type and obviously they were defined by Kautilya in view of the aberrant or delinquent nature of the community; such as immoral sex, desisting from giving assistance to a person in distress, feeding monks or *Sakya, Ajivaka* and other heretical sects at rites in honour of gods and the *pitrs* (dead parents), impersonation a state employee, putting under bondage a minor or an innocent person, causing abortion of a female slave, releasing from bondage a lawfully bound person etc.

Kautilya treated the law in the most systematic manner and made it as engulfing and as comprehensive as possible in order to deal with all types of aberrants or delinquents concerning the state, the king, territory and an individual subject including his property, person and reputation, and the mode and quantum of punishment to be awarded. The punishments variedly ranged from fine, corporal, maiming, amputation, prison term and lastly death. Offences against the state and the king like treachery, treason, misappropriation or embezzlement of state's or king's property were meted out with stringent punishment. The inherent idea was to nip in the bud criminal propensities or criminality. What was important that this code was as much, if not more, rooted in tradition as the *Dharmasastra* work.

It is perhaps, a pity and great injustice that the full code of law which we find in the Arthasastra of Kautilya, and which could well have been the basis even of modern legislation on a number of topics, came to be ignored; and its breadth of outlook, despite its adherence to the *varna* system, its warm humanitarism, and its undertakings of the realities of actual life, were set aside in favour of rather one-sided and narrow minded teaching of others in the post-Kautilyan period.

10

Internal Security

For the well-being of the subjects, the security, *inter alia*, the protection of their persons and property, became the most important priority of the state. Such security was often disturbed by criminals, who were not aliens to their fellow citizens. Therefore, some necessary checks were required against the ambivalence of human nature, which made men to live in society, but want to exercise their wits, breaking the most elementary rules designed to protect their fellow citizens' life, person and property and to maintain order in the society.

As mentioned earlier, the suppression of crime and the maintenance of law and order, especially, in the countryside was ultimately the responsibility of the *samadhartr*. Through his secret agents, he had to be on the look out for criminals and anti-social elements, including corrupt officers. He was also required to take steps to round up gangs of dacoits and thereby assert the power of the king. All the officers, who were directly concerned with the investigation of crime and punishment of criminals were subordinate to him. In the modern parlance he was the Home Minister of the state. He was assisted by three *pradestrs* and they were stationed at the headquarters of a group of 5 to 10 villages. The detection of crime and the punishments of criminals in the city was the responsibility of the *nagarikas*. They were thus, primarily police officers, within their jurisdiction and they had also the power of inflicting punishment and contrarily they were liable to be punished themselves if they inflicted monetary or corporal punishment wrongfully. They had, thus, magisterial powers without sending the proven guilty person to the trial courts. That was the reason why very great emphasis was placed on the thoroughness of the investigation in the case of major crimes like theft, murder and why these officers themselves were made liable to punishment for wrong or perverse decision. These officers were divested of powers to try civil suits, and they were merely to deal with crimes, criminality, their investigation and punishment of the proven guilty persons.

These officers were also concerned with the enforcement of the regulation, concerning the fraudulent or deceitful practices of traders, artisans, craftsmen like weavers, washermen, smiths etc. who were prone to cheat the public with respect to the quality or quantity of the goods produced or sold by them. Thirteen types of persons, whose ostensible means of subsistence were not known and who earned their livelihood by dubious means, were also required to be dealt with and controlled by these officers as they had the potentiality to corrupt other fellow citizens, including state employees. Generally, these shady characters included persons, who were prepared to give false evidence for money, practitioners of black magic, makers and dealers of counterfeit coins, poison, stupefying drugs and so on. The punishment recommended by Kautilya was banishment, which could be avoided by payment of redemption amount, to be determined in accordance with the offence.

The state took suitable measures under the direct supervision of the king when the subjects were overtaken by natural calamity like floods, epidemics, famines etc.

Almost all the crimes connected with person, property, mischief, fraud, forgery, public nuisance etc. and the state were elaborately dealt with by Kautilya in the Arthasastra. The list is so elaborate that it would become a book itself in case they are described here; but suffice it to state that any criminal act affecting the preconception stage to post-death situation of a person was very intelligently conceived of by Kautilya, who suggested the various methods of investigation including permissible torture to detect the criminal and the entailing punishment to be awarded. Kautilya was distinguishedly specific about *modus operandi* of the criminals and the rudiments of Forensic Science of the modern time. He even did not fail to state the various inferences to be drawn from the minutest clues left behind by the perpetrators. Whether a hanging was suicidal or homicidal, whether a death was due to poison, or drowning, or whether the injuries were self-inflicted or otherwise and such varied details were mentioned by Kautilya, who did not leave anything to chance or discretion of the investigating officer. In fact, Arthasastra was, and even today, constitutes the perfect manual of the modern Science of Criminology.

Kautilya had given considerable thought how basically the offences could be prevented. He had instructed to arrest a person on three grounds: on suspicion; when in possession of stolen goods; or on consideration of the circumstances attending the crime. A very exhaustive list had been given about these circumstances under which a person could be arrested on suspicion and they are cognate and germane in the modern day preventive sections of the various laws of the country. A person spending lavishly, addicted to crime, or women or gambling; found moving stealthily in disguise or at night, or making enquiries about other's property, wife etc. was the fit subject for arrest and that led to the prevention of the impending offence. When a person was found in possession of stolen goods, or articles involved in a crime, he had to prove that he acquired them lawfully; else he was treated guilty of the offence concerning these objects.

Various methods of investigation were suggested and of reading the clues left behind by the criminals; and the sequential inferences to be drawn from them by the investigating officer were mentioned. A very thorough investigation was mandatory. Ordinarily four kinds of permissible tortures are found in the Arthasastra. They are: (1) beating with a stick up to six strokes, (2) whipping upto seven lashes, (3) suspension from a height twice, and (4) giving the water tube. Fourteen other ways were also mentioned, most of them appear to be ambiguous as perfect translation of the words used in Sanskrit at that time could not be so far made. There are references to 'nine canes; twelve whipping; thirty-two slaps; two scorpion binding; burning of a finger point; heating in the sun; exposure to severe cold etc.' Torture, to be applied, had also some restriction, such as, only one type of torture was to be applied in a day; and after that there should be no torture for the next two days in succession. In the case of a pregnant woman, or a woman in the first month after her delivery, Brahmins and ascetics were exempted from torture, but other ingenious ways of their questioning were suggested until they were found to be ingenuous. Some persons were necessarily put to torture, namely, an habitual criminal, a person retracting his confessional statement, possessing stolen property, concerned with state revenue; and a person who is condemned to death by the king. In the last case nature of the torture to death was ordered by the king. These open recommendations of third degree methods for securing a confession were so thoroughly realistic in all matters connected with the running of the state, and these methods were practised, even more drastically, in all the countries, and in all the ages. Modern methods of torture are based on scientific gadgets, and even in them physical or mental torture is ingrained, as no person who has committed a crime of any nature, would speak of it and submit himself to the punishment, unless he is coerced to squeal his crime. The very fact that he is a violator of the rules adopted by the society for their benefit, shows that he violated them deliberately and with a specific intention, and unless he is corrected and retrieved to the society, he would patently remain a potential danger to the well-being of the society, and eventually he would multiply his species to the detriment of the society. This ethical code is followed throughout the world. The means available during the days of Kautilya to improve this ethical code had no other alternative than the recommended tortures.

In cases of suspected murders, post-mortem examinations were held in order to find out the cause of death. There are vivid details in the Arthasastra about the condition and appearance of the body in the case of death from different causes; such as, strangulation, hanging, drowning, poisonous substances. Kautilya had cautioned the investigating officers to be very careful and thorough while investigating into a case of suspected murder. Various poison detecting methods were suggested in order to arrive at a definite conclusion about the nature of the poison used in the commission of the offence. Kautilya had also declared the motives of murder—women, property, professional rivalry and pending law suit. In the case of suicide, it was necessary to fathom out the cause leading to the commission of suicide and the person who created the cause was to be punished; as abetment of suicide was an offence; and together with suicide it was considered to be a sinful act.

For murder, death penalty was naturally prescribed, and it took different forms according to the nature of the offence. Skinning the head and then setting it on fire was the punishment for murdering either of the parents and close relatives. Tearing asunder by bullocks was prescribed for the woman killing her husband or some elder person. Death by drowning was recommended for one who killed by poison. To impose a deterrent and inspire awe, most of these punishments were given in public view.

A large number of sex offences had been mentioned and they range from ordinary sex abuse, carnal acts, sodomy, rape and incest. Outraging the modesty of a woman was also included in that list. Those who helped the commission of these offences were similarly punished. Corporal punishment was ordinarily given.

A large number of miscellaneous offences were mentioned and they covered the entire gamut of every day life of a person, such as nuisance, mischief, negligent acts, injury, assault etc.

A special chapter has been allotted in the Arthasastra for the offences by the state officers themselves. Any dereliction of duty was made punishable, as 'example is better than precept'. Offences committed by state employees were to receive more stringent and drastic punishment than those committed by other persons. For stealing an article worth ten *panas* belonging to the state was punished with death. On this analogy, misappropriation, embezzlement, fraud, theft etc. relating to state property were punished.

A striking feature of these penal laws was the absence of any mention of imprisonment as punishment for any of the crimes, though there were prison-houses. Punishment, as a rule, took the form of fines, which were allowed to be substituted even when originally corporal punishment was ordered. Fines ranged from a few *panas* to 1000 *panas* and additional surcharge of five per cent was also levied on fines above 100 *panas*. The quantum of the fine to be imposed was to be strictly in accordance with what was prescribed and there should be no greediness in imposing them. The preference for fines was due to the circumstance that they were an important source of state revenue.

Imposition of these punishments was not arbitrary. The *pradestr* was required to use his discretion in imposing them by taking into consideration the character of the offender, the nature of the offence, extenuating or aggravating or provocating circumstances, if any, the time and place of the offence, and the immediate and future consequences of the crime and the punishment. He was to show partiality neither to the king, nor to the subjects. He was not to swell state coffers by imposing exorbitant fines, nor deprive the state of its dues by imposing light fines.

In this Book a full penal code together with a police manual was prescribed by Kautilya. The code did not have the sanctity of tradition behind it, as was the case with the law administered in the courts of *dharmasthas*. But even this code must be supposed to be the result of a long process of evolution in the field of suppression of crime, which is one of the most important functions of the state. We find relics or vestiges of the old forms of crude punishment, with effort at mitigating their vigour in many cases. These laws generally correspond to the modern civil and criminal laws. Modern courts were introduced to meet the growing needs of an increasingly complex social economy and to implement the decision of a highly organized bureaucracy on matters unknown to the old legal system. The crimes mentioned by Kautilya were committed in every society of the world, and they would continue to be committed now, and in future also, as human nature is prone to delinquency in the absence of any deterrent, for crimes always existed whatever was the form of social economy, and the need for their suppression must have arisen long before the days of Kautilya, and even during the vedic period, irrespective of the changing pattern of the government. Wherein antiquity can one find models for the detailed regulations concerning the investigation of cases of housebreaking and murder, or rules about the rounding up of dacoit gangs, or about post-mortem examination?

Far from strengthening the position of the bureaucracy, the rules were likely to make all officers, which included the judges and the police officers-*cum*-magistrate themselves, feel insecure about their position, as they would be aware that their acts were watched by secret agents, or agents provocateurs might be used to trap them. Patently the king's position was intended to be strengthened.

Obviously, there was no prison system as such. All imprisonments were supposed to be made for those unable to pay fines, or until the fines were paid; the period of imprisonment was to be determined by the amount of fine to be paid out of the wages earned for the work done for the state during the confinement. Rules about the prison-house show that there were separate wards for male and female prisoners, with sanitary arrangement, provision for worship and fire protection. Punishments were laid for prison officers exceeding their authority by harassing prisoners, preventing them from taking their meals, or answering call of nature and so on. More serious punishments were laid down for assaulting or maiming prisoners or criminally approaching a female prisoner. On certain occasion, like the acquisition of new territory by the king, or the coronation of the crown prince, or birth of a son to the king, there was to be a general amnesty and jail delivery.

The internal security of a state and its stability were prone to be disturbed by seditious elements, and the king through his secret agents dealt with them effectively, either by awarding other punishment or eliminating them secretly. A number of ways and strategies were suggested, on many occasions immoral or unethical: and women and wine often played an important role. Various distasteful ways of getting rid of traitors, treacherous persons etc. were suggested and they were to be resorted to only in the case of those who were suspected of high treason and their positional/political influence, either in the society or state hierarchy, as an open accusation and trial were fraught with danger of a mutiny or rebellion by their protagonists against the king. Its condemnation on moral or ethical grounds had no relevance when it was the question of the ruler's survival. The Arthasastra has openly acknowledged the necessity of such liquidation and that shows more Kautilya's thorough going realism than downright unscrupulousness.

Kautilya can rightly be called the primogenitor of the criminal justice system of the entire modern world.

11

Defence and External Affairs

The defence of the state was based on forts and the army, which were the first priority of the king. In his fortified capital of the state, where the king, if hard pressed by strong enemy, could entrench himself and withstand a siege over a long period, during which diplomatic moves could be made to ease the enemy's presence and avert a calamity. The army could be used for offence as well as for defence; but if it is defeated the king becomes altogether helpless and was at the mercy of the enemy. Therefore, Kautilya recommended the construction of series of forts all along the territorial borders of which the most important were one each in the principal direction. Four types of fastness-*cum*-ground were indicated with protection secured by water, desert, mountain or deep forest. The principal fort was at the state capital and all the forts had a very strong garrison. Elaborate details about the mode of constructions were given, of which were three moats outside supported by ramparts of earth with a parapet on top one after the other. They were constructed in such a manner that the enemy could not negotiate the main entrance gate until he crossed these moats and ramparts. Moats were filled with water and crocodiles and a draw bridge on each of them was operated only by the guards on duty. Outsiders could not operate these draw bridges, and therefore, they rendered themselves incapable to approach the main gate. On the rampart were to be turrets at intervals and non-vulnerable arrangements were made for the archers to shoot the intruder without exposing themselves. The approaches to the forts were to be strewn with various kinds of booby traps and contrivances intended for hindering the progress of enemy troops.

The army had four wings — infantry, cavalry, elephant division and chariot division; besides there were sappers and miners. The fortified capital was to be garrisoned by loyal troops belonging to these wings and they were under more than one commander, the reason being, to thwart any possibility to succumb to the instigation of an enemy to turn traitor, as the commanders would be afraid of one another. A unified command for the entire garrison was not necessary since the king was the Commander-in-Chief of all the army, and he was in a position to check inter-command rivalries, and in consequence insure loyalty of all the troops. Since forts were places of refuge in times of distress caused by the enemy, sufficient supply of water, food and fodder was to be categorically ensured for a prolonged siege. In the successive generations rulers had adopted *in toto* all these arrangements for effecting a strong fort.

Recruitment from all the four *varnas* was made. Ksatriya and Sudras formed a large part of the fighting forces. From a common pool recruits were trained in the art of warfare in accordance with the strategy of each of the four wings to which they were subsequently drafted and absorbed. The horses, camels, bullocks and elephants were also thoroughly trained accordingly. The training of each wing was assigned to an expert designated as *patiya dhyaksa* (Infantry); *ratha dhyaksa* (Chariot division); *hastya dhyakasa* (Elephant division); and *ashawa dhyaksa* (Cavalry).

Troops recruited belonged to the following six categories: (1) natives of the state and belonging to the family of soldiers, whose loyalty to the king and probity were not disputed. They belonged to the standing army. (2) natives of the states like serial number one, but not for the standing army. During peace time they followed their normal avocation and were drafted for army work whenever called upon to do so. (3) professional soldiers, mercenary bands having state origin and heredity, (4) the troops of any ally, (5) troops of the conquered enemy, and (6) troops of the forest tribes. Kautilya had advised cautious surveillance over number 3 to 6 categories of soldiers as they were considered vulnerable to the interest of the king in preference to their own interest, involving loot and plunder whenever an occasion came their way.

Though the existence of navy has not been mentioned in the Arthasastra, fighting in water has been indicated. The superintendent mentioned in the text was not an admiral of the fleet with military duties, as his principal duties were to control ferrying across rivers, regulate shipping at ports, collect ferry charges as well as hire for use of state boat and control riverine trade. In addition, he was vested with police duties on all waterways. It is possible that on occasions he was also required to do military duties whenever called upon to do so, such as destruction of enemy vessels, or carrying troops, ordnance etc.

Various strategic and tactical formations of warfare had been mentioned and the entire army was divided into sections of ten men, platoons, company, regiment, brigade, corps etc. These divisions were almost the same as one finds all over the world in modern army. The importance of regular training and daily fighting practices has been emphasized, and the king personally carried out inspection at regular intervals in order to ensure that the troops remained always battle worthy.

The armoury was in-charge of a separate officer. He was responsible for getting weapons manufactured and safely storing them in such a way that they do not deteriorate through heat, moisture or insects. Each weapon was to bear the king's emblem. Various fighting weapons have been described for fighting on the battlefield, for battering down an enemy's fortifications, and they included shields, armour, various accoutrements of war, catapults to throw huge stones or incendiary objects at enemy troops; and they were of indigenous origin. In order to frightening the enemy elephants and prevent them from battering the gates of the forts, pointed and strong iron nails were welded to the gates; and to prevent further opening of these gates three strong cross bars from top to bottom of the gate were arranged horizontally.

The problem of the defence of the state was interlinked with its foreign relations and policies. It was from the hostile state that the state needed to be defended. As the king was supposed to extend his kingdom by acquiring new territories, Kautilya had described foreign relationship from that standpoint. The foreign policy was summed up in the formula of six measures—*sadgunya*. This formula was associated with the theory of circle of kings, which was constituted by the following twelve categories of king: (1) The would be conqueror — *vijigisu*. (2) The enemy whose territory was contiguous to that of serial number one. (3) An ally whose territory was immediately beyond that of serial number two. (4) The enemy's ally whose territory was immediately beyond serial number four. (5) The ally of serial number one's ally with territory beyond that of serial number four. (6) The ally of the enemy's ally beyond serial number five. (7) The enemy in the rear of serial number one. (8) The ally of serial number one in the rear with the territory behind that of serial number seven. (9) The ally of serial number seven behind serial number eight. (10) The ally of serial number eight behind serial number nine. (11) The middle king with the territory adjoining those of serial numbers one and two and stronger than either of these. (12) The king lying outside or indifferent or neutral king more powerful than serial number one, two and eleven. The scheme was based on the experience everywhere that two neighbouring states with a common enemy tend to be allies. The would-be conquering king *vijigisu* who was contemplating the expansion of his dominion, was regarded as the centre of a number of states which he was supposed to overcome in his quest for suzerainty. This idea of Kautilya is very complicated and it would not conform in its entirety with the actual state of things prevailing at any time anywhere. Perhaps, it was his utopian dream that Candragupta Maurya, whose ascension to the throne of Magadha Empire was contrived and caused by him, should become invincible if his kingdom was to be centralized and surrounded by various states belonging to allies and counter-allies; and enemy and counter-enemies in such a way that any invasion on Magadha territory was initially counter-marched, counter-irritated and finally nipped in the bud. These computations and permutations were resilient and depended on various situations prevalent at the time of forging allies. However, the idea is hypothetical with great potency and relevant when a certain state endeavoured to establish supremacy over a number of neighbouring states, which Kautilya wanted Candragupta to achieve and emerge Magadha as the strongest and invincible kingdom of that era.

Relation with foreign states were to be established and negotiation carried on with them through an envoy—*duta*, or ambassadors which were of three types: one with limited assignment or power; the plenipotentiary and only the message bearer. Ambassadors were permanently posted in foreign kingdom's courts, whereas an envoy used to be sent on specific occasion with a particular purpose in view. Although by common convention, the person of the envoy was regarded as inviolable, there were feasible chances of his being detained by the enemy king. Kautilya envisaged the envoy to play the role of a dignified spy and secret agent by sending information to his own king concerning all the aspects and loopholes *vis-a-vis* vulnerable points of the state to which he was accredited as an envoy. He was also supposed to continue insurgency in that state and cause its destruction by all possible means including robbing of the treasury, killing the prince, encourage seduction, treason and treachery by loyal officers and so on with the ulterior object of making it a satellite of his own king after its complete subjugation.

The formula which summed up foreign policy consisted of six policies: (1) the policy of peace, (2) the policy of hostility, (3) the policy of remaining quiet, but on keen watch and alert, (4) the policy of marching on an expedition, (5) the policy of taking refuge, and (6) the double-cross policy of peace treaty with one king and hostility with another at the same time. The only two policies of peace and war were diversified by

Kautilya into six-fold classifications as there were different situations at that time and Kautilya desired Magadha to become the strongest kingdom in the Indian sub-continent by reducing the potential strength of other rulers. Any foreign policy was amenable to change in consideration of the accrued benefits to the state. Kautilya had mentioned three types of conquests: (1) conquest for the sake of glory and expanding territory, (2) conquest out of greed, and (3) demonical conquest out of avaricious greed for land, money, women-folk etc., and only favoured the first.

Before starting on an expeditions the king was to satisfy himself that he was superior in all essential respects/aspects to the enemy against whom he proposed to march. These included energy, bravery and personal drive of the king himself, material resources consisting of treasury and army and good counsel and diplomacy, besides the knowledge about the terrain and topography of the enemy territory and the season. At the same time the king should take great precaution that in his absence no insurrection should be allowed to take place. The overwhelming factor for the consideration of the king for any invasion was that what benefit or gain he would receive from the expedition and the impending losses, and the gains should not be commensurate with the losses, but many folds more. Before embarking on the actual expedition he should ensure that in his absence the appointed regent should be able to safeguard the kingdom.

Kautilya had described various forms of battle arrays and subterfuges to achieve victory, together with diverse strategies and counter-stratagems. He suggested frontal attack supported by flanks on either side and a strong rearguard action at the back of the enemy. Four basic types of battle arrays were recommended: (1) Staff array, (2) Serpent array, (3) Circular array, and (4) Loose array; and the choice was subject to and dependent on terrain as well as the disposition of enemy troops. Presence of a medical corps was compulsory dining an expedition, along with veterinary experts. Lucrative awards for outstanding acts of bravery during the fight were to be announced and given to the worthy soldiers. For instance, killing the enemy king, or the prince or the Commander-in-Chief was to be rewarded by the payment of 100,000 or 50,000 *panas* respectively, and 20 *panas* for killing an ordinary soldier. War trophies were liberally allowed to be acquired by the soldiers. Officers were supposed to make a note of the exploits of their soldiers. There was 'fair play' in the battle.

Kautilya, himself was a perfect soldier, fully conversant with all the facets of the martial and battle arts and he himself had trained many pupils, including Candragupta Maurya. The opportune time and place of the use of chariot division, elephant division, cavalry and infantry division were elaborately described by him in Arthasastra and these descriptions included guerilla warfares, sedition, treachery and treason in the enemy rank and file. To sum up, Kautilya had referred to the commonly used tactics that were adopted on the battlefields, and contained nothing to which objection can be taken from the military point of view, as the total rout of the enemy is the only aim of an expedition. The modern day principles are no different.

Kautilya had cautioned against destruction of enemy subjects by describing it ruinous policy, because a country without people would make no sense and there could be no kingdom without a country. Conquest of a territory meant its annexation. By successive conquests an empire could be built in which the *vijigisu*, the conqueror king, would be the sole ruler. The *vijigisu* was advised to win over the people in the vanquished territory and not to terrorize or exploit them for self-aggrandizement. He was supposed to do what was beneficial and agreeable to his new subjects and show venerence for their customs, culture, mode of living, religion, deities, fairs, festivals etc. He should behave as if he was one of them, and for them. At the same time efforts should be made to prove his bona-fides and eliminating mischievous and harmful elements. The text also described how a vassal, or feudatory king should conduct himself in relations with the suzerain in his dealing with the feudatories so that they should remain completely loyal to him and his successors over the generations. The ideal of the conquest of the world was restricted to the sub-continent of India. These conquests were an innocuous affair when one thinks of the numerous conquests in antiquity, including those of Alexander and in the medieval era of Muslims, when cities after cities were razed to the ground, predated, the male population, irrespective of age and physical inability, put to sword, and along with their women-folk and children molested and sold as slaves along with their children; and carried out complete devastation in the course of their expedition.

Arthasastra preached the ideal conquest, and, therefore, it is rightly regarded as the manual of Imperial Polity. It is also a guide to the withstanding of imperialism, whereby protection of a weak king against his strong enemy has been recommended.

One would thus, find in the text as full an advise on how to foil an ambitious king's imperialistic designs as how to conquer and build-up an empire. The teachings of Arthasastra are intended to benefit all kings—weak, strong and ambitious and that is what makes it so comprehensive as it is not a treatise on general principles, but a work concerned with recommending practical policies in any conceivable situation that could arise in actual political life. And its visualization of such situations and the courses that could be then open to a state was characterised by a realism that still continues to be unique, for its teaching has not lost its relevance in these matters even to-day. The great depth and penetration of Kautilya's political teaching and the principles he enumerated were widely applied in the First and Second World Wars, by Germany, Russia, Briton and almost all the continental countries at war.

Some of the means recommended in the text for achieving success over hostile elements might, to some, appear to be abhoring or abnoxious from moral or ethical point of view, when they forget that such means were intended to be used against intractable enemies of the state. These means were not as barbarous as the genocide of Jews by Hitler in the gas-chamber in a bid to the total extirpation of Jews.

It should be remembered that the characteristic features of the realism of this text is that the question of morality or ethics is not allowed to intrude when politics are considered, and they are to be pursued towards enemies of the state when they jeopardize its security and independence, and this position has to be tactically recognized as necessary practical politics. The dream that politics must be thoroughly ethical may, perhaps, be realised at some far distant future date. It is, however, unfair in the meanwhile to condemn an author of over two thousand years ago —an author, moreover, frankly the most realistic and practical whoever wrote on this subject—for not recommending something that is found impracticable in politics even today.

12

Introduction to English Translation

Kautilyan Arthasastra is the single treatise on the science of politics and had been specially composed by the great Kautilya for the guidance of the kings of his generation in efficiently running the administration of state in all its various aspects. It is obvious that Kautilya has taken great pains in the composition of the Arthasastra, keeping in mind the then existing political situation in the country, at the same time he has ensured to include in this treatise the principles of this science propounded by equally great teachers of the anterior generations. Thus, it is the complete and all pervading science governing the acquisition and protection of the earth (State).

Arthasastra described multidimensional matters concerning the administration/governance of a State, and ultimately it aims at the preparation of the ground for the establishment of a benevolent monarchy.

The work is in Sanskrit and begins, as usual with the sacred syllabus *Om* and homage to *Sukra* and *Brahaspati*, the precetpors of the demons and the gods respectively and the supposed promulgators of the science of politics. The Arthasastra is a treatise dealing with the fifteen principle topics into which the entire science (*sastra*) has been divided.

The topics are :

(1) Training, (2) Activity of the heads of various departments, (3) Judges, (4) Suppression of criminals, (5) Secret conduct, (6) Circle of kings as the basis, (7) Foreign policy, (8) Dealing with calamities, (9) Activity of the king on the march to war, (10) War, (11) Policy towards oligarchies, (12) Weaker king, (13) Capturing of fort, (14) Secret practice, and (15) Devices used in science.

Each topic represents a Book and accordingly it has been numbered and captioned. These Fifteen Books comprise the paraphrastic English translation, and they are spread over the following 180 sections seriated below:

TABLE OF CONTENTS

Book One: Concerning the Topic of Training

Book Two: The Activity of the Heads of Departments

Book Eight: Concerning the Topic of Calamities

Book Nine: The Activity of the King About to March

Book Ten: Concerning War

13

BOOK ONE

Concerning the Topic of Training

There are 21 chapters in this book and they are split up in 18 different sections. The topics are enumerated in sections 1 to 4 as indicated below:

Chapter	1 to 4	Enumeration of the science—
Chapter	5)	Association with elders.
Chapter	6 & 7)	Control over the senses.
Chapter	8)	Appointment of ministers.
Chapter	9)	Appointment of councillors and Chaplain.
Chapter	10)	Ascertainment of the Integrity or the absence of integrity of ministers by means of secret tests.
Chapter	11)	Appointment of persons in Secret Service.
Chapter	12)	Rules for Secret Servants.
Chapter	13)	Keeping a watch over seducible and non-seducible parties in one's own territory.
Chapter	14)	Winning over the seducible and non-seducible parties in the enemy's territory.
Chapter	15)	The topic of counsel.
Chapter	16)	Rules for the envoy.
Chapter	17)	Guarding against princes.
Chapter	18)	The conduct of the Prince in disfavour. Behaviour towards a prince in disfavour.
Chapter	19)	Rules for the king.
Chapter	20)	Regulations for the royal residence.
Chapter	21)	Concerning the protection of the king's own person.

CHAPTER ONE AND TWO

SECTION 1: IMPORTANCE OF VARIOUS SCIENCES

In this chapter Kautilya has dealt with the importance of the necessity of philosophy. According to him the Vedas — *RIGVED, SOMA* and *UAJUR* complete the triple Vedas. These together with *Atharv* and the *Itisha* Vedas are known as Vedas.

These three Vedas, Economics and Science of Politics are the only sciences according to the followers of *Manu*: whereas Economics and the Science of Politics are the only sciences propounded by *Brahaspati*, as he considered the Vedic lore a cloak for one conversant with the ways of the world. The Science of Politics is the only science according to the followers of *Usanas*, because with it are bound up undertakings connected with all the sciences. Through these sciences one can learn what is spiritual good and material well-being. *Sankhya*, *Yoga* and *Lokayata* together constitute philosophy. Investigation by means of reasoning, what is spiritul good and evil in the Vedic Lore, material gain or loss in economics, good and bad policy in the Science of Politics; as well as the relative strength and weakens of these sciences, is a useful method. Philosophy confers benefit on the people, keep the mind steady in adversity and in prosperity, and brings about proficiency in thought, speech and action. Philosophy is ever thought of as the lamp of all sciences, as the means of all actions and as the support of all laws *vis-a-vis* duties.

CHAPTER THREE

SECTION 1 (CONTINUED): DUTIES OF INDIVIDUAL AS PER *VARNAS*

Phonetics, Ritual, Grammar, Etymology, Prosody, and Astronomy are auxiliary sciences. The laws, laid down in the Vedic Lore is beneficial, as it proscribes the respective duties of the four *Varnas* and *four Arsharmas*— stages of life. They have been enumerated below:

I. Duties of Brahmins are: Studying, teaching, performing sacrifices for self, officiating at other people's sacrifices, sacrifices, making gifts and receiving gifts.

II. Duties of Ksatriya are: Studying, performing sacrifices, for self, making gifts and living by the profession of arms and protecting the kings.

III. Duties of Vaisya are: Studying, performing sacrifices for self, making gifts, agriculture, cattle-rearing and trade.

IV. Duties of Sudra are: Service of the twice born (Brahmins), engaging in an economic calling, namely agricultural, cattle-rearing and trade, and the profession of the artisan and the actor.

V. Duties of the householder are: Earning his living in accordance with his own special duties, marrying into family of the same caste but not of the same *Gotra*, approaching wife during the period (after fourth day after the beginning of the menstruation period), worship of the gods, manes and the guests, making gifts to dependents and eating after the others have eaten.

VI. Duties of the students of Vedas are: Studying the Vedas, tending the sacred fires, and ceremonial bathing, keeping the vow of living on alms only, residing till the end of his life with the preceptor or, in his absence, with the preceptor's son, or with a fellow student.

VII. Duties of forest anchorite are: Observing celibacy, sleeping on bear ground, wearing matted locks and an antelope-skin, worship of the sacred fire, and ceremonial bathing, and worshipping the gods, manes and guests; and living on forest produce only.

VIII. Duties of wandering ascetics are: Having full control over the senses, refraining from all active life, being without any possession, giving up all attachment to worldly ties, keeping the vow of begging alms, residing not in one place and in the forest, and observing external and internal, cleanliness.

IX. Duties common to all are: Abstaining from injury to living creatures, truthfulness uprightness, freedom from malice, compassionateness and forbearance. Observance of one's own specified duty leads to heaven and to endless bliss. In case of its transgression, people would be exterminated from their caste. Therefore, the king should not allow the specified duties of the different beings to be transgressed by them; for ensuring adherence to each one's special duties, he finds joy after death as well as in this life. For, people among whom the bounds of the *Aryan* rule of the life are fixed, among whom the *Varnas* and the stages of life are securely established, and who are guarded by the three *Vedas*, prosper and they do not perish. Thus, Kautilya propounded the necessity of establishing the *Vedic* Lore in the society.

CHAPTER FOUR

SECTION 1 (CONTINUED): ESTABLISHING THE NECESSITY OF ECONOMICS, AND THE SCIENCE OF POLITICS

1. Agriculture, cattle-rearing and trade, — these constitute economics, which are beneficial, as they yield grains, cattle, money, forest produce and labour.
2. Through them, the king brings under his sway his own party as well as the party of the enemies, by the use of the treasury and the army.
3. The means of ensuring the pursuit of philosophy, the three Vedas and economics is the Rod wielded by the king; its administration constitutes the science of politics, having for its purpose the acquisition of things not possessed, the preservation of things possessed, the augmentation of things preserved and the bestowal of things augmented on a worthy recipient.
4. On it is dependent the orderly maintenance of worldly life.
5. 'Therefore, the king, seeking the orderly maintenance of worldly life, should ever hold the Rod lifted up to strike.
6. For, there is not such means for the subjugation of beings as the Rod, say the ancient teachers.
7. 'No,' says Kautilya.
8. For, the king, severe with the Rod, becomes a source of terror to beings.
9. The king, mild with the Rod, is despised.
10. The king, just with the Rod, is honoured.
11. For, the Rod, used after full consideration, endows the subjects with spiritual good, material well-being and pleasures of the senses.
12. Used unjustly, whether in passion or anger, or in contempt, it enrages even forest-anchorites and wandering ascetics, how much more then the householders?
13. If not used at all, it gives rise to the law of the fishes.
14. For, the stronger swallows the weak in the absence of the wielder of the Rod.
15. Protected by him, he prevails.
16. The people, of the four *varnas* and in the four stages of life, protected by the king with the Rod, and deeply attached to occupations prescribed as their special duties, keep to their respective paths.

CHAPTER FIVE

SECTION 2: ASSOCIATION WITH ELDERS

1. Therefore, the three sciences have their root in the just administration of the Rod.
2. Administration of the Rod, rooted in self-discipline, brings security and well-being to living beings.
3. Discipline is two-fold, acquired and inborn.
4. For training disciplines, suitable stuff is necessary.
5. A science imparts discipline to one, whose intellect has the qualities of the desire to learn, listening, learning, retention, thorough understanding, reflection, rejection of false views and intentions on truth, not to any other person.
6. But training and discipline in the sciences are acquired by the authoritativeness of the teachers in the respective sciences.
7. When the ceremony of tonsure is performed, the prince should learn the use of the alphabet and arithmetic.
8. When the initiation with the preceptor is perfumed, he should learn the three, Vedas and philosophy from the learned, economics from the heads of departments and the science of politics from the theoretical and practical exponents.
9. And he should observe celibacy till the sixteenth year.
10. Thereafter should follow the cutting of the hair and marriage for him.
11. And he should have constant association with elders in learning for the sake of improving his training, since training has its root in that.
12. During the first part of the day, he should undergo training in the arts of using elephants, horses, chariots and weapons.
13. In the latter part, he should engage in listening to Itihasa.
14. The Puranas, Itivrtta, Akhyayika, Udaharana, Dharmasastra and Arthasastra — these constitute Itihasa.
15. During the remaining parts of the day and the night, he should learn new things and familiarise himself with those already learnt, and listen repeatedly to things not learnt.
16. For, from continuous study comes a trained intellect, from intellect comes practical application, and from practical application results self-possession; such is the efficacy of sciences.
17. For, the king, trained in the sciences, intent on the discipline of the subjects, enjoys the earth alone without sharing it with any other ruler, being devoted to the welfare of all beings.

CHAPTER SIX

SECTION 3: CONTROL OVER THE SENSES

(i) Casting out the Group of Six Enemies

1. Control over the senses, which is motivated by training in the sciences, should be secured by giving up lust, anger, greed, pride, arrogance and foolhardiness.
2. Absence of improper indulgence in the pleasures of sound, touch, colour, taste and smell by the senses of hearing, touch and sight, the tongue and the sense of smell, means control over the senses; or, the practice of this science gives such control.
3. For, the whole of this science means control over the senses.
4. A king, behaving in a manner contrary to that, and hence having no control over his senses, quickly perishes, though he be ruler right up to the four ends of the earth.
5. For example, the Bhoja king, Dandakaya by name, entertaining a sinful desire for a Brahmin maiden, perished along with his kinsmen and kingdom; and so did Karala, King of the Videhas.
6. Janamejaya, using violence against Brahmins, out of anger, likewise perished; Talajangha, using violence against the Bhrgus.
7. Aila, extorting money from the four *varnas* out of greed; perished and Ajabindu of the Sauviras.
8. Ravana, not restoring the wife of another through pride, perished; and Duryodhana not returning a portion of the kingdom.
9. Dambhodbhava, treating creatures with contempt out of arrogance perished; and so did Arjuna of the Haihayas.
10. Vatapi, trying to assail Agastya, out of foolhardiness, perished; and so did the clan of the Vrnis Hying to assail Dvaipayana.
11. These and many other kings, giving themselves up to the group of six enemies, perished with their kinsmen and kingdoms, being without control over their senses.
12. Casting out the group of six enemies, Jamadagnya, who had full control over his senses, as well as Ambarisa, the son of Nabhaga, enjoyed the earth for a long time.

CHAPTER SEVEN

SECTION 3 (CONTINUED)

(ii) The Life of a Sage-like King

1. Therefore, by casting out the group of six enemies he should acquire control over the sense, cultivate his intellect by association with

elders, keep a watchful eye by means of spies, bring about security and well-being by energetic activity, maintain the observance of their special duties by the subjects by carrying out his own duties, acquire discipline by receiving instruction in the sciences, attain popularity by association with what is of material advantage and properly maintain behaviour by what is beneficial.

2. With his senses thus under control he should avoid another man's wife or property as well as doing injury to others, also sleepiness, capriciousness, falsehood, wearing an extravagant dress, association with harmful persons and any transaction associated with unrighteousness or harm.
3. He should enjoy sensual pleasures without contravening his spiritual good and material well-being; he should not deprive himself of pleasures.
4. Or, he should devote himself equally to the three goals of life which are bound up with one another.
5. For, anyone of the three, *viz.*, spiritual good, material well-being and sensual pleasures, if excessively indulged in, does harm to itself as well as to the other two.
6. 'Material well-being alone is supreme,' says Kautilya.
7. For, spiritual good and sensual pleasures depend on material well-being.
8. He should set the preceptors or ministers as the bounds of proper conduct for himself, who should restrain him from occasions of harm, or, when he is erring in private, should prick him with the goad in the form of the indication of time for the performance of his regular duties by means of the shadow of the gnomon or the *alika* water clock.
9. Rulership can be successfully carried out only with the help of associates. One wheel alone does not turn. Therefore, he should appoint ministers and listen to their opinion.

CHAPTER EIGHT

SECTION 4: APPOINTMENT OF MINISTERS

1. 'He should make his fellow-students his ministers, as their integrity and capability are known,' says Bharadvaja.
2. 'For, they enjoy his confidence.'
3. 'No,' says Visalaksa.
4. 'Having been his play-mates, they treat him with disrespect.

5. He should make those his ministers who are of a like nature to him in secret matters, since they have the same character and vices.
6. For, through fear that he is conversant with their secrets they do not offend him.'
7. 'This defect is common, to both,' say the followers of Parasara.
8. 'For, through fear that they too are conversant with their secrets, he would acquiesce in what they do and what they omit to do.
9. 'To as many persons the lord of men communicates a secret, to so many does he become subservient being helpless by that act of his.
10. 'He should make those his ministers who may have helped him in calamities involving danger to life, since their loyalty is thus proved.'
11. 'No,' says Pisuna.
12. 'This is devotion, not a trait of intellect.
13. He should make those his ministers who, when appointed to tasks, the income from which is calculated, beforehand, would bring in the income as directed or more, since thus their qualities are proved.'
14. 'No,' says Kaunapadantah.
15. 'For, these are not endowed with other qualities necessary in a minister.
16. He should make those his ministers who have come, as hereditary servants from his father and grandfather, since their pure conduct is known.
17. They do not desert him even when he misbehaves, being of the same kin.
18. This is observed even among animals.
19. 'For, cattle, passing by a herd of cattle not their kin, abide only with those that are their kin.'
20. 'No,' says Vatayadhi.
21. 'For, bringing under their control everything belonging to him, they behave like masters.
22. Therefore, he should make new men well-versed in politics his ministers.
23. New men, indeed, looking upon the wielder of the Rod as occupying the position of Yama, do not give offence.'
24. 'No,' says Bahudantiputra.
25. 'One conversant with the science, but not experienced in practical affairs, would come to grief in carrying out undertakings.

26. He should appoint as ministers such persons as are endowed with nobility of birth, intellect, integrity, bravery and loyalty, because of the supreme importance of qualities in this matter.'
27. 'Everything stated above is justifiable,' says Kautilya.
28. For, from the capacity for doing work is the ability of a person judged.
29. And in accordance with their ability by suitably distributing rank among ministers and assigning place, time and work to them, he should appoint all these as ministers, not, however, as counsellors.

CHAPTER NINE

SECTION 5: APPOINTMENT OF COUNCILLORS AND CHAPLAIN

1. A native of the country, of noble birth, easy to hold in check, trained in the arts, possessed of the eye of science, intelligent, persevering, dexterous, eloquent, bold, possessed of a ready wit, endowed with energy and power, able to bear troubles, upright, friendly, firmly devoted, endowed with character, strength, health and spirit, devoid of stiffness and fickleness, amiable and not given to creating animosities — these are the excellences of a minister.
2. One, lacking in a quarter and a half of these qualities is the middling and the lowest type respectively.
3. Of these qualities he should make inquiries about nationality, nobility of birth and tractability from his kinsmen, test his training in arts and possession of the eye of science through those learned in the same sciences, learn about his intelligence, perseverance and dexterity from his handling of undertakings, test his eloquence, boldness and presence of mind on occasions of conversation, his energy and power as well as ability to bear troubles during a calamity, his uprightness, friendliness and firmness of devotion from his dealings with others, learn about his character, strength, health and spirit as well as about freedom from stiffness and fickleness from those living with him, and about his amiability and absence of a disposition to animosity by personal observation.
4. For, the affairs of a king are of three kinds, *viz.*, directly perceived, unperceived and inferred.
5. What is seen by the king himself is directly perceived.
6. What is communicated by others is unperceived by him.
7. Forming an idea of what has not been done from what is done in respect of undertakings is inferred.

8. But, because of the simultaneity of undertakings, their manifoldness and their having to be carried out in many different places, he should cause them to be carried out by ministers, unperceived by him, so that there may be no loss of place and time.
9. He should appoint a chaplain, who is very exalted in family and character, thoroughly trained in the Veda with its auxiliaiy sciences, in divine signs, in omens and in the science of politics and capable of counteracting divine and human calamities by means of Atharvan remedies.
10. And he should follow him as a pupil does his teacher, a son his father or a servant his master.
11. Ksatriya power, made to prosper by the Brahmin chaplain, sanctified by spells in the form of the counsel of ministers, and possessed of arms in the form of compliance with the science of politics, triumphs, remaining ever unconquered.

CHAPTER TEN

SECTION 6: ASCERTAINMENT OF THE INTEGRITY, OF THE ABSENCE OF INTEGRITY OF MINISTERS BY MEANS OF SECRET TESTS

1. After appointing ministers to ordinary offices in consultation with the councillors and the chaplain, king should test their integrity by means of secret tests.
2. The king should seemingly discard the chaplain on the ground that he showed resentment when appointed to officiate at the sacrifice of a person not entitled to the privilege of a sacrifice or to teach such a person.
3. He should then get each minister individually instigated, through secret agents, under oath, in this manner: 'This king is impious; well, let us set up another pious king, either a claimant from his own family or a prince in disfavour or a member of the royal family or a person who is the one support of the kingdom or a neighbouring prince or a forest chieftain or a person suddenly risen to power; this is approved by all; what about you?'
4. If he repulses the suggestion he is loyal. This is the test of piety.
5. The commander of the army, seemingly dismissed by reason of support given to evil men, should get each minister individually instigated, through secret agents, to bring about the king's destruction, with the offer of a tempting material gain, saying: 'This is approved by all; what about you?'

6. If he repulses, he is upright. This is the test of material gain.
7. A wandering nun, who has won the confidence of the different ministers and is treated with honour in the palace, should secretly suggest to each minister individually: 'The chief queen is in love with you and has made arrangements for a meeting; besides, you will obtain much wealth.'
8. If he repulses the proposal, he is pure. This is the test of lust.
9. On the occasion of a festive party, one minister should invite all the other ministers.
10. Through seeming fright at this conspiracy, the king should put them in prison.
11. A sharp pupil, imprisoned there earlier, should secretly suggest to each of those ministers individually, when they are deprived of property and honour, in this manner: 'This king is behaving wickedly; well, let us kill him and install another; this is approved by all; what about you?'
12. If he repulses, he is loyal. This is the test of fear.
13. From among them, he should appoint those proved loyal by the test of piety to posts in the judiciary and for suppression of criminals, those proved upright by the test of material gain to offices of the Administrator and in the stores of the Director of Stores, those proved pure by the test of lust to guardianship of places of recreation inside the palace as well as outside, those proved loyal by the test of fear to duties near the person of the king.
14. Those proved honest by all tests, he should make his counsellors.
15. Those found dishonest by every test, he should employ in mines, in forests for material produce, in elephant-forests and in factories.
16. 'He should appoint ministers, who have been cleared by the tests of the group of three goals of life and fear, to duties appropriate to them in accordance with their integrity; thus have the ancient teachers laid down.
17. 'However, under no circumstances must the king make himself or the queen the target for the sake of ascertaining the probity of ministers'; this is the opinion of Kautilya.
18. He should not effect the corruption of the uncorrupted as of water by poison; for, it may well happen that a cure may not be found for one corrupted.
19. And the mind, perverted by the four-fold secret tests, may not turn back without going to the end, remaining fixed in the will of spirited persons.

20. Therefore, the king should make an outsider the object of reference in the four-fold work of testing and thus investigate through secret agents the integrity or otherwise of ministers.

CHAPTER ELEVEN

SECTION 7: APPOINTMENT OF PERSONS IN SECRET SERVICE: (I) CREATION OF ESTABLISHMENTS OF SPIES

1. With the body of ministers proved upright by means of secret tests, the king should appoint persons in secret service, *viz.*, the sharp pupil, the apostate monk, the seeming householder, the seeming trader and the seeming ascetic, as well as the secret agent, the bravo, the poison-giver and the begging nun.
2. A pupil, knowing the secrets of others and bold, is the sharp pupil.
3. Encouraging him with money and honour, the minister should say, 'Regarding the king and me as your authority, report to us at once any evil of any person which you may notice.'
4. One, who has relinquished the life of a wandering monk, and is endowed with intelligence and honesty, is the apostate monk.
5. Equipped with plenty of money and assistants, he should get work done in a place assigned to him, for the practice of some occupation.
6. And from the profits of this work, he should provide all wandering monks with food, clothing and residence.
7. And to those among them, who seek a permanent livelihood, he should secretly propose, 'In this very garb, you should work in the interest of the king and present yourself here at the time of meals and payment.'
8. And all wandering monks should make similar secret proposals to monks in their respective orders.
9. A farmer, the means of whose livelihood are depleted, and is endowed with intelligence and honesty, is the seeming householder.
10. In a place assigned to him for agricultural work, he should act exactly as before.
11. A trader, the means of whose livelihood are depleted, and who is endowed with intelligence and honesty, is the seeming trader.
12. In a place assigned to him for his trade, he should act exactly as before.
13. A hermit with shaven head or with matted hair, who seeks a permanent livelihood, is the seeming ascetic.

14. Living in the vicinity of a city with plenty of disciples with shaven heads or with matted hair, he should eat, openly, a vegetable or a handful of barley at intervals of a month or two, secretly, however meals as desired.
15. And assistants of traders who are secret agents should adore him with occult practices for becoming prosperous.
16. And his disciples should announce, 'That holy man is able to secure prosperity for any one.'
17. And to those who have approached him with hopes of securing prosperity, he should specify events happening in their family, which are ascertained by means of the science of interpreting the touch of the body and with the help of signs made by his disciples, events such as a small gain, burning by fire, danger from thieves, the killing of a traitorous person, a gift of gratification, news about happening in a foreign land, saying, 'this will happen today or tomorrow,' or 'the king will do this.'
18. Secret servants and agents should cause that prophecy of his to be fulfilled.
19. To those among the visitors who are richly endowed with spirit, intelligence and eloquence, he should predict good fortune at the hands of the king and speak of their imminent association with the minister.
20. And the minister should arrange for their livelihood and work.
21. And he should pacify with money and honour those who are resentful for good reason, those resentful without reason, by silent punishment, also those who do what is inimical to the king.
22. And favoured by the king with money and honour, they should ascertain the integrity of the king's servants. Thus, these five establishments of spies have been described.

CHAPTER TWELVE

SECTION 7 (CONTINUED): (II) APPOINTMENT OF ROVING SPIES

SECTION 8: RULES FOR SECRET SERVANTS

1. And those who are without relations and have to be necessarily maintained, when they study the science of the interpretation of marks, the science of the touch of the body, the science of magic, that pertaining to the creation of illusions, the duties of the *asramas*, the science of omens, the 'wheel with the spaces' and so

on, are the secret agents; or, when they study the art of association with men.

2. Those in the land who are brave, have given up all thought of personal safety and would fight, for the sake of money, an elephant or a wild animal, are the bravoes.
3. Those who are without affection for their kinsmen and are cruel and indolent are the poison-givers.
4. A wandering nun, seeking a secure livelihood, poor, widowed, bold, Brahmin by caste and treated with honour in the palace, should frequently go to the houses of high officers.
5. By her office are explained similar offices for the shaven nuns of heretical sects.

These are the roving spies:

6. The king should employ these with a credible disguise as regards country, dress, profession, language and birth, to spy, in conformity with their loyalty and capability, on the councillor, the chaplain, the commander-in-chief, the crown-prince, the chief palace usher, the chief of the palace guards, the director, the administrator, the director of stores, the magistrate, the commandant, the city-judge, the director of factories, the council of ministers, the superintendents, the chief of the army staff, the commandant of the fort, the commandant of the frontier-fort and the forest chieftain, in his own territory.
7. Bravoes, serving as bearers of umbrella, water-vessel, fan, shoes, seat, carriage and riding animal, should spy on and ascertain the out-of-door activity of those officers.
8. Secret agents should communicate that information to the establishments.
9. Poison-givers, serving as cooks, waiters, bath-attendants, shampooers, bed-preparers, barbers, valets and water-servers, those appearing as humpbacks, dwarfs, Kiratas, dumb, deaf, idiotic or blind persons, and actors, dancers, singers, musicians, professional storytellers and minstrels as well as women should spy on and ascertain the indoor activity.
10. Nuns should communicate that information to the establishments.
11. Assistants of the establishments should carry out the transmission of spied out news by means of sign-alphabets.
12. And neither the establishments nor these assistants should know one another.

13. In case of prohibition of entry into the house for nuns, secret agents appearing at the door one after another or appearing as the mother or father or posing as female artists, singers or female slaves, should get the secret information that is spied out conveyed outside by means of songs, recitations, writings concealed in musical instruments or signs.
14. Or, a secret get-away from the house should be made by the spies by taking advantage of a pretended long illness or madness or by setting something on fire or administering poison to someone.
15. When there is agreement in the reports of three spies, credence should be given.
16. In case of continuous mistakes on their part, 'silent' punishment is the means of their removal.
17. And spies mentioned in 'The Suppression of Criminals' should live with enemies receiving wages from them, in order to find out secret information, without associating with one another.
18. They are 'persons in the pay of both'.
19. And he should appoint 'persons in the pay of both', after taking charge of their sons and wives. And he should know such agents when they are employed by the enemies. And he should ascertain their loyalty through spies of their type.
20. Thus, he should sow spies among the enemy, the ally, the middle king, the neutral king, as well as among the eighteen high officers of each of those kings.
21. Humpbacks, dwarfs, eunuchs, women skilled in arts, dumb persons and different types of Mleccha races should be employed as spies living inside their houses.
22. In fortified towns traders should constitute the spy establishments, on the outskirts of fortified towns ascetics, farmers and apostate monks in the countryside and herdsmen on the borders of the country.
23. In the forest should be placed forest-dwellers such as monks, foresters and others—a series of spies, quick in their work,—in order to find out news of the activity of the enemy.
24. And such spies of the enemy should be found out, those of the different types by his own spies of the same types, whether roving spies or spy-establishments, secret servants not bearing the marks of a secret servant.
25. In order to discover espionage by enemies, he should station at frontiers principal officers, who are non-seducible, but are shown

to be impelled by motives for action that are associated with seducible parties.

CHAPTER THIRTEEN

SECTION 9: KEEPING A WATCH OVER THE SEDUCIBLE AND NON-SEDUCIBLE PARTIES IN ONE'S OWN TERRITORY

1. When he has set spies on the high officials, he should set spies on the citizens and the country people.
2. Secret agents, opposing one another, should carry on a disputation at holy places, in assemblies, in communal gathering and other congregations of people.
3. One of them should say, 'This king is said to be endowed with all virtues and yet no virtue is to be seen in him, as he oppresses citizens and country people with fines and taxes.
4. The other should contradict him as well as those who may commend his views there.
5. He should say, 'People, overwhelmed by the law of the fishes, made Manu, the son of Vivasvat, their king.
6. And they assigned one-sixth of the grains, one-tenth of the commodities and money as his share.
7. Maintained by that, kings bring about the well-being and security of the subjects.
8. Those who do not pay fines and taxes take on themselves the sins of those kings and who do not bring about well-being and security of the subjects.
9. Therefore, even forest-dwellers offer a sixth part of their gleaned grains, saying, "This is the share for him who protects us."
10. This is the office of Indra and Yama, *viz.*, that of the kings, whose wrath and favour are visibly manifest.
11. Even divine punishment strikes those who slight them.
12. Therefore, kings must not be slighted.
13. Thus, he should restrain the common people.
14. And they should also find out rumours spreading among the subjects.
15. And spies appearing as ascetics with shaven heads or with matted hair should ascertain the contentedness or discontentedness of those, who live on his grains, cattle or money, who help him with these in calamity or prosperity, who restrain a rebellious kinsman or region, or who repel an enemy or a forest chieftain.

16. He should favour those who are contented, with additional wealth and honour.
17. He should propitiate with gifts and conciliation those, who are discontented, in order to make them contented.
18. Or, he should divide them from each other as well as from neighbouring princes, forest-chieftains, pretenders from his family and princes in disfavour.
19. If they are even then discontented, he should make them incur the odium of the country by appointing them to the office of collecting fines and taxes.
20. When they have incurred the odium, he should bring about their end by 'silent' punishment or by an insurrection in the country.
21. Or, he should post them in mines or factories, after taking their sons and wives under his protection, for fear that they might be the object of designs by enemies.
22. Those, however, who are enraged or greedy or frightened or proud, are likely to be seduced by enemies.
23. Spies appearing as fortune-tellers, soothsayers and astrologers should ascertain their mutual relations as well as their contacts with enemies or forest chieftains.
24. He should favour those, who are contented, with wealth and honour.
25. He should manage those who are discontented by means of conciliation, gifts, dissension or force.
26. In this way, the wise king should guard from the secret instigations of enemies those likely to be seduced and those not likely to be seduced in his own territory, whether prominent persons or common people.

CHAPTER FOURTEEN

SECTION 10: WINNING OVER THE SEDUCIBLE AND NON-SEDUCIBLE PARTIES IN THE ENEMY'S TERRITORY

1. The winning over of the seducible and non-seducible parties in one's own territory has been explained; that in the enemy's territory is being described.
2. One who is cheated after being promised certain things, of two persons equally skilled in some art or useful service the one who is humiliated, one who is in disfavour because of a favourite of the king, one who is defeated after being challenged to a contest, one who is distressed by banishment, one who has not achieved his

object after incurring expenditure, one who is hindered from doing his duty or receiving his inheritance, one deprived of honour or office, one held back by members of the family, one whose women-folk are molested by force, one who is put in prison, one who is fined after losing his suit in court, one prevented from indulging in wrong conduct, one whose entire property is confiscated, one tormented in confinement, one whose kinsmen are exiled or killed,—this is the group of the enraged.

3. One who has himself thwarted someone, one who has committed a serious wrong, one who has become known for a sinful act, one frightened by punishment meted out to another with a like offence, one who has seized someone's land, one who is subdued by force, one in any state department who has suddenly amassed wealth, one hoping for a pretender from the king's family coming to the throne, one disliked by the king, and one who entertains hostility towards the king,—this is the group of the frightened.
4. One who is impoverished, one whose property is taken by another, a miser, one in a calamity or, indulging in a vice and one indulging in rash transactions, — this is the group of the greedy.
5. One who is filled with self-conceit, one desirous of honour, one resentful of the honour done to his enemy, one placed in a low position, one fiery in temper, one given to violence, and one dissatisfied with his emoluments, — this is the group of the proud.
6. Among them, he should cause instigation through spies appearing as holy men with shaven heads or matted hair, — of each person of the seducible party by that spy to whom he may be devoted.
7. 'Just as an elephant, blinded by intoxication and mounted by an intoxicated driver, crushes whatever it finds on the way, so this king, not possessed of the eye of science, and hence blind, has risen to destroy the citizens and the country people; it is possible to do harm to him by inciting a rival elephant against him; show your resentment;'—in this way he should cause the group of the enraged to be instigated.
8. 'Just as a serpent, lying in hiding, emits poison at the place from which it expects danger, so this king, having become apprehensive of harm from you, will long emit the poison of anger at you; go elsewhere;'—in this way he should cause the group of the frightened to be instigated.
9. 'Just as the cow of the hunters is milked for hounds, not for Brahmins, so this king is milked for those devoid of spirit,

intelligence and eloquence, not for those endowed with qualities of the self; that other king knows how to appreciate persons of distinction; go to him'—in this way he should cause the group of the greedy to be instigated.

10. 'Just as the well of the Candalas is of use only to the Candalas, not to others, so this king, being low, is of benefit only to low persons, not to Aryas such as you; that other king knows how to appreciate persons of distinction; go to him;'—in this way he should cause the group of the proud to be instigated.
11. When they have agreed with the words 'So we shall do' and have become allied to him by the making of terms, he should employ them according to their capacity in his own works, with spies to watch over them.
12. And he should win over the seducible in the enemy's territories by means of conciliation and gifts and those not seducible by means of dissension and force, pointing out to them the defect of the enemy.

CHAPTER FIFTEEN

SECTION 11: THE TOPIC OF COUNSEL

1. When he has secured the allegiance of his own party and the party of the enemy, he should think of the undertaking of works.
2. All undertakings should be preceded by consultation.
3. The place for that should be secluded, not allowing talks to be heard outside, incapable of being peeped in even by birds.
4. For, it is known that deliberations are divulged by parrots and starlings, even by dogs and other animals.
5. Therefore, an unauthorised person must not approach the place of counsel.
6. One who divulges secret counsel should be extirpated.
7. Secret counsel is indeed betrayed by the gestures and the expressions of the envoy, the minister and the monarch.
8. Gesture is behaviour other than normal.
9. The putting on of an expression on this face is expression.
10. Concealment of that and vigilance over officers appointed should be maintained till the time of completion of the undertaking.
11. For, their prattle through negligence or in intoxication or during sleep, their immoderation such as amorousness and the like, or, a person concealed or despised, betrays secret counsel.
12. Therefore, he should guard counsel.

13. 'The divulgence of secret counsel is fatal to the security and well-being of the king and the officers appointed by him.
14. Therefore, he should deliberate alone over a confidential matter,' says Bharadvaja.
15. 'For, even councillors have councillors, and these have others still.'
16. Thus, this series of councillors leads to the divulgence of secret counsel.
17. 'Therefore, other should not know about any work sought to be done by him. Only those who undertake it should know when it is begun or even when it is actually completed.'
18. 'There is no attainment of deliberation by a single person', says Visalaksa.
19. 'For, the affairs of a king are three-fold directly perceived, unperceived and inferred.
20. Coming to know what is not known, definite strengthening of what has become known, removal of doubt in case of two possible alternatives in a matter, finding out the rest in a matter that is partly known,—this can be achieved with the help of ministers.
21. Therefore, he should sit in counsel with those who are mature in intellect.
22. 'He should despise none, but should listen to the opinion of every one. A wise man should make use of the sensible words of even a child.'
23. 'This is ascertainment of counsel, not guarding of counsel,' say the followers of Parasara.
24. 'He should ask the councillors concerning a matter exactly similar to the undertaking he has in mind, "this work was like this, or, if it were to happen like this, how then should it be done?"
25. As they might advise, so should he do that work.
26. In this way is counsel ascertained and secrecy maintained at the same time.'
27. 'No,' says Pisuna.
28. 'For, councillors, questioned about a remote affair, whether it has taken place or not, give their opinion with indifference or disclose
29. That is a defect.
30. Therefore, he should deliberate with those who are approved for the particular undertakings.
31. Holding counsel with these only he achieves success in consultation as well as its secrecy.'
32. 'No', says Kautilya.
33. For, this is a condition without fixity.

34. He should hold consultations with three or four councillors.
35. For, holding a consultation with one only, he may not reach a decision in difficult matters.
36. And a single councillor behaves as he pleases without restraint.
37. Holding consultations with two, he is controlled by the two if united and ruined by them if at war with each other.
38. With three or four, that becomes possible only with difficulty.
39. However, if it does become possible, it involves great danger.
40. With more councillors than that, it is with difficult that decisions on matters are reached or counsel guarded.
41. However, in conformity with the place, time and work to be done, he should deliberate with one or two, or alone by himself, according to their and his own competence.
42. The means of starting undertaking, the excellence of men and materials suitable apportionment of place and time, provision against failure and accomplishment of the work—this is deliberation in its five aspects.
43. He should ask them individually as well as jointly.
44. And he should ascertain their different opinions along with their reasons for holding them.
45. Having found a matter for deliberation he should not allow time to pass.
46. He should not deliberate for a long time, nor with the partisans of those to whom he would like to do harm.
47. 'He should appoint a council consisting of twelve ministers,' say the followers of Manu.
48. 'Sixteen,' say the followers of Brahaspati.
49. 'Twenty,' say the followers of Usanas.
50. 'According to capacity,' says Kautilya.
51. They should think over the king's own party and the enemy's party.
52. And they should bring about the commencement of what is not done, the carrying out of what is commenced, the improvement of what has been carried out and the excellence of the execution of order, in the case of works.
53. He should look into the affairs with those who are present.
54. With those who are not present he should hold consultations by sending out letters.
55. Indra indeed has a council of ministers consisting of a thousand sages.
56. He has that as his eye.

57. Therefore, they call him 'the thousand-eyed one,' though he is two-eyed.
58. In an urgent matter, he should call together the councillors as well as the council of ministers and ask them.
59. What the majority among them declare or what is conducive to the success of the work, that he should do.
60. And while he is doing that, the enemies should not come to know of his secret; he should, however, find out the weaknesses of the enemy. He should conceal, as a tortoise does his limbs, any limb of his own that may have become exposed.
61. Just as a person not learned in the Veda does not deserve to eat the Sraddha-meal of good persons, so a king who has not learnt the teaching of the science of politics is unfit to listen to counsel.

CHAPTER SIXTEEN

SECTION 12: RULES FOR THE ENVOY

1. When consultation has led to a choice of decision, the employment of the envoy should follow.
2. One endowed with the excellences of a minister is the plenipotentiary.
3. One lacking in a quarter of the qualities is the envoy with a limited mission.
4. One lacking in half the qualities is the bearer of a message.
5. He should start after making proper arrangements for vehicles, drought-animals and retinue of servants.
6. 'The message is thus to be delivered to the enemy; he will probably say this in reply; for that this will be the suitable reply; thus is the enemy to be outwitted;'—reflecting in this manner, he should proceed.
7. And he should establish contacts with forest chieftains, frontier-chiefs and chief officials in the cities and the countryside on the way.
8. He should observe terrains suitable for the stationing of an army, for fighting, for reserves and for retreat, for his own state and for the enemy.
9. And he should find out the size of the forts and the country as well as the strong points, sources of livelihood, defences and weak points in the enemy's territory.
10. He should enter the enemy's residence with permission.

11. And he should deliver the message as given to him, even when danger to his life is seen in so doing.
12. He should notice graciousness in speech, expression and eyes of the enemy, esteem of the envoy's words, inquiries about his wishes, keen interest in talk about the qualities of the envoy's master, offer of a seat close by, respectful welcome, remembering on pleasant occasions, and putting trust in him, as the signs of one placed; the opposite of these as the signs of one displeased.
13. To such a one he should say, 'Kings indeed have envoys as their mouthpieces, you no less than others.
14. Therefore, envoys speak out as they are told even when weapons are raised against them.
15. Of them even the lowest born are immune from killing; what to speak then of Brahmins?
16. These are the words of another.
17. This is the duty of an envoy.'
18. If not permitted to depart, he should stay on, not feeling elated by honour shown.
19. Among the enemies he should not think of himself being possessed of strength.
20. He should put up with disagreeable words.
21. He should avoid women and drink.
22. He should sleep alone.
23. For, it is often seen that the intentions of a person are revealed in sleep or intoxication.
24. He should find out about the instigation of seducible parties, the employment of secret agents against non-seducible parties, the loyalty or disaffection of the enemy's subjects towards their master and the weak points in the constituent elements of the enemy's realm, through spies appearing as ascetics or traders, or through their disciples or assistants or through agents in the pay of both appearing as physicians or heretics.
25. In case conversation with them is not possible, he should find out secret information from the utterances of beggars, drunken persons, insane persons or persons in sleep, or, from pictures, writings or signs in holy places or temples of gods.
26. When such information found out, he should make use of instigation.
27. And when asked by the enemy, he should not declare the size and strength of his own constituents.

28. He should say, 'Your Majesty knows everything,' or should say what is conducive to the success of his mission.
29. When he is being detained although his mission has not succeeded, he should thus—reflect—'Is he detaining me because he sees an imminent calamity befalling my master, or because he wants to take remedial steps against his own calamity, or because he wants to rouse against my master the enemy in the rear or his ally or to stir up an internal revolt or a forest chieftain, or because he wishes to obstruct my master's ally in front or ally in the rear, or because he wants to take remedial steps in a war of his own with another enemy or against an internal revolt or a forest chieftain of his own or because he wants to spoil the season for expedition for which my master has thoroughly prepared, or because he wants to collect stores of grains, commodities and forest produce or carry out fortifications or raise troops, or because he is awaiting time and place suitable for the operations of his own forces, or because of a feeling of contempt or through negligence, or because he seeks a continuation of close association with my master?'
30. Having found out the enemy's motive, he should stay on or escape.
31. Or, he should take into consideration some purpose regarded as desirable.
32. After delivering an unpleasant message, he should, for fear of imprisonment or death, go away even when not permitted; else he might be put under restraint.
33. Sending communications, guarding the terms of a treaty, upholding his king's majesty, acquisition of allies, instigation, dividing friends, conveying secret agents and troops into the enemy's territory.
34. Kidnapping the enemy's kinsmen and treasures, ascertainment of secret information, showing valour, helping in the escape of hostages, and resort to secret practices, — these are the functions of an envoy.
35. He should cause all this to be carried out by his envoys, and should cause a watch to be kept over the envoys of the enemy by means of counter-envoys and spies as well as through open and secret guards.

CHAPTER SEVENTEEN

SECTION 13: GUARDING AGAINST PRINCES

1. A king protects the kingdom only when he is himself protected from persons near him and from enemies, first from his wives and sons.

2. Protection from wives shall be explained in 'Regulations for the Royal Residence.'
3. As to protection from sons, however:
4. 'He should guard against princes right from their birth.
5. For, princes devour their begetters, being of the same nature as crabs.
6. Before love for them is produced in the father, silent punishment for them is best;' says Bharadvaja.
7. 'This is cruel, as it involves the killing of innocent persons and the destruction of the Ksatriya race,' says Visalaksa.
8. 'Therefore, confinement in one place is best. '
9. 'This is danger as from a snake,' say the followers of Parasara.
10. 'For, the prince, realising "through fear of my valour my father has confined me," might get the father himself in his power.
11. Therefore, making him stay in a frontier fortress is best.'
12. 'This is danger as from a fighting ram', says Pisuna.
13. 'For, realising that alone to be the means of his return, he might become the ally of the frontier chief.
14. Therefore, making him stay in the fortress of a neighbouring prince, far removed from his own territory, is best.'
15. 'This the position of a calf, for the prince, says Kaunapadanta.
16. 'For the neighbouring prince might milk his father as one milks cow with the help of the calf.
17. Therefore, making him stay with the kinsmen of his mother is best.'
18. 'This is the position of a flag for the prince, says Vatavyadhi.
19. 'For, with him as the flag, his mother's kinsmen would be making demands like Aditikausikas.
20. Therefore, he should let him free to indulge in vulgar pleasures.
21. For, sons kept engrossed in pleasures do not become hostile to the father.'
22. 'This is living death,' says Kautilya.
23. For, like a piece of wood eaten by worms, the royal family, with its princes undisciplined, would break the moment it is attacked.
24. Therefore, when the chief queen is in her *rtu* (-period), priests should offer a *caru* oblation to Indra and Brahaspati.
25. When she is pregnant, a children's specialist would arrange for the nourishment of the foetus and for delivery.
26. When she has given birth, the chaplain should perform the sacraments for the son.
27. When he is ready for it, experts should train him.

28. 'And one of the secret agents should tempt him with hunting, gambling, wine and women, suggesting to him "Attack your father and seize the kingdom".
29. Another secret agent should dissuade him from that,' say the followers of Ambhi.
30. 'This awakening of one not awake is highly dangerous', says Kautilya.
31. For, a fresh object absorbs whatever it is smeared with.
32. Similarly, this prince, immature in intellect, understands as the teaching of the science whatever he is told.
33. Therefore, he should instruct him in what conduces to spiritual and material good, not in what is spiritually and materially harmful.
34. On the contrary, secret, declaring 'We belong to you,' should guard him.
35. If in the exuberance of youth he were to entertain a longing for the wives of others, they should produce abhorrence in him through unclean women posing as noble ladies in lonely houses at night time.
36. If he were to long for wine, they should frighten him with drugged liquor.
37. If he were to long for gambling, they should create aversion in him through deceitful players.
38. If he were to long for hunting, they should frighten him through agents disguised as highway robbers.
39. If he were to entertain the idea of attacking his father, they should enter into his confidence by pretending to agree and then dissuade him saying, 'The king should not be attacked; if the attack fails, there will be death; if it succeeds, a fall in hell, an uproar and annihilation by the subjects as of a single clod of earth.'
40. They should inform if the prince is disaffected.
41. He should put an only, favourite son in prison.
42. If he has many sons, he should send the disaffected son to the frontier or some other region where he may not become as a child in the womb for the people there or a commodity for sale for those people or a source of disturbance.
43. If he is possessed of the excellences of self, he should install him in the position of the commander-in-chief or the crown prince.
44. One possessed of sagacity, one with intellect requiring to be goaded and one of evil intellect—these are the different kinds of sons.
45. He who, when taught, understands spiritual and material good and practises the same is one possessed of sagacity.

46. He who understands but does not practise is one with intellect requiring to be goaded.
47. He who is ever full of harm and hates spiritual and material good is one of evil intellect.
48. If such be the only son, he should endeavour to get a son born of him.
49. Or, he should get sons begotten on an appointed daughter.
50. An old or a diseased king, however, should get a child begotten on his wife by one of the following *viz.*, his mother's kinsman, a member of his own family, and a virtuous neighbouring prince.
51. But he should not install on the throne an only son, if undisciplined.
52. Of many sons, who are undisciplined confinement in one place is best; however the father should be beneficiently disposed towards the sons. Except in case of calamity, sovereignty passing on to the eldest son is praised.
53. Or, the kingdom should belong to the royal family; for a family oligarchy is difficult to conquer, and remains on the earth for ever without having to face the danger of a calamity befalling the king.

CHAPTER EIGHTEEN

SECTION 14: CONDUCT OF A PRINCE IN DISFAVOUR

SECTION 15: BEHAVIOUR TOWARDS A PRINCE IN DISFAVOUR

1. The disciplined prince, who finds living difficult, should obey his father when appointed to an unworthy task, except when it is dangerous to life or rouses the subject against him or involves a heinous sin.
2. If he is assigned some agreeable task, he should ask for an officer to supervise his work.
3. And under supervision of the officer, he should carry out the task assigned with special zest.
4. And he should get dispatched to his father the normal of the work as well as any extra gain received as a present.
5. If the father is even then not pleased and shows affection for another son or wife other than his mother, he should ask for leave to repair to the forest.
6. Or, in case of fear of imprisonment or death he should seek refuge with a neighbouring prince who is justly behaved, pious, truthful in speech, not given to breach of faith and welcomes and honours those who have approached him for help.

7. Staying there and becoming enriched with treasure and troops, he should enter into marriage relations with heroic men, make contacts with forest chieftains and win over seducible parties from his father's kingdom.
8. If he has to act alone, he should maintain himself by working mines and factories for gold-smelting, colouring gems and manufacturing gold and silver articles.
9. Or, he should secretly rob the wealth of heretical corporations or the wealth of temples except that to be used by Brahmins learned in the Vedas or the wealth of rich widows after entering into their confidence, and plunder caravans and sailing vessels after cheating by administering a stupefying drink.
10. Or, he should practise 'the stratagems for the conquest of an enemy town.'
11. Or, he should act after securing the support of persons from the side of his mother.
12. Or, with his appearance changed by disguising himself as an artisan, an artist, a minstrel, a physician, a professional story-teller or a heretical monk, and accompanied by associates in the same disguise, he should enter by taking advantage of some vulnerable point, and, striking the king with weapon or poison, announce, 'I am that prince; this kingdom is to be enjoyed jointly; a single person does not deserve to enjoy it; those who desire to serve me, them will I reward with double food and wages.'
13. But sons of principal officers acting as secret agents should bring the prince in disfavour to the king after securing his consent; or the mother; if she enjoys favour, should bring him.
14. If he is given up as incorrigible, secret agents should kill him with weapon or poison.
15. If not given up, they should make him addicted to women of the same character or to drinking or hunting, and seizing him at night, should bring him to the king.
16. And when he has come, he should conciliate him by the offer of the kingdom, saying, 'After me, this is yours.' Then he should confine him in one place, if still recalcitrant; but if he has other sons, he should kill him.

CHAPTER NINETEEN

SECTION 16: RULES FOR THE KING

1. When the king is active, the servants become active following his example.

2. If he is remiss, they too become remiss along with him.
3. And they consume his works.
4. Moreover, he is over-reached by enemies.
5. Therefore, he should himself be energetically active.
6. He should divide the day into eight parts as also the night by means of *nalikas*, an instrument to measure time or by the measure of the shadow.
7. A shadow measuring three *paurusas*, one *paurusa* and four *angulas*, and the mid-day when the shadow disappears, these are the four earlier eight parts of the day.
8. By them are explained the later-four.
9. Out of them, during the first eight part of the day, he should listen to measures taken for defence and accounts of income and expenditure.
10. During the second, he should look into the affairs of the citizens and the country people.
11. During the third, he should take his bath and meals and devote himself to study.
12. During the fourth, he should receive revenue in cash and assign tasks to heads of departments.
13. During the fifth, he should consult the council of ministers by sending letters, and acquaint himself with secret information brought in by spies.
14. During the sixth, he should engage in recreation at his pleasure or hold consultation.
15. During the seventh, he should review elephants, horses, chariots and troops.
16. During the eighth, he should deliberate on military plans with the commander-in-chief.
17. When the day is ended, he should worship the evening twilight.
18. During the first of the eight parts of the night, he should interview secret agents.
19. During the second, he should take a bath and meals and engage in study.
20. During the third, he should go to bed to the strains of musical instruments and sleep during the fourth and the fifth parts.
21. During the sixth, he should awaken to the sound of musical instruments and ponder over the teaching of the science of politics as well as over the work to be done.
22. During the seventh, he should sit in consultation with councillors and dispatch secret agents.

23. During the eighth, he should receive blessings from priests, preceptors and chaplain, and see his physician, chief cook and astrologer.
24. And after going round a cow with her calf and a bull, he should proceed to the assembly hall.
25. Or, he should divide the day and night into different parts in conformity with his capacity and carry out his tasks.
26. Arriving in the assembly hall, he should allow unrestricted entrance to those wishing to see him in connection with their affairs.
27. For, a king difficulty of access is made to do the reverse of what ought to be done and what ought not to be done, by those near him.
28. In consequence of that, he may have to face an insurrection of the subjects or subjugation by the enemy.
29. Therefore, he should look into the affairs of temple deities, hermitages, heretics, Brahmins learned in the Vedas, cattle and holy places, of minors, the aged, the sick, the distressed and the helpless and of women, in this order, or, in accordance with the importance of the matter or its urgency.
30. He should hear at once every urgent matter, and not put it off. An affair postponed becomes difficult to settle or even impossible to settle.
31. He should look into the affairs of persons learned in the vedas and of ascetics after going to the fire sanctuary and in the company of his chaplain and preceptor, after getting up from his seat and saluting those suitors.
32. But he should decide the affairs of ascetics and of persons versed in the practice of magic, in consultation with person learned in the three Vedas, not by himself alone, for the reason that they might be roused to anger.
33. For the king, the sacrificial vow is activity, sacrifice the administration of affairs; the sacrificial fee, however, is impartiality of behaviour, sacrificial initiation for him is the coronation.
34. In the happiness of the subjects lies the happiness of the king and in what is beneficial to the subjects his own benefit. What is dear to himself is not beneficial to the king, but what is dear to the subjects is beneficial to him.
35. Therefore, being ever active, the king should carry out the management of material well-being. The root of material well-being is activity, of material disaster its reverse.

36. In the absence of activity, there is certain destruction of what is obtained and of what is not yet received. By activity reward is obtained, and one also secures abundance of riches.

CHAPTER TWENTY

SECTION 17: REGULATIONS FOR THE ROYAL RESIDENCE

1. On a site recommended by experts in building, he should cause the royal residence to be built, with a rampart, a moat and gates and provided with many halls.
2. He should cause to be constructed a living chamber in the centre in accordance with the procedure laid down for the treasury, or a maze-house with concealed passages in wall and in its centre a living chamber, or an underground room with its opening covered by the wooden image of a deity in a nearby sanctuary and having many subterranean passages and above it a place with a stair-case concealed in a wall or having an entrance and an exit through a hollow pillar as a living chamber with the floor fixed to a mechanism and thus capable of sinking below, in order to counteract a calamity or when a calamity is apprehended.
3. Or he should vary the construction in ways other than these, because of the fear of fellow-students.
4. When fire churned from bones is taken round the royal residence three times from right towards the left, no other fire burns it nor does another fire blaze up there; also when it is smeared with ashes caused by lighting and hailwater mixed with earth.
5. Serpents or poisons do not have their power in a residence protected by a string of shoots of the *Asvattha* growing on wet land together with shoots of *Jivanti*, *Sveta*, *Muskaka and Puspawandaka* plants.
6. Letting loose peacocks, inchneumons and spotted deer on the premises destroys serpents.
7. The parrot, the starling or the fork-tailed shrike shrieks when there is fear of serpents or poison.
8. The heron becomes frantic in the proximity of poison, the pheasant becomes faint, the intoxicated cuckoo dies, the eyes of the cakora-partridge become discoloured.
9. Thus, he should take precautions against fire, poison and serpents.
10. In a part of the apartments at the back should be ladies' rooms, establishments for maternity and sickness and places for trees and water.
11. Outside that should be quarters for princesses and princes.

12. In front should be the dressing room, the council chamber, the assembly hall and a place for the ministers in-charge of princes.
13. In the open spaces between the apartments, the palace guards should be stationed.
14. In the inner apartments he should visit the queen after she is cleared of suspicion by old women.
15. For, concealing himself in the queen's chamber, his brother killed Bhadrasena, and lying in his mother's bed his son killed Karusa.
16. The queen killed the king of Kasi by mixing fried grain with poison under the guise of honey; the queen killed Vairatya with an anklet smeared with poison, the king of the Sauviras with a poison smeared girdle-jewel, Jalutha with a poison-smeared mirror; the queen killed Viduratha by keeping a weapon concealed in the braid of her hair.
17. Therefore, he should avoid these occasions.
18. He should forbid the queens contact with ascetics with shaven heads or matted hair and with jugglers as well as with female slaves from outside.
19. Nor should members of their families visit these queens except in establishments for maternity and sickness.
20. Courtesans should see them after bodies are cleansed by a bath and rubbing and after changing their garments and ornaments.
21. Men eighty years of age or women fifty years of age, appearing as a father or a mother, and aged and eunuch domestic servants should ascertain the purity or impurity of the inmates of the harem and should make them firmly devoted to what is beneficial to the master.
22. And every one in the palace should live in his own quarters and should not move to the quarters of another. And no one staying inside should establish contacts with an outsider.
23. And every object should go out of or come into the palace after it is examined and its arrival or departure recorded, its transport to its destination being under a seal.

CHAPTER TWENTYONE

SECTION 18: CONCERNING THE PROTECTION OF THE KING'S OWN PERSON

1. When risen from the bed, he should be surrounded by female guards bearing bows, in the second hall by eunuch servants wearing robes and turbans, in the third by humpbacks, dwarfs and Kiratas, in the fourth by ministers, kinsmen and door-keepers, lances in hand.

2. He should keep near him persons descended hereditarily from his father and grand-father, bound by some relationship, trained, loyal and of proved service, not anyone belonging to another country who has not been given money and honour, not even anyone belonging to his own country if taken in service after he had been harmed.
3. The palace guards should protect the king and the royal residence.
4. The head cook should cause all cooking work to be done in a guarded place by tasting it many times.
5. The king should partake of that in that same condition, after first making an offering to the sacred fire and to birds.
6. Blue colour of the flames and smoke, and a crackling sound of the fire are signs of a thing mixed with poison, also the death of birds who eat it.
7. Of boiled rice, steam having the colour of the peacock's neck, coldness, sudden change of colour as when stale, being full of unabsorbed water, and not being moist; of broths, quick drying up as well, remaining in a state of boiling, having a soiled appearance, presence of foam, becoming curdled and the destruction of smell, touch and flavour; among liquids, the appearance of a shade of colour fainter or deeper than usual and the appearance upwards lines at the edges of the mass of foam,—in the case of juice a blue line in the middle, of milk a reddish line, of wine and water black, of curds dark, of honey white; of wet substances, becoming quickly faded, becoming overcooked and having a dark blue colour in boiling; of dry substances, a quick falling to pieces and loss of colour; of hard substances softness and of soft substances hardness, and in their proximity the death of small creatures; of bed-sheets and covers, possession of dirty circles and the shedding of threads, wool or hair; of objects made of metals and gems, being smeared with mud-like dirt and the destruction of the smoothness, colour, weight, power, class and touch;—these are the indications of these objects when mixed with poison.
8. The signs of one who has administered poison, however, are: having a dry, dark face, hesitation in speech, excessive perspiration and yawning, trembling, stumbling, looking about during speech, agitation in work and not remaining steady in his own place.
9. Therefore, experts in the science of poison-cure and physicians should be in attendance on him.

10. The physician, taking from the medicine-store a medicine proved pure by tasting, and making the cook, the pounder and himself taste it beforehand, should offer it to the king.
11. Precautions for drink and water are explained by those for medicine.
12. Barbers and valets, with their garments and hands clean after a bath, should wait on the king after receiving sealed implements from the hands of palace-attendants.
13. Female slaves of proved integrity should do the work of bath-attendants, shampooers, bed-preparers, laundererss and garland-makers, or artists supervised by them should do it.
14. They should offer garments and flowers after first putting them to their eyes, and unguents to be used after bath, rubbing powder, perfumes and bath-cosmetics after first putting them on their own bosoms and arms.
15. By this is explained what has come from another person.
16. Actors should entertain avoiding plays involving weapons, fire or poison.
17. And their musical instruments should remain inside the palace as also trappings of horses, chariots, and elephants.
18. He should ride a carriage or an animal when these are attended by trustworthy servants, and a boat when it is attended by a trustworthy boatman.
19. He should not go to a boat which is tied to another boat or is caught in a violent wind.
20. At the water's edge, troops should stand on guard.
21. He should plunge in water that has been cleared by fish-catchers.
22. He should go to a park after it is cleared by snake-catchers.
23. He should go to a forest containing game, for practising on moving targets, after the danger of harm from thieves, wild animals and enemies has been removed from it by fowlers and hunters.
24. He should grant an interview to a holy ascetic in the company of trusted armed guards, to an envoy of a neighbouring prince in the company of the council of ministers.
25. Being fully armoured and riding a horse, an elephant or a chariot, he should inspect fully equipped troops.
26. At the time of his departure from and entry into the palace he should go along the royal highway, with guards stationed on both sides and with persons carrying arms, ascetics and cripples removed from it by armed men and staff-bearers.

27. He should not plunge in a crowd of men.
28. He should go to fairs, gatherings, festivals and parties only when these are supervised by officers in command of ten soldiers each.
29. And just as the king keeps a watch over others through secret agents, so should he, being self-possessed, guard himself against danger from others.

Herewith ends the First Book of the Arthasastra of Kautilya

'CONCERNING THE TOPIC OF TRAINING'

14

BOOK TWO (Part One)

The Activities of the Heads of Departments

In the original Book Two Kautilya has described the functions *vis-a-vis* the duties of the 36 heads of the different departments in equal number of chapters and their names have been serialised below:

1. Settlement of the Countryside, 2. Disposal of Non-agricultural Land, 3. Construction of Forts, 4. Lay-out of the Fortified City, 5. The Work of Store-keeping by the Director of Stores, 6. The Setting up of Revenue by the Administrator, 7. The Topic of Accounts in the Records and Audit Office, 8. Recovery of Revenue Misappropriated by State Employees, 9. Inspection of the Work of Officers, 10. The Topic of Edicts, 11. Examination of the Precious Articles to be Received into the Treasury, 12. The Starting of Mines and Factories, 13. The Superintendent of Gold in the Workshop, 14. The Activity of the Goldsmith in the Market highway, 15. The Superintendent of the Magazine, 16. The Director of Trade, 17. The Director of Forest-produce, 18. The Superintendent of the Armoury, 19. Standardisation of Weights and Measures, 20. Measures of Space and Time, 21-22. The Collector of Customs and Tolls, 23. The Superintendent of Yarns (and Textiles), 24. The Director of Agriculture, 25. The Controller of Spirituous Liquors, 26. The Supervisor of (Animal) Slaughter, 27. The Superintendent of Courtesans, 28. The Controller of Shipping, 29. The Superintendent of Cattle, 30. The Superintendent of Horses, 31-32. The Superintendent of Elephants, 33. The Superintendent of Chariots, Foot-soldiers and the Commandant of the Army, 34. The Superintendent of Passports, The Superintendent of Pasture-lands, 35. The Activity of the Administrator, Secret Agents in the Disguise

of House-holders, Traders and Ascetics, 36. Rules for the City Superintendent.

For the facility of the readers, it has been deemed expedient to split this voluminous Book comprising of about 100 pages into 3 smaller sub-books as under:

Book Two—Part one up to first 11 Chapters

Book Two—Part two from Chapter No. 12 to 24

Book Two—Part three from Chapter No. 25 to 36

BOOK TWO—(PART ONE)

Initially, the following eleven chapters have been dealt with:

1. Settlement of the Countryside, 2. Disposal of Non-agricultural Land, 3. Construction of Forts, 4. Lay-out of the Fortified City, 5. The Work of Store-keeping by the Director of Stores, 6. The Setting up of Revenue by the Administrator, 7. The Topic of Accounts in the Records and Audit Office, 8. Recovery of Revenue Misappropriated by State Employees, 9. Inspection of the work of Officers, 10. The Topic of Edicts, 11. Examination of the Precious Articles to be Received into the Treasury.

CHAPTER ONE

SECTION 19: SETTLEMENT OF THE COUNTRYSIDE

1. He should cause settlement of the country, which had been settled before or which had not been settled before, by bringing in people from foreign lands or by shifting the overflow of population from his own country.
2. He should cause villages to be settled consisting mostly of Sudra agriculturists, with a minimum of one hundred families and a maximum of five hundred families, with boundaries extending over one *krosa* or two *krosas*, and affording mutual protection.
3. He should fix, as the boundary lines, a river, a mountain, a forest, a stretch of pebbles, sand etc., a cavern, and embankment, a *Sami* tree, a *salmalt* tree or a milk-tree like *Asvattha*, *Nyagrodha* etc. (Krosa is about 1 km.).
4. He should establish a *sthaniya* in the middle of eight hundred villages, settlement a *dronamukha* in the middle of four hundred villages, a *karvatika* in the middle of two hundred villages and a *samgrahana* in a group of ten villages.
5. On the frontiers, he should erect the fortresses of frontier chiefs as the gates of the country, under the command of frontier chiefs.

6. Trappers, Gates of country and forest-dwellers should guard the intervening regions between them.
7. He should grant to priests, preceptors, chaplains and learned in the Vedas gifts to Brahmins, exempt from fines and taxes, with inheritance passing on to corresponding heirs, to head of department, accountants and others, and to *gopas*, *sthanikas*, elephant-trainers, physicians, horse-trainers and couriers, without the right of sale or mortgage.
8. He should allot to tax-payers arable fields for life.
9. Unarable fields should not be taken away from those who are making them arable.
10. He should take away fields from those who do not till them and give them to others.
11. Or, village servants and traders should till them.
12. Or, those who do not till should make good the loss to the treasury.
13. And he should favour them with grains, cattle and money.
14. These they should pay back afterwards at their convenience.
15. And he should grant to them favours and exemptions which would cause an increase in the treasury, avoid such as would cause loss to the treasury.
16. For, a king with a small treasury swallows up the citizens and the country people themselves.
17. He should grant exemptions at the time of settlement or as people come.
18. He should, like a father, show favours to those whose exemptions have ceased.
19. He should set going work in mines, factories, produce-forests, elephant-forests, cattle-herds and trade-routes and establish water-routes, land-routes and ports.
20. He should cause irrigation works to be built with natural water sources or with water to be brought in from elsewhere.
21. Or, to others who are building, he should render aid with land, road, trees and implements, and to holy places and parks.
22. If one walks out of the joint building of an irrigation work, his labourers and bullocks should do the work.
23. And he should be a sharer in the expenses and yet should receive no portion.
24. The ownership of the fish, ducks, and green vegetables in the irrigation works should go to the king.

25. The king should enforce discipline on slaves, persons kept as pledges and kinsmen who do not obey their masters etc.
26. And the king should maintain children, aged persons and persons in distress when these are helpless, as also the woman who has borne no child and the sons of one who has when these are helpless.
27. The elders of the village should augment the property of a minor till he comes of age, also the property of a temple.
28. If a person with means does not maintain his children and wife, his father and mother, his brothers who have not come of age, and his unmarried and widowed sisters, a fine of twelve panas shall be imposed, except when these have become outcasts, with the exception of the mother (Pana is a silver coin).
29. If one renounces home to become an ascetic without providing for his sons and wife, the lowest fine for violence shall be imposed, also if one induces a woman to renounce home.
30. One who has lost his capacity for activity may renounce home after securing permission from the judges.
31. Otherwise, he shall be put under restraint.
32. An ascetic sect other than the Brahmanical forest hermit, a corporation other than that of those born in the same place or an association with agreements except one for a joint undertaking shall not settle in his countryside.
33. And there should be no parks there, nor halls for recreation.
34. Actors, dancers, singers, musicians, professional story-tellers or minstrels shall not create obstruction in the work of the people.
35. Because of villages being without shelter for outsiders and because of men being engrossed in work on the fields, an increase in the treasury, labourers, goods, grains and liquids follows.
36. The king should exempt from taxes a region laid waste by the army of an enemy or by foresters, or afflicted by disease or famine, and he should prohibit expensive sports.
37. He should protect agriculture that is oppressed by the troubles of fines, labourers and taxes, and herds of cattle oppressed by thieves, wild animals, poison and crocodiles as well as by disease.
38. He should keep clear trader-routes that are harassed by the king's favourites, works-officers, robbers and frontier-chiefs or are reduced by herds of cattle.
39. Thus, the king should protect produce-forests, elephant-forests, irrigation works and mines that were made in ancient times and should start new ones.

CHAPTER TWO

SECTION 20: DISPOSAL OF NON-AGRICULTURAL LAND

1. On land unsuitable for agriculture, he should allot pastures for cattle.
2. And he should grant to ascetics wildernesses for Veda-study and *soma* sacrifices, with safety promised to everything immovable and movable in them, one *goruta* in extent at the most.
3. He should cause an animal park for the king's recreation to be laid out, with the same extent *i.e.* one *goruta*, with a single entrance, protected by a moat, containing shrubs and bushes bearing sweet fruits, having trees without thorns, with shallow pools of water and stocked with tamed deer and other animals, containing wild animals with their claws and teeth removed and having male and female elephants and cubs useful for hunting.
4. And he should establish on its border or in conformity with the suitability of the land, another animal park where all animals are welcomed as guests are given full protection.
5. And he should establish forests, one each for the products indicated as forest produce, as well as factories for goods made from forest produce, and settle foresters, attached to the produce-forests.
6. On the border of the kingdom, he should establish a forest for elephants guarded by foresters.
7. The superintendent of the elephant-forest should, with the help of guards of the elephant-forest, protect the elephant-forest on the mountain, along a river, along lakes or in marshy tracts, with its boundaries, entrances and exits fully known.
8. They should kill anyone slaying an elephant.
9. To a person bringing in the pair of tusks of an elephant dying naturally, a reward of four panas and a quarter shall be given.
10. Guards of elephant-forests, aided by elephant keepers, foot-chainers, border guards, foresters and attendants, with their own odours suppressed by the urine and dung of elephants, with their bodies covered with branches of the *Bhallataki*, and moving with five or seven female elephant decoys, should ascertain the size of the herds of elephants, by means of indications provided by sleeping places, foot-prints, dung and damage caused to river-banks.
11. They should maintain a record in writing of every elephant, whether moving in a herd, moving alone, lost from a herd or lord of a herd, and whether wild, intoxicated, cub or released from captivity.

12. They should catch elephants whose outward marks and behaviour are excellent in the judgment of elephant-trainers.
13. Victory in battle for a king depends principally on elephants.
14. For, elephants, being possessed of very big-sized bodies and being capable of life-destroying activities, pound the troops, battle-arrays, fortresses and camps of enemies.
15. Elephants form the *Kalingas* and the *Angaras* are best; those from the east, those from *Cedi* and *Karusa* and those from the *Dasarnas* and the *Aparantas* are considered as of medium quality among the elephants.
16. Those from the *Surastras* and the *Pancanadas* are declared to be of the lowest quality among them. Of all of these, valour, speed and spirit increase by training.

CHAPTER THREE

SECTION 21: CONSTRUCTION OF FORTS

1. In all four quarters, on the frontiers of the country, he should cause a nature-made fortress, equipped for fight, to be made: a water-fort either an island in the midst of water or high land shut in by water, or a mountain fort either consisting of rocks or a cave, or a desert fort either one without water and shrubs or a salty region, or a jungle fort either a marshy tract with water or a thicket of shrubs.
2. Among them a river fort and a mountain fort are places for the protectors of the country, a desert fort and a jungle fort are places for foresters or places of retreat in times of calamity.
3. In the centre of the country, he should lay out a *sthaniya*, the headquarters for revenue, on a site recommended by experts in the science of building, at the confluence of rivers or on the bank of a lake that never dries up, either a natural lake or a man-made tank, round, rectangular or square or in accordance with the nature of the building site, with water flowing from left to right, a market town, served by a land-route and a water-route.
4. He should cause three moats to be dug round it, at a distance of one *danda* from each other, fourteen, twelve and ten *dandas* broad, three-quarters or a half of the breadth deep, one-third of the surface-breadth at the bottom or square with the bottom, paved with stones or with the sides only built of stones or bricks, reaching down to natural springs of water or filled with water coming from elsewhere, with arrangements for draining excess water, and stocked with lotuses and crocodiles (Danda is about six feet in length).

5. At a distance of four *dandas* from the moat, he should cause a rampart to be made out of the earth dug out, six *dandas* high, made compact, twice that in breadth, piled upwards with a platform like flat surface at the top or with a jug-like side, pounded by elephants and bullocks having on the sides clusters of thorny bushes and poisonous creepers.
6. With the remainder of the earth, he should cause the low places in the residential areas or palace grounds to be filled up.
7. On top of the rampart, he should cause a parapet to be built, double the breadth in height, built of bricks, from twelve *hastas* upwards up to twenty-four *hastas*, either odd or even in number of *hastas* in height, with a passage for the movement of chariots, shaped like a palm-stem and with the top decked with 'drums' and 'monkey-heads'. (*Hasta* = one cubit).
8. Or, he should cause it to be made of stones, close-knit with big slabs, but under no circumstances should he have it made of wood.
9. For, fire remains lurking in it.
10. He should cause turrets to be made, square with the breadth, provided with steps for going down, of the same length as the height and at a distance of thirty *dandas* from each other.
11. Midway between every two turrets, he should cause a tower to be built, with two stories inclusive of a hall and one and a half times in length.
12. Between each turret and tower, in the centre, he should cause to be erected a board, compact with planks having holes with coverings, as a place form which to fight for three archers.
13. In the intervening spaces, he should cause a 'gods' way' to be made, two *hastas* in breadth and four times that in length, at the side.
14. He should cause tracks to be made of a width of one *danda* or two *dandas*, and in an unassailable place a run-way and an exit-door.
15. Outside the fort he should cause a covered road to be made that is strewn with knee-breakers, a mass of pikes, pits, concealed traps, barbed wires, 'serpent-backs', 'palm-leaves', 'three peaks', 'dog's jaws', bars, 'jumping sandals,' frying pans and ponds. (These are contrivances of iron or wood to cause injury to intruders.)
16. Having made on both sides of the parapet a 'ram's head' one *danda* and a half in extent he should cause the gate-way to be laid out, with space for six beams of the tower, from five *dandas* square onwards increased by one *danda* upto eight *dandas* square, or one-sixth part more than the length or one-eight part more.

17. From fifteen *hasta* onwards increased by one *hasta* upto eighteen *hastas* should be the height of the floor.
18. The circumference of a pillar one-sixth of the length, double than the portion fixed in the ground; the capital should be one-fourth the length in circumference.
19. Occupying one-fifth part of the ground floor should be a hall, a well and a border-room.
20. There should be two platforms facing each other, occupying one-tenth part of the space and in between two doors and a room.
21. And at half the height of the floor, there should be a structure with pillars.
22. There should be an upper chamber measuring half the built-in area or having a space one-third of it, with sides constructed with bricks, with a stair-case on the left running from left to right and on the other side a stair-case concealed in the wall.
23. The crest of the arch should be two *hastas* in height.
24. The two door-leaves should occupy three-fifths of the space.
25. There should be two bars to the doors.
26. The stake should be one *aratni* in height.
27. There should be a side-door five *hastas* in height.
28. There should be four elephant-bars.
29. The 'elephant nail' passage should be half the width of the structure.
30. The bridge should be equal in width to the opening and capable of being withdrawn, or it should be made of earth where there is no water.
31. Having fixed an opening equal to the width of the parapet, he should cause the *gopura*-gate to be made, with one-third shaped like a lizard's mouth.
32. Having made a well in the middle of the parapet, he should erect the *puskarini*-gate; with four halls at a distance of one *danda* and a half from each other and with holes, the *kumaripura*; a bare house with two storeys, as the *maundaka-gate*; or he should erect gates in accordance with the availability of land and materials.
33. He should cause channels to be made for storing goods, one-third more in length than the breadth.

34-35. In them should be stored stones, spades, axes, arrows and choppers, clubs and hammers; sticks, discuses, machines and 'hundred killers', pikes prepared by smiths and bamboos with piercing points, 'camel-necks', incendiary objects as well as all the materials described in the section on forest produce. They are missiles to be used in emergency.

CHAPTER FOUR

SECTION 22: LAY-OUT OF THE FORTIFIED CITY

1. Three royal highways running west to east and three running south to north, that should be the division of the residential area.
2. It should have twelve gates and be provided with suitable places for water, drains and underground passages.
3. Roads should be of a width of four *dandas*.
4. The royal highway and roads in a *dronamukha*, a *sthaniya*, the countryside and pasture-lands as well as paths in a harbour town, a battle array, a cremation ground and a village should be eight *dandas* in width.
5. Paths on irrigation works and in forests four *dandas*, paths for elephants and along fields two *dandas*, five *aratnis* the chariot path, four the cattle-path and two the path for small animals and men.
6. On an excellent buildings site, fit for the four *varnas* to live on, the royal residence should be erected.
7. In the ninth part to the north of the heart of the residential area he should cause the royal palace to be built in accordance with the procedure laid down, facing the east or the north.
8. The residence of the preceptor and the chaplain, the places for sacrifices and for water as well as counsellors should occupy its north by east part, the kitchen, the elephants stables and the magazine the south-by-east part.
9. Beyond that, dealers in perfumes, flowers and liquids, makers of articles of toilet and Ksatriyas should live in the eastern quarter.
10. The store-house for goods, the records and audit office, and workmen's quarters should occupy the east-by-south part, the storehouse for forest produce and the armoury the west-by-south part.
11. Beyond that, grain-dealers of the city, factory officers and army officers, dealers in cooked food, wine and meat, courtesans, dancers and Vaisyas should live in the southern quarter.
12. Stables for donkeys and camels and the workshop should occupy the south-by-west part, stables for carriages and chariots the north-by-west part.
13. Beyond that, workers in wool, yarn, bamboo, leather, armours, weapons and shields, and Sudras should live in the western quarter.
14. The rooms for wares and medicines should occupy the west-by-north part, the treasury and cattle and horses the east-by-north part.

15. Beyond that, the tutelary deities of the city and the king, and workers in metals and jewels and Brahmins should live in the northern quarter.
16. In enclosures in the non-residential areas, quarters for guilds and foreign merchants should be situated.
17. He should cause to be built in the centre of the city shrines for Aparajita, Apratihata, Jayanta and Vaijayanta as well as temples of Siva, Vaisravana, Asvins, Sri and Madira.
18. He should install the presiding deities of the dwelling places according to their respective regions.
19. The eight gates should be presided over by Brahman, Indra, Yama and Senapati.
20. Outside the city, at a distance of one hundred *dhanuses* from the moat, should be made sanctuaries, holy places, groves and waterworks, and the deities of the quarters in the respective quarters.
21. The northern or the eastern part of the cremation ground should be for the best among the *varnas*, to the south the cremation ground for the lower *varnas*.
22. For transgression of that, the lowest fine for violence shall be imposed.
23. The quarters for heretics and Candalas should be on the outskirts of the cremation ground.
24. He should fix boundaries for householders in accordance with areas necessary for their workshops.
25. In them they should make, with permission, flower-gardens and fruit-orchards, as well as stores of grains and commodities.
26. An enclosure for a group of ten families should be a place for a well for them.
27. He should cause to be made stores, capable of being used over a number of years, of all kinds of fats, grains, sugar, salts, perfumes, medicines, dried vegetables, fodder, dried meat, hay, wood, metals, hides, charcoal, tendons, poisons, horns, bamboos, barks, strong timber, weapons, shields and stones.
28. He should cause the old to be constantly replaced by new.
29. He should station a force consisting of elephants, horses, chariots and infantry-men, under more than one chief.
30. For, a force under more than one chief does not fall a prey to enemy instigations, through mutual fear.
31. This is explained the making of frontier forts.

32. And he should not allow in the city 'outsiders' who cause harm to the country. He should cast them out in the countryside or make them pay all the taxes.

CHAPTER FIVE

SECTION 23: THE WORK OF STORE-KEEPING BY THE DIRECTOR OF STORES

1. The Director of Stores should cause to be built a treasury, a warehouse, a magazine, a store for forest produce, an armoury and a prison-house.
2. Having caused to be dug a four-cornered well free from water and dampness, and having paved the walls on both sides and the bottom with big slabs of stone, he should cause an underground cellar to be made with a framework of strong timber, level with the ground, with three floors, with various arrangements, with ground and upper floors having well-made surfaces, with a single door, and with a staircase provided with a mechanism.
3. On that he should cause a treasure-house to be made with a prohibition to enter on two sides, with an entrance-hall, built of bricks, and surrounded by channels storing goods; he should cause to be built only an above-the-ground palace.
4. On the border of the country, he should cause a permanent treasure to be laid by persons condemned to death, as a provision against calamity.
5. He should cause to be made a warehouse and a magazine with pillars of baked bricks, with four halls opening on to a quadrangle, with many, ground and upper floors, a passage for escape through hollow pillars on two sides, in-between, a store for forest produce with many long halls with the walls surrounded by rooms, a similar with an underground cellar as an armoury, separate prison-houses for those convicted by judges and for those punished by high officers, with separate apartments for women and men with their rooms well-guarded against escape.
6. And in all structures he should cause the halls to be provided with a ditch, a well, a latrine and a bath room, with precautions against fire and poison, with protection by means of cats and ichneumons and with arrangements for worship of their respective deities.
7. In the magazine, he should place a basin with a mouth one *aratni* as in width a rain-gauge.

8. Presiding over bureaus of experts for the different products, he should receive gems, articles of high value, articles of small value and forest produce whether old or new.
9. Among these articles, in case of fraud concerning gems the highest fine for violence shall be imposed on the perpetrator and the instigator, in case of fraud concerning articles of high value the middle fine for violence, in case of fraud concerning articles of small value and forest produce the same and an equal amount in addition as fine.
10. He should accept money certified as genuine by the Examiner of Coins.
11. He should cut counterfeit coins.
12. One who brings such coins shall be fined the lowest fine for violence.
13. He should accept corn that is clean, full in measure and new.
14. In case the opposite kind is brought in, the fine shall be double the price.
15. Thus, are explained the commodities, the forest produce and the weapons.
16. In all departments, the punishments for officers, subordinates and servants, in cases of defalcation up to one *pana* and beyond that increases by one *pana* by upto four *panas*, shall be the lowest, the middle, the highest fines and death respectively.
17. For one in charge of the treasury, execution shall be the punishment for robbing the treasury.
18. For those who help them, the punishment half the fines.
19. Reproof only, if they were not aware.
20. For thieves, in case of breaking open the treasury, death by torture shall be the punishment.
21. Therefore, with trustworthy men under him, the Director of stores should bring the stores into being.
22. He should be conversant with receipts from outside and inside even after a hundred years, so that when asked he would not falter in respect of expenditure, balance and collections.

CHAPTER SIX

SECTION 24: THE SETTING UP OF REVENUE BY THE ADMINISTRATOR

1. The administrator should attend to the fort, the country, mines, irrigation works, forests, herds and trade-routes as they are main sources of revenue.

2. Custom duties, fines, standardization of weights and measures, the city-superintendent, the mint master, the superintendent of passports, spirituous liquors, animals slaughter, yarn, oil, ghee, sugars, the goldsmith, the prostitutes, gambling, buildings, the group of artisans and artists, the temple-superintendent, and what is to be received at the gates and from outsiders—these constitute the source of income called 'fort'.
3. Agricultural produce, share, tribute, tax, the trader, the river-guard, the ferry, ships, the port, pastures, road-cess, land survey and their catching,—these constitute 'country'.
4. Gold, silver, diamonds, gems, pearls, corals, conch-shells, metals, salt and ores derived from the earth, rocks and liquids,—these constitute 'mines'.
5. Flower gardens, fruit orchards, vegetable gardens, wet crop fields, and sowings of roots,—these constitute 'irrigations works'.
6. Enclosures for beasts, deer parks, forests for produce and elephant forest—these constitute 'forests'.
7. Cows and buffaloes, goats and sheep, donkeys and camels and horses and mules,—these constitute 'herds'.
8. The land-route and the water-route constitute 'trade-routes'.
9. This is the corpus of income.
10. Price, share, surcharge, monopoly tax, fixed tax, manufacturing charge and penalty constitute the heads of income.
11. What is intended for the worship of gods and manes and for charity, gifts for benedictions received, the royal palace, the kitchen, the employment of envoys, the magazine, the armoury, the warehouse, the store for forest produce, factories, labourers, maintenance of foot-soldiers, horses, chariots and elephants, herds of cattle, enclosures for beasts, deer, birds and wild animals, and stores of fuel and grass,—these constitute the corpus of expenditure.
12. The king's regnal year, the months, the fortnight and the day, thus, the date-entry, the third and seventh forthnights of the rainy season, winter and summer short by one day, the rest full and a separate intercalary month,—this is time.
13. The revenue estimate, accrued revenue, outstanding revenue, income and expenditure and balance are items in accounting.
14. The place, the sphere of activity, laying down the corpus of income receipts, the total of all items of revenue and the grand total,—this is revenue estimate.

15. Deliveries into the treasury, what is taken by the king, and the expenses of the city, these as paid in, what is carried forward from last year, what is released by a decree and what is ordered by word of mouth, these as not to be remitted,—this is accrued revenue.
16. Acquiring the fruits on completion of an undertaking the remainder of fines, these as what has to be recovered, what is withheld by force and what is used by officers, these as what must be cleared,—this is outstanding revenue, not containing goods of high value, and containing few goods of high value.
17. Current, outstanding and derived from other sources is the three-fold income.
18. What comes in from day-to-day is current income.
19. What belongs to the preceding year or what is transferred from another sphere of activity, is outstanding income.
20. What is lost and forgotten, fines imposed on employees, extra income, compensation for loss, gifts, property of a person involved in a riot, property of an issueless person and treasure-trove is income derived from other sources.
21. Balance due to army disbandment and from undertakings given up in the middle because of sickness, is return from expenditure.
22. Accretion, *viz.*, increase in the price of commodities at the time of sale, excess in weights and measures called surcharge or the increase in price because of competition for purchase,—this is also income.
23. Current, expenditure that arising out of current, gain and that arising out of gain,—this is four-fold expenditure.
24. What is spent from day-to-day is current expenditure.
25. Receipts by officers, servants etc. after a fortnight, a month or a year is gain.
26. That arising out of these two is expenditure arising out of current expenditure and out of gain respectively. This is expenditure.
27. What is left over after calculation of income and expenditure from the total of revenue items is the balance, received and carried forward.
28. Thus, the wise administrator should fix the revenue and show an increase in income and decrease in expenditure and should remedy the opposite of these.

CHAPTER SEVEN

SECTION 25: THE TOPIC OF ACCOUNTS IN THE RECORDS AND AUDIT OFFICE

1. The Superintendent should cause the Records Office to be built facing the east or the north, with separate halls, as a place for record-books.
2. There he should cause to be entered in the record-books: the extent of the number, activity and total income of the departments; the amount of increase or decrease in the use of the various materials, expenses, excess, surcharge, mixing, place, wages and labourers in connection with factories; the price, the quality, the weight, the measure, the height, the depth and the container in connection with jewels, articles of high value, of low value and forest produce; laws, transactions, customs and fixed rules of regions, villages, castes, families and corporations; the receipt of favours, lands, use, exemptions, and food and wages by those who serve the king; the receipt of jewels and land and the receipt of special allowances and payments for remedial measures against sudden calamities, by the king and his queens and sons; and payments and receipts in connection with peace and war with allies and enemies.
3. From that he should hand over in writing the revenue estimate, accrued revenue, outstanding revenue, income and expenditure, balance, the time for attendance for audit, sphere of activity, customs and fixed rules, to all the departments.
4. And overworks of the highest, the middling and the lowest kinds, he should appoint a superintendent of that class, but overworks bringing in revenue, a suitable officer by injuring whom if necessary, the king would not regret.
5. His co-receivers, sureties, those living on his work, his sons, brothers, wives, daughters and servants shall bear the loss in the work.
6. Constitute the year of work.
7. He should fix that as ending on the full moon day in Asadha, whether short or full.
8. He should provide the intercalary month with a separate bureau.
9. And he should have the activity of departments watched by spies.
10. For, the person in question *viz.*, the officer if not conversant with the activity, customs and fixed rules, causes loss of revenue through ignorance, if unable to endure the trouble of energetic activity, through laziness, if addicted to the pleasures of the senses,

sound and others, through remissness, if afraid of an uproar among subjects or of an unrighteous or harmful act, through fear, if inclined to show favour to those who have work with him, through love, if inclined to do them harm, through anger, because of reliance on learning or wealth or the support of a royal favourite, through arrogance, and because of deceit in introducing a difference in weight, measure, assessment or counting, through greed.

11. 'Among those causes of loss of revenue, the fine is as much as the loss of money, increased by one-fold in each succeeding case according to the order as stated above', say the followers of Manu.
12. In all cases the fine shall be eight times the loss,' say the followers of Parasara.
13. 'Ten times', say the followers of Brahaspati.
14. 'Twenty times', say the followers of Usanas.
15. 'In conformity with the offence', says Kautilya.
16. The accounts should come in on the Asadha full moon day.
17. When the officers have come with sealed account books and balances in sealed containers, he should impose restriction in one place, not allowing conversation among them.
18. After hearing the totals of income, expenditure and balance, he should cause the balance to be taken away to the treasury.
19. And he should make the superintendent pay eight-fold whatever may increase in the balance over the total of income as shown on the page inside the account-books or whatever the officer may cause to decrease from the balance because of the inflation of expenditure.
20. In the reverse cases, it shall fall to the lot of the officer himself.
21. For officers not coming at the proper time or coming without the account books and balances, the fine shall be one-tenth of the amount due.
22. And if, when the works officer presents himself, the accounts officer is not ready for audit, the lowest fine for violence shall be imposed.
23. In the reverse case, the fine for the works officer shall be double.
24. The high officers should render accounts in full in accordance with their activity, without contradicting themselves.
25. And among these he who makes a divergent statement or speaks falsely shall pay the highest fine for violence.
26. He should wait for one month, if the officer has not brought in the day-to-day accounts.

27. After the month, the officer shall pay a fine of two hundred *panas* increased by that amount for each succeeding month.
28. If an officer has a little of written balance due from him, he should wait for five days.
29. If he brings in the day-to-day accounts after that period, preceded by delivery of the balance into the treasury, he should look into the case with reference to laws, transactions, customs and fixed rules and by totalling up, and by looking at the work actually carried out, by inference and the use of spies.
30. And he should check the accounts for each day, group of five days, fortnight, month, four months and year.
31. He should check the income with reference to the period, place, time, head of income, source, bringing forward, quantity, the payer, the person causing payment to be made, the recorder and the receiver.
32. He should check the expenditure with reference to the period, place, time, head of expenditure or gain, occasion, the thing given, its use and amount, the person who orders, the person who takes out, the person who delivers and the receiver.
33. He should check the balance with reference to the period, place, time, head, bringing forward, the article, its characteristics, amount, the vessel in which it is deposited and the person guarding it.
34. If, in an affair of the king, the accounts officer is not ready for audit or disregards an order or changes the income and expenditure in a way different from the written order, the lowest fine for violence shall be imposed.
35. For one writing down an item in the accounts without any order or in a wrong order or in an illegible manner, or twice over, the fine is twelve *panas*.
36. For one writing down the balance in any of these ways the fine is double that.
37. For one who swallows it, the fine is eight-fold.
38. For one who destroys it, the fine is one-fifth of the amount and restitution of what is lost.
39. In case of false statement, the punishment is that for theft.
40. If admitted afterwards, the fine is double, so also if an item is forgotten and then brought in.
41. The king should put up with a minor offence and should be content even when the revenue is small; and he should honour with favours the officer who confers great benefit on the state.

CHAPTER EIGHT

SECTION 26: RECOVERY OF REVENUE MISAPPROPRIATED BY STATE EMPLOYEES

1. All undertakings are dependent first on the treasury.
2. Therefore, he should look to the treasury first.
3. Prosperousness of activities, cherishing of customs, suppression of thieves, control over employees, luxuriance of crops, abundance of commodities, deliverance from trouble, reduction in exemptions, and presents in cash,—these are the means of increase in the treasury.
4. Hindrance, lending, trading, concealment, causing loss, use, interchange and misappropriation,—these are the causes of depletion of the treasury.
5. Failure to carry out a work, failure to realize its fruit, or failure to deliver it in the treasury, constitutes hindrance.
6. For that the fine is one-tenth the amount involved.
7. Lending at interest of goods from the treasury is lending.
8. Trading in state commodities is trading.
9. In those cases, the fine is double the fruit.
10. If the officer makes the due date as not due of the date not due as due, that is concealment.
11. For that the fine is one-fifth.
12. If the officer causes a diminution of the revenue fixed or causes an increase in the expenditure sanctioned, that is causing loss.
13. For that the fine is four times the amount lost.
14. The use of the king's goods by oneself or allowing it by others is use.
15. For that, the punishment is execution for use of jewels, the middle fine for violence for use of articles of high value, restitution of that and an equal amount as fine for use of articles of small value and forest produce.
16. The appropriation of the king's goods by the substitution of other goods is interchange.
17. That is explained by rules concerning use.
18. If the officer does not deliver the income that has accrued or does not pay the expenses put down in writing or denies the balance received,—that is misappropriation.
19. For that the fine is twelve times the amount.
20. Of those officers the ways of embezzlement are forty.

21. What has accrued first is realized afterwards, what is to accrue later is realized first, what is to be carried out is not carried out, what is not to be carried out is carried out, what is carried out is made out as not carried out, what is not carried out is made out as carried out, what is carried out a little is made out as much, what is carried out much is made out as little, one thing is carried out while another is made out as carried out, what is carried out from one source is made out as from another, what is to be paid is not paid, what is not to be paid is paid, payment is not made in time, payment is made untimely, a little paid is made out as much, what is overpaid is made out as little, one thing is given while another is made out as given, what is paid to one is made out as paid to another, what is delivered into the treasury is made out as not delivered, what is not delivered is made out as delivered, forest produce for which the price has not been paid is delivered, that for which the price has been paid is not delivered, concentration of goods is made out as dispersal, or dispersal made out as concentration, an object of high value, the price is raised, or the price is reduced, the year is made discrepant as to months, or the month discrepant as to days, discrepancy as to source, discrepancy as to head of income etc., discrepancy as to workmen, discrepancy in performance, discrepancy in the sum-total, discrepancy in quality, discrepancy in price, discrepancy in weighing, discrepancy in measuring and discrepancy as to container vessels, these are the forty ways of embezzlement.
22. In these cases, he should interrogate, each individually, the subordinate officer, the store-keeper, the recorder, the receiver, the person who pays, the person who causes the payment to be made, the adviser and the help-mate.
23. And in case of a false statement by these, the fine shall be the same as for the officer concerned.
24. And he should issue a proclamation in the sphere of his activity. Those wronged by such and such an officer should communicate it to me.
23. To such as communicated he should cause payment to be made in accordance with the injury suffered.
26. And in case of many accusations, if the officer denies all charges, and is proved guilty in a single case, he shall be liable for all.
27. In case of partial admission, he shall stand trial in all cases.

28. And in case of misappropriation of a large amount of money, if proved guilty with respect to even a small part of it, he shall be liable for all.
29. An informer, to whom a guarantee is given against reprisal by the officer should receive one-sixth part if the matter is proved, one-twelfth part if he happens to be a state servant.
30. If in an accusation concerning a large amount, only a small portion is proved, he shall receive a share of what is proved.
31. In case it is not proved, he shall receive corporal or monetary punishment, and no favour shall be shown to him.
32. But if when the charge is being proved, the informer, at the instigation of the accused officer, were to throw up the case or to make himself scarce, he shall be condemned to death.

CHAPTER NINE

SECTION 27: INSPECTION OF THE WORK OF OFFICERS

1. All superintendents, endowed with the excellences of a minister, should be appointed to works according to their capacity.
2. And he should constantly hold an inspection of their works, men being inconstant in their minds.
3. For, men being of a nature similar to that of horses change when employed in works.
4. Therefore, he should be cognizant of the worker, the office, the place, the time, the work to be done, the outlay and the profit in these undertakings.
5. They should carry out the works according to orders, without concerting together or quarrelling amongst themselves.
6. Concerting together, they might swallow up the fruits of the undertakings, quarrelling, they might ruin them.
7. And they must not commence any work without informing the king, excepting measures against calamities.
8. And in cases of remissness on their part, he should fix a fine double the day's wages and other expenses.
9. And he who, amongst them, carries out the work as ordered or better, should receive a high position and honour.
10. 'If an officer with small income has a large expenditure, he consumes state revenue.
11. In the reverse case and when an officer spends in conformity with his income, he does not consume,' thus say the teachers.
12. Only through spies would this be ascertained, says Kautilya.

13. He who causes loss of revenue consumes the property of the king.
14. If he causes loss through ignorance and other causes, he should make him pay that, suitably multiplied.
15. He who procures double the normal revenue, consumes the countryside.
16. If he brings in the whole for the king, he should be warned in case of a minor offence, in case of a major offence should be punished according to the offence.
17. He who makes out as expenditure the revenue he has raised consumes the works of men.
18. He should be punished according to the offence in cases of loss or waste of days of work, the price of goods and the wages of men.
19. Therefore, he who is appointed by an order to a particular department shall communicate to him *i.e.*, the king the real nature of that work and the income and expenditure both in detail and in the aggregate.
20. And he should keep in check the patrimony-squanderer, the immediate-spender and the niggardly.
21. He who consumes in unjust ways the property inherited from the father and the grand-father is the patrimony-squanderer.
22. He who straightway consumes whatever is produced is the immediate-spender.
23. He who amasses wealth by putting his dependents and himself to suffering is the niggardly.
24. If he has a large party dependent on him, he is not to be deprived of property; in the opposite case, he should be deprived of all property.
25. Of that niggardly officer who, placed in charge of a large amount of revenue, stores it, deposits it or sends it out,—stores it in his own house, deposits it with citizens or country people, sends it out to an enemy's territory,—a secret agent should find out the party of advisers, friends, dependents and kinsmen as well as the coming in and going out of goods.
26. And having insinuated himself into the confidence of that servant of his who might be making movement to and fro in the enemy's territory, he should find out the secret.
27. When it is fully ascertained, he should cause him to be executed on the pretext of a letter from the enemy.
28. Therefore, his superintendents should carry out the works accompanied by accountants, writers, examiners of coins, receivers of balances and supervisors.

29. Supervisors are those who ride elephants, horses and chariots.
30. Their assistants, endowed with skill and integrity, should work as spies over the accountants and others.
31. He should establish each department with many heads and without permanency of tenure of office.
32. Just as it is not possible not to taste honey or poison placed on the surface of the tongue, even so it is not possible for one dealing with the money of the king not to taste the money in however small a quantity.
33. Just as fish moving inside water cannot be known when drinking water, even so officers appointed for carrying out works cannot be known when appropriating money.
34. It is possible to know even the path of birds flying in the sky, but not the ways of officers moving with their intentions concealed.
35. And he should make those who have amassed money wrongfully yield it up and should change them in their works, so that they do not consume the king's property or disgorge what is consumed.
36. But those who do not consume the king's goods and increase them in just ways, should be made permanent in their offices, being devoted to what is agreeable and beneficial to the king.

CHAPTER TEN

SECTION 28: THE TOPIC OF EDICTS

1. They declare that as *sasana* edict which is used for giving directions or orders.
2. For, kings principally depend on edicts, peace and war being rooted in them.
3. Therefore, the scribe should be endowed with the excellences of a minister, conversant with all conventions, quick in composing, with a beautiful hand and capable of reading a document.
4. He should listen with an attentive mind to the command of the king and set it down in writing, which is precise in meaning, with a courteous mention of the country, the sovereignty, the family and the name in the case of a king, and with the customary mention of the country and the name in the case of one who is not a king.
5. Having taken into consideration, in every matter, the caste, the family, the position, age and learning, the profession, property and character, also the place and time and connections by marriage, he should compose the document in conformity with the person addressed.

6. Arrangement of subject-matter, connection, completeness, sweetness, exaltedness and lucidity constitute the excellences of writing.
7. Among them, arranging in a proper order, the statement first of the principal matter, is arrangement of subject-matter.
8. The statement of a subsequent matter without its being incompatible with the matter in hand, right up to the end, is connection.
9. Absence of deficiency or excess of matter, words and letters, description in detail of the matter by means of reasons, citations and illustrations, and expressiveness of words, is completeness.
10. The use of words with a charming meaning easily conveyed is sweetness.
11. The use of words that are not vulgar is exaltedness.
12. The employment of words that are well-known is lucidity.
13. The letters in the alphabet beginning with *a* are sixty-three.
14. A combination of letters is a word.
15. That is four-fold: noun, verb, preposition and particle.
16. Among them, a noun signifies being.
17. A verb, not having a specific gender, is indicative of action.
18. Those that qualify an action, *pra* and others, are prepositions.
19. Indeclinables, *ca* and others, are particles.
20. A collection of words constitutes a sentence, when the sense is completed.
21. A group with a minimum of one word and a maximum of three words should be made, not conflicting with the meaning of the others words.
22. For concluding the writing, the word *iti* and the sub-script 'These are the words of so and so' should be used.

23-24. Censure, praise, query, statement, request, refusal, reproof, prohibition, injunction, appeasement, help, threatening and propitiation,—with these thirteen are matters arising out of writing concerned.

25. Among these, mention of defects concerning birth, body or actions is censure.
26. Mention of the merits of these same is praise.
27. 'How is this so?' is query.
28. 'Thus it is' is statement.
29. 'Give it to me' is request.
30. 'I will not give' is refusal.
31. 'This is unworthy of you' is reproof.

32. 'Do not do so' is prohibition.
33. 'Let this be done' is injunction.
34. 'What I am is you; what object belongs to me is your's this conciliation' is appeasement.
35. Aid in calamities is help.
36. Pointing to the future as full of danger is threatening.
37. Propitiation is threefold, in doing a thing, in case of transgression and during the calamity of a person and so on.
38. Documents of communication, command and gift, documents of exemption and authorization, the document giving news of happenings, the document in reply and the document applicable everywhere,—these are types of decrees.
39. 'So and so has communicated; he has said so; hence let it be given if there be truth in it'. 'He has spoken of an excellent deed in the presence of the king,' this is communication stated to be of various kinds.
40. Where there is the command of the king concerning punishment of favour, especially in the matter of servants, that is the characteristic of a decree of command.
41. Where honour, rendered in accordance with merits, is to be seen, whether in distress or when making a gift, those two become decrees of favour.
42. The favour, which is conferred at the command of the king, on the various castes and on the different cities, villages and regions, the expert should designate as the decree of exemption.
43. The delegation of authority in the matter of doing a work and in the matter of issuing orders, this may be a document authorizing the issuing of orders or even containing an authorization for doing a work.
44. With respect to a document, they designate happenings as of two kinds, *viz.*, those associated with the divine, of various kinds, and those concerning men, based on facts.
45. After seeing the document as it really is and then after reading it out, the document in reply should be prepared exactly as the words of the king may be.
46. That, in which the king asks the princes and officers to ensure protection and comforts for travellers, would be the decree called applicable everywhere; it should be known on the road, in the country and everywhere else.
47. The means are conciliation, gifts, dissension and force.

48. Among them, conciliation is five-fold, praising of merits mention of relationship, pointing out mutual benefits, showing advantages in the future, and placing oneself at the other's disposal.
49. Amongst these, appreciation of the merits of birth, body, occupation, nature, learning, property and so on, praise, adulation, this is praising of merits.
50. The praising of common kinship, marriage relationship, through teaching, relationship through sacrificial performances, common family, affection of the heart, and common friend, this is mention of relationship.
51. The praising of mutual benefits accruing to one's party of the other, this is pointing out mutual benefits.
52. 'If this were done in this way, this will happen to us both', this raising of hope is showing advantages in the future.
53. 'What I am is you, what object belongs to me, should be used by you in your works', this is placing oneself at the other's disposal.
54. Conferring benefits of money is making gifts.
55. Creating apprehension and reprimanding is dissension.
56. Killing, tormenting and seizure of property constitute force.
57. Absence of charm, contradiction, repetition, incorrect use of a word, and confusion,—these are the defects of writing.
58. Among them, the use of a black leaf, and writing unattractive, uneven and faint letters constitute absence of charm.
59. The incompatibility of the later with the earlier is contradiction.
60. Statement a second time of what is said without any distinction is repetition.
61. The wrong use of gender, number, tense and case is incorrect use of a word.
62. The making of a group where there should be no group and not making a group where should be a group, this reversal of qualities is confusion.
63. After going through all the sciences in detail and after observing the practice in such matters, Kautilya has made these rules about edicts for the sake of kings.

CHAPTER ELEVEN

SECTION 29: EXAMINATION OF THE PRECIOUS ARTICLES TO BE RECEIVED INTO THE TREASURY

1. The Superintendent of the Treasury should receive jewels, articles of high value, articles of small value or forest produce, to be

received into the treasury, while presiding over bureaus of experts in the various lines.

2. That from the *Tamraparni* that from *Pandyaka-vata* that from the *Pasika*, that from the *Kulai*, that from the *Curni*, that from Mt. *Mahendra*, that from the *Kardama*, that from the *Srotasi*, that from the Lake, and that from the *Himavat* — these are pearls.
3. The shell, the conch and miscellaneous are the sources of pearls.
4. A pearl that is lentil-shaped, triangular, tortoise-shaped, semi-spherical, with a layer, coupled, cut up, rough, spotted, goured-shaped, dark, blue, and badly perforated, is defective.
5. That which is big, round, without a flat surface, lustrous, white, heavy, smooth and perforated at the proper place, is excellent.
6. *Sirsaka, upasirsaka, prakandaka, avaghataka* and *taralapratibaddha*, —these are varieties of pearl-strings.
7. One thousand and eight strings make the *indracchanda* necklace.
8. Half that number make the *vijayacchanda*.
9. Sixty-four make the *ardha-hara*.
10. Fifty-four make the *rasmi-kalapa*.
11. Thirty-two make the *guccha*.
12. Twenty-seven make the *naksatra-mala*.
13. Twenty-four make the *ardha-guccha*.
14. Twenty strings make the *manavaka*.
15. Half that number make the *ardha-manavaka*.
16. These same, with a gem in the centre, become their respective *manavakas*.
17. A necklace of only *sirsakas* is an unmixed *hara*.
18. Like that, are the rest.
19. With a gem in the centre, it is an *ardhamanavaka*.
20. One with three strips is a *phalaka-hara* or one with five strips.
21. A single string is the unmixed *ekavali*.
22. The same, with a gem in the centre, is the *yasti*.
23. Variegated with gold and gems, it is the *ratnavali*.
24. With gold, gems and pearls at intervals, it is the *apavartaka*.
25. With stringing in a gold thread, it is the *sopanaka*.
26. Or, with a gem in the centre, it is the *mani-sopanaka*.
27. Thus, are explained varieties of strings and networks for the head, hands, feet and waist.
28. Gems come from *Koti* from the *Mala* and from beyond the sea.
29. The ruby, of the colour of the red lotus, of the colour of saffron, of the colour of *parijata-flower*, and of the colour of the morning sun.

30. The beryl, of the colour of the blue lotus, of the sirisa-flower, of the colour of water, of the colour of green bamboo, of the colour of the parrot's wing, yellow-coloured, of the colour of cow's urine and of cow's fat.
31. The sapphire, with blue lines, like the *kalaya*-flower, deep blue, having the luster of the *jambu-fruit*, having the luster of the dark cloud, the 'delighter' and the 'streaming interior'.
32. The pure crystal, of the colour of *mulata*-flower, shedding a cool shower and the sun-stone. These are the gems.
33. Hexagonal, square or round, of a flashing colour, having a suitable form, clear, smooth, heavy, lustrous, with luster inside and imparting luster,—these are the excellences of gems.
34. With a dull colour and luster, with grains, with a hole in the bloom, broken, badly bored, and covered with scratches,—these are blemishes.
35. The *vimalaka*, the *sasyaka*, the *anjanamulaka*, the *pittaka*, the *sulabhaka*, the *lohitaksa*, the *mrgasmaka*, the *jyotrasaka*, the *maleyaka*, the *ahicchatraka*, the *kurpa*, the *pratikurpa*, the *sugandhikurpa*, the *ksiravaka*, the *sukticurnaka*, the *silapravalaka*, the *pulaka*, the *suklapulaka*,—these are subsidiary types of gems.
36. The rest are glass-crystals.
37. Diamonds come from Sabharastra, from Tajjamarastra, from Kastirarastral, from Mt. Srikatanaka, from Mt. Manimanta and from Indravana.
38. The mine, the stream, and miscellaneous are the sources.
39. Like the cat's eye, the *sirisa*-flower, cow's urine, cow's fat, pure crystal, or the *mulata*-flower, and of the colour of any one of the gems,—these are the colours of diamonds.
40. A diamond that is big, heavy, capable of bearing blows, with symmetrical points, capable of scratching a vessel, revolving like a spindle and brilliantly shining, is excellent.
41. That with points lost, without edges and defective on one side, is bad.
42. The coral from Alakanda and from Vivarna, red and of the colour of the lotus is excellent, with the exception of that which is eaten by insects and which is bulging in the middle.
43. Sandal-wood from Satana is red and has the smell of the earth.
44. That from Gosirsa is blackish red and smells like fish.
45. The sandal-wood from Haritis of the colour of the parrot's feather and has the smell of a mango, also that from the Trnasa.

46. That from Grameru is red or red black and has the smell of goat's urine.
47. That from Devasabha is red and has the smell of a lotus, also that from Japa.
48. That from Jongal is red or red-black and smooth, also that from Turupa.
49. That from the Mala is whitish red.
50. Kucandana is rough, black like aloe or red or reddish black.
51. That from kala mountain is reddish black or of the colour of saffron.
52. That from Kosagara mountain is black or black-variegated.
53. That from the Sakalal is brown.

54-56. Light, smooth, not dry, unctuous with oil like butter, pleasant in smell, penetrating the skin, unobtrusive, not losing colour, capable of bearing heat, allaying heat and pleasant to the touch,—these are the excellences of sandal-wood.

57. Aloe from Jonga is black, black-variegated or variegated with round spots.
58. That from Donga is dark.
59. That from beyond the sea has a variegated appearance and has the smell of *usira* or the fragrance of *navamalika*.
60. Heavy, smooth, of a pleasant smell, widespreading in fragrance, burning well, without a thick smoke, of a uniform fragrance, capable of standing a rubbing — these are the excellences of aloe.
61. *Tailaparnika* incense from *Asokagrama* has the colour of flesh and the fragrance of a lotus.
62. That from Jonga is reddish yellow and has the fragrance of blue lotus or the smell of cow's urine.
63. That from Grameru is smooth and has the smell of cow's urine.
64. That from Suvarnakudya is reddish yellow and has the smell of the citron fruit.
65. That from Purnakadvipa has the fragrance of a lotus or the smell of butter.
66. *Bhadrasriya* from beyond the *Lauhitya* is of the colour of the *jati*-flower.
67. That from *Antaravati* is of the colour of *ustra*.
68. And both have the smell of *kustha*.
69. *Kaleyaka* from *Svarnabhumi* is smooth and yellow.
70. That from the northern mountain is reddish yellow. These are objects of high value.

71. Capable of retaining fragrance when formed into a lamp or boiled or producing smoke, not losing colour, and amenable to mixing with other substances.
72. And qualities similar to those of sandal-wood and aloe,—these are their excellences.
73. The *kantanavaka* and the *praiyaka* are skins from the northern mountain.
74. The *kantanavaka* has the luster of the peacock's neck.
75. The *praiyaka* is variegated with blue, yellow and white lines and spots.
76. Both these are eight *angulas* in length.
77. The *bisi* and the *mahabisi* come from *Dvadasagrama*.
78. The *bisi* is of an indistinct colour, hairy or variegated.
79. The *mahabisi* is rough, mostly white.
80. Both are twelve *angulas* in length.
81. The *syamika*, the *kalika*, the *kadali*, the *candrottara* and the *sakula* are produced in Aroha.
82. The *syamika* is brown or variegated with spots.
83. The *kalika* is brown or dove-coloured.
84. Both these are eight *angulas* in length.
85. The *kadali* is rough and one *hasta* in length.
86. The same, variegated with 'moons', is the *candrottara*.
87. The *sakula* is one-third the kadali in length, variegated with circular spots or variegated with natural knots in the skin. (1 *Hasta* = 1 cubit).
88. The *samura*, the *cinasi* and the *samuli* are from Bahlava.
89. The *samura* is thirty-six *angulas* and of the colour of collyrium.
90. The *cinasi* is reddish black or pale black.
91. The *samuli* is of the colour of wheat.
92. The *satina*, the *nalatula*, and the *vrttapuccha* are from Odra.
93. The *satina* is black.
94. The *nalatula* is of the colour of the flower-panicle of the *nala*-reed.
95. And the *vrttapuccha* is brown.

These are the varieties of skins.

96. Of skins, the soft, the smooth and the hairy are best.
97. Woollen cloth is white, all red and part red, with threads laid in with the needle, variegated in weaving, with pieces joined together and with broken off threads.
98. The blanket, the *kaucapaka*, the *kulamitika*, the *saumitika*, the horse's saddle-cloth, the coloured blanket, the *talicchaka*, the

armour, the *paristoma* and the *samantabhadraka* are varieties of woollen cloth.

99. Slippery and wet as it were, fine and soft is best.

100. The black *bhingisi*, made out of a collection of eight woven strands and the *apasaraka* which keeps off rain,—that is woollen cloth from *Nepala*.

101. The *samputika*, the *caturasrika*, the *lambara*, the *katavanaka*, the *pravaraka* and the *sattalika* are products from the hair of animals.

102. The *dukula* from the Vangas is white and smooth.

103. That from the Pundras is dark and smooth like a gem.

104. That from Suvarnakudya is of the colour of the sun, with gem-smooth water-weave, with a uniform weave and with a mixed weave.

105. Of these there is cloth with a single yarn or with one and a half yarns or with two, three or four yarns.

106. Thus is explained the *ksauma* from Kasi and the Pundras.

107. The *Patrona* silk comes from the Magadhas the Pundras and Suvamakudya.

108. The *naga-tree*, the *likuca*, the *bakula* and the banyan tree are the sources.

109. That from the *naga-tree* is yellow.

110. That from the *likuca* is wheat-coloured.

111. That from the *bakula* is white.

112. The remaining one is of the colour of butter.

113. Of these, that from *Suvarnakudva* is best.

114. Thus are explained the silk and silk cloth from the land of Cina (China). Cotton fabric from Madurai, the Aprantas, the Kalingas, Kasi, the Vangas, the Vatsas and the Mahaisas are the best.

115-116. Of precious articles other than these, he should be conversant with the amount, price, characteristics, class and appearance, their storing, manufacturing of new ones and repair of old ones secret treatment, tools, their use according to place and time, and remedies against things destructive to them.

15

BOOK TWO (Part Two)

Activities of Heads of Departments (Continued)

In this sub-book of original Book-Two composed by Kautilya information from Chapter No. 12 to 24 has been dealt with. These chapters are: 12. The starting of Mines and Factories, 13. The Superintendent of Gold in the Workshop, 14. The Activity of the Goldsmith in the Market Highway, 15. The Superintendent of the Magazine, 16. The Director of Trade, 17. The Director of Forest-produce, 18. The Superintendent of the Armoury, 19. Standardisation of Weights and Measures, 20. Measures of Space and Time, 21-22. The Collector of Customs and Tolls, 23. The Superintendent of Yarns and Textiles, 24. The Director of Agriculture.

CHAPTER TWELVE

SECTION 30: STARTING OF MINES AND FACTORIES

1. The Director of Mines, being conversant with the science of metal veins in the earth and metallurgy, the art of smelting and the art of colouring gems, or having the assistance of experts in these, and fully equipped with workmen skilled in the work and with implements, should inspect an old mine by the marks of dross, crucibles, coal and ashes, or a new mine, where there are ores in the earth, in rocks or in liquid form, with excessive colour and heaviness and with a strong smell and taste.
2. Those liquids that flow inside a hole, a cave, a table-land at the foot, a rock-cut cave, or a secret dug-out in mountains whose regions are known to contain gold-ore, that are of the colour of the

jambu —the mango—or the palm-fruit or of a cross-section of ripe turmeric or of jaggery or of orpiment or red arsenic or honey or vermilion or white lotus or of the feather of a parrot or a peacock, that have in their environs water and plants of the same colour, and that are viscous, clear and heavy, are gold-bearing liquids.

3. If, when thrown in water, they spread on the surface like oil and absorb mud and dirt, they are capable of transmuting copper and silver up to one hundred times their own weight.
4. Exactly similar to that in appearance, but with a strong smell and taste, he should know to be bitumen.
5. Ores in earth or rocks, which are yellow or copper-coloured or reddish-yellow, which, when broken, show blue lines or are of the colour of the *mudga* or *masa*-bean or *krsara*, which are variegated with spots or lumps as of curds, which are of the colour of turmeric or myrobalan or lotus-leaf or moss or liver or spleen or saffron, which, when broken, show lines, spots or svastikas of fine sand, which are possessed of pebbles and are lustrous, which, when heated, do not break and yield plenty of foam and smoke, are gold-ores, to be used for insertion, as transmuters of copper and silver.
6. Ores of the colour of a conch-shell or camphor or crystal or butter or a dove or a pigeon, or *vimalaka* or the peacock's neck, of the colour of *sasyaka*-gem or *goṃedaka*-gem or jaggery or unrefined sugar, of the colour of the flower of *kovidara*, or lotus or *patali*-flower or *kalaya*-flower or the flower of flax or of linseed, and containing lead, containing antimony, smelling like raw flesh, when broken black with a white shimmer or white with a black shimmer, or all variegated with lines and spots, soft, which when being smelted do not split and yield plenty of foam and smoke, are silver-ores.
7. In the case of all ores, when there is increase in heaviness there is increase in metal-content.
8. Of these, those that are impure or dim in the interior flow in a pure form when infused in strong urine and caustic, when formed into lumps a paste of with the *rajavrksa*, the banyan tree, the *pilu*, cow's bile, pigment and the urine and dung of the buffalo, the donkey and the young camel, either mixed with this during boiling or smeared with this paste.
9. The insertion in the ore of the bulbous roots of the *kadali* and the *vajra*, along with the caustic of the ashes of barley, *masa*-bean, sesamum, *palasa* and *pilu* or along with the milk of the cow and the goat, is productive of softness.

10. Honey and liquors, goat's milk with sesamum-oil, mixed with ghee, jaggery and fermenting stuff, together with the *kandali*,—with only three infusions in this, a metal ore that may have been broken even a hundred-thousand-fold becomes soft.
11. The insertion of the powder of the teeth and horns of the cow is the remover of softness in metals.
12. Ore from rocks or a region of the earth, which is heavy, unctuous and soft and which is tawny, green, reddish or red in colour is copper-ore.
13. That which is crow-black or of the colour of the dove or yellow pigment or studded with white lines and smelling like raw flesh, is lead-ore.
14. That which is grey like saline earth or of the colour of a backed lump of earth, is tin-ore.
15. That which is made up mostly of smooth stones, is whitish-red or of the colour of *sinduvara*-flower, is iron-ore.
16. That which is of the colour of *kakanda* ('crow's egg') or birch-leaf, is *vaikrntaka-ore.*
17. That which is clear, smooth, lustrous, possessed of sound, cold, hard and of a light colour, is gem-ore.
18. What is produced from ores, he should put to use in factories for the respective metals.
19. He should establish trade in manufactured goods in a single place, and lay down a penalty for those who manufacture, purchase or sell elsewhere.
20. He should make a miner who robs pay eight-fold, except in the case of jewels.
21. The thief and the person who lives by mining without permission, he should bind and force to work in the mines, also the person who offers personal labour in place of a fine.
22. He should let for part-share or on lease a mine that is burdensome in point of expenses or working; a light one, he should work himself.
23. The Director of Metals should establish factories for copper, lead, tin, *vaikrnataka*, brass, steel, bronze, bell-metal and iron, also trade in metal-ware.
24. The Mint Master should cause to be minted silver coins with one-fourth part copper and containing a hardening alloy one *masa* in weight of one of the following, *viz.*, iron, tin, lead and antimony,

of the denominations of one *pana*, a half *pana*, a quarter *pana* and a one-eight *pana*; further coins with one-quarter sustenance of an alloy, of the denominations of one *masaka*, a half *masaka*, a *kakani* and a half *kakani*.

25. The Examiner of Coins should establish the currency of *panas*, for trade and for receipts in the treasury.
26. He should also fix a coining fee of eight per cent, a commission of five per cent, an inspection fee of one eighth per cent, and a penalty of twenty-five *panas* for those who manufacture, purchase, sell and examine in other places.
27. The Superintendent of Mines should establish factories for articles of conch-shells, diamonds, gems, pearls, corals and caustics as well as commerce in them.
28. The Salt Commissioner should collect at the proper time the share of salt as released after crystallization as well as the lease-rent, also the price, the inspection fee and the surcharge from the sale.
29. Imported salt shall pay one-sixth part as duty.
30. Its sale shall be allowed only after the share and the dues are paid *viz.*, five per cent surcharge, the inspection fee and the manufacturing fee.
31. The purchaser shall pay the duty and a protective duty corresponding to the loss sustained by the king's goods; one who purchases at another place shall pay a fine of six-hundred *panas* in addition.
32. A person selling adulterated salt shall pay the highest fine for violence, also the person living by salt-manufacture without permission, except forest hermits.
33. Brahmins learned in the Vedas, ascetics and labourers may take salt for their food without payment.
34. All other varieties of salt and sugar shall pay only the duty.

35-36. Thus, from the mines he should collect, the price, the share, the surcharge, the monopoly tax, penalty, duty, compensation, fine, inspection fee, and manufacturing charges as well as the twelve kinds of metals and commodities made from them. In this way he should fix the collection of income under various heads in the case of all commodities.

37. The treasury has its source in the mines; from the treasury the army comes into being. With the treasury and the army, the earth is obtained with the treasury as its ornament.

CHAPTER THIRTEEN

SECTION 31: THE SUPERINTENDENT OF GOLD IN THE WORKSHOP

1. The superintendent of Gold should cause to be built a workshop with a court-yard having four work-halls without inter-communication with a single door, for the manufacture of gold and silver.
2. In the middle of the market highway he should establish the goldsmith, skilled in his profession, of noble birth and trustworthy.
3. That from the Jambu river, that from (Mt.) Satakumbha, that from Hataka, that from Venu, that produced in Srngasukti, that found in a natural condition, that transmuted by means of liquids and that produced from mines,—these are types of gold.
4. Gold of the colour of the lotus-filament, soft, smooth, not producing a sound and lustrous is best, reddish-yellow is of a middling quality, red of the lowest quality.
5. Of the best varieties, the pale-yellow and the white are impure.
6. He should cause that because of which it is impure to be removed by means of lead four times that quantity.
7. If it becomes brittle by the admixture of lead, he should cause it to be smelted with dried lumps of cow-dung.
8. If it is brittle because of its own roughness, he should cause it to be infused in sesamum-oil and cow-dung.
9. Gold produced from the mines, becoming brittle by the admixture of lead, he should turn into leaves by heating and cause them to be pounded on wooden anvils, or should cause it to be infused in the pulp of the bulbous roots of the *kadali* and the *vajra*-plants.
10. That originating in Tuttha, that from Gauda, that from Kambu and that from Cakravala—these are silver, white, smooth and soft is best.
11. Silver which is white, smooth and soft is best.
12. The opposite kind and that which tends to burst is bad.
13. He should purify that with one-fourth part of lead.
14. That in which a crest has appeared at the top, which is clear, lustrous and of the colour of curds is pure.
15. One *suvarna* of pure, turmeric-coloured gold is the standard.
16. Thence by the substitution of one *kakani* copper onwards in a *suvarna* of gold up to the limit of four *masakas*, sixteen standards are obtained.

17. After first rubbing the gold to be tested on the touchstone, he should afterwards rub the standard gold on it.
18. That with a streak of the same colour as the standard on places on the stone that are neither depressed nor elevated, he should know as properly tested; what is over-rubbed or lightly rubbed or powdered over with red chalk from underneath the finger-nail, he should know as deception.
19. Gold, touched with the forepart of the hand smeared with *jati*-vermilion or sulphate of iron dissolved in cow's urine, becomes white.
20. The streak of the gold on the touchstone, that has filaments, is smooth, soft and lustrous is best.
21. Stone from the Kalingas or from the Tapi, which is of the colour of the *mudga*-bean, is the best touchstone.
22. That which shows the exact colour is advantageous for either sale or purchase.
23. That which has the colour of an elephant, with a green tinge, is over-sensitive to colour and is advantageous for sale.
24. That which is firm, hard and of uneven colour, is not sensitive to colour and is advantageous for purchase.
25. The cut of gold that is sticky, of even colour, smooth, soft and lustrous, is best.
26. The heating that is uniform outside and inside, and has the colour of the lotus-filament or the colour of *kurandaka*-flower, is best.
27. That which is dark or blue, shows impurity.
28. Weights and measures shall be explained in the Section in the 'Superintendent of Standardisation'.
29. In accordance with those rules he should give and receive silver and gold.
30. An unauthroized person shall not approach the workshop.
31. One approaching is to be extirpated.
32. Even an officer, if carrying gold and silver inside, shall be deprived of the same.
33. Artisans doing the work of setting in gold, bead-making, plating and gilding and ornamental gold, and blowers, servants and dust-washers, shall enter and leave after their garments, hands and private parts are searched.
34. And all their tools and incompleted works shall remain just there.
35. He should hand over the gold received and the work being carried out into the office.

36. In the evening and in the morning, he should deposit, the gold and the articles, marked with the seals of the maker and the overseer.
37. Setting, stringing and minor work, these are ways of working.
38. Setting is the fixing of binding and so on.
39. Stringing is weaving in threads and so on.
40. Making a solid article, a hollow article or one with beads and so on is minor work.
41. In the work of setting, he should use one-fifth part as fastening at base and tenth part as side-fastening.
42. Silver with a quarter part copper, or gold with a quarter part silver is artificial; against that he should guard.
43. In the work of fixing of beads, there should be three parts enclosing at the sides and two parts base, or four parts base and three parts enclosing at the sides.
44. In the work of the gold-plater, he should plate an article of copper with an equal amount of gold.
45. An article of silver, whether solid or hollow, he should cover with half the amount of gold.
46. Or, he should gild the silver article with one-fourth part gold by means of the liquid or powder of sand-vermilion.
47. Ornamental gold of the best kind, possessed of excellent colour, passed through an equal amount of lead, turned into leaves by heating and Indus-earth, made bright with, becomes the base of blue, yellow, white, green and parrot-feather colours.
48. And iron of the colour of the peacock's neck, white at the cut, shimmering, and powdered after being heated, is for this gold a colouring matter one *kakani* in measure for one *suvarna* of gold.
49. Or, silver, purified, four times in a crucible of bones, four times in one with an equal amount of lead, four times in a dry crucible, three times in a pot-sherd twice in cow-dung, thus passed through seventeen crucibles, made bright with Indus-earth.
50. From this one *kakani* onwards up to two *masas* should be inserted in one *suvarna*; afterwards the adding of colouring matter should follow; it becomes white silver.
51. Three parts of ornamental gold, strengthened with thirty-two parts of white silver, it becomes white-red.
52. It makes copper yellow.
53. Making the ornamental gold bright, he should give one-third part colouring; it becomes yellowish red.
54. With two parts of white silver, one part of ornamental gold produces the colour of the *mudga*-bean.

55. When smeared with half a part of black iron, it becomes black.
56. Ornamental gold twice smeared with an enveloping liquid gets the colour of the parrot's feather.
57. In undertaking that work, he should take a test regarding the various colours.
58. And he should be conversant with the treatment of iron and copper.
59. Therefore, he should know also loss in the case of articles made of diamonds, gems, pearls and corals and the amounts required for the making of gold and silverwares.

60-61. Of an even colour, symmetrical, with beads not sticking to each other, firm, well-burnished, not soaked for a false glitter, divided into suitable parts, pleasant to wear, not gaudy, full of luster, with a charming shape, even, and pleasing to the mind and eye, — these are declared to be the excellent qualities of an ornament.

CHAPTER FOURTEEN

SECTION: 32 THE ACTIVITY OF THE GOLDSMITH IN THE MARKET-HIGHWAY

1. The Goldsmith should cause the gold and silver work of the citizens and the country people to be carried out by workshop artisans.
2. They should do the work with the time and the nature of the work stipulated, without stipulation as to time when there is the excuse of the nature of the work.
3. In case the work is done otherwise than ordered there shall be as ordered loss of wage and a fine double that amount.
4. In case the time limit is exceeded, he shall receive a wage reduced by one-quarter and a fine double that amount.
5. The artisans shall deliver in the same condition as to quality and quantity as they receive the entrusted metal.
6. And even after a lapse of time, customers shall receive it in the same condition, except what is lost in manufacture and worn away by time.
7. The Goldsmith should be conversant with every detail in connection with the characteristics and the manufacture of gold and its articles by workshop artisans.
8. In the case of gold and silver used in the manufacture of articles, a loss of one *kakani* in a *savarna* may be allowed.
9. One *kakani* of iron—twice that in the case of silver—is the insertion for colour; one-sixth part of that is the loss allowed.

10. In case of diminution of quality to the extent of one *masa* at least, the lowest fine for violence, shall be imposed in case of diminution of quantity, to that extent the middle fine, in case of deceit in scales and weights, the highest fine, also in case of fraud in an article manufactured.
11. For a person causing the manufacture of an article unseen by the Goldsmith or in some other place, the fine shall be twelve *panas.*
12. For the artisan, the fine shall be double, if there is a valid excuse.
13. If there is no excuse, the person shall be taken to the magisterial court.
14. And for the artisan, the punishment shall be a fine of two hundred *panas* or the cutting off of the fingers of his hand.
15. They shall purchase the scales and weights from the Superintendent of Standardisation.
16. Otherwise, there shall be a fine of twelve panas.
17. Making solid objects, making hollow objects, plating, coating, fixing and gilding constitute an artisan's work.
18. Fraud in the balance, removal, tapping, boxing and embedding are the means of pilfering by artisans.
19. Easily bending, carved out, with split top, with a subsidiary neck, with bad strings, with defective scales, given to swinging, and magnetic,—these are false balances.
20. Two parts of silver and one part of copper constitute *triputaka.*
21. By means of that, mineral gold is removed; that is 'removal by *triputaka.*'
22. By substitution of copper, that is 'removal by copper', by substitution of vellaka, that is 'removal by *vellaka,*' by substitution gold containing half copper, that is 'removal by gold'.
23. A dummy crucible, foul dross, the 'crane's beak', the blowpipe, the pair of tongs, the water-vessel, borax, and the same gold, these are the ways of removal.
24. Or, sand made into lumps and placed there beforehand, is taken out of the fire-place on the breaking of the crucible.
25. At the time of fixing together afterwards or at the time of testing the laid-on plating leaf, interchange of a gold article by a silver article is tapping, or the interchange of sand lumps containing gold by sand lumps containing iron.
26. A firm and a removable enclosing is made in cases of plating, coating and fixing.
27. A piece of lead covered with a leaf of gold, with the interior fixed with lac, is the firm enclosing.

28. The same, when there are casings of layers, is the removable enclosing.
29. A leaf that is compact or a twinleaf is made in cases of coating.
30. Copper or silver is made the interior of leaves in cases of fixing.
31. An article of copper, fixed with a leaf of gold and polished is *suparsva* with a well-made side; the same, fixed with a twin-leaf and polished, and an article of copper and silver similarly treated are *uttaravarnaka* with quality outside.
32. He should find these two out by heating and testing on the touchstone or by failure of right sound and by scratching.
33. The removable encasing they set down in the acid of the *badara*-fruit or in salt-water. Thus, is the 'enclosing'.
34. In a solid or a hollow article, gold-mixed earth or the pulp of *maluka* and vermilion, when heated, remains embedded.
35. Or, in an article with a firm base, lac mixed with sand or the paste of red lead, when heated, remains embedded.
36. Of these two, heating or breaking is the test of purity.
37. Or, in an article containing an encircling metal, salt heated by a fire-brand along with soft pebbles, remains embedded.
38. Boiling is the test of its purity.
39. Or, a layer of mica is fixed in an article with a double base by means of lac.
40. Of that, in which the fixing has been covered, one part sinks down when it is placed in water, or it is pierced with a needle in the spaces between the layers.
41. Gems, silver or gold form the embedding in solid or hollow articles.
42. Of that, heating or breaking is purity. Thus, is the embedding.
43. Therefore, the Goldsmith should ascertain the class, appearance, quality, quantity, the ornament made and the characteristics of articles made of diamonds, gems, pearls and corals.
44. In the course of testing articles that are made or in the course of repairs to old articles, four ways of stealing: knocking off, cutting out, scratching out or nibbing off.
45. When under the pretext of discovering an 'enclosing', they cut out a bead or a string or a casing, that is knocking off.
46. Or, when in an article with a double base, they insert an object of lead and cut the interior out, that is cutting out.
47. When from solid objects they scratch out with a sharp tool, that is scratching out.

48. When after coating a piece of cloth with the powder of one of the following, *viz.*, yellow orpiment, red arsenic or vermilion, or with powder of *kuruvinda* stone they rub the article with it, that is rubbing off.
49. By that articles of gold and silver lose in weight and yet no part of these articles gets bruised.
50. Of plated articles that are broken or cut or rubbed off, he should form an inference as to loss with the help of a similar article.
51. Of coated articles he should form an estimate by cutting out as much as has been cut out by the artisan.
52. Or, of those that have changed their appearance, he should do heating and rubbing in acid water a number of times.
53. Sudden movement of the hand, the weights, the fire, the wooden anvil, the tool-box, the receptacle, the peacock's feather, the thread, garment, talk, the head, the lap, the fly, attention to one's person, the bellows-skin, the water-platter, and the fire-pan,—these he should know as the means of pilfering.
54. Of silver articles he should know that as fraudulent which smells like raw flesh, easily catches dirt, is rough, very hard or changed in colour.
55. In this manner he should test the new and the old as well as the article that has changed its appearance, and should impose penalties on the artisans as prescribed.

CHAPTER FIFTEEN

SECTION 33: THE SUPERINTENDENT OF THE MAGAZINE

1. The Superintendent of the Magazine should know about agricultural produce, revenue from the countryside, purchase, barter, begging, borrowing, labour in place of taxes, income from other sources, return from expenditure and additional income.
2. The various kinds of grains brought in by the Director of Agriculture, constitute agricultural produce.
3. The aggregate tax, the one-sixth share, provisions for the army, tribute, tax, the 'lap', the 'side', compensation for loss, presents, and income from stores, constitute revenue from the countryside.
4. The price of grains, disposal of treasury and recovery of what is given at interest, constitute purchase.
5. Exchange of different kinds of grains at a different price, is barter.
6. Asking for grains from another source, is begging.
7. The same, intended to be returned, is borrowing.

8. The work of pounding, splitting, frying, fermenting, and grinding from those who live by these, the pressing of oil from oilmen using the hand press and the round press, and the work of extracting and treating juice of sugar-canes,—these constitute labour in place of taxes.
9. What is lost, forgotten and so on, is income from other sources.
10. Balance due to army disbandment and from undertakings given up in the middle because of sickness, is return from expenditure.
11. Difference in weights and measures, hand-filling, residue of the heap, surcharge, outstanding revenue, and earned income, constitute additional income.
12. As regards grains, fats, sugars and salts, shall be stated under state rules concerning grains in the Section on the Director of Agriculture.
13. Butter, oil, suet and marrow are fats.
14. Treacle, jaggery, unrefined sugar and granulated sugar constitute the group of sugars.
15. Salt from the Indus-land, sea-salt, *bida*-salt, salt-petre, borax and salt from saline soil constitute the group of salts.
16. That made by bees and the juice of grapes, are honey.
17. One of the following, *viz*., sugar-cane juice, jaggery, honey, treacle, the juice of *jambu*-fruit and the juice of *panasa*-fruit, infused with a decoction of *mesasrngi* and long pepper, kept for one month, six months or a year, and then mixed with *cidbhita, urvaruka*, sugar-cane stalk, mango fruit and myrobalan, or unmixed with these, constitute the group of fermented juices.
18. Tamarind, *karanarda*, mango, pomegranate, myrobalan, citron, *kola, badara, sauviraka, parusaka* and others form the group of sour fruit-juices.
19. Curds, sour gruel and others, are the group of sour liquids.
20. Long pepper, blade pepper, ginger, cumin-seed, the bitter *kirata*, white mustard, coriander, *coraka, damanaka, maruvaka*, the stalk of sigru and other, constitute the group of spices.
21. And dried fish and dried meat, bulbous roots, roots, fruits, vegetables and other, constitute the group of vegetables.
22. From these he should set apart one half for times of distress for the country people, and use the other half.
23. And he should replace old stock with new.
24. He should personally observe the amount of increase or decrease in the grains when pounded, rubbed, ground or fried, and when they are moistened, dry or cooked.

25. Of *kodrava* and *vrihi*-rice, one-half is the substance, of *sali*-rice, one-half less of *varaka*, one-third less.
26. Of *priyangu*, one-half is the substance with an increase of one-ninth.
27. *Udaraka* has the same mass, also barley and wheat when pounded, and sesame, barley, *mudga* and *masa* when rubbed.
28. Wheat increases by one-fifth, also fried barley.
29. *Kalaya*-meal is less by one quarter.
30. Meal of *mudga* and *masa* is half a quarter less.
31. Of legumes, one-half is the substance, that of lentils, one-third less.
32. Ground flour uncooked, and *kulmasa* become one and a half times in volume.
33. Barley-meal becomes double, also *pulaka* and cooked flour.
34. Of *Kodraya varaka, udaraka* and *priyangu*, the cooked preparation is three-fold, of *sali*-rice five-fold.
35. Later grains, when moistened, become double, one-half more, when sprouted.
36. There is an increase of one-fifth in the case of fried grains.
37. *kalaya* becomes double, also fried rice and barley.
38. One-sixth is the amount of oil from linseed.
39. From *nimba*, *kusa*, mango, wood-apple and others, one-fifth part is the amount of oil.
40. Oils from sesame, *kusumbha*, *madhuka* and *ingudi* amount to one-fourth.
41. Of cotton and flax, five *palas* yield one pala yarn.
42. Twelve adhakas of rice-grains from five dronas of *sali*-rice arc for the feeding of a young elephant, eleven for that of vicious elephants, ten for riding elephants, nine for war-elephants, eight for infantry-men, seven for chiefs, six for the queens and the princes, five for kings or one prastha of rice-grains, unbroken and cleansed.
43. One prastha of rice-grain, one-fourth of that broth, a quantity of salt, one-sixteenth of broth, one-fourth part butter or oil, constitute one meal of an Arya male.
44. One-sixth of a prastha broth, and half the quantity of fat is for the lower classes.
45. One-quarter less for women.
46. One-half for children.
47. For twenty *palas* of meat, half a kuduba of fat, one pala of salt, one pala of sugar, two dharanas of spices and half a prastha of curds should be used.

48. By that higher quantities are explained.
49. For vegetables, one and a half times as much, for dried meat twice as much and the same ingredients.
50. Later is stated the amount of food ration for elephants and horses in the section on the Superintendents of these.
51. For bullocks, one drona of masa or a pulaka of barley, the rest as laid down for horse.
52. The special ration for bullocks is one tula of oil-cake from the press or ten *adhakas* of broken grains and bran.
53. Twice that for buffaloes and camels.
54. Half a *drona* for donkeys, spotted deer and red deer.
55. One *adhaka* for *ena* and *kuranga*-deer.
56. Half an *adhaka* for goats, rams and boars or double that broken grains.
57. And one *prasta* of boiled rice for dogs.
58. Half a *prasta* for swans, herons and peacocks.
59. For deer, beasts, birds and wild animals other than these, he should cause an estimate to be made from one meal consumed by them.
60. He should cause charcoal and husks to be taken to metal workshops and for plastering walls.
61. He should give the broken grains to slaves, labourers and broth-makers, and things other than these to dealers in cooked rice and in cakes.
62. Implements for weighing and measuring, grinding-stones, pestle and mortar, pounding and crushing machines, scatterer, winnowing, basket, sieve, cane-basket, box and broom are the implements.
63. Sweeper, watchman, weigher, measurer, supervisor of measuring, giver, supervisor of delivery, receiver of tallies, and the group of slaves and labourers,—these are the workmen.
64. On high should be the storing place for grains; close-knit grass bags for sugar; earthen jars and wooden casks for fats; and the earth for salt.

CHAPTER SIXTEEN

SECTION 34: THE DIRECTOR OF TRADE

1. The Director of Trade should be conversant with the differences in the prices of commodities of high value and of low value and the popularity or unpopularity of goods of various kinds, whether produced on land or in water and whether they have arrived along

land-routes or water-routes, also should know about suitable times for resorting to dispersal or concentration, purchase or sale.

2. And that commodity which may be plentiful, he should collect in open place and raise the price.
3. Or, when the price is reached, he should fix another price.
4. He should establish in one place trade in royal commodities that are produced in his own country; in many places, in those produced in foreign lands.
5. And he should cause both to be sold so as to favour the subjects.
6. And he should avoid even a big profit that would be injurious to the subjects.
7. He should not create a restriction as to time or the evil of a glut in the market in the case of commodities constantly in demand.
8. Or, traders should sell royal goods in many places with the price fixed.
9. And they should pay compensation in accordance with the loss.
10. One-sixteenth part is the surcharge in measure by capacity, one-twentieth part in measure by weighing, one-eleventh part of commodities sold by counting.
11. He should encourage the import of goods produced in foreign lands by allowing.
12. And to those who bring such goods in ships or caravans, he should grant exemption from taxes that would enable a profit to be made by them.
13. And no law suit in money matters should be allowed against foreign traders, except such as are members of native concerns and their associates.
14. Officers in charge of royal goods shall deposit the price of goods sold, in one place, in a wooden box having a lid with one opening.
15. And in the eighth part of the day, they should hand it over to the Director of Trade, declaring, 'This much is sold; this is left over'.
16. They should also hand over the implements of weighing and measuring.
17. Thus, the sale of goods in one's own territory has been explained.
18. In foreign territory, however, he should ascertain the price and the value of the commodity taken out and the commodity to be brought in exchange and should calculate the profit after clearing expenses for duty, road-cess, escort-charges, picket- and ferry-dues, food and fodder and share.
19. Should there be no profit, he should see if there is any advantage in taking out goods or in bringing in goods in exchange for goods.

20. Then with a quarter of the goods of high value, he should set going trade by land along a safe route.
21. And he should establish contacts with forest chieftains, frontier officers, and chiefs in the city and the countryside, to secure their favour.
22. In case of a calamity, he should rescue the goods of high value or himself.
23. Or, if he has reached his destination, he should carry on the trade after paying all dues.
24. And on the water-route he should ascertain hire for boats, provisions on the journey, price and amount of goods and of the goods in exchange, seasons suited for voyage, precautions against dangers and regulations at the ports.
25. And along river-routes, he should ascertain conditions of trade from the regulations and should proceed to where there is profit and avoid absence of profit.

CHAPTER SEVENTEEN

SECTION 35: THE DIRECTOR OF FOREST PRODUCE

1. The Director of Forest Produce should cause forest produce to be brought in by guards in the produce forests.
2. And he should start factories for forest produce.

3-4. And he should fix dues from those cutting produce forests, also penalty, except in cases of distress *Saka, tinisa, dhanvana, arjuna, madhuka, tilaka, sala, simsapa, arimeda, rajadana, sirisa, khadira, sarala, tala, sarja, asvakarna, somavalka, kusa, amra, priyaka, dhava* and others constituting the group of hard trees with hard wood.

5. *utaja, cimiya, capa, venu, vamsa, satina, kantaka, bhalluka* and others constituting the group of reeds.
6. *vetra, sikavalli, vasi, syamalata, nagalata* and others constituting the group of creepers.
7. *malati, muruva, arka, sana, gavedhuka, atasi* and others the group of fibre-plants.
8. *munja, balbaja* and others constituting raw materials for ropes.
9. The leaves of *tali, tala and bhurja*.
10. The flowers of *kimsuka, kusumbha and kunkuma*.
11. Bulbous roots, roots, fruits and others constituting the group of medicinal plant products.
12. *kalakuta, vatsanabha, halahata, measringa, musta, kustha, mahavisa, vellitaka, gaurardra, balaka, markata, haimavata,*

kalingaka, daradaka, ankolasara, austraka, and other poisons, serpents, and insects, these same kept in jars, all constituting the group of poisons.

13. Skin, bones, bile, tendons, eyes, teeth, horns, hooves and tails of the lizard, *seraka,* leopard, bear, dolphin, kion, tiger, elephant, buffalo, *camara*, *srmara*, rhinoceros, bison and *gavaya*, and also of other deer, beasts, birds and wild animals should be stored.
14. Iron, copper, steel, bronze, lead, tin, *vaikrntaka* and brass constituting the group of metals.
15. Vessels made of split bamboo-cane and of clay.
16. Charcoal, husks and ashes; enclosures for deer, beasts, birds and wild animals and enclosures for fuel and grass.
17. Separate factories milking all kinds of goods should be erected, outside as well as inside, by the Director of Forest Produce, for ensuring livelihood and protection of the city.

CHAPTER EIGHTEEN

SECTION 36: THE SUPERINTENDENT OF THE ARMOURY

1. The Superintendent of the Armoury should cause to be made machines for use in battles, for the defence of forts and for assault on the enemies' cities, also weapons, armours and accoutrements by artisans and artists expert in those lines, producing goods with an agreement as to the amount of work, time allowed and wages, and should store them in places suitable for each.
2. He should frequently change their places and expose them to sun and wind.
3. He should store in a different way what is being damaged by heat, moisture or insects.
4. And he should know them by their class, appearance, characteristics, quantity, source, price and place of storing.
5. *sarvatobhadra, jamadagnya, bahumukha, visvasaghatin, samghati, yanaka, parijanyaka, bahu, urdhuvadhu, and ardhababahu* are fixed machines.
6. *panacalika, devadanda, sukarika, musalayasti, hastivaraka, talavrnta,* hammer, mace, *sprktala,* spade, *asphatima, utpatima, udghatima, sataghni*, trident and discus are mobile machines.
7. *sakti, prasa, kunta, hataka, bhindipala, sula, tomara, varahakarna, karpana, kanaya, trasika* and others are weapons with piercing points.
8. Made from tala, capa, wood and horn and known as *karmuka, kodanda* and *druna* are the bows.

9. *muruva, arka, sana, gavedhu, venu* and sinews of animals are bow-strings,
10. *venu, sara, salaka, dandasana and naraca* are arrows.
11. Their tips for cutting, piercing and striking are made of iron, bone or wood.
12. *nistrimsa, mandalagra* and *asiyasti* are swords.
13. The horn of the rhinoceros and buffalo, the tusk of the elephant, wood and bamboo-root form the hilts.
14. *parasu, kuthara, pattasa, khanitra,* spade, saw, and *kandacchedana* are razor-type weapons.
15. Stones for use in machines, in slings and by hand, and mil-stones are stone-weapons.
16. A coat of mail of metal rings or metal plates, an armour of fabrics, and combinations of skin, hooves and horns of dolphin, rhinoceros, dhenuka, elephant and bull, are armours.
17. Helmet, neck-guard, cuirass, robe, coat of mail, breast-plate and thigh-guard, box, leather shield, *hastikarna, talamula, dhamnika, kapata, kitika, apratihata and balahakanta* are shields.
18. Objects used in giving training to elephants, chariots and horses, objects used for their decoration and arrangements for their equipment are the accoutrements.
19. Illusion magic and secret practices are work.
20. And concerning the factories: the Master of the Armoury should know the desire, the carrying out of the undertaking, the use, fraud if practised, gain, loss and expenditure of the various types of forest produce.

CHAPTER NINETEEN

SECTION 37: STANDARDISATION OF WEIGHTS AND MEASURES

1. The Superintendent of Standardisation should cause factories to be established for the manufacture of standard weights and measures.
2. Ten *masa*-beans make one *masaka* of gold, or five *gunja*-berries.
3. Sixteen of these make one *suvarna* or *karsa*.
4. A *pala* is equivalent to four *karsas*.
5. Eighty-eight white mustard-seeds make one *masaka* of silver.
6. Sixteen of these make one *dharana*, or twenty *simba*-beans.
7. A *dharana* of diamond weighs twenty rice-grains.
8. A half-*masaka*, a *masaka*, two, four, eight *masakas*, a *suvarna*, two, four, eight *suvarnas*, also ten, twenty, thirty, forty and one hundred *suvarnas*, are denominations of weights.

9. By that are explained *dharanas.*
10. Weights should be made of iron or stone from the Magadhas or the Mekala hills or such as would not increase in weight by water and smearing or decrease in weight by heat.
11. Beginning with six *angulas* in length and rising successively by eight *angulas*, he should cause ten balance-beans to be made, one *pala* of metal onwards in weight increased successively by one *pala*, with scale-pans on the two sides of the fulcrum or a pan on one side only.
12. He should cause the *samavrtta* balance to be made of metal thirty-five *palas* and seventy-two *angulas* in length.
13. Fixing a ball of metal five *palas* in weight at one end, he should cause the level to be secured for marking zero.
14. From that point onwards, he should cause markings to be made for one *karsa*, increased by a *karsa* up to one *pala*, then increased by a *pala* up to ten *palas*, then for twelve, fifteen and twenty *palas.*
15. Thereafter, he should cause markings to be made increased by ten up to one hundred *palas.*
16. In the 'fives' he should cause it to be covered with *nandi* the *svastika* mark.
17. He should cause a balance called *parimani* to be made with double this amount of metal and ninety-six *angulas* in length.
18. On that he should cause markings to be made beyond one hundred for twenty, fifty-two and hundred *palas.*
19. A *bhara* contains twenty *tula* weights.
20. A *pala* contains ten *dharanas.*
21. One hundred of these *palas* is the revenue measure.
22. Less by five *palas* successively are measures for trade, for payments and for measuring out to the palace.
23. Of these, the *pala* is successively less by half a *dharana*, the metal of the upper beam successively less by two successive *palas* and the length successively less by *six angulas.*
24. In the case of the former two, an excess in weight of five *palas* is to be received except in cases of meat, metals, salt and gems.
25. The balance made of wood should be eight *hastas* long, provided with markings or with weights and supported by 'peacock's feet'.
26. Twenty-five *palas* of fire-wood are a means of cooking one *prastha* of rice.
27. This is an indication for more and for less.
28. Thus, weights and balances have been explained.

29. Now, two hundred *palas* of *masa*-beans make one drona for revenue measures, one hundred and eighty-seven and a half *palas*, for trade, one hundred and seventy-five *palas*, for making payments, and one hundred sixty-two and a half *palas*, for measuring out to the palace.
30. Of these, *adhaka*, *prastha* and *kudaua* are smaller measures, being each one-fourth of the preceding.
31. Sixteen *dronas* make one *khari*.
32. Twenty *dronas* make one *kumbha*.
33. Ten *kumbhas* make one *vaha*.
34. He should cause measures to be made of dry, hard wood, even, with one-fourth as top-head, or with the heap included inside.
35. However, in the case of liquids, wine, flowers and fruits, husk and charcoal, and lime, the measure of the top-heap is an increase that is double.
36. One *pana* and a quarter the price of a *drona*; three-quarters, of an *adhaka*; six *masakas*, of a *prastha*; one *masaka*, of a *kuduba*.
37. The price of the measures for liquids and other should be double.
38. The price of the weights should be twenty *panas*.
39. One-third that the price of the balance.
40. He should cause a stamping of the weights and measures to be made every four months.
41. The penalty for unstamped weights etc. is twenty-seven *panas* and a quarter.
42. Traders shall pay a stamping fee amounting to one *kakani* every day to the Superintendent of Standardisation.
43. One-thirty-second part is the surcharge for heating in the case of clarified butter, one-sixty-fourth part in the case of oil.
44. One-fiftieth part is the flow from the measure in the case of liquids.
45. He should cause measures of a half-*kuduba*, a quarter-*kuduba* and one-eighth *kuduba* to be made.
46. Eighty-four *kudubas* of clarified butter are known as a *varaka*; but sixty-four *kudubas* make a *varaka* of oil; and one-quarter of these is known as a *ghatika*.

CHAPTER TWENTY

SECTION 38: MEASURES OF SPACE AND TIME

1. The Superintendent of Measurements should be conversant with the measurements of space and time.
2. Eight atoms make one *rathacakraviprus*-chariot-wheel particle.

3. Eight of them make one *liksa*-nit.
4. Eight of them make one *yuka*-louse.
5. Eight of them make one *yavamadhaya*-barley middle.
6. Eight *yavamadhyas* make one *angula*-finger.
7. Or, the maximum width of the middle part of the middle finger of a middling man is an *angula*.
8. Four *angulas* make a *dhanurgraha*.
9. Eight *angulas* make a *dhanurmusti*.
10. Twelve *angulas* make a *vitasti* span and the height of the shadow-gnomon.
11. Fourteen *angulas* make a *sama*, a *sala*, a *pariraya* and a *pada* (foot).
12. Two spans make an *aratni*-cubit, the *hasta* of Prajapati.
13. A *hasta* with a *dhanurgraha* is the measure of a *hasta* for weights and measures and for pastures.
14. A *hasta* with a *dhanurmusti* makes a *kisku* or a *kamsa*.
15. Forty-two *angulas* make a carpenter's sawing *kisku*, a measure for the camp, the fort and royal property.
16. Fifty-four *angulas* make a *hasta* for measuring forest produce.
17. Eighty-four *angulas* make a *vyama*, a measure for ropes and a *paurusa* man's height for measuring moats or diggings.
18. Four *aratnis* make a *danda*, a *dhanus*, a *nalika*, and a *paurusa* for the householder.
19. One hundred and eight *angulas* make a *dhanus*, measure for roads and city-walls and a *paurusa* for measuring the piling of fire-altars.
20. Six *kamsas* make a *danda*, a measure for gifts to Brahmins and to guests.
21. Ten *dandas* make a *rajju*.
22. Two *rajjus* make a *paridesa*.
23. Three *rajjus* make a *nivartana* on one side.
24. A *bahu* has two *dandas* more.
25. Two thousand *dhanuses* make a *goruta*.
26. Four *gorutas* make a *yojana*.
27. Thus, measurements of space have been explained.
28. Hereafter measurements of time.
29. *tuta*, lava, *nimesa*, *kastha*, *kala*, *nalika*, *muhurta*, forenoon and afternoon, day, night, fortnight, month, season, ayana, year and cycle of years are divisions of time.
30. Two *tutas* make a *lava*.
31. Two *lavas* make a *nimesa*.
32. Five *nimesas* make a *kastha*.

33. Thirty *kasthas* make a *kala*.
34. Forty *kalas* make a *nalika*.
35. Or, a hole in a jar with a dimension of four *masakas* of gold made four *angulas* in length, with an *adhaka* of water running throughout it measures one *nalika*.
36. Two *anlikas* make a *muhurta*.
37. A day of fifteen *muhurtas* and a night of the same length occur in the months of Caitra and Asvayuja.
38. After that, one of them first increases and then decreases by three *muhurtas* during a period of six months and *vice versa* the other.
39. When the shadow of the gnomon is eight *paurusas*, one-eighteenth part of the day is past, when six *paurusas*, one-fourteenth part is past, when three *paurusas*, one-eighth part, when two *apurusas*, one-sixth part, when one *paurusa*, one-fourth part, when eight *angulas*, three-tenth part is past, when four *angulas*, three-eighth part, and when there is no shadow, it is mid-day.
40. When the day has turned, one should understand the remaining parts in like manner.
41. In the month of Asadha, the mid-day loses shadow.
42. After that, in the six months beginning with Sravana, the shadow at mid-day increases by two *angulas* in each month and in the six months beginning with Magha, it decreases by two *angulas* in each month.
43. Fifteen days and nights make a fortnight.
44. That in which the moon waxes is the bright.
45. That in which the moon wanes is the dark.
46. Two fortnights make a month.
47. Thirty days and nights make a works' month.
48. A half day more makes a solar month.
49. A half day less makes a lunar month.
50. Twenty-seven days and nights make a month of constellations.
51. Thirty-two make a month for the army.
52. Thirty-five, a month for maintenance of horse.
53. Forty, a month for maintenance of elephants.
54. Two months make a season.
55. Srvana and Prausthapada are the rainy season.
56. Asvayuja and Karttika are autumn.
57. Margastrsa and Pausa are winter.
58. Magha and Phalguna are the season of frost.
59. Caitra and Vaisakha are spring.
60. Jyesthamuliya and Asdha are summer.

61. The *uttarayana* begins with the season of frost.
62. The *daksinayana* begins with the rainy season.
63. Two *ayanas* make a year.
64. Five years make one cycle.
65. The sun takes one-sixtieth part of a day; thus in one season he brings about the loss of one day, and so does the moon cause loss of one day.
66. Thus, in every period of two years and a half the two beget an additional month, the first in summer and the second at the end of the cycle of five years.

CHAPTER TWENTYONE

SECTION 39: THE COLLECTOR OF CUSTOMS AND TOLLS

1. The Collector of Customs and Tolls should establish the customs house and the flag facing the east or the north in the vicinity of the big gates of the city.
2. The receivers of duty, four or five in number, should record details in writing about traders who have arrived in a caravan, who they are, from what place, with how much merchandise and where the identity pass was issued or the stamping was made.
3. For goods without the stamp the penalty is double the dues.
4. For those with a forged stamp, the fine is eight times the duty.
5. For those with broken stamps, the penalty is distraint in the warehouse.
6. In case of change of the royal stamp or of change in the name, he should make the trader pay a fine of one *pana* and a quarter per load.
7. Traders shall declare the quantity and price of the goods that have arrived at the foot of the flag, 'Who is willing to purchase these goods, so much in quantity, at this price?'
8. When it has been thrice proclaimed, he should give it to those who have sought it.
9. In case of competition among purchasers, the increase in price together with the duty shall go to the treasury.
10. If for fear of duty a trader declares the quantity of the goods or the price to be less than it actually is, the king shall confiscate that excess.
11. Or, the trader shall pay eight times the duty.
12. He should impose the same penalty in case of depreciation of price of a package containing goods by showing a sample of lower value

and in case of concealment of goods of high value by goods of low value.

13. Or, if through fear of a rival purchaser a trader increases the price beyond the due price of a commodity, the king shall receive the increase in price, or make the amount of duly double.
14. The same penalty eightfold shall be imposed on the Superintendent concealing the trader's offences.
15. Therefore, the sale of goods should be made by weighing, measuring or counting; an appraisal of value should be made of goods of small value and goods enjoying concessions.
16. And for goods that have passed beyond the foot of the flag without the duty being paid, the fine is eight times the duty.
17. Secret agents operating on roads and in places without roads should find out such evasion.
18. Goods intended for marriage, marriage-gifts accompanying the bride, goods intended as gifts, goods required on the occasion of a sacrifice or a ceremony or a birth and goods used in various rituals like worship of the gods, tonsure rite, initiation for Veda study, hair-cutting rite, consecration for a vow and so on, should go duty-free.
19. For a person making a false declaration in this respect the punishment for theft, shall be imposed.
20. For the trader taking out a commodity for which duty has not been paid along with one for which duty has been paid, or carrying off a second commodity under one stamp after breaking open the package, forfeiture of the same and an equal amount as fine shall be the punishment.
21. For the trader carrying off goods of high value from the customs house after securing acceptance of cowdung cakes or straw as the basis for calculating duty, the highest fine for violence shall be the punishment.
22. For the trader taking out any one of the unexportable articles, *viz.*, weapons, armours, coats of mail, metals, chariots, jewels, grains and cattle, there shall be a fine as proclaimed as well as loss of the goods.
23. In case any one of these is brought in, its sale shall be effected duty-free outside the city-gate itself.
24. The frontier officer should charge a road cess of one *pana* and a quarter for a cart-load of goods, of one *pana* for a one-hoofed animal, of half a *pana* for cattle, of a quarter *pana* for small animals, of one *masaka* for a shoulder-load.

25. And he shall make good what is lost or stolen on the way.
26. He should send on to the Superintendent a caravan from a foreign land after making an investigation as to goods of high and low value and giving them an identity-pass and stamp on the goods.
27. Or, a secret agent appearing as a trader should communicate to the king the size of file caravan.
28. In accordance with that information, the king should tell the Collector of Customs about the size of the caravan, in order to make his omniscience known.
29. Then the Collector, on meeting the caravan, should say, 'These are goods of high and low value belonging to such and such a merchant. It should not be concealed. This is the king's power.'
30. For one concealing goods of low value the fine shall be eight times the duty, for concealing goods of high value, confiscation of everything shall be the punishment.
31. He should cut out goods that are harmful to the country and that are worthless. He should make goods that are highly beneficial duty-free, also seeds that are rare.

CHAPTER TWENTYTWO

SECTION 39 (CONCLUDED): THE TARIFF OF DUTIES AND TOLLS

1. Goods are from the countryside, from the city and from foreign lands.
2. That on goods going out and that on goods coming in is duty.
3. On goods coming in the duty shall be one-fifth of the price.
4. Of flowers, fruits, vegetables, roots, bulbous roots, fruits of creepers, seeds, dried fish and meat, he should take one-sixth part as duty.
5. Of conch-shells, diamonds, gems and necklaces of pearls and corals, he should make a valuation through men expert in the line, making an agreement with them as to the amount of work, time allowed and wages.
6. On *ksauma*, *dukula*, silk yarn, armours, yellow orpiment, red arsenic, antimony, vermilion, metals of various kinds and ores, on sandal-wood, aloe, spices, fermentation, and minor substances, on skins, ivory, bed-spreads, coverings and silk cloth, and on products of goats and rams, the duty to be charged is one-tenth part or one-fifteenth part.

7. On clothes, four-footed and two-footed creatures, yarn, cotton, perfumes, medicines, woods, bamboos, barks, leather goods and earthenware, and on grains, fats, sugars, salts, wine, cooked food and so on the duty is one-twentieth part or one-twenty-fifth part.
8. To be received at the gate is one-fifth of the normal duty, or he should fix it with a concession in accordance with the benefit derived by the country.
9. And no sale of commodities shall be allowed in the places of their origin.
10. For taking metal goods from mines the penalty is six hundred *panas*.
11. For taking flowers and fruits from flower-gardens and fruit-orchards, the fine is fifty-four *panas*.
12. For taking vegetables, roots and bulbous roots from vegetable-gardens, the fine is fifty-one and three quarter *panas*.
13. For taking all kinds of crops from fields, the fine is fifty-three *panas*.
14. One *pana* and one *pana* and a half is the penalty in case of agricultural produce.
15. From this, he should fix the duties for new and old commodities in accordance with the customs of the country and the community, and penalty according to the offence.

CHAPTER TWENTYTHREE

SECTION 40: THE SUPERINTENDENT OF YARNS AND TEXTILES

1. The Superintendent of Yarns should cause trade to be carried out in yarns, armours, cloth and ropes through men expert in the work.
2. He should get yarn spun out of wool, bark-fibres, cotton, silk-cotton, hemp and flax, through widows, crippled women, maidens, women who have left their homes and women paying off their fine by personal labour, through mothers of courtesans, through old female slaves of the king and through female slaves of temples whose service of the gods has ceased.
3. He should fix the wage after ascertaining the fineness, coarseness or medium quality of the yarn, and the largeness or smallness of quantity.
4. After finding out the amount of yarn, he should favour them with oil and myrobalan unguents.

5. And on festive days, they should be made to work by honouring and making gifts.
6. In case of diminution in yarn, a diminution in wage, according to the value of the stuff.
7. And he should cause work to be carried out by artisans producing goods with an agreement as to the amount of work, time and wage, and should maintain close contact with them.
8. And when starting mills for the weaving of cloth from *ksauma*, *dukula*, silk yarn, hair of the *ranku* deer, and cotton yarn, he should gratify the workmen by gifts of perfumes and flowers and by other means of showing good-will.
9. He should bring about the production of varieties of cloth, bed-sheets and coverings.
10. And he should start factories for armours by artisans and craftsmen expert in the line.
11. And those women who do not stir out—those living separately, widows, crippled women or maidens,—who wish to earn their living, should be given work by sending his own female slaves to them with a view to support them.
12. Or, if they come themselves to the yarn-house, he should cause an interchange of goods and wages to be made early at dawn.
13. The lamp should be there only for the inspection of the yarn.
14. For looking at the face of the woman or conversing with her on another matter, the lowest fine for violence shall be imposed, for delay in the payment of wages, the middle fine, also for payment of wages for work not done.
15. If a woman after receiving the wage does not carry out the work, he should make her forfeit the tongs formed by the thumb and the middle finger, also those who have misappropriated or stolen and then run away.
16. And in the matter of wages, there shall be a fine for workmen in accordance with their offence.
17. And he should himself keep in touch with rope-makers and makers of armours.
18. And he should cause articles, such as straps and others to be manufactured.
19. He should cause ropes to be made of yarn and fibres, and thongs of canes and bamboos, as trappings for war and bindings for vehicles and drought-animals.

CHAPTER TWENTYFOUR

SECTION 41: THE DIRECTOR OF AGRICULTURE

1. The Director of Agriculture, himself conversant with the practice of agriculture, water-divining and the science of rearing plants, or assisted by experts in these, should collect, in the proper seasons, seeds of all kinds of grains, flowers, fruits, vegetables, bulbous roots, roots, creeper fruits, flax and cotton.
2. He should cause them to be sown in land, suitable for each, which has been ploughed many times, through serfs, labourers and persons paying off their fines by personal labour.
3. And he should cause no delay in the work of these on account of ploughing machines, implements and bullocks, and on account of the work of artisans, such as smiths, carpenters, basket-makers, rope-makers, snake-catchers and others.
4. In case of loss of fruit of a work through their negligence, the fine shall be equal to the loss of that fruit.
5. Sixteen *dronas* is the amount of rain in dry lands, one and a half times that in wet lands, where sowings are in conformity with the nature of the region, thirteen *dronas* and a half in the Asmaks, twenty-three in the Avantis, unlimited in the Aparantas and the snowy regions, and unlimited as to time, in lands where sowings are made with the help of canals.
6. One-third of the annual rainfall in the first and the last months, together two-thirds in the intervening two months,—this is the form of excellence of the season.
7. Its ascertainment is made from the position, motion and impregnation of Jupiter, from the rise, setting and movements of Venus and from modification in the natural appearance of the sun.
8. From the sun is known the successful sprouting of seeds, from Jupiter the formation of stalks in the crops, from Venus rain.
9. Three clouds raining continuously for seven days each, eighty clouds showering drops of rain and sixty clouds accompanied by sunshine, this rainfall is even and beneficial.
10. Where it rains distributing wind and sunshine properly and creating three periods for the drying of cowdung cakes, there the growth of crops is certain.
11. In conformity with that, he should cause crops to be sown, requiring plenty of water or little water.

12. *sali*-rice, *urihi*-rice, *kodrava*, sesamum, *priyangu*, *uddraka* and *varaka* are the first sowings.
13. *mudga*, *masa* and *saimubya* are the middle sowings.
14. Sunflower, lentils, *kulatta*, barley, wheat, *kalaya*, linseed and mustard are the last sowings.
15. Or, the sowing of seeds should be in conformity with the season.
16. What is left over from sowing, farmers cultivating for half the produce should till, or those who live by personal labour should work it for a one-fourth or one-fifth share.
17. The farmers shall pay a share for uncultivated land as desired by the king, except in times of distress.
18. The farmers shall pay a water-rate of one-fifth in the case of water set in motion by the hand from their own water-works, one-fourth when set in motion by shoulders and one-third when set flowing in channels by a mechanism, one-fourth when lifted from rivers, lakes, tanks and wells.
19. According to the amount of water available for the work, he should decide on wet crops, winter crops or summer crops.
20. *sali* and others are the best crops, vegetables middling, sugar-cane worst.
21. For, sugar-canes are fraught with many dangers and require much expenditure.
22. A region where the foam strikes the banks is suited for creeper fruits, regions on the outskirts of overflows, for long pepper, grapes and sugarcanes those on, the borders of wells, for vegetables and roots, those on the borders of moist beds of lakes, for green grasses, ridges for plants reaped by cutting, such as perfume-plants, medicinal herbs, *usira*-grass, *ribera*, *pindaluka* and others.
23. And on lands suitable for each, he should raise plants that grow on dry lands and that grow in wet lands.
24. Soaking in dew by night and drying in the heat by day for seven days and nights is the treatment in the case of seeds of grains, for three days and nights or five in the case of seeds, and of pulses, smearing at the cut with honey, ghee and pig's fat, mixed with cowdung in the case of stalks that serve as seeds, with honey and ghee in the case of bulbous roots, smearing with cowdung in the case of stone-like seeds in the case of trees, burning in the pit and fulfilment of the longing with cow-bones and cowdung at the proper time.

25. And when they have sprouted, he should feed them with fresh acrid fish along with the milk of the *snuhi*-plant.
26. He should collect and burn the seeds of cotton and the slough of a serpent. Serpents do not remain where there is this smoke.
27. However, at the first sowing of all kinds of seeds, he should sow the first handful after it is immersed in water containing gold and should recite the following *mantra*:
    'Salutation to Kasyapa, the Lord of Creation and to the god of rain always. May the divine Sita prosper in my seeds and my grains.'
28. To watchmen in vegetable-gardens and in fruit and flower enclosures, to cowherds and serfs and labourers, he should supply food in accordance with persons dependent on them, and pay a wage of one *pana* and a quarter per month.
29. To artisans, he should give food and wages in conformity with their work.
30. And those learned in the Vedas and ascetics may take flowers and fruits that have fallen on the ground for worship of the gods, rice and barley for the *agrayana* sacrifice, and those who live by gleaning may take what is left at the base of a heap of grains.
31. And at the proper time he should bring in the crops and other things as they are harvested. The wise man should not leave anything in the field, not even husk.
32. He should make high walls, or roofs of the same kind. He should not make the tops compact nor very light.
33. He should make the heaps situated at the border of the threshing circular floor. At the threshing ground, workmen should carry no fire and should be provided with water.
    All these activities would result good agricultural yields.

16

BOOK TWO (Part Three)

Activities of Heads of Departments (Concluded)

In this Sub-Book of original BOOK TWO composed by Kautilya information from chapter No. 25 to 36 has been described. These departments are: 25. The Controller of Spirituous Liquors, 26. The Supervisor of (Animal) Slaughter, 27. The Superintendent of Courtesans, 28. The Controller of Shipping, 29. The Superintendent of Cattle, 30. The Superintendent of Horses, 31-32. The Superintendent of Elephants, 33. The Superintendent of chariots, Foot-soldiers and the Commandant of Army, 34. The Superintendent of Passports, The Superintendent of Pasture-lands, 35. The Activity of the Administrator, Secret Agents in the Disguise of House-holders, Traders and Ascetics, 36. Rules for the City Superintendent.

CHAPTER TWENTYFIVE

SECTION 42: THE CONTROLLER OF SPIRITUOUS LIQUORS

1. The Controller of Spirituous Liquors should cause trade in wines and ferments to be carried on in the fort, the country or the camp, through persons dealing in wines and ferments, being born to that work, either in one place or in many places or according to convenience for purchase and sale.
2. He should fix six hundred *panas* as the penalty for those who manufacture, purchase or sell in other places.

3. He should enforce prohibition of taking wine out of the village and its accumulation, because of the danger of remissness in duties by those appointed, because of the danger of transgression of the bounds of propriety by Aryas and because of the danger of rash acts by bravoes.
4. Or, those of known integrity may carry out a small quantity, well marked, either one-fourth of a *kuduba*, half a *kuduba*, a *kuduba*, half a *prastha*.
5. Or, they should drink in the drinking-houses without moving about.
6. In order to find out things that are misappropriated after being received in trust or as a deposit or a pledge and that are acquired in undesirable ways, he should, on finding an article or money not belonging to a person, get the person offering it arrested in another place under some other pretext, also the person who spends lavishly and the person who spends without having a source of income.
7. And the vintner shall not sell liquor at a different price or on credit, except spoiled liquor.
8. He should get the latter sold in another place.
9. Or, he should pay it as wages for slaves and labourers.
10. Or, he should give it as a strong drink for drought animals or as nourishment for pigs.
11. He should cause ale-houses to be built with many rooms, and provided with separate beds and seats, and drinking bars provided with perfumes, flowers and water, and pleasant in all seasons.
12. Secret agents, placed there, should exertion the normal and occasional expenditure of customers and get information about strangers.
13. They should make a note of the ornaments, clothes and cash of customers who are intoxicated or sleeping.
14. In case of loss of these, the traders shall pay the same and a fine of equal amount.
15. Traders, on their part, should find out through their own female slaves of beautiful appearance, the intentions of strangers and natives, who have the outward appearance of Aryas, when they are intoxicated or asleep in secluded parts of the rooms.
16. Concerning the *medaka*, the *prasanna*, the *asava*, the *aristas*, the *marieya* and *madhu*.
17. One *drona* of water, one half *adhaka* of rice-grains and three *prasthas* of ferment form the mixture for the *medaka*.

18. Twelve *adhakas* of flour, five *prasthas* of ferment or the mixture of its class along with the bark and fruit of the *kramuka*, form the mixture for the *prasanna*.
19. One *tula* of the wood-apple fruit, five *tulas* of treacle, and a *prastha* of honey form the mixture for the *asava*.
20. One quarter more of this mixture is the best *asava*, one quarter less the lowest kind.
21. The *aristas* are as prescribed by physicians for each separate malady.
22. The *maireya* is distilled from a decoction of the bark of the *mesasrngi* with the addition of jaggery, having a mixture of long pepper and black pepper or mixed with the three fruits.
23. Or, there should be a mixture of the three fruits in all liquors mixed with jaggery.
24. The juice of grapes is *madhu*.
25. Its name derived from the place of origin is *kapisayana* and *harahuraka*.
26. One *drona* pulp of *masa*-beans, raw or cooked, with one-third part more rice-grains, mixed with a part weighing one *karsa* each of *morata* and others is the formation of ferment.
27. A mixture weighing five *karsas* each of *patha, lodhra, tejovati, cardamum, valuka,* lacquers, *madhurasa, priyangu, daruharidra,* black and long pepper is the addition for the *medaka* and the *prasanna.*
28. And *katasarkara*, mixed with a decoction of liquorice makes the colour clear.
29. The mixture for the *asava* is one *karsa* each of cinnamon bark, *citraka, vilanga* and *gajapippali* and two *karsas* each of *kramuka,* liquorice, *musta* and *lodhra.*
30. And one-tenth part of these is the formation of the essence.
31. The mixture for *prasanna* is that for white liquor.
32. Mango-liquor, with a higher proportion of juice or a higher proportion of essence, is *mahasura*, or when it contains the mixture.
33. The powder of burnt *katasarkara*, infused in a decoction of *morata, palasa, pattura, mesarngi, karanja* and *ksiravrksa*, mixed with half its quantity of the pulp of *lodhra, citraka, vilanga, patha, musta, kalinga-yava, daruharidra, indivara, satapuspa, apamdrga, saptaparna, nimba and asphota*, a handful of this with nails invisible, makes one *kumbhi* of those liquors clear, fit to be drunk by the king.

34. And jaggery, five *palas* in weight, should be added to it to increase the sweet juice.
35. Householders should be free to manufacture white liquor on festival occasions or an *arista* for medicinal use, or other spirituous preparations.
36. On the occasions of festivals, gatherings and fairs, permission to manufacture and sell liquor should be granted for four days.
37. On those days, he should charge a penalty per day from those not permitted, till the end of the festivity.
38. Women and children should make a search for ingredients used in liquors and ferments.
39. Dealers in goods not manufactured by the state shall pay a duty of five per cent on *sura, medaka, arista, madhu,* sour fruit juices, and sour liquors.
40. And after ascertaining the day's sale and the surcharge on measures and on cash, he should fix the compensation accordingly and should keep doing what is customary.

CHAPTER TWENTYSIX

SECTION 43: THE SUPERVISOR OF ANIMAL SLAUGHTER

1. The Supervisor of Slaughter should impose the highest fine for violence for binding, killing or injuring deer, beasts, birds or fish for whom safety has been proclaimed and who are kept in reserved parks, the middle fine on householders for these offences in reserved park enclosures.
2. For binding, killing or injuring fish and birds whose slaughter is not current, he should impose a fine of twenty-six *panas* and three quarters for binding deer and beasts, double that.
3. Of those whose slaughter is current and who are not protected in enclosures, he should receive one-sixth part, of fish and birds one-tenth part more, of deer and beasts, duty in addition.
4. He should release in sanctuary parks the live one-sixth part of birds and deer.
5. Sea-fish having the form of an elephant or a horse or a man or a bull or a donkey, or those from lakes, rivers, tanks or canals, curlew, osprey, gallinule, swan, ruddy goose, pheasant, *bhrngaraja, cakora, mattakokila,* peacock, parrot and *madanasarika*, which are birds for sport and auspicious birds, also other creatures whether birds or deer, should be protected from all dangers of injury.

6. For transgression of this protection, the first fine for violence shall be imposed.
7. Traders shall sell meat without bones, of deer and beasts freshly killed.
8. For meat containing bones, they should give a compensation for loss.
9. For what is short in weight, the fine be eight times the short measure.
10. The calf, the bull and the milch-cow among these animals are not to be killed.
11. For one killing them, there shall be a fine of fifty *panas*, also for one torturing them to death.
12. They shall not sell meat that is swollen without head, feet and bones, foul-smelling and of a naturally dead animal.
13. Otherwise, there shall be a fine of twelve *panas*.
14. Beasts, deer, wild animals and fish, belonging to sanctuaries, should, when harmful, be killed or bound in places other than the place of their protection.

CHAPTER TWENTYSEVEN

SECTION 44: THE SUPERINTENDENT OF COURTESANS

1. The Superintendent of Courtesans should appoint as a courtesan, with one thousand *panas*, a girl, from a courtesan's family or a family not of courtesans, who is richly endowed with beauty, youth and arts, and a deputy courtesan for half the family establishment.
2. If a courtesan has run away or died, her daughter or sister shall run the family-establishment, or the mother shall provide a deputy courtesan.
3. In the absence of these, the king should take away the establishment.
4. In conformity with superiority in point of beauty and ornaments, he should, with one thousand *panas*, assign the lowest, middle most or highest turn for attendance, in order to add distinction to attendance with the parasol, the water-jug, the fan, the palanquin, the seat and the chariot.
5. In case of loss of beauty, he should appoint her as the 'mother'.
6. The ransom price is twenty-four thousand *panas* for a courtesan, twelve thousand for a courtesan's son.
7. From the age of eight, the latter should do the work of the king's minstrel.

8. The female slave of a courtesan, whose professional career is over, should do work in the magazine or the kitchen.
9. One, not going for such work, should be kept under restraint, be made to pay the monthly wage of one *pana* and a quarter.
10. He should keep an account of the payment by visitors, gifts, income, expenditure and gains of a courtesan, and should prohibit an act of excessive expenditure.
11. For handing over her ornaments to the keeping of any one else but the mother, the fine shall be four *panas* and a quarter.
12. If she sells or pledges her belongings, the fine shall be fifty *panas* and a quarter, twenty-four *panas* in case of verbal injury, double that in case of physical injury, fifty *panas* and a quarter and one *pana* for cutting off the ear.
13. In case of violence against a maiden who is unwilling, the highest fine shall be imposed, the lowest fine for violence, if she is willing.
14. If a man keeps under restraint a courtesan who is unwilling, or helps her to run away or spoils her beauty by cutting up a wound, the fine shall be one thousand *panas*.
15. Or, there shall be an increase in fine in accordance with the importance of her position, up to double the ransom amount.
16. If a man causes the death of a courtesan who has been appointed to the office, the fine shall be three times the ransom amount.
17. For killing a mother, a daughter or a female slave living by her beauty, the highest fine for violence shall be imposed.
18. In all cases, the prescribed fine shall be imposed for the first offence, double that for the second offence, three-fold for the third offence, in case of the fourth repetition of the offence he may do what he pleases.
19. A courtesan, not approaching a man at the command of the king, shall receive one thousand strokes with the whip, or a fine of five thousand *panas*.
20. If a courtesan, after receiving payment, shows dislike, she shall be fined double the amount of payment.
21. In case she cheats in connection with attendance on visitors staying overnight, she shall pay eight times the amount of payment, except in case of her illness or defects in the man.
22. If she kills a man, the punishment shall be burning on the funeral pyre or drowning in water.
23. If a man robs a courtesan of her ornaments, her goods or the payment due to her, he shall be fined eight times the amount.

24. The courtesan shall communicate to the Superintendent the payment, the gain and the name of the man.
25. By this are explained rules for the women of actors, dancers, singers, musicians, story-teller, bards, rope-dancers, showmen and wandering minstrels, who deal in women, and women who follow a secret profession.
26. Their musical instruments, when coming from foreign lands, shall be charged a fee per show of five *panas*.
27. Prostitutes who live by their beauty, shall pay per month a tax double the normal fee charged by them.
28. He should provide maintenance from the king's exchequer to the teacher who imparts to courtesans and female slaves who live by the stage, the knowledge of the arts of singing, playing on the lute, the flute and the drum, reading the thoughts of others, preparing perfumes and garlands, entertaining in conversation, shampooing and the courtesan's art.
29. And the teachers should train the sons of courtesans to be the chiefs of those who live by the stage and also of all types of dancers.
30. And their women, who are conversant with various kinds of signs and languages, should be employed, under the lead of their kinsmen, against the wicked, for spying, killing or making them blunder.

CHAPTER TWENTYEIGHT

SECTION 45: THE CONTROLLER OF SHIPPING

1. The Controller of Shipping should look after activities concerning sea voyages and ferries at the mouths of rivers, as well as ferries over natural lakes, artificial lakes and rivers, in the *sthaniya* and other towns.
2. Villages on their shores and banks shall pay a fixed tax.
3. Fishermen shall pay one-sixth of their catch as rent for the boats.
4. Traders shall pay a part of the goods as duty according as it may be current at the ports, those travelling by the king's ships shall pay hire for the voyage.
5. Those fishing for conch-shells and pearls shall pay a rent for the boats, or sail in their own boats.
6. And the duty of the Supervisor of these is explained by that of the Superintendent of Mines.
7. The Controller of Shipping shall observe the regulations in a port town as fixed by the Commissioner of Ports.

8. He should rescue boats that have gone out of their course or are tossed about by a gale, like a father.
9. He should make goods that have fallen in water either duty-free or pay half the duty.
10. And he should send these boats on, as commissioned, at times suitable for voyage from the port.
11. He should demand duty from ships sailing on sea when they come within the domain.
12. He should destroy boats that cause harm, also those coming over from the enemy's territory and those violating the regulations of the port.
13. And he should keep in use boats in-charge of a captain, a pilot, a manipulator of the cutter and ropes and a bailer of water, on big rivers that have to be ferried on even in winter and summer, small ones on small rivers flowing only in the rainy season.
14. And these should have their crossing places fixed because of the danger of crossing by traitorous persons.
15. For one crossing out of time or elsewhere that at the crossing, the punishment shall be the lowest fine for violence.
16. For one who crosses without authority even at the proper time and at the crossing, the penalty for crossing is twentysix *panas* and three quarters.
17. There shall be no penalty for fishermen, carriers of loads of wood and grass, attendants at flower gardens, fruit orchards and vegetable gardens and cowherds, also for those whose going after an envoy is conceivable, and for those carrying out activity in connection with goods for the army, when these cross in their own barges, as well as for those who ferry across seeds, food stuffs and articles for household use in villages along the water courses.
18. Brahmins, wandering monks, children, old persons, sick persons, carriers of royal edicts and pregnant women should cross with a sealed pass from the Controller of Shipping.
19. Persons from foreign lands may enter when permission to enter is granted or on the testimony of the caravan.
20. He should cause to be arrested a person carrying off the wife, the daughter or the property of another, a person who is frightened or agitated, a person hiding behind a heavy load, a person concealing his face by a load on the head containing heavy goods, a wandering monk who has just put on the marks or who is without the marks, a person whose illness cannot be seen, a person showing a changed

appearance because of fear, a person secretly carrying goods of high value, letters, weapons or means of fire, a person with poison in hand, a person who has travelled a long distance and a person without a sealed pass.

21. A small animal and a man with a load in hand shall pay one *masaka*, a load on the head, a load on the back, a cow and a horse shall pay two *masakas*, a camel and a buffalo four, a small vehicle five, one driven by bullocks six, a cart seven, a load of commodities one quarter of a *pana*.
22. By that is explained fare for a load of goods.
23. The fare for ferries on big rivers is double.
24. Villages on water-ways shall pay a fixed amount of food and wages for the ferrymen.
25. At the frontiers, ferrymen should recover the duty, the escort-charges and the road cess, and should confiscate the goods of one going out without a seal, also those of a person crossing with a heavy load at an improper time and elsewhere than at the regular crossing.
26. When a boat, that is lacking in men or equipment or is unseasonworthy, comes to grief, the Controller of Shipping shall make good what is lost or ruined.
27. Between the eight days, after the full moon day of Asadha and that of Karttika, ferrying shall be provided. The workman should give a surety and should bring in the regular daily earnings.

CHAPTER TWENTYNINE

SECTION 46: THE SUPERINTENDENT OF CATTLE

1. The Superintendent of Cattle should know about cattle looked after in return for a wage, tended with a tax and a fixed return, become useless and cast off, entered in the state herds by payment of a share, the total number of cattle in herds, cattle that are lost or have perished, and the total produce of milk and ghee.
2. The cowherd, the buffalo herdsman, the milker, the churner and the hunter should look after one hundred milch cows, receiving a wage in cash.
3. For if given a wage in milk and ghee, they might do harm to the calves. These are cattle looked after for a wage.
4. One person should look after one hundred animals containing an equal number of aged cows, milch-cows, cows with young, cows with calf for the first time and heifers.

5. He should give eight *varakas* of ghee, one *pana* per animal and the hide with the mark, every year. This is tending with a tax and a fixed return.
6. Herdsmen looking after one hundred animals divided into an equal number of cows that are diseased, that are crippled, that do not allow another person to milk them, that are difficult to milk and that kill their calves, should give a share appropriate to that class. These are cattle become useless and cast off.
7. Of cattle that have entered the king's herds through fear of an enemy invasion or forest tribes the owners should give one-tenth part according to the law of protection. These are cattle entered by payment of a share.
8. Calves, weaned calves, young bulls being broken in drought, bullocks, and stud bulls are made cattle; buffaloes drawing a yoked vehicle or a cart, stud buffaloes, slaughter-buffaloes and those carrying loads on their backs and shoulders are male buffaloes; thc heifer, the weaned heifer, the cow with calf for the first time, the cow with young, the milch-cow, the cow that has not borne a calf and the sterile cow, are cows and she-buffaloes; those a month or two old, are their offsprings as calves and heifers.
9. He should make those that are a month or two old.
10. He should mark an animal that has stayed in the herd for a month or two.
11. The branded mark, the natural mark, the colour, the peculiarity of the horns, with these characteristics, he should record addition to the herd. This is the total of cattle in the herds.
12. An animal that is stolen by thieves, has gone into another herd or has disappeared is lost.
13. An animal that has sunk in mud or has got in an inaccessible place, or is struck down by illness or old age or has suffered because of water or food, or is struck by a tree, a bank, wood or rock, or is struck by lightning or killed by a wild animal, a serpent, a crocodile or in a forest conflagration, is destroyed.
14. They should make good what is lost or destroyed through negligence.
15. Thus, he should be cognisant of the number of animals.
16. He who himself kills an animal or incites another to kill or steals or incites another to steal, shall be executed.
17. He who changes the cattle of another with the royal mark, shall pay the lowest fine for violence per animal.

18. After recovering what is stolen by thieves from cattle belonging to his own country, a person shall receive the animal agreed upon.
19. He who recovers cattle belonging to a foreign country, shall receive half the animals.
20. Cowherds shall care for and treat the young, the old and the diseased.
21. They shall graze the cattle in a forest from which the fear of danger from thieves, wild animals and enemies has been removed by flowers and hunters and which is suitable in different seasons.
22. And in order to frighten serpents and wild animals and to know the movements in the pastures, they should tie a bell round the necks of timid animals.
23. They should take cattle down to water, to which the descent is even and broad, and which is free from mud and crocodiles, and should guard them at the time.
24. They should report cattle seized by robbers, wild animals, serpents or crocodiles and cattle that have died because of disease or old age; otherwise, they shall be liable to pay the price of the animal.
25. Of an animal dying through a valid cause, they shall deliver the marked hide in the case of the cow and the buffalo, the mark on the ear in the case of the goat and the sheep, the tail and the marked skin in the case of the horse, the donkey and the camel, and the hair, skin, bladder, bile, tendons, teeth, hooves, horns and bones in the case of all.
26. They may sell the flesh, either fresh or dried.
27. They should give the butter-milk to the dogs and pigs.
28. They should bring in the solidfied curds as food for the army.
29. The whey is for moistening the oil cake from the oil press.
30. The seller of cattle shall pay one quarter of a *pana* per animal.
31. In the rainy season, autumn and winter, they should milk the cattle both times, in the season of frost, spring and summer, once only.
32. For one milking a second time then, the cutting off of the thumb shall be the punishment.
33. For one allowing the milking time to pass, the fine shall be equal to the loss of that fruit.
34. By this are explained punishment for neglect of proper times for putting the nose-string, for breaking in, for accustoming to the yoke and for training in going round.
35. From a *drona* of cow's milk, a *prastha* of ghee is the normal yield, one-fifth more in the case of she-buffaloes, one half more in the case of goats and sheep.

36. Or, actual churning shall decide the amount in the case of all.
37. For in accordance with the excellence of the ground, the grass and water, there is an increase in the yield of milk and ghee.
38. For one causing a bull of the herd to be hurled down by another bull, the lowest fine for violence shall be the punishment for causing his death, the highest fine.
39. By grouping according to class, groups of ten cattle should be guarded.
40. The arrangements at the place of stay should be according to the movements of the cattle or according to the strength of the cattle, and in conformity with capability for guarding.
41. He should cause the wool of goats and sheep to be gathered every six months.
42. Thus are explained rules concerning herds of horses, donkeys, camels and pigs.
43. For bullocks, with nose-string and capable of driving at the speed of a gentle horse, the ration shall consist of half a *bhara* of green fodder, grass double that, a *tula* of oil cake from the press, or ten *adhakas* of broken grains and bran, five *palas* of rock-salt, one *kuduba* of oil for the nose and one *prastha* as drink, a *tula* of meat and an *adhaka* of curds, a *drona* of barley or of half cooked *masa* beans; a *drona* of milk or half an *adhaka* of liquor, a *prastha* of fat, ten *palas* of sugar and a *pala* of ginger as a strength giving drink.
44. One quarter less is the ration for mules, cows and donkeys, double for buffaloes and camels.
45. For bullocks used for work and for milch-cows suckling their calves, the giving of rations shall be according to the time of work and the yield of milk respectively.
46. For all, there shall be abundance of grass and water.
47. Thus, is explained the care of herds of cattle.
48. He should provide a herd of one hundred donkeys and horses with five stallions, of one hundred goats and sheep with ten rams, and of cows, buffaloes and camels with four bulls.

CHAPTER THIRTY

SECTION 47: SUPERINTENDENT OF HORSES

1. The Superintendent of Horses should cause to be registered the total number of horses, received as gift, acquired by purchases, obtained in war, bred in the stables, received in return for help, stipulated in a treaty or temporarily borrowed, according to their pedigree, age, colour, marks, class and source.

2. And he should report such as are not good or are crippled or diseased.
3. The horse-attendant shall receive from the treasury and the magazine a month's allowance for the horse and carefully look after it.
4. He should cause stables to be constructed, in length according to the number of horses, in width double of a horse's length, with four doors and a rolling ground in the centre, with an entrance-hall, provided with boards for sitting at the main gate, and crowded with monkeys, peacocks, spotted deer, ichneumons, *cakoras*, parrots and *sarikas.*
5. He should cause a stall for each horse to be built, square with the length of a horse, with a flooring of smooth planks, with a receptacle for fodder, with outlets for urine and dung, and facing the east or the north.
6. Or, he should arrange the direction according to the nature of the stables.
7. For mares, stallions and foals the stalls shall be at separate ends.
8. For a mare that has borne a foal, a drink of a *prastha* of ghee shall be provided for three nights.
9. After that, a *prastha* of barley meal and an invigorating drink of fat and medicines shall be given for ten nights.
10. Thereafter, half cooked barley or beans, green fodder and a diet according to the season shall be given.
11. After ten nights from birth, a foal should have a diet of one *Kuduba* barley-meal, ghee one-quarter and a *prastha* of milk, till it is six months old.
12. After that, it should be given a *prastha* of barley, increased by half a *prastha* every month, till it is three years old, *then* a *drona* of barley till it is four years old.
13. After, that, when four-year old or five-year old, it is fit for work, being fully developed.
14. The face of the best type of horse is thirty-two *angulas*, its length five times the face, its shank twenty *angulas* and height four times the shank.
15. Three *angulas* less successively, are the measurement for the middling and lowest types.
16. One hundred *angulas* is the girth of the best type.
17. One-fifth part less that of the middling and lowest types successively.

18. For the best type of horse the ration is two *dronas* of *sali*-rice, *vrihi*-rice, barely or *priyangu*, either half-dry or half-cooked, or a half-cooked meal of *mudga* or *masa* and a *prastha* of fat, five *palas* of salt, fifty *palas* of meat, an *adhaka* of juice or double that curds for moistening the lumps of dry food, a *prastha* of liquor with five *palas* of sugar or double that quantity of milk as an *invigro rating* drink.
19. And for whetting the appetite of those fatigued by a long journey or a heavy load, a *prastha* of fat should be given as a clyster, one *kudaba* of fat for the nose, half a *bhara* of green fodder, grass double that or a collection of bundles of grass six *aratnis* in circumstance.
20. This, less by one quarter successively, is for the middling and lowest types.
21. Equal to the best type in point of ration is the chariot-horse and the stallion of the middling type.
22. Equal to the middling are those of the lowest types.
23. One quarter less is the ration for mares and mules.
24. And half of this is for foals.
25. These are rules for rations of horses.
26. Those who cook the food for horses, who hold the reins and who treat them should taste the food beforehand.
27. Horses incapacitated for work by war, disease, or old age should receive food for maintenance.
28. Horses unfit for use in war should be used, as stallions, to breed on mares in the interests of the citizens and the country people.
29. Of those fir for use, the best come from Kamboja, Sindhu, Aratha and Vanayu, the middling from Bahlika, Papeya, Sauvira and Titala, the rest are inferior.
30. In accordance with their fiery, gentle of dull mettle, he should assign to them work connected with war or ridding.
31. The all-sided work of a horse is work connected with war.
32. Moving at a gallop, moving at a canter, leaping, moving at a trot, and responding to signals are movements of riding-horses.
33. Among them, *aupavenuka*, *vardhamanaka*, *yamaka*, *alidhapluta*, *prthuga* and trikacali are varieties of gallop.
34. The same, with head and ears unaffected, is canter, or it has sixteen types of paces.
35. *prakirnaka, prakirnottara, nisanna, parsvanuvrtta, urminmarga, sarabhakridita, sarabhapluta, tritala, bahyanuvrtha, pancapani, simhayata, sudduta, klista, slingita, brmhita and puspabhikirna* are the paces in canter.

36. Monkey leap, frog leap, antelope leap, one-foot leap, cuckoo move, breast-movement and crane move are types of leap.
37. Heron gait, heron-or-water gait, peacock gait, half-peacock gait, ichneumon gait, half-ichneumon gait, boar gait, half-boar gait are varieties of trot.
38. Acting in accordance with signals is signal-responding.
39. Six, nine and twelve yojanas, is the road covered in a day for chariot-horses, five yojanas, seven and a half, and ten, the road for riding and pack horses.
40. The stride, the gait with gentle breath and the load-carrying are the gaits.
41. Striding, galloping, leaping, near-fast and fast are the speeds.
42. Teachers of training should give directions concerning straps and implements for them, and charioteers concerning accoutrements of chariot-horses necessary in war.
43. Physicians of horse should prescribe remedies against decrease or increase in the weight of the body, and diet varying according to season.
44. The holder of reins, the binder of horses, the fodder-giver, the food-cook, the stall-guard, the hair-trimmer and the specialist in poison-cure, should wait upon horses with their respective duties.
45. And in case of transgression of duties by them, he should cut down their day's wage.
46. For one riding a horse kept apart for the rite of lustration or kept apart for treatment by a physician, the fine shall be twelve *panas*.
47. In case of a worsening of the disease because of withholding treatment or medicine, the fine shall be double the cost of cure.
48. In case of an untoward happening through their fault, the fine shall be the price of the animal.
49. Thus, are explained rules for attendance on herds of cattle, donkeys, camels and buffaloes and goats and sheep.
50. He should cause a bath to be given to horses twice a day, also perfumes and garlands. On the junctures of the dark halves of months, offerings to spirits should be made and on those of the bright halves, reciting of blessings by Brahmins.
51. He should cause the lustration rite to be performed on the ninth day in Asvayuja, at the beginning or the end of an expedition or in case of illness, being intent on a pacificatory rite.

CHAPTER THIRTYONE

SECTION 48: THE SUPERINTENDENT OF ELEPHANTS

1. The Superintendent of Elephants should carry out the guarding of elephant-forest and look after the stables, stalls, places for lying down and the amount of work, food and fodder for male and female elephants and cubs, that are being trained or are competent for work, the assignment of tasks to them, the straps and implements and the accoutrements of war, and physicians, trainers and groups of attendants.
2. He should cause a stable to be constructed double an elephant's length in height, breadth and length, with additional stalls for female elephants, with an entrance-hall, with a collection of beams, and facing the east or the north.
3. He should cause a stall for each elephant to be built, square in conformity with an elephant's length, with a smooth tying-post and plank flooring, and with outlets for urine and dung.
4. There should be a place for lying down equal in size to the stall and half in height, in the fort, for elephants used in war and used for riding, outside the fort for those under training and rogue-elephants.
5. The first and seventh of the one-eight parts of the day are times for bath, after that for feeding.
6. In the forenoon is the time for exercise, the afternoon is the time for invigorating drink.
7. Two parts of the night are the time for sleep, one-third part for lying down and getting up.
8. The time for catching elephants is in summer.
9. A twenty-year old should be caught.
10. A cub, an elephant with small tusks, one without tusks, one diseased, a female elephant with young and a suckling female elephant are not to be caught.
11. A forty-year old elephant with measurements of seven *aratnis* as height, nine as length and ten as girth is best, a thirty-year old one is middling, a twentyfive-year old one lowest.
12. For those two, the ration is less by a quarter than that for the preceding type.
13. For each *aratni* of height, the ration is a *drona* of rice-grains, half an *adhaka* of oil, three *prasthas* of melted butter, ten *palas* of salt,

fifty *palas* of meat, an *adhaka* of juice or double that quantity of curds for moistening dry lumps, an *adhaka* of liquor with ten *palas* of oil for smearing the limbs, an eight part of a *prastha* of oil for the head and for the lump, two *bharas* and a quarter of green fodder and two *bharas* and a half of dry grass; of leaves of plants etc. there is to be no limit.

14. Equal in the matter of food to the seven *aratni* elephant is the eight *aratni* one when beyond rutting.
15. According to the size in *hastas*, the rest, *viz.* the six *aratni* and the five *aratni* ones.
16. A cub, fed on milk and green fodder may be caught for play.
17. With redness formed, covered, with smoothened sides, with an even girth, with flesh spread evenly, level with the backbone, and with a trough formed, these are appearances of an elephant.
18. In conformity with the appearance, he should give exercise to the gentle and the dull elephant and to the animal with mixed characteristics, in various types of work, or in accordance with the season.

CHAPTER THIRTYTWO

SECTION 48: SUPERINTENDENT OF ELEPHANT (CONCLUDED)

The Activity of Elephants:

1. Classes of elephants corresponding to work are four: one in training, one used in war, one for riding and the rogue elephant.
2. Among them one under training is of five kinds: getting used to a man on the shoulder, getting used to the lying post, getting used to the place for catching elephants, getting used to the trap, and getting used to a herd.
3. The accompanying treatment for him is the work of bringing up a cub.
4. The war elephant has seven ways of doing work: standing in attendance, going round, marching together, killing and trampling, fighting with elephants, assaulting towns, and fighting in battles.
5. The accompanying treatment for him is the work of putting on the girth, the work of putting on the neck-chain, and the work of moving in a herd.
6. The riding elephant is of eight kinds: one who is led, one ridden with the help of another elephant, one trotting, one trained in

various gaits, one ridden with a stick, one ridden with a goad, one ridden without any help, and one used for hunting.

7. The accompanying treatment for him is the work of keeping fit, the work of recouping what is lacking and the work of responding to signals.
8. The rogue-elephant has one way of activity: he is frightened, restrained, abnormal, in rut, with rut fixed and with a fixed cause of intoxication.
9. The accompanying treatment for him is the work of guarding in solitary confinement.
10. One who is lost for all activity is a rogue-elephant, pure, firmly resolved, vehement and spoiled by all defects.
11. The tying equipment and implements for them should be in accordance with the instructions of trainers.
12. The tying post, the neck-chain, the girth, the stirrup-rope, the foot-chain, the upper chain and so on constitute the tying equipment.
13. The goad, the bamboo, the machine and so on are implements.
14. The *vaijayanti* garland, the *ksurapra*-necklace, the covering, the carpet and so on are ornaments.
15. The armour, lance, quiver, machines and so on are accoutrements for war.
16. The physician, the trainer, the rider, the driver, the guard, the decorator, the cook, the fodder-giver, the foot chainer, the stall guard, the night-attendant and so on form the group of attendants.
17. The physician, the stall guard and the cook should receive a *prastha* of boiled rice, a *prasrti* of fat and two *palas* of sugar and salt, also ten *palas* of meat, excepting the physicians.
18. Physicians shall treat elephants afflicted by long journey, illness, work, rut or old age.
19. Uncleanliness of the stall, non-receipt of fodder, making elephants sleep on bare ground, striking them at an improper place, mounting by another person, riding at an improper time, or on unsuitable land, leading down to water where there is no crossing, and a thicket of trees are occasions for penalty.
20. He should take that from their food and wages.
21. Three lustration rites should be performed in the four-monthly junctures of seasons, offering on the junctures of dark halves should be made to spirits and on the junctures of the bright halves to Senani.

22. Leaving a length double the circumference at the root of the tusks, he should cut, these, every two years and a half in the case of those from river-banks, every five years in the case of those from mountainous regions.

CHAPTER THIRTYTHREE

SECTION 49: THE SUPERINTENDENT OF CHARIOTS

SECTION 50: THE SUPERINTENDENT OF FOOT SOLDIERS

SECTION 51: THE ACTIVITY OF THE COMMANDANT OF THE ARMY

1. The duty of the Superintendent of Chariots is explained by that of the Superintendent of Horses.
2. He should establish factories for the manufacture of chariots.
3. One with ten *purusas* of height and twelve *purusas* interior is the biggest chariot.
4. Less that by one *purusa* interior space successively up to six *purusas* interior space are smaller ones; thus, there are seven sizes of chariots.
5. He should cause to be made chariots, such as temple chariot, festival chariot, war chariot, travelling carriage, chariot for marching against an enemy's city and chariot for training.
6. He should be conversant with arrangements concerning bows, striking weapons, armours and accoutrements, and the employment of charioteers, chariot-attendants and chariot-horses in various works, also look after food and wages till the conclusion of the works of servants hired and not hired, giving practice to and protecting them, as well as making gifts and showing honour to them.
7. Thus, is explained the duty of the Superintendent of Foot Soldiers.
8. He should be conversant with the strength or weakness of hereditary, hired, banded, allied, alien and forest troops, with military operations in water or on high ground, with open or tactical fighting, in trenches or in the open, by day or by night, and with the employment or absence of employment of the foot soldiers in different types of work.
9. The Commandant of the Army, trained in the science of all kinds of fights and weapons, and renowned for riding on elephants,

horses or in chariots, should be conversant with the same, and with the direction of the work carried out by the four-fold troops.

10. He should look out for suitable ground for one's side, suitable season for fighting, arraying a force against enemy arrays, breaking unbroken ranks, re-forming broken ranks, breaking compact ranks, destroying broken ranks, destroying the fort and the season for an expedition.
11. Being devoted to the training of the troops, he should arrange signals for the arrays by means of musical instruments, banners and flags, when halting, marching or attacking.

CHAPTER THIRTYFOUR

SECTION 52: THE SUPERINTENDENT OF PASSPORTS

SECTION 53: THE SUPERINTENDENT OF PASTURE LANDS

1. The Superintendent of Passports should issue a sealed pass for one *masaka.*
2. Only a person with a sealed pass shall be entitled to enter or leave the countryside.
3. A native of the land, without a sealed pass, shall pay twelve *panas.*
4. In case of a forged pass, the lowest fine for violence shall be imposed, the highest for one not belonging to the country.
5. The Superintendent of Pasture Lands should ask for the sealed pass.
6. And he should establish pasture land in regions between villages.
7. He should clear low lands and forests of the danger of robbers and wild animals.
8. In waterless regions, he should establish wells, water-works and springs, also flower- and fruit-enclosures.
9. Flowers and hunters should go round in the forest.
10. At the approach of robbers or enemies, they should produce a sound with conch shells or drums, not allowing themselves to be caught, either climbing mountains or trees, or riding swift vehicles.
11. And he should convey to the king movements of enemies and forest-tribes by means of domesticated pigeons carrying sealed letters or by a series of smokes and fires.
12. He should ensure the livelihood of those in produce forests and elephant forest and secure the road cess, protection against robbers, escort of caravans, protection of cattle and trade.

CHAPTER THIRTYFIVE

SECTION 54: THE ACTIVITY OF THE ADMINISTRATOR

SECTION 55: SECRET AGENTS IN THE DISGUISE OF HOUSEHOLDERS, TRADERS AND ASCETICS

1. Dividing the countryside into four divisions, the Administrator should cause to be entered in a register the number of villages, classifying them as best, middling and lowest, recording this is exempt from taxes, this provides soldiers, this much is the revenue in grains, cattle, cash, forest produce, labour and produce in place of tax.
2. Under his direction, the revenue officer should look after a group of five villages or ten villages.
3. He should record the number of villages by fixing their boundaries, the number of fields by an enumeration of ploughed and unploughed fields, dry and wet fields, parks, vegetable gardens, flower and fruit enclosures, forest, structures, sanctuaries, temples, waterworks, cremation grounds, rest houses, sheds for drinking water, holy places, pasture lands and roads, and in conformity with that he should keep records of the size of boundaries, forests and roads, and of grants, sales, favours and exemptions, concerning village-boundaries and fields, and keep records of houses by an enumeration of tax-payers and non-tax-payers.
4. And in them, he should record so many are persons belonging to the four *varnas*, so many are farmers, cowherds, traders, artisans, labourers and slaves, so many are two-footed and four-footed creatures, and so much money, labour, duty and fines arise from them.
5. And of males and females in the families, he should know the number of children and old persons, their work, customs and the amount of their income and expenditure.
6. And in the same manner, the divisional officer should look after a fourth part of the countryside.
7. In the headquarters of the revenue and divisional officers, magistrates should carry out their duties and secure the recovery of dues.
8. And agents in the guise of householders, directed by the Administrator, should find out the number of fields, houses and families in those villages in which they are stationed, fields with respect to their size and total produce, houses with respect to

taxes and exemptions and families with respect to their *varna* and occupation.

9. And they should find out the number of individuals in them and their income and expenditure.
10. And they should find out the reason for departure and stay of those who have gone on a journey and those who have arrived respectively, as also of men and women who are harmful, and find out the activity of spies.
11. In the same manner, spies in the guise of traders should find out the quantity and price of the king's goods produced in his own country, obtained from mines, water-works, forest, factories and fields.
12. And in activities concerning goods of high and low value produced in foreign lands and imported along a water route or a land route, they should find out the amount of duty, road cess, escort charges, dues at the police station and the ferry, share, food and gifts.
13. In the same manner, agents in the guise of ascetics, directed by the Administrator, should ascertain the honesty or dishonesty of farmers, cowherds and traders and of the departmental heads.
14. And assistants disguised as old thieves should find out the reasons for entry, stay and departure of thieves and brave men of the enemy, in sanctuaries, cross-roads, deserted places, wells, rivers, pools, river crossings, temple compounds, hermitages, jungles, mountains forests and thickets.
15. Thus, the Administrator, being ever diligent, should look after the countryside; and those establishments of spies should also look after it, also other establishments having their own different origin should look after it.

CHAPTER THIRTYSIX

SECTION 56: RULES FOR THE CITY SUPERINTENDENT

1. The City Superintendent should look after the city in the manner of the Administrator.
2. The section officer should look after a group of ten families or twenty or forty families.
3. He should find out the number of individuals, men and women, in that group, according to caste, family-name and occupation, also their income and expenditure.
4. In the same manner, the divisional warden should look after a fourth part of the fortified city.

5. Officer in charge of charitable lodging-houses should allow lodging to heretical travellers; after informing the section officer and to ascetics and Brahmins learned in the Vedas, after satisfying themselves about their bona fides.
6. Artisans and artists should lodge persons of their own profession in their own places of work, and traders should lodge each other in their own place of work.
7. They shall report one who sells goods at an unauthorized place or time, as well as one without a title to the goods.
8. Vintners, vendors of cooked meat, vendors of cooked rice, and prostitutes shall give lodging only to one thoroughly known to them.
9. They shall report one who spends lavishly and one who does a rash deed.
10. The physician, after reporting to the section officer and the ward officer, a person who has made him treat a wound secretly and a person who does an unwholesome act, would become free, and so would the house-owner; otherwise, he shall be held equal in guilt.
11. And the house-owner shall report those who have departed and those who have arrived; otherwise he shall be held liable for any offence committed during the night.
12. On safe nights, he shall pay three *panas.*
13. And agents operating along roads and away from roads should arrest, outside the city and inside, in temples, holy places, forests and cremation grounds, a person with a wound, one with harmful tools, one hiding behind a heavy load, agitated, one in a long sleep, one tired after a journey or a stranger.
14. Similarly, inside the city, they should make a search in deserted places, workshops, ale-houses, cooked-rice houses, cooked meat houses, gambling dens and quarters of heretics.
15. And citizens shall take steps against an outbreak of fire in summer.
16. In the two middle quarters of the day, one-eight of a *pana* is the fine for kindling fire.
17. Or they should do their cooking outside the house.
18. One quarter of a *pana* is the fine for not providing five jars, also a big jar, a trough, a ladder, an axe, a winnowing-basket, a hook, a 'hair-seizer' and a skin-bag.
19. The City Superintendent should remove things covered with grass or matting.
20. He shall make those who live by the use of fire reside in one locality.
21. House-owner should live near the front doors of their own houses, not collecting together at night.

22. Collection of water-jars should be placed in thousands on roads and at cross-roads, gates and in royal precincts.
23. For the owner, not running to save the house on fire, the fine shall be twelve *panas*, six *panas* for a tenant.
24. In case of houses catching fire through negligence, the fine shall be fiftyfour *panas*.
25. The incendiary should be put to death by fire.
26. For throwing dirt on the road the fine shall be one-eight of a *pana*, for blocking it with muddy water, one quarter.
27. On the royal highway, the fines shall be double.
28. Fines for voiding faces in a holy place, in a place for water, in a temple and in royal property are one *pana* rising successively by one *pana* half these for passing urine.
29. If these are due to medicine, illness or fear, the persons are not to be fined.
30. For throwing the dead body of a cat, a dog, an ichneumon or a serpent inside the city, the fine shall be three *panas*, for throwing the dead body of a donkey, a camel, a mule, a horse or cattle, six *panas*, for a human corpse, fifty *panas*.
31. In case of a change of route or in case of taking the corpse out by a gate other than the gate for corpses, the lowest fine for violence shall be imposed.
32. The fine for gate-keepers allowing this, shall be two hundred *panas*.
33. For depositing and burning a corpse elsewhere than in a cremation ground, the fine shall be twelve *panas*.
34. The watch-drum shall be sounded at both ends of the night excluding a period six *nalikas*.
35. At the sound of the drum, punishment for moving at the prohibited time, near the king's palace, is a fine of one *pana* and a quarter, in the first and the last watches, double that in the middle watch, four times, that inside the palace-grounds.
36. He should question a person arrested in a suspicious place or with a suspicious mark or because of a previous offence.
37. For approaching royal property and for scaling the city's fortifications, middle fine for violence shall be imposed.
38. Those moving at night on account of a woman in delivery, for a doctor, on account of a death, with a lamp, in a carriage, at the City Superintendent's drum, for a show or on account of a fire, and those moving with sealed passports are not to be arrested.
39. During nights of unrestricted movements, those disguised in dress or in a dress contrary to their sex, wandering monks, and men with

sticks and weapons in hand, shall be punished in accordance with their offence.

40. For guards preventing what ought not to be prevented and not preventing what ought to be prevented, the fine shall be double that for movement during the forbidden watches.
41. For guards misbehaving with a woman who is a slave, the lowest fine for violence shall be imposed with one not a slave, the middle fine, with one in the exclusive keeping of some one the highest, with a woman from a respectable family the punishment shall be death.
42. For a guard not reporting to the City Superintendent an offence committed during the night whether by the animate or the inanimate, the punishment shall be in conformity with the offence, also in case of negligence.
43. Constant inspection of places supplying water, roads, watercourses, covered paths, ramparts, parapets and other fortifications, and the guarding of what is lost, forgotten or has run away are the duties of the Superintendent.
44. And in prison house, there should be a release of children, old persons, the sick and the helpless on the day of the king's birth constellation and on full moon days.
45. Persons of a pious disposition or persons bound by an agreement may give a ransom for the offence.
46. Every day or every five days, he should clear out those in prison by getting them to do work, by inflicting corporal punishment or by receiving the favour of cash in ransom.
47. On the occasion of the acquistion of a new territory, on the occasion of the installation of the crown prince or on the occasion of the birth of a son to the king, a release of all in the prison is ordained.

Herewith ends the Second Book of the Arthasastra of Kautilya
'THE ACTIVITY OF THE HEADS OF DEPARTMENTS'.

17

BOOK THREE

Cocerning Judges

In this BOOK THREE, there are 20 chapters, wherein details and systematic guidance have been propounded by Kautilya for the benefit of judges in due discharge of their judicial functions. The most remarkable and astounding is the fact that these instructions which were given by Kautilya before 2300 years are still useful in arriving at the just and positive conclusions in the entire judicial process of the country even today. The guidelines are on the following subjects: (1) Valid and Invalid Transaction. (2) Concerning Marriage. (3) Concerning Marriage (Continued). (4) Concerning Marriage (concluded). (5) Partition of Inheritance. (6) Partition of Inheritance (Continued). (7) Partition of Inheritance (Concluded). (8) Concerning Immovable Property. (9) Concerning Immovable Property (Continued). (10) Concerning Immovable Property (Concluded). (11) Non-payment of Debt. (12) Concerning Deposits. (13) Law Concerning Slaves and Labourers. (14) Undertaking in Partnership. (15) Recision of Sale and Purchase. (16) Non-conveyance of Gifts, Sale Without Ownership and the Relationship of Ownership. (17) Forcible Seizures. (18) Verbal Injury. (19) Physical Injury. (20) Gambling and Betting, Miscellaneous.

CHAPTER ONE

SECTION 57: DETERMINATION OF VALID AND INVALID TRANSACTIONS

SECTION 58: FILING OF LAW-SUITS

1. Three judges, all three of the rank of ministers, should try cases arising out of transactions at frontier posts, in the *sangrahanas, dronamukhas* and *sthaniyas*.

2. They should declare as invalid transactions concluded in absence, inside a house, at night time, in a forest, by fraud or in secret.
3. For one who concludes such a transaction or induces its conclusion, the lowest fine for violence shall be the punishment.
4. The fines shall be half for witnesses, each one of them.
5. For trustworthy persons, however, there shall be only annulment of the object.
6. Contracting a debt with a pledge in its absence or transactions in absence that are accepted as free from blame shall succeed.
7. Those concluded inside a house, concerning inheritance, things handed over, deposits and marriage, or by women who do not stir out of their homes, or by sick persons who are not unsound in mind, shall succeed.
8. Those concluded at night, concerning forcible seizure, trespass with criminal intent, strife, marriage and a royal order or by persons carrying on their business in the fore-part of the night, shall succeed.
9. Those concluded in the forest, by persons moving in forests, from amongst caravans, herds, hermitages, hunters and wandering minstrels, shall succeed.
10. And among persons earning a secret livelihood, those fraudulently made shall succeed.
11. And in case of secret association, those concluded in secret shall succeed.
12. Transactions other than these shall not succeed, also those concluded by dependents, such as by a son dependent on the father, by a father dependent on the son, by a brother excluded from the family, by a younger son whose share has not been allotted to him, by a woman dependent on her husband or son, by a slave or a person kept as a pledge, by a minor or a person grown too old for doing any business, and by a person accused of a crime, by a wandering monk, by a cripple or by one overcome by a calamity, excepting by those to whom authority for the transaction has been given.
13. Even among such, transactions concluded by a person in rage, a person in distress, an intoxicated person, an insane person or a person or a person in another's power, shall not succeed.
14. For those who conclude, who induce the conclusion of and who bear witness to such transactions, the fines shall be as prescribed for each one separately.

15. All transactions, however, in each respective group, concluded with full title at the proper place and time, with all formalities duly observed, with admissible evidence, with the appearance, marks, quantity and qualities duly noted, shall succeed.
16. And in their case, the last document shall be authoritative, except in the case of direction and pledge. Thus, ends the determination of valid and invalid transactions.
17. After writing down the year, the season, the month, the fortnight, the day, the office, the place, the debt, and the country, village, caste, family, name and occupation of the plaintiff and the defendant, who have given adequate sureties, the clerk shall put down the questions with answers to the plaintiff and the defendant, in due order of the subject-matter.
18. And he shall look into them when put down.
19. A party to a suit who gives up the disputes as put down and changes to another dispute, does not corroborate the first statement by a subsequent matter, remains silent after challenging an unchallengeable statement of the other party after making an affirmation does not indicate the evidence when asked to do so, indicates weak evidence or false evidence, produces evidence other than that indicated, when evidence is produced denies a statement in the matter saying, 'it is not so', does not accept what is confirmed by witnesses, talks secretly with witness in a place where no conversation is allowed,—these are reasons for loss of suit.
20. The fine for loss of suit is one-fifth the amount in dispute.
21. The fine for one who voluntarily admits is one-tenth.
22. Wages for the servant shall be one-eight part of a *pana*.
23. Food on the way will be according to the prices at the time.
24. The defeated party shall pay both these.
25. The accused shall not file a counter-complaint, except in cases of strife, forcible seizure and association in caravans.
26. And there shall be no suit against the accused by another party.
27. If the plaintiff, to whom a reply had been given by the defendant, does not counter-reply on the same day, he shall lose the suit.
28. For, it is the plaintiff, who has decided beforehand what is to be done, not the defendant.
29. If the latter does not reply, a period of three days or seven may be allowed.
30. After that, the judge shall impose a fine of three *panas* minimum and twelve *panas* maximum.

31. After three fortnight, if he does not reply, the judge shall impose the fine for loss of suit and indemnity to the plaintiff from goods belonging to him, excepting the tools of his profession.
32. He shall impose the same penalty on the defendant who absconds.
33. In the case of the plaintiff, there shall be loss of suit the moment he absconds.
34. The statement of a witness who dies or suffers from a misfortune is without value.
35. The successful plaintiff may, after paying the fine, make a poor defendant work for him.
36. Or, the defendant may keep a pledge, if he so desires.
37. Or, he may indemnify him by work, guarded by charms destructive of evil spirits, with the exception of a Brahmin.
38. When all laws are perishing, the king here is the promulgator of laws, by virtue of his guarding the right conduct of the world consisting of the four *varnas* and four *asramas*.
39. A matter in dispute has four feet, law, transaction, custom and royal edict; among them the latter one supersedes the former one.
40. Of them, law is based on truth, a transaction, however, on witnesses, customs on the commonly held view of men, while the command of kings is the royal edict.
41. Carrying out his own duty by the king, who protects the subjects according to law, leads to heaven; of one who does not protect or who inflicts an unjust punishment, the condition is the reverse of this.
42. For, it is punishment alone that guards this world and the other, when it is evenly meted out by the king to his son and his enemy, according to the offence.
43. For, a king, giving decisions in accordance with law, transaction, settled custom and edict as the fourth, would conquer the earth up to its four ends.
44. He shall decide, with the help of law, a matter in which a settled custom or a matter based on a transaction contradicts the science of law.
45. Where a text of the science may be in conflict with any edict in a matter of law, there the edict shall prevail; for, there the written text loses its validity.
46. A distinctly seen offence, a voluntary admission, straight forwardness in questions and answers to one's own and the opposite party, reasoning, and oath, lead to a decision in a case.

47. In case of contradiction between an earlier and a later statement, in case of the blame-worthiness of witnesses and in case of escape from the custody of the prison-guard, loss of suit shall be decreed.

CHAPTER TWO

SECTION 59: CONCERNING MARRIAGE

(i) The Law of Marriage; (ii) Rules Concerning Woman's Property; (iii) Concerning Supersession of a wife by Second Marriage.

1. All transactions begin with marriage.
2. Making a gift of the daughter, after adoring her with ornaments is the Brahma form of marriage.
3. The joint performance of sacred duties is the Prajapatya.
4. On receiving a pair of cattle from the bride-groom, it is Arsa.
5. By making a gift of the daughter to the officiating priest inside a sacrificial altar, it is the Daiva.
6. By a secret association between lovers, it is the Gandharva.
7. On receiving a dowry, it is the Asura.
8. By forcible seizure of a maiden, it is the Raksasa.
9. By the seizure of sleeping or intoxicated maiden, it is the Paisaca.
10. The first four are lawful with the sanction of the father, the remaining with the sanction of the father and the mother.
11. For, those two receive the dowry of the daughter, or one of them in the absence of the other.
12. The woman shall receive the second dowry.
13. In the case of all forms of marriage, giving pleasure to the bride by means of gifts is not forbidden.
    Thus, ends the law of marriage.
14. Maintenance and ornaments constitute woman's property.
15. Maintenance is an endowment of a maximum of two thousand *panas*; as to ornaments, there is no limit.
16. It is not an offence for the wife to use that for the maintenance of her sons and daughters-in-law or if no provision is made when the husband is away on a journey, or for the husband to use it for taking steps against robbers, diseases, famine and other dangers and for religious acts, or for the couple to use it jointly when they have begotten a son and a daughter.
17. And if it has been used for three years, the wife shall not question, in the case of the pious marriages.

18. If used in the Gandharva and Asura marriages, the husband shall be made to return both with interest, if used in the 'Raksasa' and 'Paisaca' marriages, he shall pay the penalty for theft.
19. When the husband is dead, the widow, if desirous of leading a life of piety, shall forthwith receive the endowment and ornaments and the remainder of the dowry.
20. If, after receiving these, she marries again, she shall be made to return both with interest.
21. If however, she is desirous of having a family, she shall receive, at the time of remarriage, what was given to her by her father-in-law and her late husband.
22. Later is explained the time for remarriage in "Long absence from home".
23. If she remarries against the wishes of her father-in-law, she shall forfeit what was given her by her father-in-law and her late husband.
24. If the widow is snatched away from the protection of her kinsmen, the kinsmen by the new marriage shall return her woman's property of the first marriage as it may have been received by her.
25. If she has approached for remarriage in a legitimate manner, the acceptor shall protect her woman's property of the first marriage.
26. A widow remarrying shall forfeit what was given by her late husband.
27. She shall use it if desirous of a pious life.
28. If a widow, who has sons, marries again, she shall forfeit her woman's property.
29. The sons, however, shall receive that woman's property.
30. Or, if she remarries for the maintenance of her sons, she shall augment the woman's property for the sake of the sons.
31. The woman shall settle on sons born to her from many husbands her woman's property as given by the respective fathers.
32. A widow marrying again shall settle on her sons her woman's property even when she is entitled to do what she pleases with it.
33. A widow without sons, remaining faithful to her husband's bed, shall use her woman's property in the proximity of elders, till the end of her life.
34. For, a woman's property is meant for calamities.
35. After her death, it shall go to the heirs.
36. If a woman dies while her husband is living, her sons and daughters shall divide her woman's property among themselves, daughters

only if she has no sons, in the absence of these the husband shall receive it.

37. The dowry, the post-marriage gifts and other things given by her relations, the relations shall receive. Thus, end rules concerning woman's property.
38. The husband shall wait for eight years if the wife does not bear offsprings or does not bear a son or is barren, for ten if she bears dead offspring, for twelve if she bears only daughters.
39. After that, he may marry a second wife with the object of getting a son.
40. In case of transgression of that rule, he shall hand over the dowry, the woman's property and half that as compensation for supersession, and pay a fine of twentyfour *panas* maximum.
41. By paying the dowry, the woman's property, and in the case of a wife without a dowry or woman's property of her own a compensation for supersession equal in amount to that, and a suitable maintenance he may marry even a number of wives.
42. For, wives are necessary for having sons.
43. And in case of simultaneity of the menstrual periods of these, he shall approach according to the time of marriage, first that wife whom he had married first, or the wife who has living sons.
44. In case of concealment of the period or failure to approach at the time, ninetysix *panas* shall be the fine.
45. The husband may not approach a wife who has sons, who is desirous of a pious life, who is barren, who hears dead offspring or whose menstruation has stopped, if she is unwilling.
46. And if unwilling, the man may not approach a wife who is leprous or insane.
47. A woman, however, shall approach a husband even of this type, for bearing a son.
48. A husband, who has become degraded or gone to a foreign land or has committed an offence against the king or is dangerous to her life or has become an outcast or even an impotent one may be abandoned.

CHAPTER THREE

SECTION 59 (CONTINUED): CONCERNING MARRIAGES

(iv) Marital Duty; (v) Maintenance; (vi) Cruelty; (vii) Disaffection; (viii) Misconduct; and (ix) Prohibition of Favours and Dealings.

1. A woman twelve years of age attains majority, a man when sixteen years of age.
2. If after this there is a failure to carry out marital duties, there shall be a fine of twelve *panas* for the woman, twice that for the man. Thus, ends the topic of marital duty.
3. When maintenance is not payable at stipulated intervals of time, the husband shall give the necessary food and clothing according to the dependents or more in a generous measure.
4. If payable at stipulated intervals of time, he shall calculate the same and pay in instalments.
5. And also in case she has not received a dowry, a woman's property and compensation for supersession, the same procedure shall be followed.
6. If the wife is staying in her father-in-law's family or has become separated, the husband is not to be used. Thus, ends the topic of maintenance.
7. The inculcation of modest behaviour shall be done without the use of expressions such as 'thou lost one', 'thou ruined one', 'thou fatherless one' or 'thou motherless one'.
8. Or, striking on the back three times with one of the three, *viz.*, a split bamboo-cane, rope or hand may be done.
9. In case of transgression of this fines half those for verbal and physical injury shall be imposed.
10. The same shall be the punishment for the wife whose offence against her husband is well-known.
11. On occasions of her enjoying herself outside the home out of jealousy, the penalty shall be as laid down. Thus, ends the topic of cruelty.
12. A wife disliking her husband and not adorning herself for fulfilment of marital duty during seven menstrual periods, shall forthwith set down her endowment and ornaments and consent to her husband lying with another woman.
13. A husband disliking the wife shall consent to her staying alone in the family of one of the following *viz.*, a female mendicant, a guardian or a kinsman.
14. One who speaks a falsehood, when indications are clear, when there is a refusal of intercourse or when an approach is made to a person of the same *varna* through a secret emissary, shall pay a fine of twelve *panas*.
15. A disaffected wife is not to be granted divorce from the husband who is unwilling, nor the husband from the wife.

16. By mutual disaffection alone a divorce shall be granted.
17. Or, if the husband seeks divorce because of the wife's offence, he shall give to her whatever he may have taken.
18. Or, if the wife seeks divorce because of the husband's offence, he shall not give her whatever may have been received.
19. There is no divorce in pious marriages. Thus, ends the topic of disaffection.
20. The wife who, though prohibited, indulges haughtily in the sport of drink, shall pay a fine of three *panas*.
21. In case she goes by day to a show by women or on a pleasure trip with women, the fine shall be six *panas*.
22. At night, the fines shall be double.
23. For leaving home when the husband is asleep or intoxicated and for not opening the door to the husband, twelve *panas* is the fine.
24. For going out at night the fine is double.
25. If a man and a woman, with sexual intercourse in view, indulge in gestures with limbs or indecent conversation in secret, twentyfour *panas* is the fine for the woman, double that for the man.
26. For touching the hair, the knot of the lower garment, teeth or nails, the lowest fine for violence shall be imposed, double that for the man.
27. And in case of conversation in a suspicious place, punishment by whipping may be substituted for the fine in *panas*.
28. To women, the Candala shall give five strokes with the last in the region between the sides *i.e.* on the back in the centre of the village.
29. Or, she may free herself by paying a *pana* for each stroke.
    Thus, ends the topic of misconduct.
30. When a man and a woman, who are forbidden, make a gift to one another of small articles, a fine of twelve *panas* shall be imposed, if of big articles, twentyfour *panas*, if of money or gold, a fine of fiftyfour *panas* for the woman, double these for the man.
31. Half these same fines shall be imposed in case the two are unapproachable for each other, also in cases of forbidden dealings with men.
    Thus, ends the topic of prohibition.
32. On account of disaffection towards the king, and misconduct, and by wilfully running away, a woman loses her ownership over the woman's property, what she has brought from her kinsmen and dowry.

CHAPTER FOUR

SECTION 59: CONCERNING MARRIAGE (CONCLUDED)

(x) Leaving Home; (xi) Going Away with a Man; (xii) Short Absence from Home; and (xiii) Long Absence from Home.

1. For a woman who leaves the house of her husband, the fine is six *panas*, except in case of ill-treatment.
2. If she was forbidden to do so the fine is twelve *panas*.
3. If she has gone to a neighbour's house, the fine is six *panas*.
4. In case a neighbour, a mendicant or a trader gives her shelter, food or goods respectively, the fine shall be twelve *panas*.
5. If these have been forbidden, the lowest fine for violence shall be imposed.
6. If she has gone to the house of a stranger, the fine is twenty-four *panas*.
7. In case a stranger gives shelter to another man's wife, a fine of a hundred *panas* shall be imposed, except in cases of distress.
8. In case he has prohibited her or is ignorant about her coming, he is guiltless.
9. 'There is no offence in going to the house of one of the following, *viz.*, a kinsman of the husband, a trustee, the village headman, a guardian, a female mendicant or her own kinsman, if there are no males in it, on account of the husband's ill-treatment', say the teachers.
10. 'To the house of a kinsman, even if there are males in it.
11. For, how can there be deceit by a chaste woman?
12. This is easy to understand', says Kautilya.
13. Going to the house of kinsman on the occasion of death, illness, calamity or childbed is not at all forbidden.
14. For the husband preventing her on such an occasion, the fine is twelve *panas*.
15. If even on such occasions she conceals herself, she shall forfeit her woman's property, or the kinsmen, concealing her, shall forfeit the balance of the dowry.

    Thus, ends the topic of leaving home.
16. In case a wife leaving the house of her husband, goes to another village, the fine is twelve *panas* as well as the loss of her endowment and ornaments.
17. Or, in case she goes in the company of a man with whom sex-intercourse is permissible, the fine shall be twentyfour *panas* and

the loss of all rights, excepting the giving of maintenance and approaching during the period.

18. For the man the punishment is the lowest fine for violence, if equal or superior in *varna*, the middle fine if inferior.
19. A blood relation is not to be punished.
20. In case there is prohibition, half the above fines shall be imposed on him.
21. In case she goes to a secret place midway on her way or if she accompanies on the way, with carnal intentions, a man who is suspected or forbidden, one should know that as adultery.
22. Accompanying a man on the way is no offence in the case of the women of dancers, wandering minstrels, fishermen, fowlers, cowherds, vintners and others who give freedom to their women.
23. Or, in case of prohibition, for the man taking the woman with him or the woman going with him, the fines shall be half the same as above.

    Thus, ends the topic of going with a man.
24. The wives of a Sudra, a Vaisya, a Ksatriya and a Brahmin, who are away on a short journey, shall wait for a period of one year increased successively by one year, if they have not borne children, for one year more, if they have borne children.
25. Those who are provided for shall wait for double the period.
26. The trustee shall maintain those unprovided for, kinsmen for four or eight years after that.
27. Thereafter, they shall release them after taking back according as they had given.
28. The wife shall wait for a Brahmin who is away studying, for ten years if she has no child, for twelve if she has a child, for a royal servant she shall wait till the end of her life.
29. And if she bears a child from a man of the same *varna*, she shall not incur blame.
30. Or, when the affluence of the family has disappeared, she, being released by the trustee, may marry again as she desires, or when she is in distress, for the sake of livelihood.
31. After a pious marriage, the maiden shall wait for her husband who has gone away without informing her, for seven periods if no news is heard about him; for one year if news is heard.
32. If he has gone away after informing her, she shall wait for five periods when no news is heard, for ten if news is heard.
33. If he had paid only a part of the dowry, shall wait for three periods if there is no news, seven periods if there is news about him.

34. If he paid the dowry in full, she shall wait for five periods if there is no news, ten if there is news.
35. After that, she may remarry as she desires, with the permission of the judges.
36. For frustration of the period is destruction of sacred duty, says Kautilya. Thus, ends the topic of short absence from home.
37. The wife of a man who has gone away on a long journey or has become a wandering monk or is dead shall wait for seven periods, for one year if she has borne children.
38. After that she may approach for marriage a full brother of the husband.
39. If there are many such brothers, she should approach one who is proximate to the husband, one who is pious, one capable of maintaining her, or the youngest if without a wife.
40. In the absence of these, even one who is not a full brother, a *sapinda* or a member of the family who is near.
41. Among these, this alone shall be the order of preference.
42. In case she marries setting aside these heirs of her husband, or in case she has a lover, the lover, the woman, the bestower of the woman and the man who marries her receive the penalty for adultery.

CHAPTER FIVE

SECTION 60: PARTITION OF INHERITANCE

(i) Order of Inheritance

1. Sons, having fathers,—with the father and mother alive—are not masters of the property.
2. After the father's death, there may be a partition of the father's property among them.
3. What is acquired by oneself is not to be divided, except what is brought into being out of the father's property.
4. Sons or grandsons up to the fourth generation shall be receivers of shares of goods come down without a partition from the father's property.
5. Till then the funeral cake remains unbroken.
6. When the cake is discontinued, all shall divide in equal shares.
7. Those who had received no property from the father or those who had divided the father's property, when they live together, may divide again.

8. And he, through whom the property may raise, shall receive two shares.
9. Full brother or those living with him shall receive the property of a sonless man, and daughters shall receive it.
10. The sons shall inherit the estate of a man with sons, or the daughters, born in the pious marriages.
11. In the absence of these, the father if alive.
12. In the absence of the father, the brothers and sons of brothers.
13. And a brother's sons, if without their father, shall receive only a single share of the father, even if they are many in number, along with the brothers.
14. Of uterine brothers born of more than one father, the partition of inheritance is to be from the respective father.
15. As between the father, the brother and the son, so long as the earlier one is alive, they do not depend on the later one, and so long as the eldest is alive, on the youngest even if he had received wealth.
16. In the case of partition during his life-time, the father shall not show special favour to any one.
17. And he shall not, without ground, exclude any one from inheritance.
18. When there is no property of the father, the eldest shall support the younger brothers except those who are wrongly behaved.
19. There is partition only among those who have attained majority.
20. They shall deposit with the mother's kinsmen or with village elders, the share of those who have not attained majority, clearing it of debts, till they come of age, also the share of one who is away on a journey.
21. To brother who are not established in life they shall give an amount for their marriage, equal to that of those already settled, and to daughters an amount for bestowal in marriage.
22. There is to be an equal division of debts and property.
23. 'Those without any property shall drive even water-vessels', say the teachers.
24. 'This is play with words', says Kautilya.
25. There is division of an object that exists, not of one that does not exist.
26. He should cause partition to be made in the presence of witnesses, declaring with specific mention, 'so much property is joint, of that so much is each one's share.'

27. They shall divide again what is wrongly divided, what is robbed by one from the other, what is hidden, or what, being unknown, comes to light later.
28. The king shall take that to which there are no heirs, excluding maintenance for the wife and what is needed for funeral rites, with the exception of the property of a Brahmin learned in the Vedas.
29. He shall bestow that on those well versed in the three Vedas.
30. An outcast, a son born to an outcast and an impotent person are not entitled to a share, also an idiot, a lunatic, a blind and a leprous person.
31. If these have a wife, their progeny, not of the same kind as the father, shall receive a share.
32. The others shall receive only food and clothing excepting the outcasts.
33. And if, after they have been married, their potency is lost, the kinsmen shall beget sons for them, and he shall assign shares to them.

CHAPTER SIX

SECTION 60: ORDER OF INHERITANCE (CONTINUED)

(ii) Division into shares

1. Among sons of the same wife, the special share of the eldest is to be goats in the case of Brahmins, horses in the case of Ksatriyas, cattle in the case of Vaisyas and sheep in the case of Sudras.
2. One eyed or lame among them are to be the share of the middle-most and those of mixed colours the share of the youngest.
3. In the absence of animals, the eldest shall receive one part of every ten articles, with the exception of jewels.
4. For, he has the fetters of the duty of offering oblations to the manes tied round him.
5. This is the partition recommended by Usanas.
6. From the personal belongings of the father, the carriage and ornaments are to be the share of the eldest; the bed and seat, and bell-metal dishes used for meals, the share of the middle-most; black grains, iron objects, household furnishing and the bullock-cart, the share of the youngest.
7. Of the remaining articles or of a single there is to be an equal division.
8. The sisters do not inherit, receiving only a share of the bell-metal dishes used for meals and ornaments from the mother's personal belongings.

9. The eldest, if devoid of manly qualities, shall receive only a third of an eldest son's share, one-fourth only if he behaves in an unjust manner or has given up religious duties.
10. If he behaves wantonly, he shall forfeit the whole.
11. By that are explained the middle-most and youngest sons.
12. Among these, he who is endowed with manly qualities shall receive a half of an eldest son's special share.
13. In the case of sons of different wives however, seniority is to be in accordance with priority of birth, in the absence of one wife married according to the sacrament and another not married according to the sacrament, and in the absence of one wife married while a virgin and another married when she had lost her virginity, also among two sons born of the same wife or among twins.
14. In the case of Suta, the Magadha, the Vratya and the Rathakara, partition is to be in accordance with mastery in the profession.
15. The rest shall live under him.
16. If all are without mastery, they shall receive equal shares.
17. Among a Brahmin's sons from wives belonging to the four *varnas*, the son of the Brahmin wife shall receive four shares, the son of the Ksatriya wife three shares, the son of the Vaisya wife two shares, the son of Sudra wife one.
18. By that is explained partition among sons from wives belonging to three and two *varnas* of a Ksatriya and a Vaisya respectively.
19. A Brahmin's son born of a wife belonging to the immediately next *varna* is to have an equal share.
20. That of a Ksatriya or a Vaisya is to have half a share, or an equal share if endowed with manly qualities.
21. The only son among two wives, one of the same *varna* as the husband and the other of a different *varna*, shall receive everything, and shall maintain the kinsmen.
22. In the case of Brahmins, however, the son born of a Sudra wife shall receive only one-third of the property as his share, a *sapinda* or a proximate member of the family shall receive two-thirds for the sake of offering the funeral oblations.
23. In the absence of these, the father's teacher or pupil shall receive the two-thirds.
24. Or, a person appointed, either a mother's kinsman or a person of the same *gotra*, may beget on his wife a *ksetraja* son; to him he shall allot that property.

CHAPTER SEVEN

SECTION 60: ORDER OF INHERITANCE (CONCLUDED)

(iii) Classification of Sons

1. 'Seed, dropped in the property of another, belongs to the owner of the field', say some teachers.
2. 'The mother is only a leather-bag for holding the seed; who owns the seed, to him belongs the child', say others.
3. 'Both are to be found,' says Kautilya.
4. A son begotten by oneself on a duly married wife is the legitimate son.
5. Equal to him is the son of the appointed daughter.
6. A son begotten on the wife of a man by a person appointed, whether of the same *gotra* or of a different *gotra*, is the *ksetraja* son.
7. If the begetter has no other son, he belongs to both fathers or both *gotras* and offers funeral offerings to and inherits property from both.
8. With the same duties and rights as he, is the son secretly born, who is, however, secretly begotten in the house of the kinsmen.
9. One abandoned by the kinsmen is the cast-off, a son to him who performs the sacraments for him.
10. The offspring of a maiden is the 'maiden's son'.
11. The son of a bride married when *enceinte* and pregnant is brought with the marriage.
12. The son of a woman remarried is 'the remarried woman's son'.
13. If begotten by oneself, he becomes an heir to his father and kinsmen.
14. If begotten by another, he is an heir only to him who performs the sacraments for him, not to the kinsmen.
15. With the same rights is the adopted son, given with water by the parents.
16. One who himself or through his kinsmen has offered to be a son is the son approached.
17. One appointed to the position of a son is the son made.
18. One purchased is the son bought.
19. When, however, a legitimate son is born, the others, if of the same *varna*, receive a one-third share, if not of the same *varna*, receive only food and clothing.
20. The sons of a Brahmin and a Ksatriya born of a wife belonging to the immediately next *varna* are of the same *varna* as the father, of a wife belonging to the next but one *varna*, are not of the same *varna*.

21. A Brahmin's son from a Vaisya wife is *Ambastha*, from a Sudra wife a *Nisada* or a *Parasava*.
22. A Ksatriya's son from a Sudra wife is *Urga*.
23. A Vaisya's son from a Sudra wife is nothing but a Sudra.
24. And of these three *varnas* sons begotten on wives of the same *varna* by those who have not practised the vows, are *Vratyas*.
25. These are the 'right order' sons.
26. From a Sudra are born of a Vaisya, a Ksatriya and a Brahmin wife respectively the *Ayogava*, the *Ksatta* and the *Candala*.
27. From a Vaisya are born the *Magadha* and the *Vaidehaka* of a Ksatriya and a Brahmin wife respectively.
28. From a Ksatriya is born the *Suta* of a Brahmin wife.
29. The *Suta* and the *Magadha* mentioned in the Purana, however, are different, a special type from the Brahmin and the Ksatriya.
30. These are the 'reverse order' sons, who come into existence because of the transgression of his own duties by the king.
31. From an *Urga* on a *Nisada* wife is begotten the *Kukkuta*; in the opposite case, the *Pulkasa*.
32. From an *Ambastha* on a *Vaidehaka* wife is born the *Vaina*; in the opposite case, the *Kusilava*.
33. From an *Ugra* on a *Ksatta* wife is born the *Svapaka*.
34. These and others are the intermediate castes.
35. A *Rathakara* is a Vaisya, so-called because of his profession.
36. Among them, marriage is to be in their own caste of origin, there is to be observance of precedence and the pursuit of the hereditary occupation.
37. Or, they are to have the same special duties as the Sudra, expecting the *Candala*.
38. Only the king, behaving in this manner, obtains heaven, otherwise hell.
39. In the case of all intermediate castes, partition is to be in equal shares.
40. Whatever be the customary law of a region, a caste, a corporation or a village, in accordance with that alone shall he administer the law of inheritance.

CHAPTER EIGHT

SECTION 61: CONCERNING IMMOVABLE PROPERTY

(i) Concerning Dwelling Places

1. Disputes concerning immovable property are to be decided on the testimony of neighbours.

2. A house, a field, a park, an embankment, a tank or a reservoir is immovable property.
3. Along the house is to be a boundary, fixed with iron wires in pillars at the corners.
4. He should cause the house to be made in conformity with the extent of the boundary.
5. Or, he should cause a new fixing of the boundary to be made two *aratnis* or three *padas* away from the wall of a neighbour's house.
6. He should make the dung-hill, the water-course or the well, not in a place other than that suited to the house, except the water-ditch for a woman in confinement till the end of ten days from delivery.
7. In case of transgression of that, the lowest fine for violence shall be imposed.
8. By that are explained the work of cutting fire-wood and channels for water used for rinsing on festive occasions.
9. He should cause to be made a deep-flowing water-course or one falling in a cascade, three *padas* away from a neighbour's wall or one *aratni* and a half away.
10. In case of transgression of that, the fine is fifty-four *panas*.
11. He should cause to be made a place for carts and quadrupeds, a fire-place, a place for the large water-jar, the grinding mill or the pounding machine, one *pada* away or one *aratni* from a neighbour's wall.
12. In case of transgression of that, the fine is twenty-four *panas*.
13. Between all two structures or two projecting rooms, there is to be an open lane one *kisku* wide or three *padas*.
14. Between them, the distance between the eaves of roofs is to be four *angulas*, or one may over-lay the other.
15. He should cause to be made a side-door in the intervening lane, measuring one *kisku*, for making repairs to what is damaged, not allowing crowding.
16. For light, he should cause a small window to be made high up.
17. When the dwelling is occupied, he should cause it to be covered.
18. Or, house-owners, by mutual agreement, may get things done as desired, and should avoid what is undesirable.
19. And he should cause that part above the verandah which requires protection, to be covered by matting, or a wall touching the roof, for fear of damages by rain.
20. In case of transgression of that, the lowest fine for violence shall be imposed, also in case of obstruction by doors or windows contrary to natural arrangement, except on royal highways and roads.

21. The same fine is to be imposed in case of obstruction outside the house by parts of a ditch, stair-case, water-channel, ladder or dung-hill and in case of prevention of the use of their rights by others.
22. For one causing damage to the wall of another's house the fine is twelve *panas*, double that in case of spoiling it with urine or dung.
23. A free flow of water must be allowed in the channels when it is raining, else the fine is twelve *panas*.
24. And the same fine shall be imposed on one staying on when forbidden and on one ejecting a tenant, except in cases of verbal and physical injury, theft, forcible seizure, adultery and wrongful use.
25. The tenant leaving of his own accord shall pay the balance of the annual rent.
26. For one rendering help in a common dwelling, for one obstructing a thing used in common and in case of prevention of rightful use by others twelve *panas* is the fine.
27. Double that is the fine for destroying what is used in common.
28. Of sheds, court-yards and latrines, of fire-place and pounding sheds, and of all open spaces, use in common is desired.

CHAPTER NINE

SECTION 61 (CONTINUED): CONCERNING IMMOVABLE PROPERTY

(ii) Scale of Immovable Property; (iii-v) Fixing of Boundaries; (vi) Concerning Encroachment and Damage.

1. Kinsmen, neighbours and creditors, in this order, shall have the right to purchase landed property on sale.
2. After that, others who are outsides may bid for purchase.
3. Owners shall proclaim a dwelling as for sale in front of the house, in the presence of members of forty neighbouring families, and a field, a park, an embankment, a tank or a reservoir as for sale at the boundaries, in the presence of village elders who are neighbours, according to the extent of the boundary, saying 'at this price who is willing to purchase?'
4. What has been thrice proclaimed and not objected to, the purchaser shall be entitled to purchase.
5. Or, in case of increase in price because of competition, the increase in price together with the tax shall go to the treasury.
6. The successful bidder at the sale shall pay the tax.

7. In case of a bid by one who is not an owner, the fine shall be twentyfour *panas*.
8. If the bidder does not come to take possession, the owner whose property was auctioned may sell again after seven days.
9. In case of transgression by one whose property was auctioned, the fine is two hundred *panas* in the case of immovable property, a fine of twentyfour *panas* in other cases.
   Thus, ends the topic of sale of immovable property.
10. A group of neighbouring five villages or ten villages shall decide a dispute regarding boundaries between two villages, by means of boundary-marks, immovable or artificial.
11. Elders among farmers and cowherds, or outsiders who formerly had possessions there, conversant with the boundary-marks, either many or even one, should, after declaring the boundary-marks, point out the boundary, putting on a contrary dress.
12. In case the boundary marks as declared are not found, the fine shall be a thousand *panas*.
13. He shall impose the same fine on those who, after the boundary is pointed out, remove the boundaries or destroy the boundary-marks.
14. Or, the king shall fix, according as it may be beneficial, the boundary, the extent of the marks of which is lost.
15. Village elders who are neighbours shall decide disputes concerning fields.
16. In case of difference of opinion among them, they shall arbitrate in favour of which are the majority, the honest or the approved, or they shall follow the middle course.
17. The king shall take that property to which the claim of both is rejected, also that the owner of which has disappeared.
18. Or, he may allot it as it may be beneficial.
19. In case of forcible seizure, the fine for theft shall be imposed in the case of immovable property.
20. In case of seizure on good grounds, he shall pay an amount to the owner after calculating his labour and profit.
21. For removing the boundary marks the lowest fine for violence shall be imposed.
22. For breaking the boundary, twentyfour *panas* shall be the fine.
23. By that are explained disputes concerning penance-groovers, pasture lands, highways, cremation grounds, temples, sacrificial grounds and holy places.
    Thus, ends the topic of fixing of boundaries.

24. All disputes whatever shall be, decided on the testimony of neighbours.
25. As between a pasture land, dry land, wet-crop field, a vegetable garden, a threshing floor, a shed and a stall for vehicles, the earlier one may suffer encroachment from the later one.
26. Dry regions are those with the exception of groves for Vedic study and *soma*-sacrifices, temples and holy places.
27. In case of damage to the ploughing or seeds in another's field by the use of a reservoir, channels or a field under water, they shall pay compensation in accordance with the damage.
28. In case of mutual damage to fields under water, parks and embankments, the fine shall be double the damage.
29. A tank on a lower level, constructed afterwards, shall not flood with a field watered by a tank on a higher level.
30. A tank constructed on a higher level shall not prevent the flooding with water of a lower tank, except when its use has ceased for three years.
31. For transgression of that, the punishment shall be the lowest fine for violence and the emptying of the tank.
32. The ownership of a water-work, not in use for five years, shall be lost except in cases of distress.
33. When tanks and embankments are newly constructed, an exemption from taxes for five years should be granted, when those that are ruined and abandoned are renovated, an exemption for four years, when those that are over-grown with weeds are cleared, for three years, when dry land is newly brought under cultivation, for two years.
34. He is free to mortgage or sell.
35. Owner may give water in return for share of produce of various kinds from sowings in fields, parks and gardens watered by their dug out channels, structures based on rivers or tanks, or to others as it may be advantageous.
36. And those who use these on lease, on hire, as a pledge, for a share or with authorization for use, shall keep them in repair.
37. In case of failure to repair, the fine in double the loss.
38. For one letting out water from the dams out of turn, the fine shall be six *panas*, also for one obstructing, through negligence, the water of other when it is their turn.

CHAPTER TEN

SECTION 61: CONCERNING IMMOVABLE PROPERTY (CONCLUDED)

(vii): Damage to Pastures, Fields and Roads

SECTION 62: NON-OBSERVANCE OF CONVENTIONS

1. If one obstructs a customary water-course in use or makes a new one that is not customary, the lowest fine for violence shall be imposed, also if one constructs in another's land a dam, a well, a holy place, a sanctuary or a temple.
2. If a person himself or through others puts to mortgage or sale a charitable water-work, continued since old times, the middle fine for violence is to be imposed, the highest on witnesses, except when it is in ruins and abandoned.
3. In the absence of the owner, villages or persons of a pious disposition should repair these.
4. The size of roads has been explained in the 'Lay-out of the Fort'.
5. For encroaching on a path for small animals or men the fine is twelve *panas*, on a path for small animals or men the fine is twelve *panas*, on a path for large animals twentyfour *panas*, on a road for elephants or fields fiftyfour *panas*, on a road to a dike or a forest one hundred and six, on a road to a cremation ground or a village two hundred, on a road in a *dronamukha* five hundred, on a road in a *sthaniya*, the countryside or pasture land one thousand.
6. In case of reducing the size of these roads, the fines are one-quarter of the fines mentioned.
7. In case of ploughing on them, the fines are as prescribed.
8. If the owner of the field takes away the field or the tenant leaves it at the time of sowing, the fine shall be twelve *panas*, except in cases of defect, calamity or unbearable conditions.
9. Tax-payers shall mortgage or sell only to tax-payers, Brahmin owners of gift-lands only to Brahmin owners of gift-lands.
10. Otherwise, the lowest fine for violence shall be imposed.
11. Or, the same fine is to be imposed on a tax-payer settling in a village exempt from taxes.
12. But one settling in a tax-paying village shall have freedom to get all things, excepting a house.
13. That also he may give him.
14. If one does not till land that is inalienable, another may use it for five years and return it after receiving compensation for his exertions.

15. Non-tax-payers, living in a different place, may live on the produce of their fields.
16. Tenants shall accompany, by turns, the village headman journeying on village business.
17. Those who do not accompany shall pay a penalty per *yojana* of one *pana* and half a *pana*.
18. For the village headman ejecting from the village one who is not a thief or an adulterer, the fine is twenty-four *panas*, for the village the highest fine for violence.
19. The entry of one who has been ejected is explained by trespass.
20. He should cause a fence to be made with pillars all round the village at a distance of one hundred *dhanuses* from it.
21. They shall live on pasture land, intended for the grazing of cattle, by cutting the grass.
22. They shall receive one quarter of a *pana* per animal in the case of camels and buffaloes that have grazed on the pasture and moved away, half a quarter in the case of cattle, horses, and donkeys, one sixteen part in the case of small animals.
23. If after grazing, the animals sit down, these same fines shall be double, four-fold if they stay overnight.
24. Bulls belonging to village temples or a cow within ten days of her calving, and stud bulls are exempt from fines.
25. In case the cattle eat the crops, he shall make their owner pay double the damage to the crops after calculating it in accordance with the harvest.
26. And if the owner allows the cattle to graze without informing the owner of the field, the fine shall be twelve *panas* if he lets them loose.
27. For herdsmen the fines shall be half of these.
28. The same fines he shall impose in case the cattle eat the produce in plantations.
29. The fines shall be double if the fence is broken, also if the cattle eat grains in the sheds or the threshing circle.
30. He shall take steps against injury to cattle.
31. Animals from reserved parks or those that are protected, if found eating, should, after intimating the owner, be so driven off as not to cause injury to them.
32. Cattle should be driven off with a piece of rope or a whip.
33. For causing injury to them in other way, the fines for physical injury shall be imposed.

34. Those that attack or whose offence is clear may be restrained by all possible means. Thus, ends the topic of damage of fields and roads.
35. The village itself shall receive the penalty of a farmer who, after accepting residence in a village, does not do his share of work.
36. He shall pay double the wage for the work if he does not do work, double each individual's share if he does not contribute money, and a double share if he does not contribute food and drink on festive occasions.
37. One who does not contribute his share in a stage-show shall not witness it with his people.
38. If he listens to or witnesses it secretly, he shall perforce give a double share, also in an undertaking beneficial to all.
39. They shall obey the orders of one who proposes what is beneficial to all.
40. For not carrying them out the fine is twelve *panas*.
41. If, on the other hand, they conspire together and beat him, the punishment for each severally shall be double the prescribed punishment for the offence.
42. The punishment shall be severe for those who injure him.
43. And seniority among them shall be fixed from the Brahmin downwards.
44. And in their festivities, Brahmins, if unwilling, may not do any work and yet receive their share.
45. By that is explained the non-observance of conventions in the case of a region, a caste, a family and a corporation.
46. The king should do what is agreeable and beneficial to these, when they build dikes that are of benefit to the country or bridges on roads or carry out works beautifying the villages or defences of the villages.

CHAPTER ELEVEN

SECTION 63: NON-PAYMENT OF DEBTS

1. One *pana* and a quarter is the lawful rate of interest per month on one hundred *panas*, for purposes of trade, ten *panas* for those going through forests, twenty *panas* for those going by sea.
2. For one charging or making another charge a rate beyond that, the punishment shall be the lowest fine for violence, for witnesses, each one of them, half the fine.
3. If, however, the king is unable to ensure protection, the judge should take into consideration the usual practice among creditors and debtors.

4. Interest on grains shall be up to a half, on the harvesting of crops; thereafter it may increase being turned into capital.
5. Interest on capital shall amount to half the profit, to be paid for one year, being set apart in a store.
6. One away on a long journey or become obstinate in making payments shall pay double the capital.
7. For one recovering interest without fixing it or increasing its rate or claiming through witnesses the capital with interest added to it, the fine shall be four times the one-fifth or one-tenth part.
8. For claiming through witnesses a small amount that was never lent, the fine shall be four times the non-existent amount.
9. Of that, the receiver shall pay one-third, the rest he who helped him to receive it.
10. Debt shall not increase in the case of a person confined in a long sacrificial session or by illness or in the preceptor's house, or in the case of a minor or an insolvent.
11. For one not receiving back the debt being paid off, the fine shall be twelve *panas*.
12. If it is done by pleading a valid reason, it shall remain in another's custody with further interest stopped.
13. A debt not taken notice of for ten years shall be irrecoverable, except in the case of a minor, an aged person, a sick person, a person in a calamity, a person away on a journey or in case of migration from the country or disorder in the kingdom.
14. Sons shall pay the debt with interest of deceased person, or heirs inheriting the property or co-debtors or sureties.
15. There shall be no other suretyship.
16. The suretyship of a minor is void in law.
17. But sons, grandsons or heirs inheriting the property shall be liable to pay a debt about the repayment of which the place and the time are not fixed.
18. Sons or grandsons shall bear liability for suretyship concerning life, marriage or land, to which no restriction as to place or time applies.
19. In case many debts become due at the same time, two creditors shall not simultaneously sue one debtor except when he is about to leave the place.
20. Even, in that case, he shall secure payment in the order of contracting the debts or first the dues of the king and of a Brahmin learned in the Vedas.

21. The debt mutually contracted between a husband and a wife or a father and son or between undivided brothers, is irrecoverable through a court of law.
22. Agriculturists and the king's servants are to be held at the time of their work.
23. And the wife shall not be held liable for the debt incurred by her husband, if she has not assented to it, except in the case of cowherds and farmers tilling for half the produce.
24. The husband, however, shall be held liable for the debt incurred by the wife, if he has gone abroad without providing for her.
25. In case of admission of the claim, it is best.
26. In case of non-admission, however, witnesses shall decide, those who are trustworthy, honest or approved, three at least in number.
27. Or, two will suffice if both parties agree, but never a single witness in the case of debt.
28. Not allowed as witnesses are a wife's brother and associate, a dependent, a creditor, a debtor or an enemy, a cripple, and a convicted person also those mentioned before of unfit for transaction.
29. The king, a Brahmin learned in the Vedas, a village servant, a leper and a wounded man, an outcast, a Candala, a person following a despised profession, a blind, deaf, dumb or self-invited person, a woman and king officer shall be cited as witnesses except in the case of their own groups.
30. In cases of verbal and physical injury, theft and adultery, however all may be cited as witnesses except an enemy, a wife's brother and an associate.
31. In the case of secret transactions, one woman or man, who has heard or witnessed, it may be cited as a witness, excepting the king or an ascetic.
32. Masters may bear testimony for servants, priests and preceptors for disciples, and parents for sons, without being forced, or the latter may do so for them.
33. And in case of their suing each other, the betters, if defeated, shall pay one-tenth as fine, the inferiors, one-fifth. Thus, ends the topic of witnesses.
34. The judge should exhort witnesses in the presence of Brahmins, a water-jar and fire.
35. In that connection, he should say to a Brahmin witness, 'Speak the truth.'

36. To a Ksatriya or a Vaisya he should say, 'Let there be no fruit of sacrificial and charitable deeds for you if you speak untruth; you would go, potsherd in hand, begging for alms to the house of your enemy.'
37. To the Sudra he should say, 'Whatever the reward of your merit between birth and death, that would go to the king and the king's sin come to you in case of a false deposition, and punishment will also follow; even afterwards facts as seen and heard would be found out; being of one mind, bring out the truth.'
38. For those who do not bring out the truth, the fine shall be twelve *panas* after seven days; after three fortnights, they shall pay the amount of the suit.
39. In case of differences among witnesses, the judges should decide in favour of that part in whose favour are the majority, honest or approved, or should follow the middle course.
40. Or, the king should take that object.
41. If witnesses testify to an amount less than that claimed in the suit, the plaintiff shall part of the excess claimed, as fine.
42. If, on the other hand, they testify to a larger amount, the king should take that excess.
43. What was badly heard or badly written through the folly of the plaintiff, or the affidavit of a person since deceased, shall after investigation, be decided only on the testimony of witnesses.
44. 'In case of divergent replies to question through the folly of witnesses themselves, they shall be fined the lowest, middle-most and highest fines, with regards to testimony about place, time and the matter respectively', say the followers of Usanas.
45. 'False witnesses who bring into being a non-existent thing or ruin an existing thing, shall pay ten times that thing as fine', say the followers of Manu.
46. 'Or, if through folly they lead to a wrong judgment, death by torture is to be the punishment', say the followers of Brhaspati.
47. 'No', says Kautilya.
48. For, witnesses have to testify to what is the truth.
49. For those who do not testify to the truth the fine is twentyfour *panas*, half that for those who do not speak out.
50. The plaintiff or defendant shall produce witnesses who are not at a great distance in place or time. He may secure those who are at a distance or are unwilling to come, with a summons from the king.

CHAPTER TWELVE

SECTION 64: CONCERNING DEPOSITS

1. The law of deposits is explained by that of debts.
2. If the fortified city or the countryside is pillaged by enemy forces or forest tribes, or the village, the caravan or the herd is plundered by robbers, or there is loss of the wheeled carriage, or the deposit is enveloped by flames or by the current in a calamity of fire or floods in the midst of village, or the boat has sunk or is plundered, the depository, if himself involved, shall not be liable for the deposit.
3. The user of the deposit shall pay charges for use in accordance with the place and the time, and a fine of twelve *panas*.
4. He shall be liable for what is lost or has perished in consequence of the use and shall pay a fine of twentyfour *panas*, or, if the deposit or runs away for some other reason.
5. He shall not be liable for a deposit that dies or is in distress.
6. And in case of a mortgage, sale or denial of the deposit, the fine shall be four times one-fifty its value.
7. In case of substitution or helping it to run away, the fine shall be equal to its value.
8. By that are explained the loss, use, sale, mortgage and misappropriation of a pledge.
9. A pledge, yielding benefit, shall not be forfeit nor shall its capital bear interest, except when allowed.
10. A pledge, not yielding a benefit, may be forfeited and its capital shall bear interest.
11. For one not returning the pledge to the owner who has come to redeem it the fine shall be twelve *panas*.
12. Or, in the absence of the creditor, the debtor may recover his pledge after depositing the redemption amount with village elders.
13. Or, the pledge, with further interest stopped and its value at that time fixed, may remain just there or in the charge of the office for prevention of loss and destruction.
14. Or, in the absence of the debtor, the creditor if afraid of destruction of the pledge, may sell it, with the judges permission, at the highest price, or to the satisfaction of the Guardian of Deposits.
15. But an immovable pledge that can be enjoyed after labour or enjoyed in its fruits without labour, may bring in a profit over and above the value of the interest on the capital, without causing a reduction in the capital.

16. He who enjoys it without authorization shall surrender the profit after deducting the value of the interest due and a part as fine.
17. The rest is explained by the law of deposits.
18. By that are explained the direction and the commission.
19. Or, if a person in whose charge is the object to be handed over, does not reach the place indicated while going with a caravan, or is plundered and abandoned by robbers, he shall not be liable for the object in his charge.
20. Or, if he dies on the way, even his heir shall not be liable.
21. The rest is explained by the law of deposits.
22. They shall return, in the same condition in which they received it, a thing borrowed or a thing hired.
23. They shall not be liable for a thing given with restriction as to place or time, if it is lost or ruined through deterioration or some sudden calamity.
24. The rest is explained by the law of deposits.
25. Concerning sale through agents, however, salesmen selling the commodity at the proper place and time shall pay to the owner the price as received and the profit.
26. Or, if the price is lower because of their missing the proper place and time, they shall pay the price according to the rate at the time of giving the goods to them for sale and the profit.
27. Or, if selling the goods as agreed upon they do not make a profit, they should pay only the price.
28. Or, if the price is lower because of a fall in prices, they should give the lower price as reduced.
29. Or, in the case of dealers, who are trustworthy and free from blame so far as the king is concerned, they may not pay even the price of what is lost or ruined through deterioration or a sudden calamity.
30. But of commodities removed in space or time they shall pay the price and profit after deducting losses and expenses, and a separate share in the case of each of the different kinds of goods.
31. The rest is explained by the law of deposits.
32. With this is explained the topic of sale through agents.
33. And the trust is explained by the law of deposits.
34. If he hands it over to one when it was entrusted to him by another, it shall be treated as lost.
35. In case of misappropriation of a thing entrusted, a former offence of the trustee and the persons entrusting it shall lead to decision.
36. For, artisans are dishonest.
37. There is no rule regarding trusts prevailing among them which requires evidence beforehand.

38. If he denies a thing entrusted without evidence, the person who had entrusted it may make witnesses, secretly stationed behind walls, learn about it by soliciting him in private or in a park by creating confidence on the occasion of a drinking party.
39. Some aged or sick trader should entrust to him in secret an object that is marked and go away.
40. At his direction, his son or brother should approach and demand the thing entrusted.
41. If he returns it he is honest, else he shall give the thing originally entrusted and a fine for theft.
42. Or, some credible person, about to leave home, should entrust to him a marked object and then leave.
43. Then returning after some time he should ask for it.
44. If he returns it he is honest, else he shall give the thing entrusted and a fine for theft.
45. Or, he should himself bring him round with a marked object.
46. Or, a person appearing foolish by nature should, through fear of arrest for king's dues or movement at forbidden time, entrust to him at night an object of high value and go away.
47. Being in prison, he should ask him for it.
48. If he returns it he is honest, else he shall give the thing entrusted and a fine for theft.
49. And by means of a recognition-mark, he shall demand both of people in his house.
50. If either of the two is not given, punishment etc. as stated before.
51. And the judge should question the source of the objects used by the defendant, and inquire into indications of that object being involved in the transaction, as well as the capacity of the complainant to own the object.
52. By this is explained association in secret.
53. Therefore, one should make a deal, with one's people or with strangers, in the presence of witnesses, in an open manner, properly declaring it with respect to place, time, quantity and quality.

CHAPTER THIRTEEN

SECTION 65: LAW CONCERNING SLAVES AND LABOURERS

1. For one selling or keeping as a pledge a minor Arya individual except a slave for livelihood, the fine is twelve *panas* for a kinsman

in the case of a Sudra, double that in the case of Vaisya, three times in the case of a Ksatriya, four times in the case of a Brahmin.

2. For a stranger, the lowest, the middle and the highest fines and death are the punishments respectively, also for purchasers and witnesses.
3. It is not an offence for *Mlecchas* to sell an offspring or keep it as a pledge.
4. But there shall be no slavery for an Arya in any circumstances whatsoever.
5. Or, after keeping as a pledge an Arya when the family has bound itself in times of distress of Aryas, they shall, on finding the redemption amount, redeem first a minor or one who renders help.
6. A person pledging himself shall be forfeit if he runs away once, one pledged by another if he runs away twice, both at the first attempt, if about to leave for a foreign land.
7. Or, for one depriving a slave of his Aryahood, when he has stolen money, the fine shall be half the above fines.
8. The pledger shall be liable for the capital, if the pledge has run away or is dead or is in calamity.
9. Making a pledge pick up a corpse, dung, urine or leavings of food, and making women pledges give bath to a naked person, giving corporal punishment to them and dishonouring them shall result in the loss of the capital, and shall result in freedom for a nurse, a female attendant, a woman tenant tilling for half the produce and a maid.
10. The going away of an attendant who has begotten an offspring is valid in law.
11. For one approaching a nurse who is pledged, when she is unwilling, the punishment shall be the lowest fine for violence if she is under his control, the middle if she is under the control of another.
12. If one, himself or through another, defiles a maiden who is pledged, he shall lose the capital, pay her dowry and a fine double that.
13. The progeny of one who sells himself shall be known as Arya.
14. He shall get what is earned by himself without detriment to his work for the master, also his paternal inheritance.
15. And he shall become an Arya by paying the price.
16. By that are explained the slave for livelihood and the person pledged.
17. And his ransom amount is to be in conformity with the capital.
18. One on whom a fine is imposed may pay off the fine by work.

19. An Arya individual captured under the banner should be freed by suitable work for a specified period or for half the price.
20. If one employs in vile work or in a foreign land, a slave less than eight years of age, without kinsmen and unwilling to do that work, from among any of the four types,—a slave born in the house, received in inheritance, obtained as a present and purchased, or if one sells or pledges a female slave who is *enceinte* without providing for the nourishment of the foetus,—the lowest fine for violence shall be imposed, also on purchasers and witness.
21. If a person does not make a slave an Arya for a suitable ransom, the fine is twelve *panas*, and confinement for him till he does it.
22. Kinsmen shall inherit the property of a slave, in their absence the master.
23. The offspring begotten by the master on his own female slave shall be known as free along with the mother.
24. If the mother is attached to the house and looks after the affairs of the family, her brother and sister also shall be free.
25. If, after ransoming a male or a female slave, a person again sells or pledges him, the fine is twelve *panas*, except in the case of those who themselves agree.

Thus, ends the law concerning slaves.

26. Those who are near shall note a labourer's engagement in work.
27. He should receive a wage as agreed upon, in conformity with the work and time if the wage is not agreed upon.
28. A cultivator, a cowherd and a trader should receive one-tenth part of the crops, of butter and of the goods dealt in by them respectively if the wage is not agreed upon.
29. But if the wage is agreed upon, then as agreed upon.
30. But the group of those who work in hope of remuneration such as artisans, artists, minstrels, physicians, professional story-tellers, attendants and others should get a remuneration as others of that type do or as experts fix.
31. Disputes shall be settled only on the testimony of witnesses.
32. In the absence of witnesses, the judge should inquire at the place where the work was carried out.
33. In case of non-payment of the wage, the fine is one-tenth or six *panas*.
34. In case of denial, the fine is twelve *panas* or one-fifth.
35. If a person in distress, overcome by the current of a river or flames or robbers or wild animals, calls a rescuer with the promise of all

possessions or sons and wife or himself and is rescued, he should give a reward as directed by experts.

36. By that are explained retractions of promises made in distress in all cases.
37. A harlot should get a fee in accordance with the indications of union; but she who makes an exorbitant demand shall lose it, also if she shows evil-mindedness or lack of modesty.

CHAPTER FOURTEEN

SECTION 65: LAW CONCERNING SLAVES AND LABOURERS (CONCLUDED)

Duties of Servants

SECTION 66: UNDERTAKINGS IN PARTNERSHIP

1. For a labourer not doing the work after receiving the wage, the fine is twelve *panas*, and detention till it is done.
2. If he is incapable or if the work is vile or if he is ill or in calamity, he shall get annulment, of the agreement or the right to get it done by another.
3. Or, at his cost, the employer shall have the right to get it done.
4. If, when there is a restriction 'You shall not give this work to another, nor shall I do any one else's work', the employer does not get work done by him or the labourer does not do the work, the fine shall be twelve *panas*.
5. If the labourer has received wages from another person than the employer, he may not, on completion of the work, do additional work for him if unwilling.
6. 'If the employer does not give work when the labourer has presented himself, the work shall be considered as done', say the teachers.
7. 'No', says Kautilya.
8. A wage is for work done, not for what is not done.
9. If after allowing even a little to be done, he does not allow it to be done further, his work shall be considered as done.
10. In case the labourer misses the proper place and time or does the work in a wrong manner, he may not, if unwilling, allow the work as done.
11. In case more work is done than agreed upon, he shall not make the effort vain.
12. Thus, are explained labourers from unions.

13. The workman kept on the work from among them shall remain for seven nights.
14. After that, the union shall provide another and secure the completion of the work.
15. And without informing the employer, the union shall not remove any one or bring in any one.
16. In case of transgression of that, the fine is twentyfour *panas*.
17. For the person removed by the union, the fine shall be half that. Thus, ends the topic of labourers.
18. Labourers from unions or partners in an undertaking shall divide the wages as agreed upon or in equal proportions.
19. Or, cultivators and traders shall give to a partner who has become ill in the interval between the commencement and completion of work connected with crops and goods respectively an individual share corresponding to work as done by him.
20. In case a substitute is provided, they shall give the full share.
21. But if he has fallen ill when the goods put together have brought success, they shall give his individual share there and then.
22. For, success or failure on the way is common.
23. But if when the work has begun a partner goes away even if in good health, he shall be fined twelve *panas*.
24. Nor shall he have the freedom to keep away.
25. But he should cause a misappropriator to be caught by a promise of a share for the work, preceded by a promise of safety, and he should give him the share and safety.
26. In case he steals again, he shall be exiled, also if he goes elsewhere.
27. In case of very serious offence, however, he should deal with him as with a traitor.
28. Sacrificial priests shall divide the fees as agreed upon or in equal shares, excepting objects received for each one's special duties.
29. And in the *Agnistoma* and other sacrifices, a priest falling ill after the consecration ceremony shall receive one-fifth of his share, after the sale of *soma* one-fourth, after the heating of the *pravargya*-vessel on the middle *upasad* day one-third, after the middle *upasad* day half the share, after morning pressing on the day of *soma*-pressing, three quarters of the share.
30. After the mid-day pressing, he shall receive the full share.
31. For at that time the fees are carried.
32. Except in the case of the *Brhaspatisava*, fees are indeed given at each pressing.
33. Thus are explained fees for sacrifices lasting for many days.

34. The remaining hired priests should do the work of those who have fallen ill, up to ten days and nights or others trusted by themselves should do it.
35. Should, however, the sacrificer fall ill before the sacrifice is completed, the priests should complete the work and receive the fees.
36. But if when the work is incomplete one leaves the sacrificer or the priests, the lowest fine for violence shall be imposed.

37-38. One owning a hundred cows but not keeping the sacred fires, one owning a thousand cows but not performing a sacrifice, a drunkard, one who has married a heretical woman, a slayer of a Brahmin, a violator of an elder's bed, one addicted to receiving gifts from evil persons, a thief, a priest working for a degraded person, in the case of these there is no harm in abandoning each other, because of the certainty of impurity attaching to such sacrificial work.

CHAPTER FIFTEEN

SECTION 67: RESCISSION OF SALE AND PURCHASE

1. If, after selling an article, one does not deliver it, the fine shall be twelve *panas*, except in cases of defect, a sudden calamity or unsuitability.
2. A defect in the article is defect.
3. Trouble from the king, thief, fire or water is a sudden calamity.
4. What is lacking in many qualities or what is done by one in distress is unsuitable.
5. For traders a period of retraction of one day may be allowed, for agriculturists three days, for cowherds five days.
6. In the case of the sale of the means of livelihood by persons of mixed and the highest *varnas*, a period of retraction of seven days may be allowed.
7. For perishable goods, a retraction may be allowed with the restriction 'It shall not be sold elsewhere'.
8. In case of transgression of that, the fine is twenty-four *panas* or one-tenth part of the goods.
9. If, after purchasing an article, one does not receive it, the fine is twelve *panas*, except in cases of defect, a sudden calamity or unsuitability.
10. And rescission of purchase is similar to retraction by a seller.
11. In the case of marriages, however, revocation is valid up to the ceremony of clasping the hand in the case of the first three *varnas*, and up to consummation in the case of Sudras.

12. Even in the case of those whose hand-clasping ceremony is completed, revocation is valid on discovering a defect connected with sex.
13. But under no circumstances will revocation be valid when they have begotten children.
14. For giving a maiden in marriage without mentioning the maiden's defect in connection with sex, the fine is ninety-six *panas* and the return of the dowry and woman's property.
15. Or, for the suitor marrying without mentioning the bridegroom's defect, the fine is double, and the loss of the dowry and woman's property.
16. In the case of bipeds and quadrupeds, however, for declaring dull, diseased and unclean ones as energetic, healthy and clean respectively, the fine is twelve *panas*.
17. In the case of quadrupeds revocation is allowed up to three fortnights, up to a year in the case of human beings.
18. For, it is by that time that purity or otherwise can be known.
19. The members of the court should so allow revocation in the matter of a gift or a purchase that neither the giver nor the receiver is harmed.

CHAPTER SIXTEEN

SECTION 68: NON-CONVEYANCE OF GIFTS

SECTION 69: SALE WITHOUT OWNERSHIP

SECTION 70: THE RELATION OF OWNERSHIP

1. The non-delivery of first is explained by the non-payment of debts.
2. A gift, not negotiable, shall remain in revocation in one place.
3. If, after promising to give his whole property, his sons and wife or himself, one revokes, the judges shall allow it.
4. And the judge shall annual a gift of piety to wicked persons or for destructive actions, a gift of wealth to those who are not useful or are harmful, and a gift of love to unworthy persons.
5. And experts shall fix revocation in such a way that neither the donor nor the receiver is harmed.
6. For one who accepts a gift made in fear—through fear of punishment or fear of abuse or fear of a calamity—the punishment shall be that for theft, also for him who makes it.
7. That applies also to a gift in anger for injuring another and a gift made in haughtiness above that of kings.

8. In that case the fine shall be the highest.
9. The son or heir inheriting the property may not pay, if unwilling, obligations of suretyship, balance of a fine or dowry, a gambling debt, a debt for drinks and a gift of love.
   Thus, ends the topic of non-conveyance of gifts.
10. As to sale without ownership, on findings a lost or stolen article, the owner shall cause it to be seized by the judge.
11. Or, if the place and time are likely to be missed, he should himself seize it and bring it to the judge.
12. And the judge should question the possessor, 'where did you get this'?
13. If he were to show a legitimate method of purchase but not the vendor, he shall be acquitted on handing over that article.
14. If the vendor were found, he shall pay the price to the purchaser and a fine for theft.
15. If he were to find a means of exoneration, he may clear himself and so on till the means of exoneration are exhausted.
16. When these are exhausted, the last person unable to exonerate himself shall pay the price and fine for theft.

CHAPTER SEVENTEEN

SECTION 71: FORCIBLE SEIZURE

1. Forcible seizure is a deed of force in the presence of the owner.
2. In the absence of the owner it is theft, also in case of denial.
3. 'In case of the forcible seizure of jewels, articles of high value, of low value and forest produce, the fine shall be equal to their value', say the followers of Manu.
4. 'Double the value', say the followers of *Usanas*.
5. 'In accordance with the offence', says Kautilya.
6. 'In the case of flowers, fruits, vegetables, roots, bulbous roots, cooked food, leather goods, wicker-baskets, earthenware and other trifling articles, the fine is a minimum of twelve *panas* and a maximum of twentyfour *panas*.
7. In the case of articles of iron, wood and ropes, small animals, cloth and other big articles, the fine is a minimum of twentyfour *panas* and a maximum of fortyeight *panas*.
8. In the case of articles of copper, steel, bronze, glass and ivory and other big articles, the lowest fine for violence, a minimum of fortyeight *panas* and a maximum of ninetysix *panas* shall be the punishment.

9. In the case of large animals, human beings, fields, houses, money, gold, fine cloth and other big articles, the middle fine for violence a minimum of two hundred and a maximum of five hundred shall be the punishment.
10. For one who binds or causes another to bind or releases from bondage a woman or a man by using force, the punishment shall be the highest fine for violence, a minimum of five hundred and a maximum of one thousand', say the teachers.
11. 'He who causes another to commit an act of force, saying "I accept responsibility", shall pay double the fine.
12. He who causes it saying "I shall give as much money as will be required", shall pay a four-fold fine.
13. He who causes it by stating the amount in the words "I shall give so much money", shall pay the money as stated as well as the fine', say the followers of Brhaspati.
14. 'If he were to plead anger, intoxication or delusion, he shall impose on him the single fine as prescribed', says Kautilya.
15. In all cases of fine one should know that there is an impost of eight *panas* per hundred, but in those above one hundred, a surcharge in addition of five *panas* per hundred.
16. Because of the large number of crimes by subjects or because of a defect in the condition of kings, the impost and the surcharge, which are illegal, are current, but the basic fine is alone known to be legal.

CHAPTER EIGHTEEN

SECTION 72: VERBAL INJURY

1. Defamation, vilification and threat constitute verbal injury.
2. Of defamation pertaining to body, character, learning, profession and country, in case of defamation pertaining to body, such as one-eyed, lame and so on, the fine is three *panas*, if defect is a fact, the fine is six *panas* in case of a false imputation of the defect.
3. In case of censure masquerading as praise of one-eyed, lame and other persons, such as 'with beautiful eyes', the fine shall be twelve *panas*.
4. And in case of vilification referring to leprosy, madness, impotence and so on, when it is true, false and contains ironical praise, the fines are twelve *panas* increased by twelve *panas* successively in the three cases, if it is towards equals.

5. If towards superiors the fines shall be double, if towards inferiors half the fines, if towards wives of others double, but half the fines if it is due to a mistake, intoxication, delusion and so on.
6. Of leprosy and madness, physicians and men staying near are the authority, of impotency, women, foam on the urine and stinking of ordure in water shall constitute proof.
7. In case of libel concerning character, among Brahmins, Ksatriyas, Vaisyas, Sudras and the lowest born, the fines are three *panas* successively if it is of the earlier by the later, decreasing by two *panas* successively up to two *panas* if of the later by the earlier, also in case of vilification like 'low Brahmin' and so on.
8. By that are explained defamation concerning the learning of professional story-tellers, slander of the profession of artisans and actors, and libel of the country of those from Prajjuna, Gandhara and so on.
9. The person who threatens another with doing something, saying, 'I shall do this to you,' shall pay, in case he does not actually do it, a fine half that prescribed for the doing of it.
10. If he is incapable of carrying out the threat or pleads anger, intoxication or delusion, he shall pay a fine of twelve *panas*.
11. If he has feelings of enemity and is capable of doing harm, he shall furnish a surety till the end of his life.
12. A person deserves the lowest fine for violence for reviling his own country and village, the middle fine for reviling his own caste or corporation, the highest for reviling gods and sanctuaries.

CHAPTER NINETEEN

SECTION 73: PHYSICAL INJURY

1. Touching, menacing and striking constitute physical injury.
2. For one touching another's body below the navel with the hand, mud, ashes or dust, the fine shall be three *panas*; with those same when they are impure and with the foot or with spittle, six *panas*; with vomit, urine, ordure and so on, twelve *panas*.
3. For touching above the navel the fines shall be double, on the head four-fold, in the case of equals.
4. The fines shall be double in the case of superiors, half in the case of inferiors, double in the case of wives of others, half if due to a mistake, intoxication, delusion and so on.
5. For holding another by the feet, the garment, the hand and the hair, the fines shall be six *panas* increased successively by six *panas*.

6. In cases of pressing, squeezing in one's arms; bending, dragging and sitting on another, the lowest fine for violence shall be imposed.
7. For going away after throwing down, the fine shall be half.
8. The judge shall cause the limb of a Sudra with which he strikes a Brahmin to be cut off.
9. For menacing, a ransom may be allowed, for touching the fine is half.
10. By that are explained Candalas and other impure persons.
11. For menacing with the hand the fine shall be three *panas* minimum and twelve *panas* maximum, double for menacing with the foot, the lowest fine for violence with an object causing hurt, the middle with one endangering life.
12. For one causing hurt without blood with any one of objects made of wood, earth, stone, or metal, or a stick or rope, the fine shall be twentyfour *panas*, for causing a bleeding wound double, except in the case of impure blood.
13. For one beating another to the point of death without causing bleeding, or causing dislocation of the hand or foot the punishment shall be the lowest fine for violence, also for breaking hands, feet or teeth, cutting off the ear or nose and opening up wounds, excepting festering wounds.
14. For breaking the thigh or neck or piercing the eye and in cases of hurt leading to obstruction in speech, movement or eating, the punishment shall be the middle fine for violence and the expenses for treatment and cure.
15. In case of death, he shall be taken for trial as a criminal by a magistrate.
16. If a number of persons beat one person, the fine shall be double for each one of them.
17. 'An old scuffle or trespass with criminal intent shall not be a cause for a suit', say the teachers.
18. 'There is no going scot-free for an offender', says Kautilya.
19. 'In case of a scuffle, he who comes first to the court wins, for only one unable to put up with the injury runs to the court', say the teachers.
20. 'No', says Kautilya.
21. Whether one has approached first or later, witness alone are to help in deciding the case; if there are no witnesses, the injury or the indications of the scuffle are to decide.
22. If one does not reply to an accusation of injury, he shall be convicted on the same day.

23. For taking away in a scuffle an object of another, the fine shall be ten *panas*, for destroying a small object, the same and an equal amount as fine, for destroying a big object, the same and double that as fine, for destroying clothes, ornaments, money and gold articles, the same and the lowest fine for violence.
24. For one causing the wall of another's house to shake by striking at it, the fine shall be three *panas*, for breaking or cutting it six *panas* and payment of the cost of repairs.
25. For one throwing into another's house an object causing hurt the fine shall be twelve *panas*, an object dangerous to life the lowest fine for violence.
26. For causing hurt to small animals with wood and other things, the fine shall be one *pana* or two *panas*, double than that for causing bleeding.
27. For these same offences concerning big animals, the fine shall be double and payment of expenses for treatment and cure.
28. For cutting the shoots of trees in city parks that bear flowers or fruit or yield shade the fine shall be six *panas*, for cutting small branches twelve *panas*, for cutting stout branches twentyfour *panas*, for destroying trunks the lowest fine for violence, for uprooting the tree the middle fine.
29. In the case of bushes and creepers bearing flowers or fruit or yielding shade the fines shall be half, also in the case of trees in holy places, penance-groves and cremation grounds.
30. In the case of trees at the boundaries, in sanctuaries, and of trees that are prominent, these same fines doubled shall be imposed, also in the case of trees in royal parks.

CHAPTER TWENTY

SECTION 74: GAMBLING AND BETTING

SECTION 75: MISCELLANEOUS

1. The Director of Gambling should cause gambling to be carried on in one place.
2. For one gambling with dice in another place, the fine shall be twelve *panas*, in order to find out those who follow a secret profession.
3. 'In a suit concerning gambling, the lowest fine for violence shall be imposed on the winner, the middle on the loser.
4. For, this latter being of a foolish nature and anxious to win, cannot bear a loss', say the teachers.
5. 'No', says Kautilya.

6. If the loser is punished with a double fine, no one will approach the king for justice.
7. Gamblers indeed are generally fraudulent players.
8. Masters of gambling halls shall provide for them clean cowrie-shells and dice.
9. For substituting other cowrie-shells or dice the fine shall be twelve *panas*, for fraudulent play the lowest fine for violence and confiscation of winnings, for cheating fine for theft in addition.
10. The master of the hall shall take five per hundred of the winnings, as well as hire for cowrie-shells, dice, leather-straps and ivory-cubes and charges for water, ground and the act of gambling.
11. He shall carry out the pledging and sale of articles.
12. For not prohibiting offences concerning dice, ground or the use of hand, the fine shall be double.
13. Thus, is explained 'a challenge' except challenges concerning learning or art.
14. As to miscellaneous, however: For not returning at the proper place and time a thing borrowed, hired, pledged or entrusted, for missing the place or time of meeting or staying together at a watch of the night or shadow of the gnomon by day for one making a Brahmin pay duty at the police post or fare at the ferry, and for inviting over the heads of the immediate and the next-but one neighbours, the fine shall be twelve *panas*.
15. For one not handing over an object which he is enjoined to deliver, for one touching the brother's wife with the hand, for one going to a prostitute in the exclusive keeping of another, for one purchasing goods claimed by another, for one breaking open a sealed house, and for one doing harm to members from forty neighbouring families, the fine shall be fortyeight *panas*.
16. For the receiver of the family treasure denying it, for one forcible violating a widow living by herself, for a Candala touching an Arya lady, for one not rushing to rescue another close by in distress, for one rushing without cause and for one feeding Sakya, Ajivaka and other heretical monks at rites in honour of gods and manes, the fine shall be one hundred *panas*.
17. For one putting question to suspects on oath without authorization, and for one, not an officer, doing the work of an officer, for one castrating males used for stud purposes among small animals, and for one causing the abortion of a female slave by medicines, the punishment shall be the lowest fine for violence.

18. As between father and son, husband and wife, brother and sister, maternal uncle and nephew or teacher and pupil, for one abandoning the other when not an outcast, and for one abandoning another going together in a caravan in the middle of a village, the lowest fine for violence shall be the punishment, if in a forest the middle fine, for causing harm to him thereby the highest fine; for other going with the caravan, half the fines shall be the punishment.
19. For one binding or making another bind a man not deserving to be bound or releasing a man from bondage, and for one binding or causing another to bind a child that has not attained majority, the fine shall be one thousand *panas*.
20. Special fines should be imposed according to the special nature of men and offences.
21. The head of a religious order, an ascetic, a sick person, one exhausted by hunger, thirst or a journey, a foreigner, one groaning under a fine, and an indigent person should be shown leniency.
22. The judges themselves shall look into the affairs of gods, Brahmins, ascetics, women, old persons, sick persons, who are helpless, when these do not approach the court, and they shall not dismiss their suits under the pretext of place, time or adverse possession.
23. And men are to be honoured on account of excellence in learning, intellect, valour, noble birth and deeds.
24. In this way the judges should look into affairs, without resorting to deceit, being impartial to all beings, worthy of trust and beloved of the people.

Herewith ends the Third Book of the Arthasastra of Kautilya

'CONCERNING THE JUDGES'

18

BOOK FOUR

The Suppression of Criminals

It was enjoined on a king to administer the rules in a such a way as to promote prosperity and happiness for all human pursuits without which the high ends of life were impossible to be achieved, and the human society preserved. Kautilya had visualised in those days the need of the Government for establishing socio-ethical-political order in the state and his notion of a welfare state was to ensure an ideal righteous life in the citizens. As all human beings are prone to commit sin, of one type or the other, including selfishness and abuse, to sublimate them and to make them righteous and law abiding, a set of rule and a class of administrative machinery were formulated by him. Kautilya had not left any thing to chance. All human misdemeanors were minutely and very carefully thought of by him, including of those in the service of the state and the general population: and appropriate punishments, without any discretion of infliction were suggested. However, on account of the 'Four *Varna*' community life then prevalent, Kautilya had prescribed lenient punishment to Brahmins, but as one descends the *Varna* Ladder—Ksatriya, Vaisya and Sudra, the quantum and nature of the punishment became comparatively stringent. Women were considered weaker section of the society and accordingly the women offenders were meted out with very lenient punishments. These punishments were less inhuman when compared to those inflicted in the contemporary world.

Methods of locating the likely perpetrator of offences and their consequential investigations have also been mentioned in great details in this Book—'Suppression of Criminals' containing the following subjects:

1. Keeping a Watch over Artisans, 2. Keeping a Watch over Traders, 3. Remedial Measures during Calamities, 4. Guarding against Persons with Secret Means of Income, 5. Detection of Criminals through Secret Agents in the Disguise of Holy Men, 6. Arrest on Suspicion with the Stolen Article and by Indications of the Act, 7. Inquest on Sudden Deaths, 8. Investigation through interrogation and through Torutre, 9. Keeping a Watch over Officers of All Departments, 10. Redemption from Corporal Punishment, the cutting of individual's limbs. 11. The Law of Capital Punishment, Simple and with Torture, 12. Violation of Maidens, 13. Punishment for Transgressions.

CHAPTER ONE

SECTION 76: KEEPING A WATCH OVER ARTISANS

1. Three magistrates, all three of the rank of ministers, shall carry out the suppression of criminals.
2. Employer of artisans capable of making good an article, those good at entrusting materials, and artisans working with their own capital should accept entrusted material with the guarantee of the guild.
3. In case of death, they shall be responsible for the entrusted material.
4. And they shall carry out the work with the place, time and nature of the work stipulated, without stipulation as to place or time if the nature of the work can be pointed out as the reason.
5. For exceeding the time-limit, there shall be a reduction in the wage by one quarter and double that as fine.
6. They shall be liable for what is lost or destroyed except in case of deterioration or a sudden calamity.
7. For carrying out a work otherwise than as ordered, there shall be loss of wage and double that as fine.
8. Weavers shall increase yarn to the extent of eleven *palas* from ten.
9. For diminution in increase, the fine shall be double the diminution.
10. The wage for weaving shall be equal to the value of the yarn, one and a half times in the case of *kasuma* and *kauseya*, double in the case of *patrona*, blankets and quilt.
11. For shortness in measure, there shall be a reduction in wage equal to the value of the short measure and double that as fine, for short weight the fine shall be four times the deficiency, for change of yarn the fine shall be double its value.
12. By that is explained the weaving of double cloth.

13. In one tula of wool, a reduction in carding to the extent of five palas reduction in the hair.
14. Washermen shall wash garments on wooden boards or smooth slabs of stone.
15. Those washing on anything else shall pay for damage to garments and a fine of six *panas*.
16. Wearing a garment of other than one marked with the sign of the club shall pay a fine of three *panas*.
17. For selling, hiring out or pledging the garments of others the fine shall be twelve *panas*, for change of garment the fine shall be double the price and the return of the garment.
18. They shall return a garment, which is white like a bud, which is cleansed on a slab of stone, which has the colour of washed yarn, and which is bleached white, after one day increased successively by one day.
19. One with a light red colour after five days, one dyed blue after six days, a precious garment dyed in saffron flower, lac-juice or *manjistha* the treatment of which is arduous and which has to be worked upon with great care, after seven days.
20. After that they shall lose their wage.
21. In case of dispute concerning dyeing, trustworthy experts shall fix the wage.
22. For the most precious garments the wage shall be one *Pana*, for middling one half, for lowest one-quarter, for rough garments one *masaka* or two *masaka*, double for dyed garments.
23. At the first washing there is a loss of one-fourth of the value of the garment at the second of one-fifth.
24. By that are explained later losses in value.
25. By washermen are explained tailors.
26. For goldsmith purchasing silver or gold in the same form from the hand of disreputable person without informing state officers the fine is twelve *panas*, if in a charged form twentyfour *panas*, if form the hands of a thief fortyeight *panas*.
27. In case of purchase at a low price in secret or what is changed in appearance there shall be the punishment for theft, also in case of deceit in the article manufactured.
28. For the goldsmith stealing one *masaka* from one *suvarna* of gold the fine shall be two hundred *panas*, for stealing one *masaka* from one *dharana* of silver twelve *panas*.
29. By that are explained higher values.

30. For one securing an artificial enhancement of colour or practising removal or mixture with base metals, the fine shall be five hundred *panas*.
31. In case of fraud in connection with these two metals, he shall treat it as a case of removal of colour.
32. One *masaka* is the wage for one *dharana* of silver, one-eight part of a *pana* for one *suvarna* of gold.
33. In accordance with special skill, the wage may be increased to double.
34. By that are explained further rates.
35. In the case of copper, steel, bell-metal, *vaikrntaka* and brass, the wage is five *panas* per hundred *palas*.
36. A lump of copper has a loss of one-tenth part in working.
37. In case of reduction to the extent of one *pala* beyond this, the fine shall be double the value of the loss.
38. By that are explained further cases.
39. A lump of lead or tin has a reduction of one-twentieth part.
40. And one *kakani* is the wage for one *pala* of it.
41. A lump of iron has a reduction of one-fifth.
42. And two *kakani* is the wage for one *pala* of it.
43. By that are explained further cases.
44. For the Examiner of Coins rejecting an established currency of *panas* which does not deserve to be rejected or not rejecting one deserving to be rejected the fine is twelve *panas*.
45. The currency of *panas* is effective when cleared of the payment of surcharge.
46. For one accepting one *masaka* on a *pana* sent into circulation the fine is twelve *panas*.
47. By that are explained further cases.
48. For one causing a counterfeit coin to be made receiving it or sending it into circulation the fine is one thousand *panas*, for inserting it in the treasury the penalty is death.
49. Attendants and dust-washers should receive one-third of articles of high value found by them, the king two-third and gems when found.
50. For stealing a gem, the punishment is the highest fine for violence.
51. In cases of information about mines, gems and buried treasure, the informant shall receive one-sixth part, one-twelfth part if he be a servant of the state.

52. A treasure-trove over one hundred thousand *panas* shall go to the king.
53. If less, he shall give one-sixth part to the finder.
54. A native of the land, who is upright, shall receive the entire treasure-trove buried by his forefathers after producing proof of ownership.
55. In the absence of proof of ownership, the fine is five hundred *panas*, one thousand for appropriating it secretly.
56. For the physician undertaking treatment involving danger to life without informing the authorities, the fine is the lowest fine for violence in case of death, the middle fine in case of death through a mistake in treatment.
57. In case of injury to a vital part or causing a deformity, the magistrate shall treat it as a case of physical injury.
58. Actors shall live in one place during the rainy season.
59. They shall avoid excessive gifts of love by one person and excessive praise of one.
60. For transgression of that, the fine is twelve *panas*.
61. They may, at will, entertain by making fun of the customs of countries, castes, families, schools and love-affairs.
62. By actors are explained wandering minstrels and mendicants.
63. For them the punishment shall be as many lashes with the whip as the number of *panas* the judges may pronounce as the fine, to be inflicted with an iron rod (*i.e.*, mercilessly).
64. In the case of the remaining kinds of work, he shall lay down wages for artists in accordance with what they produce.
65. In this manner the king should prevent thieves who are not known as thieves such as traders, artisans, actors, mendicants, jugglers and others from oppressing the country.

CHAPTER TWO

SECTION 77: KEEPING A WATCH OVER TRADERS

1. The Superintendent of Markets should set up the pledging of sale of old wares which are furnished with proof of ownership in the market-place.
2. And he should inspect the weights and measures because of fraud in the standard of weights and measures.
3. In the case of the *parimani* and the *drona*, half a pala, less or more is no offence.
4. For one *pala* less or more the fine is twelve *panas*.

5. By that is explained the increase in fine for each successive *pala*.
6. In the case of a *tula*, one *karsa* less or more is no offence.
7. For two *karsas* less or more the fine is six *panas*.
8. By that is explained the increase in fine for each successive *karsa*.
9. In the case of an *adhaka*, half a *karsa* less or more is no offence.
10. For one *karsa* less or more the fine is three *panas*.
11. By that is explained the increase in fine for each successive *karsa*.
12. From this, he should form an estimate of the fines for deviations in other types of weights and measures.
13. For the trader, purchasing with larger weights and measure and selling with smaller ones, these same fines are to be doubled.
14. For one robbing to the extent of one-eight part of the price of the goods, in the case of good sold by counting, the fine is ninety-six *panas*.
15. For the trader effecting the sale or pledging of an article made of wood, metal or gems, or made of ropes, leather or clay, or made of yarn, bark or hair, which is not genuine by declaring it to be genuine, the fine is eight times the price.
16. For the trader effecting the sale or pledging of an article not of high value as an article of high value or of an article not of a particular class as an article of that class or of an article which is given a false shine or in which there is fraud or the container of which is changed, the fine is fiftyfour *panas* if the price is trifling, double if the price is one *pana*, two hundred *panas*, if the price is two *panas*.
17. By that is explained the increase in fine in case of increase in price.
18. For artisans and artists who by conspiring together bring about a deterioration in the quality of a work or profit or a hindrance to purchase or sale, the fine is one thousand *panas*.
19. For traders, too, who by conspiring together hold back wares or sell them at a high price, the fine is one thousand *panas*.
20. As to difference in weight or measure of difference in price or quality the weigher or measurer who by a trick of the hand brings about a difference to the extent one-eighth part in an article priced at one *pana*, the fine is two hundred *panas*.
21. By that is explained the increase in fines by two hundred *panas* successively.
22. For mixing things of a similar kind with objects such as grains, fats, sugars, salts, perfumes and medicines, the fine is twelve *panas*.
23. The Merchant should fix, after calculating their total earnings for what the sales-agents should live on with permission.

24. What falls in between the purchaser and the seller becomes different from what is received.
25. With that they may make stores of gains and commodities, when permitted to do so.
26. The Director of Trade should confiscate what is accumulated otherwise by them.
27. With that he should trade when selling grains and commodities to the advantage of the subjects.
28. And he should fix a profit for them of five per hundred over and above the permitted purchase-price in the case of indigenous commodities, ten per hundred in the case of foreign goods.
29. For those who increase the price beyond that or secure a profit beyond that during purchase or sale, the fine shall be two hundred *panas* for an additional profit of five *panas* in one hundred *panas*.
30. By that is explained the increase in fine in case of increase in price.
31. And in case of the joint purchase by them remaining unsold, he shall not allow another joint purchase.
32. In case of damage to commodities, he should show them favour.
33. If there is a glut of commodities, the Director of Trade should sell all goods in one place.
34. So long as these are unsold, others shall not sell.
35. They shall sell those for a daily wage for the benefit of the subjects.
36. In the case of commodities distant in place and time, however, the Director of Trade expert in fixing prices, shall fix the price after calculating the investment, the production of goods, duty, interest, rent and other expenses.

CHAPTER THREE

SECTION 78: REMEDIAL MEASURES DURING CALAMITIES

1. There are eight great calamities of a divine origin: fire, floods, disease, famine, rats, wild animals, serpents and evil spirits.
2. From them he should protect the country.
3. In summer, the village shall do the cooking outside the houses or being protected by a collection of ten fire-fighting implements.
4. Prevention of fire is explained in 'Rules for the City Superindependent' and in connection with royal possession in 'Rules for the Royal Residence'.
5. And on parvan-days, he should cause religion to be made with offerings, oblations in fire and recitals of benedictions.

6. In the rainy season, village situated near water should live away from the level of the floods.
7. And they should keep a collection of wooden planks, bamboos and boats.
8. They should rescue a person being carried away by the flood by means of gourds, skin-bags, canoes, tree-stems and ropebraid.
9. For those who do not go to the rescue, the fine is twelve *panas*, except in the case of thosc without canoes.
10. And on parvan-days he should cause worship of the rivers to be carried out.
11. Experts in the practice of magic or those versed in the Vedas should use spells against rain.
12. In case of drought, he should cause worship of the Lord of Saci, the Ganges, the Mountains and Mahakaccha to be made.
13. The calamity of disease, magicians and others should counteract with secret means, physicians with medicines or holy ascetics with pacificatory and expiatory rites.
14. By that is explained the epidemic.
15. He should cause to be instituted bathing in sacred places, worship of Mahakaccha, milking of cows in cremation grounds, burning of effigies and a night festival in honour of gods.
16. In case of disease or epidemic among cattle, he should order lustration rites in connection with the sheds and objects connected with them and worship of their respective deities.
17. During a famine, the king should make a store of seeds and foodstuffs and show favour to the subjects, or institute the building of forts or water-works with the grant of food, or share his provisions with them entrust the country to another king.
18. Or, he should seek shelter with allies, or cause a reduction or shifting of the population.
19. Or, he should migrate with the people to another region where crops have grown, or settle along the sea, lakes or tanks.
20. He should make sowings of grains, vegetables, roots and fruits along the water-works or hunt deer, beasts, birds, wild animals and fish.
21. In case of danger from rats, cats and ichneumons should let loose.
22. For catching or killing these, the fine shall be twelve *panas*, also for not restraining dogs, except in the case of foresters.
23. He should strew grains smeared with the milk of snuhi-plants or such as are mixed with sacred mixtures.

24. Or, he should institute a tax on rats.
25. Or, holy ascetics should perform pacificatory rites.
26. And on *parvan*-days, he should order worship of rats.
27. By that are explained remedies against danger from locusts, birds, and insects.
28. In case of danger from wild animals, he should elave carcasses of cattle mixed with a stupefying liquid or intestines of cattle filled with *madana-kodrava*.
29. Fowlers or hunters should busy themselves with concealed cages and pits.
30. Armoured men, weapons in hand, should kill wild animals.
31. For one not going forth to help, the fine shall be twelve *panas*.
32. The same shall be the reward for one slaying a wild animal.
33. And he should order the worship of mountains on *parvan*-days.
34. By that are explained remedies against herds or deer or beasts, swarms of birds and crocodiles.
35. In case of danger from serpents, experts in poison-cure should act with charms and medicines.
36. Or persons coming together should kill snakes.
37. Or, experts in the Atharvaveda lore should use magic spells.
38. And on *parvan*-days, he should order worship of cobras.
39. By that are explained remedies against danger from acquatic creatures.
40. In the case of danger from evil spirits, experts in the Atharvaveda lore or experts in the practice of magic should perform rites for destroying evil.
41. And on *parvan*-days, he should order Religious-trees with offerings of raised platforms, umbrellas, food, small flags and goats.
42. In cases of all kinds of danger, they should make offerings day and night, saying 'we offer you the oblation'.
43. And in all cases, he should favour the stricken subjects like a father.
44. Therefore, experts in the practice of magic, and holy ascetics, capable of counteracting divine calamities, should live in the kingdom, honoured by the king.

CHAPTER FOUR

SECTION 79: GUARDING AGAINST PERSONS WITH SECRET MEANS OF INCOME

1. In 'Rules for the Administrator' the protection of the country has been described.

2. Kautilya explained the weeding of thorns in that country.
3. The Administrator should station in the country secret agents appearing as holy ascetics, wandering monks, cart-drivers, wandering minstrels, jugglers, tramps, fortune-tellers, soothsayers, astrologers, physicians, lunatics, dumb persons, deaf persons, idiots, blind persons, traders, artisans, artists, actors, brothel-keepers, vintners, dealers in bread, dealers in cooked meat, and dealers in cooked rice.
4. They should find out the integrity or otherwise of village officers and heads of departments.
5. And whomsoever among these he suspects of deriving a secret income he should cause to be spied upon by a secret agent.
6. A secret agent should say to a judge in whom confidence is inspired by him, 'Such and such a relation of mine in accused before you; save him in this misfortune and accept this amount.'
7. If he were to do so, he should be exiled as one given to receiving bribes.
8. By that are explained magistrates.
9. A secret agent should say to a village chief or a departmental head, 'Such and such a rogue has plenty of wealth; this misfortune has befallen him; by using that, extort money from him.'
10. If he were to do so, he should be exiled as an extortioner.
11. Or, an agent pretending to be an accused should induce those, who are known to bear false testimony, with plenty of money.
12. If they were to do so, they should be exiled as false witnesses.
13. By that are explained those who cause false evidence to be given.
14. Or, if he considers any one as a user of occult means for winning love with incantations or rites with herbs and rites in cremation grounds, a secret agent should say to him, 'I am in love with so and so's wife, daughter-in-law or daughter; make her reciprocate my love and take this money.'
15. If he were to do so, he should be exiled as a user of occult means for winning love.
16. By that are explained practices of black magic and sorcery.
17. Or, if he considers any one who prepares, purchases or sells poison or who deals in medicines or food, as an administerer of poison, a secret agent should say to him, 'So and so is my enemy; bring about his death and take this money.'
18. If he were to do so, he should be exiled as a poison-giver.
19. By that is explained the dealer in stupefying mixtures.

20. Or, if he considers any one as an utterer of false coins, being a frequent purchaser of various metals and acids, of coals, bellows, pincers, vices, anvils, dyes, chisels and crucibles, with indications of hands and clothes smeared with soot, ashes and smoke, and being possessed of blacksmith's tools, a secret agent should expose him by insinuating himself into his confidence as a pupil and by carrying on dealings with him.
21. If exposed, he should be exiled as an utterer of false coins.
22. By that is explained the remover of colour from precious metals and the dealer in artificial gold.
23. But the thirteen persons, having secret ways of income, when engaged in doing injury to others, should be exiled or they shall pay a redemption amount in accordance with the gravity of the offence.

CHAPTER FIVE

SECTION 80: DETECTION OF CRIMINALS THROUGH SECRET AGENTS IN THE DISGUISE OF HOLY MEN

1. After the employment of spies, secret agents appearing as holy men should entice criminals by means of lores favourite with criminals, *viz.*, robbers by means of charms inducing sleep, making invisible or opening doors, adulterers by love-winning charms.
2. When these have been enthused, to see the power of the charms, they should take a large band of them at night and proposing to go to one village should go to another village in which men and women are prepared beforehand, and say, 'Right here you can see the power of our lore; it is difficult to go to the other village.'
3. Then opening the gates by means of a gate opening charm, they should say, 'Enter'.
4. By means of an invisibility charm they should make the criminals go safely through the midst of wakeful guards.
5. Sending guards to sleep with a sleep-inducing charm they should cause them with their beds to be moved by the criminals.
6. With a love-winning charm they should make the cirminals enjoy harlots appearing as other men's wives.
7. When these are convinced of the power of their lores, they should prescribe the performance of preliminary rites and so on, so that they may be recognized.
8. Or, they should get them to do their work in houses in which goods have been marked.

9. Or, they should get them caught in one place after winning their confidence.
10. They should get them arrested while engaged in purchasing, selling or pledging articles that are marked or when they are intoxicated with drugged liquor.
11. When they are arrested, he should question them concerning former offences and their associates.
12. Or, Secret agents appearing as old thieves should, after winning their confidence, get thieves to do their work in the same manner and get them arrested.
13. When they are arrested, the Administrator should point them out to citizens and country people, saying, 'The king has studied the lore of catching thieves; it is under his instructions that these thieves have been caught; I shall catch others too; you should therefore restrain your kinsmen who may have criminal tendencies.'
14. And if he were to come to know through the information of the spies that some one among them has stolen a trifle like a yoke-pin, goad and so on, he should declare that about him among them, saying, 'This is the king's power.'
15. Old thieves, cow-herds, fowlers and hunters, winning the confidence of forest thieves and foresters, should induce them to attack caravans, herds or villages with plenty of articles made of artificial gold and forest produce.
16. When the attack is made, they should get them killed by concealed soldiers or through provisions for the journey mixed with stupefying liquids.
17. Or, they should get them arrested while sleeping after being tired by a long journey carrying in heavy load of stolen goods or when they are intoxicated by drugged liquor at festive parties.
18. And having caught them, the Administrator should show them as before, to the people causing a proclamation of the king's omniscience to be made among the inhabitants of the kingdom.

CHAPTER SIX

SECTION 81: ARREST ON SUSPICION, WITH THE STOLEN ARTICLE AND BY INDICATIONS OF THE ACT

1. After the practices of holy men comes the topic of arrest on suspicion, with the articles and because of the act.
2. He should suspect as being either a murderer, or a thief, or one living on a secret income by appropriating buried treasure or entrusted

article or through employment by enemies the following persons, *viz.*, one whose inheritance and family income are exhausted, one with a small wage, one falsely declaring his country, caste, family, name or occupation, one whose profession or work is hidden, one addicted to meat, wine, eating of food, perfumes, garlands, clothes and ornaments, one who spends lavishly, one addicted to prostitutes, gambling or drinking in bars, one travelling frequently, one whose stay and departure are unknown, one moving at an odd time in a solitary place or a forest or a house-garden, one holding long consultations and meeting frequently in a secret place or in a place with a likely victim, one secretly getting treatment for recently inflicted wounds, one always staying inside the house, one proceeding stealthily, one devoted to a beloved, one making frequent inquiries about other people's possessions such as women, goods, or houses, one in possession of tools of a condemned occupation or lore, one moving stealthily in the shadow of walls at an odd hour of the night, one selling at an improper place and time goods that are changed in appearance, one who entertains a feelings of hostility, one with a low occupation or caste concealing his appearance, one, not a monk, having the marks of a monk, or a monk with a different mode of life, one who had formerly committed an offence, one shown up by his own deeds, one who, at the sight of the City Superintendent or a big officer, conceals himself, runs away, sits without breathing, becomes agitated or has his voice and complexion of the face dry and changed, and one shying at a crowd of men carrying weapons in hand. Thus, ends the topic of arrest on suspicion.

3. As to arrest with the article, however, what is lost or stolen and is not found, he should communicate to those who deal in wares of that class.
4. If they, on coming by the article communicated, were to conceal it, they shall be liable for the offence of being accessories.
5. If they are ignorant about it, they shall be acquitted on giving up the article.
6. And they shall not pledge or sell old wares without informing the Market Superintendent.
7. If the article about which information has been given is found, he should question the person arrested with the article concerning its acquisition 'Whence did you get this?'
8. If he were to plead 'I got it in inheritance, obtained it as a gift, purchased it, got it made, received it as a secret pledge from so

and so; this is the place and time of its acquisition; this is its price, quantity, marks and value,' he shall be acquitted of statements about the acquisition being corroborated.

9. If the person who lost the article were also to prove the same, he shall hold the article as belonging to him whose possession of it was earlier and long or whose title is clear.
10. For, even among quadrupeds and bipeds there is a similarity in appearance and marks; how much more then would it be in the case of forest produce, ornaments and other articles produced from material from the same source and by the same manufacturer.
11. If he were to plead 'This is a borrowed or hired article, a pledge, a trust, a deposit or goods given for sale on agency basis, belonging to so and so,' he shall be acquitted on corroboration by the person proving his innocence.
12. If that person were to say 'It is not so' the person arrested with the article shall justify the reason for the other person giving it, the reasons for his accepting it or get the indications corroborated by the giver, the one who causes to give, the recorder, the receiver and those who have witnessed or heard the transaction.
13. In the case of an article that is left, has disappeared or run away and is afterwards found, there shall be clearance from guilt proof concerning place, time and acquisition.
14. If not cleared, he shall pay that and as much again as fine.
15. Otherwise, he shall be liable to punishment for theft. Thus, ends the topic of arrest with the article.
16. As to arrest because of the act, however, in the case of a house that has been robbed, entry or exit otherwise than by a door, the piercing of the door wtih a hole or by uprooting, the crumbling of a wall while climbing up or descending, or the digging up of the ground as a means of burying or robbing objects secretly, he should hold committed by one inside the house, if things stolen could be known through information supplied, and if the cutting, the rubbish, the breaking and the tools are on the inside.
17. In the reverse case he should hold these as committed by an outsider, if these are on both sides as committed by both inmates and outsiders.
18. If the offence is committed by an insider, he should examine a man closely related, who may be addicted to vice, may have ruthless associates or may be in possession of a thief's tools, or a woman from an indigent family or attached to another man or an attendant of a similar conduct, who is sleeping excessively, overpowered

by sleep, agitated, with voice and face dry and changed, restless, prattling too much, with limbs stiffened by climbing high up, with body or clothes cut, crushed, broken or torn, with hands and feet having scars or stiffened, with hair and nails full of dust or with hair and nails cut and bent, or who is thoroughly bathed and anointed, with limbs rubbed with oil, or with hands and feet just washed, whose footprints are similar to those found in dust or wet surface, or who has flowers, wine, perfumes, bits of cloth, unguents or perspiration similar to those found at the entrance and exit.

19. He should hold him to be a thief or an adulterer.
20. The magistrate, alongwith the village and divisional officers, should make a search for thieves outside, and the City Superintendent should do it inside the fort, according to indication just mentioned.

CHAPTER SEVEN

SECTION 82: INQUEST ON SUDDEN DEATHS

1. He shall examine a person dying suddenly, after smearing the body with oil.
2. One with urine and ordure thrown out, with the skin of the abdomen filled with wind, with swollen hands and feet, with eyes open, with marks on the throat, he should hold as killed through the stopping of breathing by strangulation.
3. The same, with arms and thighs contracted, he should hold as slain by hanging.
4. One with hands, feet and abdomen swollen, with eyes sunk in, with the navel turned out, he should hold as impaled.
5. One with the anus and eyes closed, with the tongue bitten, with the belly swollen, he should hold as dead by drowning water.
6. One bespattered with blood, with limbs broken or dislocated, he should hold as slain with sticks or stones.
7. One with limbs shattered and burst, he should hold as hurled down from a height.
8. One with dark hands, feet, teeth and nails, with loose flesh, hair of the body and skin, with the mouth covered with foam, he should hold as killed by poison.
9. The same, with bloody marks of bite, he should hold as killed by a snake or an insect.
10. One with clothes and limbs thrown about, with excessive vomiting and motions, he should hold as killed by a stupefying mixture.
11. He should find out if he is killed in one of these ways, or, if after being killed, he is hanged or has his throat cut, through fear of punishment.

12. He should examine through birds the remainder of the meal of one suspected of being killed by poison.
13. Or, if what is taken from the heart and thrown in fire produces a crackling sound and becomes rainbow-coloured, he should hold that as poisoned, or if he sees the heart not burning when the body is cremated.
14. He should seek his servant who may have received a severe verbal or physical injury at the hands of the deceased, or a woman stricken with grief or attached to another, or a kinsman coveting inheritance, livelihood or a woman.
15. He should investigate the same in the case of one hanged after being murdered.
16. Or, in the case of one who has hanged himself, he should find out if any improper wrong has been done to him.
17. In the case of all, an offence concerning a woman or property, rivalry in profession, hostility towards a rival, or association in a market place, or one of the heads of dispute in a law-court is an occasion for anger.
18. Murder is caused by anger.
19. He should investigate, through those proximate, the murder of a person, whether he is killed by some persons themselves of through agents appointed, or by thieves for the sake of money, or by enemies of some one else because of similarity.
20. He should question him by whom he had been called, with whom he had stayed or gone, or by whom he was brought to the place of murder.
21. And he should question those moving near him at the place of murder, each one separately, 'Who brought him here? Who killed him? Did you see any one with a weapon in hand or hiding himself or agitated?'
22. As they might reply, so should he question further.

23-24. Observing that objects used on the person of the helpless deceased, his belongings, clothes, dress or ornaments, he should question those who deal in those articles, concerning their meeting with him, their residence, the reason for their stay, their occupation and dealings, and then carry on the investigation.

25-26. If a person, under the influence of passion or anger, or a woman infatuated by sin, were to kill himself or herself by means of a rope, a weapon or poison, he should cause them to be dragged with a rope on the royal highway by a Candala; there is to be no cremation-rite for them nor obsequies by kinsmen.

27. If, however, some kinsman were to perform for them the rites in connection with the dead, he should meet with the same fate afterwards, or should be abandoned by his relations.
28. A person having dealings with an outcast loses caste himself after one year, by sacrificing for them, by teaching them or by entering into marriage relations with them; so does another having dealings with these.

CHAPTER EIGHT

SECTION 83: INVESTIGATION THROUGH INTERROGATION AND THROUGH TORTURE

1. In the presence of the robbed person and of witnesses, external and internal, he should question the accused about his country, caste, family, name, occupation, wealth, associates and residence.
2. And he should compare these with statements.
3. Then he should question him concerning his movements on the previous day, and place of stay during the night up to the time of arrest.
4. In case of corroboration by persons proving his innocence, he shall be cleared of guilt; otherwise, he shall be put to torture.
5. After three nights, the suspect shall not be liable to arrest, because of the inadmissibility of interrogation after that interval, except when tools of the crime are found with him.
6. For one calling another, who is not a thief, the punishment shall be that for a thief, also for one hiding a thief.
7. One accused of being a thief shall be cleared of guilt, if implicated out of enmity or hatred.
8. For one keeping under restraint, one cleared of guilt, the lowest fine for violence shall be the punishment.
9. In the case of one about whom suspicion has arisen, he should produce tools, counsellors, accomplices, stolen articles and agents.
10. And he should compare his action by reference to his entry, receiving of goods and division into shares of the stolen goods.
11. In the absence of corroboration of these grounds, showing guilt, he should hold a person, though prattling, as not a thief.
12. For, it is observed that even one not a thief, meeting by chance thieves on their way, is arrested because of similarity with the thieves in dress, weapons or goods or on account of his being found near the thieves' goods, as for instance Ani-Mandavya declaring himself to be a thief though not a thief, because of the fear of the pain of torture.

13. Hence, he should punish only such in whose case proof is fully obtained.

14-15. He shall not put to torture a person whose offence is trifling, or who is a minor or aged or sick or intoxicated or insane or overcome by hunger, thirst or travel, or who has overeaten to be secretly watched by persons of the same character, prostitutes, attendants at water-booths, giver of advice, accommodation and food to them.

16. In this way should he outwit them, or as explained in connection with misappropriation of entrusted articles.

17. He should put to torture one whose guilt is found to be probable, but under no circumstances a pregnant woman or a woman within one month of delivery.

18. For woman, however, there is to be only half the torture, or only examination by interrogation.

19. For a Brahmin there is to be the use of secret agents if he is learned in the Veda, also for an ascetic.

20. In case of transgression of this rule, the highest fine shall be imposed on one who gives and who causes him to give the torture, also for causing death by torture.

21. The ordinary four-fold torture is: six strokes with a stick, seven lashes with a whip, two suspensions from above and the water-tube.

22. In the cases of very grave offenders, there may be: nine strokes with a cane, twelve whip-lashes, two thigh-encirclings, twenty strokes with a *nakta-mala-stick*, thirty-two slaps, two scorpion-bindings, and two hangings up, needle in the hand, burning one joint of a finger of one who has drunk gruel, heating in the sun for one day for one who has drunk fat, and a bed of *balbaja*-points on a winter-night.

23. This is the eighteen-fold torture.

24. He should ascertian the tools, the amount, the manner of infliction, the determining and the limiting of it from the *kharapatta*.

25. He should cause torture to be given on alternate days and one only on one day.

26. He should cause torture to be used collectively, separately or repeatedly in the case of one who is a former offender, who after confessing, retracts, with whom a part of the stolen goods are found, who is arrested because of the act or with the article, who conceals the king's treasury or who is to be killed by torture at the king's order.

27. In all offences, a Brahmin is not to be tormented.
28. On his forehead shall be a branded mark of the guilty to exclude him from all dealings, the mark of a dog in case of theft, a headless trunk in case of murder of a human being, the female organ in case of violation of an elder's bed, the vintner's flag in case of liquor-drinking.
29. Proclaiming a Brahmin of sinful deeds and making the sear of the mark on him, the king should exile him from the country or settle him in mines.

CHAPTER NINE

SECTION 84: KEEPING A WATCH OVER OFFICERS OF ALL DEPARTMENTS

1. The Administrator and the magistrates should first keep in check the heads of departments and their subordinates.
2. For an officer stealing an article of high value or a gem from mines or factories for articles of high value, simple death without torture, shall be the punishment.
3. For stealing an article of low value or an implement from factories for articles of low value, the lowest fine for violence shall be the punishment.
4. For one stealing from places of production of articles a king's commodity, above one *masa* in value up to one-fourth of a *pana* in value, the fine is twelve *pana*s; up to two-quarters in value, twenty-four *pana*s; up to three-quarters in value, thirty-six *pana*s; up to one *pana* in value, fortyeight *pana*s; up to two *pana*s in value, the lowest fine for violence shall be the punishment; up to four *pana*s and above in value, the middle fine; up to eight *pana*s in value, the highest; up to ten *pana*s in value, death shall be the punishment.
5. For misappropriation of forest produce, goods or tools from magazines, warehouse, stores of forest produce and armouries, these same fines shall be imposed for articles half in value of those above.
6. For misappropriation from the treasury, store-rooms and the Goldsmith's workshop, these same fines shall be doubled for articles one-quarter in value.
7. For thieves, in case of breaking open the treasury etc. death by torture shall be the punishment.
8. Thus, have been explained offences concerning the king's possessions.

9. But in the case of other properties, for an officer stealing secretly by day from a field, a threshing floor, a house or a shop, forest produce, ware or tool above one masaka in value and up to one-quarter of a *pana* in value, the fine in three *panas* or smearing him with cow-dung and proclaiming his guilt; up to two-quarters, in value, six *panas* fine or smearing with cow-dung and ashes and proclaiming his guilt; up to three-quarters in value, nine *panas* fine or smearing with cow-dung and ashes and proclamation of his guilt or with a girdle of potsherds round his body; up to one *pana* in value, twelve *panas* fine or shaving of the head and exile; up to two *panas* in value, twenty-four *panas* or driving him out of the city with a piece of brick after shaving him; up to four *panas* in value, thirty-six *panas* fine; up to five *panas* in value, forty-eight *panas*; up to ten *panas* in value, the lowest fine for violence; up to twenty *panas* in value, two hundred *panas* fine; up to thirty *panas* in value, five hundred *panas* fine; up to forty *panas* in value, one thousand fine; up to fifty *panas* in value and above death shall be the punishment.
10. For one stealing forcibly by day or at night during the forbidden watches, these same shall be imposed for articles half in value.
11. For one robbing forcibly, by day or night, with weapons, these same fines shall be doubled for articles one quarter in value.
12. For making counterfeit documents and seals of householders, superintendents, principal officers and the king, the punishment is the lowest, the middle, the highest fines and death respectively, or in accordance with the offence.
13. If the judge threatens, upbraids, drives away or browbeats a litigant, he shall impose the lowest fine for violence on him, double that in case of verbal injury.
14. If he does not question one who ought to be questioned, questions one who ought not to be questioned, or after questioning dismisses the statement, or instructs, reminds or prompts him, he shall impose the middle fine for violence on him.
15. If he does not ask for evidence which ought to be submitted, proceeds with the case without evidence, dismisses it under a pretext, carries away one tried, with delays, throws out of context a statement which is in proper order, gives to witnesses help in their statements or takes up once again a case which is completed and in which judgment is pronounced, he shall impose the highest fine for violence on him.

16. In case the offence is repeated, double the fine and removal from office shall be the punishment.
17. If the clerk does not write what is said, writes what is not said, writes correctly what is badly spoken, writes inaccurately what is well spoken, or modifies the sense conveyed, he shall impose the lowest fine for violence on him or punishment in accordance with the offence.
18. If the judge or the magistrate imposes a money fine on one not deserving to be fined, he shall impose on him double the fine imposed, or eight times the shortfall or excess over the prescribed fine.
19. If he imposes corporal punishment, he shall himself suffer corporal punishment or pay double the normal redemption amount.
20. Or, he shall pay a fine eight times the just claim which he disallows or unjust claim which he allows.
21. For the hindrance of sleep, sitting down, meals, answering calls of nature or movement and for binding, in a judge's lock-up or in a prison-house, the fine shall be three *panas* increased successively by three *panas* for him who does it and for him who causes it to be done.
22. For the jailor setting free or allowing the escape of an accused from the lock-up the punishment shall be the middle fine for violence and the payment of the amount in the suit, from the prison-house confiscation of the entire property and death.
23. For the superintendent of the prison-house confiscation of allowing movement to a prisoner without informing the judge or magistrate the fine is twentyfour *panas*, for using torture double that, for making him submit to another position or withholding food and drink ninety-six *panas*, for tormenting or maiming him the middle fine for violence, for killing him one thousand *panas* as fine.
24. For the jailor violating a married woman prisoner who is a slave or a pledge the punishment shall be the lowest fine for violence, the wife of a thief or a rioter the middle, an Arya woman prisoner the highest.
25. Or, for a prisoner doing this, there shall be execution there and then.
26. He shall understand the same punishment for the offence in connection with an Arya woman caught in the prohibited period of the night, in connection with a female slave the lowest fine for violence.

27. For one helping a prisoner to escape from the lock-up without breaking it the punishment shall be the middle fine, by breaking it death, from the prison-house confiscation of the entire property and death.
28. In this manner the king should first correct those officers who deal in money matters by means of punishment; and they, being corrected, should correct the citizens and the country people by means of punishments.

CHAPTER TEN

SECTION 85: REDEMPTION FROM CORPORAL PUNISHMENT, THE CUTTING OF INDIVIDUAL LIMBS

1. In the case of the first offence of thieves at holy places, pickpockets and those with raised hands, the punishment shall be the cutting off of the middle finger and thumb or a fine of fifty-four *panas*; in case of the second, the cutting off of five fingers or a fine of one hundred; in case of the third, cutting off of the right hand or a fine of four hundred; in case of the fourth, death as desired by the magistrate.
2. In cases of theft of cocks, ichneumons, cats, dogs or pigs less than twenty-five *panas* or in value in case of killing any of these, there shall be a fine of fiftyfour *panas* or the cutting off of the tip of the nose; half the fines for Candalas of forest-dwellers.
3. For carrying away deer, beasts, birds, wild animals or fish, caught in snares, nets or concealed pits, the punishment shall be that and an equal amount as fine.
4. In case of theft of deer or objects from deer-parks or produce-forests, there shall be a fine of one hundred.
5. In case of theft of deer or birds intended for show or pleasure or in case of killing these, the fine shall be double.
6. In case of theft of small articles belonging to artisans, artists, actors or ascetics, there shall be a fine of one hundred; for theft of large articles, two hundred, also for theft of agricultural goods.
7. For one, who is not given permission to enter, entering a fort, or one going out through a hole in the city-wall taking an entrusted article with him, the punishment shall be the cutting of the sinews of the feet or a fine of two hundred.
8. For one stealing a cart, a boat or a small animal, the punishment shall be the cutting off of the one foot or a fine of three hundred.

9. For one cheating with false cowrie-shells, dice, leather-straps, ivory-cubes or by sleight of hand, the punishment shall be cutting off of one hand or a fine of four hundred.
10. In case of aiding a thief or an adulterer, and for a woman caught in adultery, the punishment shall be the cutting off of ears and nose or a fine of five hundred; for a man double that.
11. For one stealing a big animal or one male or female slave, or for one selling articles from a corpse, the punishment shall be the cutting off of both feet or a fine of six hundred.
12. In case of striking with hands or feet persons of the highest *varna* and elders, and in case of mounting the royal carriage, riding animal and so on, the punishment shall be the cutting off of one hand and one foot or a fine of seven hundred.
13. For a Sudra calling himself a Brahmin, for one concealing temple property, for one ordering what is treasonable and for one blinding both eyes of another, the punishment shall be blindness by means of poisonous collyrium or a fine of eight hundred.
14. For one setting a thief or an adulterer free, for one writing a royal edict with omissions or additions, for one kidnapping a maiden or a female slave together with money, for a fraudulent dealer, and for one selling unclean meat, the punishment shall be the cutting off of the left hand and both feet or a fine of nine hundred.
15. In case of sale of human flesh, death is the punishment.
16. For one stealing cattle, images, persons, fields, houses, money, gold, gems or crops belonging to a temple, the punishment shall be highest fine or simple death.

17-18. After taking into full consideration the person and the offence, the motive, seriousness or lightness of the offence, the consequences, the present, and the place and time, the magistrate shall fix the highest effects, the lowest and the middle in the matter of punishment, remaining neutral between the king and the subjects.

CHAPTER ELEVEN

SECTION 86: THE LAW OF CAPITAL PUNISHMENT, SIMPLE AND WITH TORTURE

1. For one killing a person on the spot during a scuffle, the punishment shall be death with torture.
2. In case of death within seven days simple death shall be the punishment, within a fortnight within a month five hundred, and the cost of treatment.

3. For one striking another with a weapon, the fine shall be the highest for violence.
4. If that is done in intoxication, the hand shall be cut off; if through delusion, a fine of two hundred shall be imposed.
5. In case of death resulting, death shall be the punishment.
6. For one causing abortion with a blow the fine shall be the highest, with medicine the middle, by causing suffering to the woman the lowest fine for violence.
7. They shall impale on the stake those who beat a man or a woman with force, who rush upon them, who hold them down, who threaten to kill, who attack them and who pierce them, also robbers on highways and house-thieves, and those who kill or steal an elephant, a horse or a chariot belonging to the king.
8. And if any one were to cremate or remove them, from the stake he shall receive the same punishment or the highest fine for violence.
9. For supplying murderers or thieves with food, accommodation, tools, fire, or giving counsel or rendering service to them, the fine shall be the highest; reprimand only in case of ignorance.
10. He should let go the sons and wives of murderers or thieves if not in concert, should seize them, if in concert.
11. He shall cause to be slain by setting fire to hands and head one who covets the kingdom, who attacks the king's palace, who rouses foresters of enemies, or who causes rebellion in the fortified city, the country or the army.
12. He shall make a Brahmin in such a case enter darkness.
13. He shall cause to be slain by setting fire to the skinless head one who has killed his mother, father, son, brother preceptor or an ascetic.
14. For reviling these, the punishment shall be the cutting of the tongue, for wounding a limb, he shall be deprived of the corresponding limb.
15. For killing a person by accident, and in case of theft of a herd of cattle, the punishment shall be simple death.
16. And he should know a herd to contain ten heads of cattle at least.
17. For one breaking a dam holding water, drowning in water at the same spot shall be the punishment, the highest fine for violence if it was without water, the middle if it was in ruins and abandoned.
18. He shall drown in water a man giving poison to another and a woman slaying a man, if not pregnant; if pregnant, at least a month after delivery.

19. He shall cause to be torn by bullocks a woman who kills her husband, an elder or her offsprings or who sets a house etc. on fire or gives poison or breaks into a house.
20. He shall cause to be burnt in fire one who sets on fire a pasture, a field, a threshing ground, a house, a produce-forest or an elephant forest.
21. He shall cause the tongue to be rooted out of one who reviles the king or divulges secret counsel or spreads evil news about the king and one who licks anything in a Brahmin's kitchen.
22. He shall cause to be slain with arrows the stealer of weapons or armours, if he is not a soldier.
23. For the soldier, the highest fine shall be the punishment.
24. Of one injuring the generating organ or testicles of another he shall cause these same limbs to be cut off.
25. For injuring the tongue or the nose, the cutting of the middle finger and the thumb shall be the punishment.
26. These painful punishments have been laid down in the texts of high-souled authors, but in the case of crimes that are not painful, simple death is prescribed as lawful.

CHAPTER TWELEVE

SECTION 87: VIOLATION OF MAIDENS

1. For one violating a maiden of the same *Varna* who has not attained puberty, the punishment shall be the cutting off of the hand or a fine of four.
2. In case she dies, death shall be the punishment.
3. Of one violating a maiden who has attained puberty, the middle and index fingers shall be cut off or a fine of two hundred imposed.
4. And he shall make good the loss to her father.
5. And he shall not have the right to marry her if she is unwilling.
6. If she is willing, there shall be a fine of fiftyfour *panas*; half that, however for the woman.
7. If she has been reserved by the dowry of another, there shall be the cutting off of the hand or a fine of four hundred, as well as the payment of the dowry.
8. A bridegroom not receiving the bride after the betrothal, when she had has seven menstrual periods, shall have the right to her by having relations with her, and he shall not make good the father's loss.

9. The latter forfeits his ownership by his acts making her periods vain.
10. It is no effence for a maiden having menstruation for three years to approach a man of the same *Varna*, after that even a man not of the same *Varna* provided she goes without her ornaments.
11. For taking her father's property, she shall be liable for theft.
12. If a man intending a maiden for another, secures her for himself, the fine shall be two hundred.
13. And he shall not have the right to her if she is unwilling.
14. For showing one maiden and giving another, the fine shall be one hundred if she is of the same *Varna*, double if she is of a lower *Varna*.
15. For a bride, not a virgin at the time of consummation, the fine shall be fiftyfour *panas*, and she shall return the dowry and marriage expenses.
16. If after maintaining that kind of condition she fails, she shall pay double.
17. For substituting other blood, the fine shall be two hundred, also for the man falsely accusing the bride of loss of virginity.
18. And he shall lose the dowry and the expenses.
19. And he shall not have the right to her if she is unwilling.
20. A maiden deflowered by a woman shall pay a fine of twelve *panas* if a willing party and of the same *Varna*; the violating woman shall pay double.
21. If the maiden was unwilling, she shall pay a fine of one hundred and her dowry, for the satisfaction of her passion.
22. A maiden deflowering herself shall become the king's slave.
23. In case a maiden violated outside the village and in case of a false accusation, the fine shall be double.
24. For one abducting a maiden by force, the fine is two hundred; if with gold ornaments the highest.
25. For many persons abducting a maiden, the fines shall be as prescribed for each one separately.
26. For one deflowering a courtesan's daughter, the punishment shall be a fine of fiftyfour *panas* and a dowry to the mother sixteen times the rate for a visit.
27. For one deflowering the daughter of a male or a female slave herself, who is not a slave the fine is twentyfour *panas* and the payment of dowry and ornaments for her.
28. For one violating a female slave due for redemption, the fine is twelve *panas* and the payment of clothes and ornaments.

29. For giving help or accommodation, the punishment shall be the same as for the offender.
30. The husband's kinsman or his servant should keep under guard the wife who misbehaves when the husband is away on a journey.
31. Kept under guard, she should wait for the husband.
32. If the husband were to tolerate, both should be set free.
33. In case he does not tolerate, the punishment shall be the cutting off of the ears and nose for the woman, and the lover shall meet with death.
34. For one making out a paramour as a thief, the fine shall be five hundred; for one releasing him with money, eight times that as fine.
35. Adultery shall be understood as committed when there is mutual caressing of the hair, or from indications of bodily enjoyment, or from the opinion of experts, or from the woman's statement.
36. After rescuing a stranger woman, who was being carried off by enemy troops or foresters, or carried away by a current, or was abandoned in a forest or during a famine, or was left under the impression of her being dead, a man may enjoy her as agreed upon.
37. If she is superior to caste to him or is unwilling, or has children, he shall give her back for a ransom.

38-40. After having rescued a woman belonging to others from the hands of robbers, from the current of a river, from a famine, from a disturbance in the country, from a forest, or when she is lost or left as dead, a man may enjoy her as agreed, but not one who is saved through the power of the king or by her kinsmen, or higher in caste nor one unwilling, nor again one who already has children; such as one; however, he should restore to her kinsmen in return for a suitable ransom.

CHAPTER THIRTEEN

SECTION 88: PUNISHMENTS FOR TRANSGRESSIONS

1. For one making a Brahmin consume drink or food which is unfit for human consumption the fine shall be the highest, the middle for making a Ksatriya do so, the lowest for making a Vaisya do so, a fine of fiftyfour *panas* for making a Sudra do so.
2. Those consuming such things of their own accord shall be exiled from the country.
3. In case of trespass in another's house by day the punishment shall be the lowest fine for violence, by night the middle.

4. For one entering with a weapon by day or by night the fine shall be the highest.
5. A mendicant and trader, an intoxicated and an insane person, very close neighbours when threatened by force or in a calamity, and those whose entry is customary, are not to be punished except when prohibited.
6. For one climbing the enclosing fence of his own house after midnight the punishment shall be the lowest fine for violence, that of another's house middle, also for one breaking the hedge of a village park.
7. Traders in caravans may stay inside the village when their valuables are made known to village officers.
8. What is stolen or killed from among these, the master of the village shall make good, if it has not gone out at night.
9. What is stolen or killed between villages, the Superintendent of Pastures shall make good.
10. In regions without pastures, the officers for catching thieves shall make good.
11. If they are unprotected even then, the villages shall allow a search according to the boundaries as fixed.
12. In the absence of fixing of boundaries, a group of five or ten villages shall allow the search.
13. In case of injury caused by making a rickety house, a cart with the pole at the head unsupported, a weapon without covering, an uncovered hollow or well or a concealed pit, he shall hold it to be a case of physical injury.
14. Once shouting 'get out of the way' when cutting a tree, leading by the rope and an animal under training, using or riding the untamed among quadrupeds, throwing about pieces of wood, clods of earth, stones, sticks, arrows or arms, and in a collision in a carriage or with an elephant, is not to be punished.
15. One desiring to be killed by an enraged elephant shall give one *drona* food, a jar of wine, flowers and unguents and a piece of cloth for wiping the tusks.
16. Death by an elephant is equal to a bath at the end of the horse sacrifice; hence this washing of the feet.
17. In case of death of one not desirous of such a death the highest fine shall be imposed on the driver.
18. For the owner not rescuing a person being injured by a horned or tusked animal of his, the lowest fine for violence shall be the punishment; the middle if he was called to come to the rescue.

19. For one allowing horned or tusked animals to kill one another, the fine shall be that and as much again.
20. For one riding a temple animal, a stud bull or a cow not yet calved the fine shall be five hundred, for killing these the highest.
21. In case of theft of small animals useful for their hair or milk or for riding or stud-purposes, the fine shall be that and as much again, also for killing these, except of rites in honour of gods and the manes.
22. In case of injury when the cart has the nose-strings of the bullocks cut or the yoke broken or when it moves crosswise towards some one or recedes backwards, or when there is a crowd of animals and men, the driver is not to be punished.
23. Otherwise he shall be liable to punishment as prescribed in case of injury to men and animals.
24. And in case of death of non-human animals, the payment of the animal as well shall be enforced.
25. When the driver is a minor, the owner if in the carriage is to be fined; if the owner is not there the person in the carrige or the driver if he has attained majority.
26. The king shall confiscate a carriage in-charge of a minor or one without a man in it.
27. What a magician brings about to another by witchcraft and black magic, that shall be meted out to him.
28. The use of love-winning magic may be allowed towards a wife who does not like her husband, or towards a maiden by a suitor or towards the husband by the wife.
29. Else, in case of injury, the middle fine for violence shall be imposed.
30. For one carnal approaching the sister of his mother or father, his maternal aunt, his preceptor's wife, his daughter-in-law, daughter or sister, the punishment shall be the cutting off of the generating organ and testicles and death thereafter.
31. The woman if willing, shall receive the same, also a woman who has had relations with a slave, a servant or a pledged man.
32. For a Ksatriya having relations with a Brahmin woman, not guarded, the fine shall be the highest, for a Vaisya confiscation of the entire priority; a Sudra shall be burnt in a fire of straw.
33. For having relations with the king's wife, the punishment in all cases shall be cooking in a big jar.
34. For having relations with a Svapaka woman, the man shall go to another land, with the mark of the headless trunk branded on his forehead, or shall become a Svapaka himself if he is a Sudra.

35. For Svapaka having relations with an Arya woman there shall be death, for the woman the cutting off of the ears and nose.
36. For having relations with a woman who has left her home, the fine is twentyfour *panas*.
37. If willing she shall receive the same.
38. For enjoyment of a prostitute by force, the fine shall be twelve *panas*.
39. For many men enjoying forcibly one prostitute, the fine shall be twentyfour *panas* for each one separately.
40. For one approaching a woman elsewhere than in the female organ the lowest fine for violence shall be imposed, also for one misbehaving with a man.
41. A fine of twelve *panas* is prescribed for the senseless wretch who carnally approaches lower animals, and double that for misbehaving with images of gods.
42. In case punishment is inflicted on those not deserving to be punished, thirty times that as a fine for the king shall be placed in water for Varuna and given to Brahmins after that.
43. Thereby the sin of the king arising from the mistake in inflicting punishment is purified. For Varuna is the chastier of kings who behave wrongly towards men.

Herewith ends the Fourth Book of Arthasastra of Kautilya
'THE SUPPRESSION OF CRIMINALS'

19

BOOK FIVE

Secret Conduct

When this Arthasastra was composed by Kautilya (about 330 B.C.), the political situation in the country was fluid in the face of Alexander's (Greek) invasion of India. The Greek troops had almost captured the North-Western region of the Indus-basin and there was no king, powerful enough, to resist the Greek advance towards other parts of the country. The triumphant progress of Alexander had demonstrated the inherent weakness of the Hindustani kings and their administrative machinery, including army. They had no organisation worth the name and no unity of direction. There was no pooling of resources. The Nanda Dynasty was ruling over the whole of the Gangetic plains under the stewardship of Dhanananda, who was avariciously greedy and vicious and most arrogantly different to the welfare of the subjects. The State officials virtually simulated the ruler and their capricious greed for wealth, wine and women made them totally sterile, lethargic and apathetic to the welfare of the State and its subjects. Under these all embracing chaotic conditions, Kautilya dethroned Dhanananda, and installed CANDRAGUPTA MAURYA on the throne of the Magadha and with the help of the latter, Kautilya succeeded in establishing a mighty kingdom in almost throughout Hindustan, and finally driving away the Greeks from the Indian soil. Obviously, Kautilya felt a very strong need to remove all the drawbacks and corrupt tendencies from the administrative machinery and make it very strong, incorruptible, impeccable, and totally faithful to the State and the duties performed by it. Officers of scrupulous probity and integrity and strictest rectitude were needed and to ensure that they do not in any way become delinquent, a close watch and counter-watch on all their activities, professional, as well as domestic, were required to be maintained.

Many of the means suggested by Kautilya appear initially to be unethical but when strategies of espionage, counter-espionage and insurgency have to be deployed, chastity of means are often relegated to the background in the race achieving the desired ends. In the present civilised world such methods are always adopted. Kautilya had dwelt upon all these aspects in this Book on the following subjects:

1. Concerning the Infliction of Secret Punishment. 2. Replenishment of the Treasury. 3. Concerning the Salaries of State Servants. 4. Conduct Proper for a Dependent. 5. Concerning Proper Behaviour for a Courtier. 6. Continuance of the Kingdom, and Continuous Sovereignty. All these constitute the Fifth Book 'Secret Conduct'.

CHAPTER ONE

SECTION 89: CONCERNING THE INFLICTION OF SECRET PUNISHMENT

1. The 'weeding of thorns' from the fortified city and the country has been explained.
2. We shall now explain that from the king and his rulership.
3. The remedy against those principal officers, who live on the king by holding him in their power or who are in league with the enemy, is the employment of secret agents or winning over of seducible parties, as explained before, or secret instigation or spying, as we shall explain in section on the capture of an enemy's town.
4. But against those treasonable principal officers, who cause harm to the kingdom, and who, being favourites or being united, cannot be suppressed openly, he should employ 'silent punishment', finding pleasure in doing this duty.
5. A secret agent, after inciting a brother of the treasonable high officer, not honoured by him, should show him to the king.
6. The king should induce him to fight against the treasonable officer by granting the use of the treasonable man's property.
7. When he has acted with a weapon or poison, he should cause him to be executed on that very ground, declaring, 'He is a murderer of his brother.'
8. By that are explained the *parasava* and the son of a female attendant.
9. Or, a brother, instigated by a secret agent, should demand inheritance from the treasonable officer.
10. As he lies down at the door of the treasonable man's house at night, or when he is staying elsewhere, assassin, slaying him, should declare. 'This claimant of the inheritance is killed.'

11. Then, giving support to the slain man's party, the king should suppress the other.
12. Or, secret agents, staying near the treasonable officer, should threaten the brother claiming inheritance with death.
13. As he at night and so on, as before.
14. When of two treasonable officers, a son has relations with the father's wife or a father with the son's wife or a brother with that of a brother, a fight between the two started by a sharp pupil is explained by the preceding.
15. Or, a secret agent should instigate a son of the treasonable officer thinking highly of himself, suggestion 'You are really the king's son, kept here through fear of the enemy.'
16. When he believes that, the king should honour him in private, 'Though the time for installing you as the crown prince has come, I am not crowning you through fear of the officer.'
17. The secret agent should induce him to murder the officer.
18. When he has acted, the king should cause him to be executed on that very ground, declaring 'He is a parricide'.
19. Or, a female mendicant, agent having won the confidence of the wife of the treasonable officer by means of love-winning potions, should cheat them by the use of poison.
20. Thus, end the stratagems through kinsmen.
21. He should dispatch the treasonable high officer with a weak army containing assassins, for destroying foresters or an enemy's town or for establishing a district officer or a frontier officer in a region separated by a wilderness or for suppressing the domain of a city-officer that has risen in revolt or for seizing a caravan-route on the frontier along with land easily recoverable by the enemy.
22. In the fight, taking place by day or night, assassins or agents appearing as highway robbers should kill him, announcing, 'He was killed during the attack'.
23. Or, when he has gone to a fair or on a pleasure trip, the king should invite treasonable officers to see him.
24. These, entering together with assassins with concealed weapons shall allow a search of their persons in the middle hall for being allowed to enter inside.
25. The assassins, seized by the door-keepers, should say, 'we are engaged by the treasonable officers.'
26. After proclaiming that, they should kill the treasonable men.
27. In place of the assassins, others *i.e.* criminal should be executed.
28. Or, going on a pleasure trip outside the city, he should honour the treasonable men by giving them quarters near him.

29. A woman of bad character, appearing as the queen, should be caught in their quarters at night and so on, as before.
30. Or, he should request the treasonable officer for food by praising 'Your cook or food-preparer is good,' or for a drink, when out on a journey some time.
31 Mixing both those with poison, he should urge the two themselves to taste them first.
32 Having announced that, he should cause them to be slain as poison-givers.
33. Or, an agent appearing as a holy man should make the officer, if he is given to black magic, believe 'You will attain your desires by eating one of the following: a lizard, a tortoise, a crab or an ox with broken horns, which is endowed with auspicious marks.'
34. When he agrees, he should get him killed in the course of the rite by poison or iron clubs, announcing, 'He was killed by a mishap in the rite.'
35. Or, an agent appearing as a physician, after establishing a malignant or incurable disease for the treasonable person, should cheat him with poison in the preparations of medicine or food.
36. Or, agents employed as cooks or food-servers, should cheat the treasonable person by means of poison.
37. Thus, ends the topic of suppression by secret means.
38. As to suppression of two treasonable persons, however:
39. He should dispatch one treasonable person himself accompanied by a weak army and assassins to where the other treasonable person is to be suppressed, saying 'Go, raise an army or money in that fortified city or region; or extract money from the favourite; or, kidnap the favourite's daughter; or, carry out any one of the undertakings, *viz.*, building a fort or an embankment, making a trade-route, setting on new land, starting mines, raising material-forests or elephant-forest; or, carry out the work of a provincial officer or frontier officer; and whoever prevents you or does not give you help should be imprisoned.'
40. In the same way he should send word to the others,'The transgression of so and so should be prevented by you.'
41. When he may be disputing on these occasions for strife or on account of hindrances in his work, assassins should secretly kill him by bringing down their weapon on him.
42. For that offence, the others should be punished.
43. Or, when strife ensues or is raised by assassins on occasions of injury to property, implements, crops or vehicles in connection

with boundaries of villages, fields threshing-floors or houses in treasonable cities, villages or families, or on occasions of shows, ceremonies or festivals, the assassins should bring down their weapons and say 'Thus, are dealt with those who dispute with this person.'

44. For that offence the others should be punished.
45. Or, assasins should set fire to fields, threshing-floors or houses, or bring down their weapons on the kinsmen, relations or draught animals of those treasonable persons whose mutual quarrels are deep-rooted, and say, 'We were engaged by so and so'.
46. For that offence the others should be punished.
47. Or, secret agents should induce treasonable officers in the fortified city and in the country to be one another's guests.
48. There poison-givers should give poison.
49. For that offence the others should be punished.
50. Or, a female mendicant agent should suggest to a treasonable chief in the country, 'The wife, the daughter-in-law or the daughter of treasonable chief in the country is in love with you.'
51. When he consents, she should take his ornaments and show them to the master, saying 'That chief, puffed up with youth, has designs on your wife, daughter-in-law or daughter.'
52. In the quarrel between the two at night and so on, as above.
53. As to treasonable vassals surrendering with troops, however,—the crown prince or the commander-in-chief should do some wrong and, after going away, show fight.
54. Then the king should dispatch against him the treasonable vassals themselves with a weak army containing assassins and so on,—all the stratagems as above.
55. And among their sons surviving them, he who is not disloyal, should get the patrimony.
56. In this way, the kingdom continues in the succession of his sons and grandsons, free from dangers caused by men.
57. He should employ 'silent punishment' towards his own party or that of the enemy, without hesitation, being possessed of forbearance in respect of the future and the present.

CHAPTER TWO

SECTION 90: REPLENISHMENT OF THE TREASURY

1. The king without a treasury should collect a treasury, when difficulties concerning money have arisen.

2. He should demand a third or a fourth part of the grains from a region, whether big or small in size, that is not dependent on rains and yields abundant crops; from a middling or inferior one, according to yield.
3. He should not make a demand on a region useful for building a fort or embankment or trade-routes or new settlements or mining or material forests or elephant forest, or on a region small in size which is on the frontier.
4. He should provide one making a new settlement with grains, cattle, money and other things.
5. He should purchase for money a fourth part of the grains after allowing for seeds and livelihood.
6. He should exempt forest produce and the property of a Brahmin learned in the Vedas.
7. Even that he may purchase so as to favour them.
8. Or, in case that does not serve the purpose, officers of the Administrator should cause preparation of the fields for sowing to be made by farmers in summer.
9. At the time of sowing seeds, they should make a deed of the seeds, laying down a penalty double that which may be lost through negligence.
10. When the crops have ripened, they should prevent the taking of green or ripe grains, except handfuls of vegetables or grains plucked by hand for the purpose of worship of gods and manes and for charity or for the sake of cows.
11. And they should leave remnants of the heap for mendicants and village servants.
12. For one appropriating his own crops, compensation for loss shall be eight-fold.
13. For one stealing another's crops, the penalty for grains shall be fifty-fold, if he is of the same class; death, however, if he is an outsider.
14. They should take a fourth part of grains, a sixth part of wild produce and of goods made of silk-cotton, lac, linen, barks, cotton, wool and silk, medicines, perfumes, flowers, fruits and vegetables, also of wood, bamboos, meat and dried meat, one half of ivory and skins.
15. For one selling these without permission, the punishment shall be the lowest fine for violence.
16. Thus, ends making demands on farmers.

17. Dealers in gold, silver diamonds, gems, pearls, corals, horses and elephants shall pay a tax of fifty.
18. Dealers in yarn, cloth, copper, steel, bronze, perfumes, medicines and wines shall pay a tax of forty.
19. Dealers in grains, liquids and metals and those carrying on trade with carts shall pay a tax of thirty.
20. Traders in glass and major artisans shall pay a tax of twenty.
21. Minor artisans and keepers of harlots shall pay a tax of ten.
22. Dealers in articles of wood and bamboo, stoneware, earthenware, cooked food and green vegetables shall pay a tax of five.
23. Actors and prostitutes shall pay half their wage.
24. They shall recover a tax in cash from those skilled in work, and shall not overlook any offence of theirs.
25. For, these might sell something by representing it as not belonging to them.
26. Thus, ends the topic of making a demand on dealers.
27. Owners of cocks and pigs shall give half; small animals one-sixth; cows, buffaloes, mules, donkeys and camels one-tenth.
28. Keepers of harlots should replenish the treasury through female servants of the king, possessed of great beauty and youth.
29. Thus, ends the making of demands on breeders of animals.
30. The demand is to be made once only not twice.
31. Or, in case that does not serve the purpose, the Administrator, pointing to some work to be done, should ask citizens and country people for contributions.
32. And secret agents should then first give large amounts.
33. Referring to that, the king should ask the citizens and country people for corresponding contributions.
34. And sharp pupils should reproach those who give little.
35. Or, he should ask money of the rich according to their wealth, or according to benefits, conferred on them, or whatever they may offer of their own will.
36. He should bestow on them position, umbrella, turban or decorations in consideration of money.
37. Administrators should bring to the treasury the property of heretical corporations or the property of temples not intended for use by a Brahmin learned in the Vedas, declaring that it was deposited with a person who is dead or whose house is burnt.
38. The Superintendent of Temples should collect the treasures belonging to temples in the fort and in the county in one place, each separately, and bring them, to the treasury in the same manner.

39. Or, after raising at night a god's temple or a sanctuary of a holy person as a miraculous happening, he should live on fairs and festival gatherings.
40. Or, he should proclaim the presence of a divinity by means of a tree in a sanctuary-park endowed with flowers and fruits out of season.
41. Or, agents appearing as holy men after showing danger from an evil spirit in a tree demanding the tax of a human being, should ward it off for the citizens and the country people for money.
42. Or, in a well connected by a subterranean passage he should show a cobra with a number of hoods in return for a gift of money.
43. In a sanctuary hole or an ant-hill hole, he should point to the manifestation of a snake in an image of a cobra concealed inside, and after 'arresting its consciousness' by means of food, should show it to the credulous.
44. To those who do not believe, he should administer poison when they are sipping water or washing themselves and declare it to be a curse of the divinity, or should cause a person condemned to death to be bitten.
45. Or, he should replenish the treasury by offering remedies against occult manifestations.
46. Or, an agent appearing as a trader should trade with plenty of goods and assistants.
47. When he has amassed wealth by entrusted deposits and loans against the value of goods, he should get him robbed at night.
48. By this are explained the Examiner of Coins and the Goldsmith.
49. Or, an agent appearing as a trader, with well-known dealings, should secure on loan or hire a large number of gold and silver articles on the occasion of a festive party.
50. Or, in a festive gathering he should obtain plenty of money and gold as a loan by a display of his entire goods, and also collect the price of each article.
51. Both these, he should cause to be stolen at night.
52. Or, after infatuating men suspected of treason with women appearing as pious ladies, and catching them in the houses of those same women, they should confiscate their entire property.
53. Or, when a dispute has arisen between members of treasonable families, poison-givers, who are employed there, should give poison.
54. For that offence, the others should be deprived of their property.

55. Or, a person condemned to death should demand of a treasonable person, on a credible pretext, a commodity or entrusted money or a loan given or an inheritance.
56. Or, he should address the treasonable person as a slave, or his wife, daughter-in-law or daughter as a slave or as wife.
57. As he lies down at the door of the treasonable person's house or when he stays elsewhere, an assassin, slaying him, should declare 'This fellow, longing for property, has been killed.'
58. For that offence the others should be deprived of their property.
59. Or, an agent appearing as a holy man, after luring a treasonable person with magical lores, should say to him, 'I know the rite for inexhaustible wealth, for opening the doors of the king's palace, for winning a woman's heart, for causing disease to the enemy, for securing a long life or for getting a son.'
60. When he consents, he should cause him to make an offering of plenty of wine, meat and perfumes in a sanctuary at night time.
61. And from a place, where money consisting of a single coin is buried beforehand and where a limb of a corpse or the corpse of an infant may have been placed, he should show him the money and say, 'This is too little.'
62. He should add 'for plenty of money, offering must again be made; hence, with this very money you yourself purchase tomorrow plenty of articles of offering.'
63. He should be arrested while purchasing article of offering with that money.
64. Or, a treasonable person should be charged by a female agent appearing as a mother, saying, 'You have killed my son.'
65. During his night sacrifice or a sacrifice in a forest or when sport in a forest has started, assassins, killing a condemned man due for execution, should smuggle him in.
66. Or, an agent working as a servant of the treasonable person should throw in a false coin in the money received as wages and point that out.
67. Or, an agent appearing as a workman should, while working in the house, place the implements or a thief or a maker of false coins there, or an agent appearing as a physician should place poison there in the guise of medicine.
68. Or, a secret agent close to the treasonable person should communicate through a sharp pupil articles for coronation and a letter from an enemy secretly planted there and should mention their purpose.

69. Thus, he should behave towards treasonable and unrighteous persons, not towards others.
70. He should take from the kingdom fruits as they ripen, as from a garden; he should avoid unripe that causes an uprising for fear of his own destruction.

CHAPTER THREE

SECTION 91: CONCERNING THE ANNUAL SALARIES OF STATE SERVANTS

1. In accordance with the capacity of the fortified city and countryside, he should fix wages for the work of servants at one quarter of the revenue, or by payments to servants that enables the carrying out of works.
2. He should pay regard to the body, of income not cause harm to spiritual good and material advantage.
3. The sacrificial priest, the preceptor, the minister, the chaplain, the commander-in chief, the crown prince, the king's mother and the crowned queen should receive fortyeight thousand *panas*.
4. With this much remuneration, they become insusceptible to instigations and disinclined to revolt.
5. The Chief Palace Usher, the Chief of Palace Guards, the Director, of labour corps, the Administrator and the Director of Stores should receive twentyfour thousand.
6. With this much, they become efficient in their work.
7. The princes, the mothers of princes, the commandant, the city-judge, the director of factories, the council of ministers, the provincial officer and the frontier officer should receive twelve thousand.
8. For, with this much, they help in strengthening the entourage of the master.
9. Heads of banded troops, commandants of elephants, horses and chariot corps, and magistrates should receive eight thousand.
10. For, with this much, they are able to cany their groups with them.
11. Superintendents of infantry, cavalry, chariots and elephants and Guardians of material and elephant forests should receive four thousand.
12. The chariot-fighter, the elephant trainer, the physician, the horsetamer and the carpenter and breeders of animals should receive two thousand.

13. The fortune-teller, the soothsayer, the astrologer, the narrator of Puranas, the charioteer and the bard, the chaplain's men and all superintendents should receive one thousand.
14. Foot-soldiers trained in the fighting arts and the groups of accountants, clerks and others should receive five hundred.
15. But actors should receive two hundred and fifty, and makers of musical instruments should receive double the wage of these.
16. Artisans and artists should receive one hundred and twenty.
17. Servants, valets, attendants and guards of quadrupeds and bipeds and foreman of labourers should receive a wage of sixty, also riders, bandits and mountain-diggers supervised by Aryas, as well as all attendants.
18. Teachers and learned men should receive an honorarium as deserved, a minimum of five hundred and a maximum of one thousand.
19. The average envoy should receive ten *panas per yojana*, a double wage beyond ten up to one hundred *yojanas*.
20. The 'King' should receive three times the fee of those equal in learning at the Rajasuya and other sacrifices.
21. The king's charioteer should get one thousand.
22. Sharp pupils, monks fallen from vow, and agents appearing as householders, traders and ascetics should get one thousand.
23. Village servants, secret agents, assassins, poison-givers and female mendicants should get five hundred.
24. Those moving about for spying should get two hundred and fifty or should have their wage increased according to their efforts.
25. Supervisors of groups of one hundred and one thousand should carry out the payment of food and wages to them, give directions and order their dispersal.
26. There is to be no dispersal in the case of royal property and guarding the fortifications in the city and the country.
27. They shall have permanent heads and many such heads.
28. Of those dying while on duty, the sons and wives shall receive the food and wages.
29. And their minor children, old and sick person should be helped.
30. And he should grant them money and do honour on occasion of death, illness and birth ceremonials.
31. If he has a small treasury, he should give forest produce, cattle and fields and a little money.

32. Or, if he has undertaken the settlement of new lands, he should give only money, not a village, in order that transactions that have taken place in the village may be established.
33. In this manner he should fix different food and wages for regular and casual servants according to their skill and work.
34. Fixing one *adhaka* for a servant with a wage of sixty, he should fix food in accordance with the cash wage.
35. Infantry, cavalry, chariots and elephants should carry out practice in their arts outside the city at sun-rise, except on juncture-days.
36. The king should constantly attend to that, and should frequently inspect their arts.
37. He should allow weapons and armours that are stamped with the king's insignia to be brought into the armoury.
38. Shall move about unarmed, except those permitted with a sealed license.
39. He shall pay double what is lost or destroyed.
40. And he shall keep an account of what has perished.
41. Frontier officers should seize the weapons and armours of caravan traders or allow them to pass after sealing them.
42. Or, when deciding on an expedition, he should make the army ready.
43. Then agents appearing as traders should give all goods to the soldiers at the time of the expedition to be recovered double later.
44. Thus, is made the secret sale of the king's goods as well as the recovery of wages.
45. Looking after income and expenditure in this manner, he does not suffer a calamity of the treasury and the army.
46. Thus, are explained different rates of food and wages.
47. And secret agents, prostitutes, artisans and actors, as well as elders of the army should ascertain, with diligence, the loyalty or disloyalty of soldiers.

CHAPTER FOUR

SECTION 92: CONDUCT PROPER FOR A DEPENDENT

1. One, conversant with the ways of the world, should seek service with a king, endowed with personal excellences and the excellences of material constituents, through such as are dear and beneficial to the king.

2. Or, he should have recourse to even one lacking in material constituents, if he thinks, 'Just as I am desirous of service, so is he desirous of training and is endowed with qualities of one easily approachable,' but never one lacking in personal excellences.
3. For, one lacking in qualities of the self, comes to an end even after receiving mighty sovereignty, as a result of contempt for the political science or as a result of association with harmful persons:
4. After securing an audience with a king endowed with qualities of the self, he should give a test in the political science.
5. For, he attains stability of position by not contradicting the science.
6. Questioned about matters requiring intelligence, he should state what is associated with spiritual and material benefit in the present and in future and what is possible, like an expert, without being afraid of the assembly.
7. If approved, he should stipulate, 'You should not question those, who are not distinguished, concerning spiritual and material wellbeing, nor inflict punishment on those who are associated with powerful persons, nor inflict punishment on the instant on those associated with me; you should not harm my party, my livelihood and my secrets; and by signs I shall prevent you from inflicting punishment under the influence of passion or anger.'
8. If appointed, he should, with permission, enter the place indicated, and should sit at the king's side neither very near nor far, on another seat.
9. He shall not indulge in bellicose talk, nor make statements that are uncultured or not based on personal knowledge or untrustworthy or untrue, nor indulge in loud laughter when there is no joke, nor break wind or spit with a sound.
10. He should avoid a secret talk with another, a quarrelsome remark during a discussion among men, a dress fit for a king or that of gaudy men or clowns, an open request for some jewel or a special favour, contracting one eye or lip, knitting or eye-brows and cutting short a remark when another person in speaking, opposition to those associated with the powerful, association working for a common objective and union with women, persons frequently meeting women, envoys of neighbouring princes, persons belonging to the party of the inimical, persons dismissed and harmful persons.
11. He should declare without loss of time what is in the king's interest, in the company of those dear and beneficial to the king what is in his own interest, at the proper place and time what is in the interest

of another, always what is connected with spiritual and material well-being.

12. When asked, he should declare what is agreeable and beneficial, should not declare what is harmful but agreeable; or, he may, with permission, declare in private what is disagreeable but beneficial, when the king is prepared to listen.

13-14. Or, when making a reply he should remain silent and should not mention enemies and others. Those cast out from his affection may, though competent, become even disagreeable, to him and harmful persons are known to have become favourites as they act according to their knowledge of his inclinations. He may laugh at laughable things, and avoid frightful laughter.

15. He should turn away from another frightful words, and should not himself use frightful words to another, and should tolerate such words addressed to himself, being full of forbearance like the earth.

16. For, self-protection must always be first secured by the wise for, the conduct of those serving a king, has been stated to be like remaining in fire.

17. Fire, when it reaches another, may burn a part or of most the whole body; but a king might kill one along with sons and wife or might cause one to prosper.

CHAPTER FIVE

SECTION 93: CONCERNING PROPER BEHAVIOUR FOR A COURTIER

1. When assigned work, he should show income, cleared of expenses.
2. And he should specify a business that is inner or outer, open or secret, urgent or brooking delay, by saying 'This is of this nature.'
3. He should not humour him by false praises when he is addicted to hunting, gambling wine or women.
4. And remaining near, he should endeavour to wean him from the vice, and should guard him from enemy's instigations, cheating and fraud.
5. And he should observe his gestures and expressions.
6. For, a wise man shows, with his gestures and expressions, a reversal of the pairs of feelings *viz.*, liking and hatred, joy and distress, resoluteness and fear, for concealing his secret counsel.
7. The king is pleased at his sight, accepts his statement, gives him a seat, gives an audience in private, does not oversuspect on an

occasion of suspicion, takes pleasure in his talk, pays regard to him in matters that are to be communicated, tolerates wholesome words spoken, appoints him to a task with a smile, touches him with the hand, does not ridicule him in a praiseworthy matter, speaks of his virtues in his absence, remembers him during meals, goes with him on a pleasure trip, helps him in a calamity, honours, those devoted to him, tells him his secret, increases his honour, does what is advantageous to him, wards off what is harmful—thus is known when the king is satisfied with him.

8. These same reversed are signs of a dissatisfied king and Kautilya has stated more:
9. Anger at sight of him, not listening to and prohibition of his statements, not giving him a seat and not looking at him, change in complexion and voice, contraction of one eye, eye-brow or lip, appearance without cause of sweat, sighs or smile, consultation with another, going away suddenly, making another prosper, scratching the ground or limbs, goading another against him, showing contempt for his learning, *varna* or country, censure of those with a like offence, censure of every single offence, praise of those against him, not paying regard to his good deeds, mentioning his evil deeds, paying attention at the back, extreme indifference, telling him a falsehood, and a difference in the behaviour towards him of those who frequently see the king.
10. And he should observe the change in behaviour even of non-human beings.
11. 'He is sprinkling water from on high,' with this thought Katyanana left his king's service; 'The heron (is flying) towards the left,' with his Kaninka Bharadvaja; 'Ah, grass,' with this Dirgha Carayana; 'The garment is cold,' with his Ghotamukha left 'The elephant has sprinkled water,' with this Kinjalka left 'He has praised the chariot and horse,' with this Pisuna left; at the barking of the dog, the son of Pisuna left.
12. And in case of deprival of emoluments and honour, leaving of the service of the king is recommended.
13. Or, knowing the master's character and his own offence, he should remedy it.
14. Or, he should approach his ally who may be close to him.
15. And staying there, he should, through friends, carry out the removal of his offence toward the master; then he should return again while the king is alive or when he is dead.

CHAPTER SIX

SECTION 94: CONTINUANCE OF THE KINGDOM

SECTION 95: CONTINUOUS SOVEREIGNTY

1. The minister should take steps in case of a calamity of the king in the following manner:
2. Even before there is fear of the danger of the king's death, he should, by winning the support of those dear and beneficial to the king, establish audience with the king at intervals of one month or two, under the pretext that, 'The king is engaged in a rite for removing the troubles of the country or for destroying enemies or for securing long life or for getting a son.'
3. He should show, at a time when the appearance cannot be distinguished, a person appearing like the king to the subjects and to the envoys of allies and enemies.
4. And he should hold suitable conversation with them through the minister.
5. And through the Chief Usher and the Chief of Palace Guards, he should cause the king's daily duties to be carried out as described before.
6. And towards those who do harm, he should cause disfavour to be shown as it may be pleasing to the subjects, favour only towards those who have conferred benefits.
7. He should cause the treasury and the army to be collected in one place, in the fortified city or on the frontier, in charge of trustworthy men, also being together members of the family, princes and principal officers under some pretext.
8. And if any principal officer, with a strong party, stationed in the fort or a forest, were to show hostility, he should get him won over.
9. Or, he should send him on an expedition full of dangers or to an ally's family.
10. And he should cause that vassal, from whom he apprehends danger, to be brought under control under the pretext of a festival, a wedding, an elephant hunt, a horse-sale, or grant of land, or through his own ally.
11. Then he should enter into a treaty that would be inviolable.
12. Or, he should bring about enmity of the vassal with forest chiefs or enemies.
13. Or, he should win over a pretender from his family or a prince in disfavour by the promise of a part of his territory.
14. Or, winning the support of members of the royal family, princes and principal officers, he should show a prince as already crowned.

15. Or, he should cause the administration to be carried on by weeding out the thorns of the kingdom in the manner described in the section 'Infliction of Punishment'.
16. If, however, any principal officer or any one of the vassals were to rise in revolt, he should invite him, saying, 'Come here, I shall make you the king,' and get him killed.
17. Or, he should get rid of him by using 'Remedies against Troubles'.
18. Or, after gradually transferring the burden of the kingdom to the crown prince, he should announce the calamity of the king.
19. In case the calamity has befallen the king in enemy territory, during war he should secure a treaty with the enemy through an ally posing as a foe and retire.
21. Or, after crowning the prince, he should fight back.
22. Or, if attacked by the enemy, he should use 'Remedies against Troubles' as described.
23. 'In this way the minister should secure continuous sovereignty,' says Kautilya.
24. 'Not so,' says Bharadvaja.
25. 'When the king is dying, the minister should make members of the family, princes and principal officers fight against one another or against other principal officers.'
26. When any one fights, he should get him slain by a rising of the subjects.
27. Or, getting rid of members of the family, princes and principal officers by silent punishment, he should seize the kingdom himself.
28. For, for the sake of the kingdom, the father fights with sons and the sons with the father, what to say then of the constituent, namely, the minister, the one support of the kingdom?
29. He should not disdain that when it has come to him of its own accord.
30. "A woman approaching of her own accord curses if discarded," such is a saying among the people.
31. 'Time comes but once to a man waiting for an opportunity; that time is difficult for that man to get again when he wants to do his work.'
32. 'This incites subjects to revolt, is unrighteous and uncertain as to result,' says Kautilya.
33. He should place on the throne a prince possessed of qualities of the self.
34. In the absence of one so endowed, he should call together high officers and, introducing a prince not addicted to vice or a princess or the queen *enceinte* should say, 'This is a trust with you; pay regard

to his father as well as to your goodness and noble birth; he is only an emblem, you alone are masters; or, what else should be done?'

35. When he says this, secret among them agents should say, 'Who else but this king, with you to guide him, would be able to protect the four *varnas*?'
36. Saying 'So be it,' the minister should invest with authority the prince or the princess or the *enceinte* queen and should introduce him or her to kinsmen and relations and to the envoys of allies and enemies.
37. He should cause an increase in the provisions and salaries of ministers and soldiers, and say, 'When grown up, this prince will again give a rise.'
38. Thus, he should speak to the principal officers in the fort and the country, and to parties of allies and enemies he should speak as deserved.
39. And he should strive to give training to the prince.
40. Or, after getting an offspring begotten on the princes by a man of the same caste, he should crown him.
41. Through fear of change of the mother's mind, he should keep near her a member of the family with small spirit and a young boy with auspicious marks.
42. And during the monthly periods he should guard her.
43. And he should not cause any excellent object of pleasure to be made for his own use.
44. For the king, however, he should cause belongings like carriages, riding animals, ornaments, dresses, women and houses, to be provided.
45. And when he has attained youth, he should ask for rest, to find out his inclination; he should leave him if he is not satisfied and continue to guard him if he is satisfied.
46. Or, if he has fallen from favour, he should repair to a forest or engage in a long sacrificial session after instructing select secret retinue to guard the prince.
47. Or, if the king is under the influence of principal officers, he, well conversant with the science of politics, should enlighten him through historical and mythological tales, with the support of those dear to king.
48. Or, putting on the appearance of a holy man and resorting to secret practices, he should get hold of the king and after getting hold of him should employ 'the Infliction of Punishment' against the treasonable.

Herewith ends the Fifth Book of the Arthasastra of Kautilya

'SECRET CONDUCT'

20

BOOK SIX

Circle of Kings as the Basis

According to the ancient Indian traditions, the scope of political science is to embrace all human activities, *vis-a-vis*, all aspects of human life and relations. Righteousness in all human pursuits was repeatedly advocated, as without which the high ends of life are impossible to be achieved. Every human being, whether a king or a commoner, was excepted to strive hard in his life to achieve the four high ends of life in order to redeem himself from the cycles of rebirth. They are: 'Virtue, Profit, Pleasure' and called the 'TRIPPLE AGGREGATE' and are supplemented by the fourth 'EMANCIPATION OF SOUL'. But as in this world men are prone to violate these religious edicts, it was then felt absolutely necessary to install an authority which would compel men to conform to these spiritual dictates and punish the aberrants or the delinquents, and maintain the socio-political order of the community. This authority was the king who was accordingly vested with the power to control the delinquents and remedy their behaviour in consonance with the spiritual dictates. Like other countries of the world, the king in India was not of divine origin, nor were his powers absolute; and he was never permitted to be a despotic ruler, although his appointment was mostly hereditary. People made him the trustee of the entire realm placed under his protection. He was merely the office bearer, and the trust was the growth of the country in area and prosperity; and the care of the material and moral well-being of the subjects. He was never considered the proprietor of the land under his sovereignty. The State in ancient India was an association in the nature of the trust created by the subjects to guard their interest according to the spiritual edicts. Therefore, the king was not entrusted with the functions of legislation. The administration of justice and the execution of laws; and the protection of the State as a whole and its subjects were the cardinal functions. The king was not allowed to rule the State all by himself and according to his likes and dislikes. He was to administer his realm with the advice and assistance of capable ministers whose morality, wisdom and administrative acumen were always superlative and beyond question, or suspicion. It was also observed that no one who had not attained the age of 50 years was considered competent to hold the post. Out of the prescribed total of thirtyseven ministers, four were Brahmins, eight Ksatriyas and twentyone Vaisyas, four Sudras (Mahabharata). Thus, there were representatives from all the four *Varnas*, and together they helped the king in the overall administration of the State and secured and also ensured its well-being along with that of the subjects. Their selection was based on such qualities as were prescribed and possessed by them (unlike the current position in the country). Each one of them was supposed to be excellent in his respective sphere. With such a tradition of generation in view, Kautilya had composed this Book and dealt with the following subjects:

1. Excellences of the Constituents, and 2. Concerning Peace and Activity.

CHAPTER ONE

SECTION 96: EXCELLENCES OF THE CONSTITUENT ELEMENTS

1. The king, the minister, the country, the fortified city, the treasury, the army and the ally are the constituent elements of the state.
2. Among them, the excellences of the king are:
3. Born in a high family, endowed with good fortune, intelligence and spirit, given to seeing elders, pious, truthful in speech, not breaking his promise, grateful, liberal, of great energy, not dilatory with weak neighbouring princes, resolute, not having a mean council of ministers, desirous of training,—these are the qualities of one easily approachable.
4. Desire to learn, listening, learning, retention, thorough understanding, reflecting, rejecting false views and intentness on truth,—these are the qualities of intellect.
5. Bravery, resentment, quickness and dexterity,—these are the qualities of energy.

6. Eloquent, bold, endowed with memory, intellect and strength, exalted, easy to manage, trained in arts, free from vices, able to lead the army, able to requite obligations and injury in the prescribed manner, possessed of a sense of shame, able to take suitable action in calamities and in normal conditions, seeing long and far, attaching prominence to undertakings at the proper place and time and with appropriate human endeavour, able to discriminate between peace and fighting, giving and withholding, and observance of conditions and striking at the enemy's weak points, well-guarded, not laughing in an undignified manner, with a glance which is straight and without a frown, devoid of passion, anger, greed, stiffness, fickleness, troublesomeness and slanderousness, sweet in speech, speaking with a smile and with dignity, with conduct conforming to the advice of elders,—these are personal excellences.
7. The excellences of a minister have been stated before.
8. Possessed of strong positions in the centre and at the frontiers, capable of sustaining itself and others in times of distress, easy to protect, providing excellent means of livelihood, malevolent towards enemies with weak neighbouring princes, devoid of mud, stones, salty ground, uneven land, thorns, bands, wild animals, deer and forest tribes, charming, endowed with agricultural land, mines, material forests and elephant forests, beneficial to cattle, beneficial to men, with protected pastures, rich in animals, not depending on rain for water, provided with water routes and land routes, with valuable, manifold and plenty of commodities, capable of bearing fines and taxes, with farmers devoted to work, with a wise master, inhabited mostly by the lower *varnas*, with men loyal and honest,—these are the excellences of a country.
9. The excellences of a fort have been stated before.
10. Acquired lawfully by the ancestors or by oneself, consisting mostly of gold and silver, containing various kinds of big jewels and cash, one that would withstand a calamity even of a long duration in which there is no income,—these are the excellences of a treasury.
11. Inherited from the father and the grandfather, constant, obedient, with the soldiers' sons and wives contented, not disappointed during marches, unhindered everywhere, able to put up with troubles, that has fought many battles, skilled in the science of all types of war and weapons, not having a separate interest because of prosperity and adversity shared with the king, consisting mostly of Ksatriyas,—these are the excellences of an army.

12. Allied from the days of the father and the grandfather, constant, under control, not having a separate interest, great, able to mobilise quickly,—these are the excellences of an ally.
13. Not of royal descent, greedy, with a mean council of ministers with disaffected subjects, unjust in behaviour, not applying himself to duties, vicious, devoid of energy, trusting in fate, doing whatever pleases him, without shelter, without a following, impotent, ever doing harm to others—these are excellences in an enemy.
14. For, an enemy of this type becomes easy to exterminate.
15. Excluding the enemy, these seven constituent elements have been described with each one's excellences manifest; those, when they operate, become subordinate to the excellences of the king.
16. A king endowed with personal qualities endows with excellences the constituent elements not so endowed. One not endowed with personal qualities destroys the constituent elements that are prosperous and devoted to him.
17. Then that king not endowed with personal qualities, with defective constituent elements, is either killed by the subjects or subjugated by the enemies, even if he be ruler up to the four ends of the earth.
18. But one possessed of personal qualities, though ruling over a small territory, being united with the excellences of the constituent elements, and conversant with the science of politics, does conquer the entire earth, never loses.

CHAPTER TWO

SECTION 97: CONCERNING PEACE AND ACTIVITY

1. Peace and activity constitute the source of acquisition and security.
2. Activity is that which brings about the accomplishment of works undertaken.
3. Peace is that which brings about security of enjoyment of the fruits of works.
4. The source of peace and activity is the six-fold policy.
5. Decline, stability and advancement are the consequences of that policy.
6. Acts of human agency are good policy and bad policy; of divine agency good fortune and misfortune.
7. For, it is acts of human and divine agency that make the world go.
8. That caused by an unseen agency is the divine act.
9. In that, the attainment of the desired fruit is good fortune; of undesired, fruit misfortune.

10. That caused by a seen agency is the human act.
11. In that, the coming into being of well-being is good policy; its ruin, bad policy.
12. That can be thought about; the divine is incalculable.
13. The king, endowed with personal excellences and those of his material constituents, the seat of good policy, is the would-be conqueror.
14. Encircling him on all sides, with territory immediately next to his is the constituent called the enemy.
15. In the same manner, with territory separated by one other territory is the constituent called the ally.
16. A neighbouring prince possessed of the excellences of an enemy is the foe; one in calamity is vulnerable; one without support or with a weak support is fit to be exterminated; in the reverse case, fit to be harassed or weakened.
17. These are the different types of enemies.
18. Beyond him, the ally, the enemy's ally, the ally's ally, and the enemy's ally's ally are situated in front in accordance with the proximity of the territories; behind, the enemy in the rear, the ally in the rear, the rear enemy's ally and the rear ally's ally one behind the other.
19. One with immediately proximate territory is the natural enemy; one of equal birth is the enemy by birth; one opposed or in opposition is the enemy made for the time being.
20. One with territory separated by one other is the natural ally; one related through the mother or father is the ally by birth; one who has sought shelter for wealth or life is the ally made for the time being.
21. One with territory immediately proximate to those of the enemy and the conqueror, capable of helping them when they are united or disunited and of suppressing them when they are disunited, is the middle king.
22. One outside the sphere of the enemy, the conqueror and the middle king, stronger than their constituents, capable of helping the enemy, the conqueror and the middle king when they are united or disunited and of suppressing them when they are disunited, is the neutral king.
23. These are the constituent of the circle of kings.
24. Or, the conqueror, the ally and the ally's ally are the three constituents of this circle of kings.

25. They, each individually united with its five constituent elements, the minister, the country, the fort, the treasury and the army, constitute the eighteen-fold circle.
26. By that is explained a separate circle for each of the enemy, the middle and the neutral kings.
27. Thus, there is a collection of four circles.
28. There are twelve constituents who are kings, sixty material constituents, a total of seventy-two in all.
29. Each of these has its own peculiar excellences.
30. Power and success are to be explained.
31. Power is possession of strength.
32. Success is obtaining happiness.
33. Power is three-fold: the power of knowledge is the power of counsel, the power of the treasury and the army is the power of might, the power of valour is the power of energy.
34. In the same way, success is also three-fold: that attainable by the power of counsel is success by counsel, that attainable by the power of might is success by might, that attainable by the power of energy is success by energy.
35. Thriving with these, the king becomes superior; reduced in these, inferior; with equal powers, equal.
36. Therefore, he should endeavour to endow himself with power and success, or, if similar, to endow with power and success the material constituents in accordance with their immediate proximity or integrity.
37. Or, he should endeavour to detract these from treasonable persons and enemies.
38. Or, if he were to see, 'My enemy, possessed of power, will injure his subjects with verbal or physical injury or appropriation of their property, or, when endowed with success, will become negligent because of addiction to hunting, gambling, wine or women, thus with subjects disaffected or himself become weakened or remiss, he will be easy to overpower for me; or, being attacked in war, he will remain in one place or not in his fort, with all his troops collected together, thus with his army brought together, and himself separated from his ally and fort, he will be easy to overpower for me; or, he will render help to me when I am attacked by a strong king thinking, "The strong king is desirous of exterminating my enemy elsewhere; after exterminating him, he might exterminate me," or help me when my undertakings have failed; and when

seeking to seize the middle king the enemy's help is needed—for these and other reasons, he may wish power and success even to the enemy.

39. Making the kings separated by one intervening territory the felly and those immediately proximate the spokes, the leader should stretch himself out as the hub in the circle of constituents.
40. For, the enemy situated between the two, the leader and the ally, becomes easy to exterminate or to harass, even if strong.

Herewith Ends the Sixth Book of the Arthasastra of Kautilya

'THE CIRCLE OF KINGS AS THE BASIS'

Please seen figures (a) and (b) for Circle of Kings.

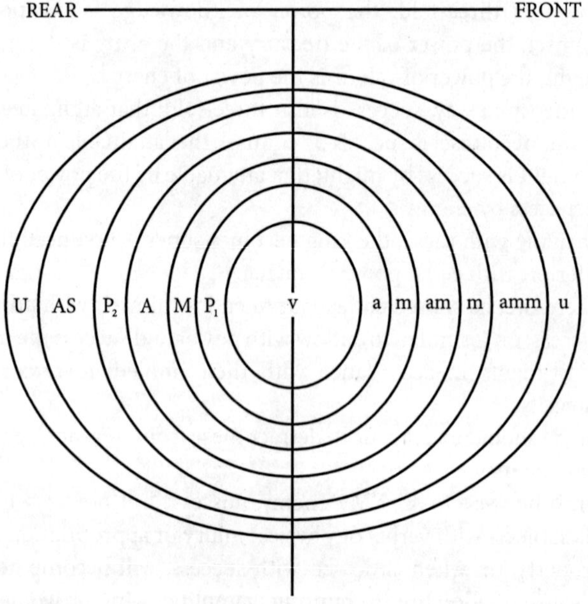

Fig. (a): Simplified View of Rajmandal Circle of kings

V: Vijigisu; a: ari; m: mitra; am: arimitra; mm: mitramitra; amm: arimitramitra; P1: parsnigraha; M: Madhyam; A: akranda: P2: parsnigrahasara; AS: akrandasara; U: Udasin

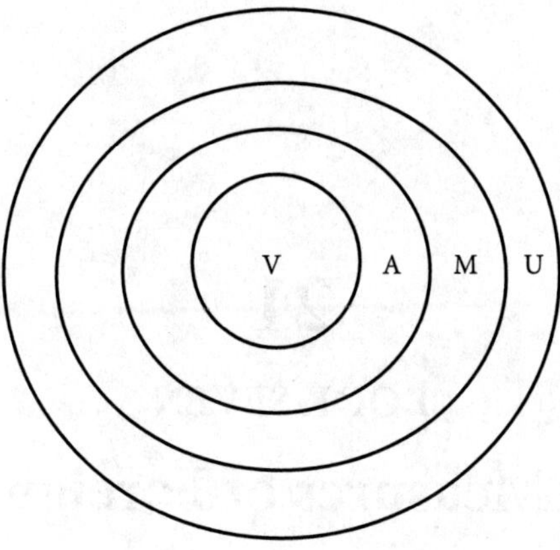

Fig. (b) Complex View of Rajmandal Circle of King
V: Vijigisu: A: Arl; M: Madhyam; Udasina (would be) (enemy)
(Middle) (Netural) (Conqueror)

21

BOOK SEVEN

The Six Measures of Foreign Policy

During the period of the Nanda Dynasty, the Hindu, Buddha and Jain religions had under their sway the population of the Empire (329 B.C.). However, during the rule of Candragupta Maurya (317-293 B.C.) Vedic religion, as propounded by Kautilya, was generally accepted by the people, more because the king himself had patronised it. The foundation of the Maurya Empire was the unique event in the Hindustani History. Its glory enhanced by the circumstances in which it was acquired. It was achieved against formidable difficulties created by the establishment of a foreign rule in the country as a consequence of Alexander's victorious campaigns in the north-west Hindustan during the shortest ever period of two years in the world history. A huge Mauryan Empire sprang into existence unifying innumerable fragments of distracted Hindustan. Gigantic world-wide religious movements were initiated, and with the flourishing of trade with the foreign countries the affairs of a secluded Hindustan were brought into close touch with those of the outer world. Religious rivalries culminating in hostilities at various places erupted. The smaller states and tributaries which were brought under the suzerainty of the Mauryan Empire required constant surveillance, vigilance in order to check and thwart any attempt at cessation from the Empire, which happened to be surrounded from all sides by such states, which were either conquered, or chose to be federated with the Mauryan Empire. A love-hate relationship existed almost throughout the Empire. The political situation was fluid and the society had become vulnerable. Obviously, Kautilya was fully conversant with these conditions; and in order to suppress and overcome them he had ingeniously formulated the foreign policy of the Mauryan Empire taking carefully into account all conceivable situations, devices and subterfuges which were required to be deployed by the king for safety, security, and stability of the Empire. The various functions discussed by Kautilya cover the following topics: 1. Enumeration of the Six Measures of Foreign Policy, Determination of measures of Decline, Stable Condition and Advancement, 2. Conduct when Seeking Shelter, 3. Adherence to Policies by the Equal, The Weaker and the Stronger King. Peace-treaties by the Weaker King, 4. Staying Quiet after Making War, Staying Quiet after Making Peace, Marching after Making War, Marching after Making Peace, Marching together with other kings, 5. Considerations regarding an Attack on a Vulnerable King and the Enemy, Causes leading to Decline. Greed and Disaffection among the Subjects, Reflection on Confederated Allies, 6. Concerning the March of Two Kings who have entered into a Treaty of Alliance, Treaties with Stipulations, without Stipulations and with Deserters, 7. Peace and War Connected with the Dual Policy, 8. Conduct for the King about to be Attacked. The Different Kinds of Allies Fit to be Helped, 9-12. Pacts for securing an Ally, Money, Land and an Undertaking, 13. Considerations regarding the King Attacking in the Rear, 14. Recoupment of Powers that have become Weak, 15. Reasons for Entrenching Oneself after Making War with a Powerful King, Conduct for the King Surrendering with his Troops, 16. Conduct Proper for the King Subjugating by Force, 17. The Making of Peace, Liberation of the Hostage, 18. Conduct towards the Middle King, Conduct towards the Neutral King, Conduct towards the Circle of Kings, — These constitute the seventh Book 'The Six Measures of Foreign Policy.'

CHAPTER ONE

SECTION 98: ENUMERATION OF THE SIX MEASURES OF FOREIGN POLICY

SECTION 99: DETERMINATION OF MEASURES IN DECLINE, STABLE CONDITION AND ADVANCEMENT

1. The circle of constituent elements is the basis of the six measures of foreign policy.
2. 'Peace, war, staying quiet, marching, seeking shelter and dual policy constitute the six measures,' say the teachers.
3. 'There are only two measures,' says Vatavyadhi.
4. 'For, out of peace and war the six measures come into being.'
5. 'These are really six measures, because of differences in the situations,' say Kautilya.
6. Among them, entering into a treaty is peace.

7. Doing injury is war.
8. Remaining indifferent is staying quiet.
9. Augmentation of power is marching.
10. Submitting to another is seeking shelter.
11. Resorting to peace with one and war with another is dual policy.
12. These are the six measures of foreign policy.
13. When in decline as compared to the enemy, he should make peace.
14. When prospering, he should make war.
15. When he thinks 'The enemy is not able to do harm to me, nor I to him,' he should stay quiet.
16. When possessed of a preponderance of excellent qualities, he should march.
17. Depleted in power, he should seek shelter.
18. In a work that can be achieved with the help of an associate, he should resort to a dual policy.
19. Thus, are the measures established.
20. Of them, he should follow that policy by resorting to which he may be able to see, 'By resorting to this, I shall be able to promote my own undertakings concerning forts, water-works, trade-routes, setting on waste land, mines, material forests and elephant forests, and to injure these undertakings of the enemy.'
21. That is advancement.
22. Perceiving 'My advancement will be quicker or greater or leading to a greater advancement in the future, the reverse will be that of the enemy,' he should remain indifferent to the enemy's advancement.
23. In case the advancement takes the same time or bears an equal fruit for both, he should make peace.
24. He should not follow that policy by resorting to which he were to see the ruin of his own undertakings, not of those of the other party.
25. This is decline.
26. Perceiving 'I shall decline after a longer time or to a lesser extent or in such a way that I shall make a greater advancement, the enemy will decline in the reverse manner,' he should remain indifferent to his decline.
27. In case the decline lasts for the same period or leads to equal results for both, he should make peace.
28. The policy, following which he were to see neither the advancement nor the decline of his own undertakings, constitutes stable condition.

29. Perceiving 'I shall remain stable for a shorter period or in such a way that I shall make a greater advancement, the enemy will do so in the opposite way,' he should remain indifferent to his stable condition.
30. 'In case the stable condition lasts for the same period or leads to equal consequences for both, he should make peace,' say the teachers.
31. 'This is not disputed', says Kautilya.
32. Or, if he were to see, 'Remaining at peace, I shall ruin the enemy's undertaking by my own undertakings bearing abundant fruits; or, I shall enjoy my own undertakings bearing abundant fruits or the undertakings of the enemy; or, by creating confidence by means of the peace, I shall ruin the the enemy's undertakings by the employment of secret remedies and occult practices; or, I shall easily entice away the persons capable of carrying out the enemy's undertakings by offering a greater remuneration from my own undertakings, with facilities of favours and exemptions; or, the enemy, in alliance with a extremely strong king, will suffer the ruin of his own undertakings; or, I shall keep prolonged his war with the king, being at war with whom he is in alliance with me but is hostile to me; or, his country, laid waste by his enemy, will come to me, so that I shall achieve advancement in my undertakings; or, the enemy, with his undertakings ruined and himself placed in a difficult situation, would not attack my undertakings; or with my undertakings started elsewhere, I shall achieve advancement in my undertaking, being in alliance with both; or, by making peace with the enemy I shall divide from him the circle of kings which is attached to the enemy, and when divided, I shall secure it for myself; or, by giving support to the enemy by favouring him with troops when he seeks to seize the circle, I shall create hostility towards him, and when he faces hostility I shall get him destroyed by that same circle,' he should secure advancement through peace.
33. Or, if he were to see, 'My country, consisting mostly of martial people or fighting bands, or secure in the protection of a single entrance through a mountain-fort, a forest-fort or a river-fort, will be able to repulse the enemy's attack; or taking shelter in an impregnable fort on the border of my territory, I shall be able to ruin the enemy's undertaking; or the enemy, with his energy sapped by the troubles caused by a calamity, has reached a time when his undertakings face ruin or, when he is fighting elsewhere, I shall

be able to carry off his country,' he should secure advancement by resorting to war.

34. Or, if he were to think, 'The enemy is not able to ruin my undertakings nor am I able to ruin his undertakings; or, when he is in a calamity, or engaged as in a conflict between a hound and a boar, I shall advance myself, being intent on carrying out my own undertakings,' he should secure advancement by staying quiet.
35. Or, if he were to think, 'The ruin of the enemy's undertakings, can be brought about by marching, and I have taken steps to secure the protection or my own undertakings,' he should secure advancement by marching.
36. Or, if he were to think, 'I am not able to ruin the enemy's undertakings nor to avert the ruin of my own undertakings,' he should seek shelter with a strong king and by carrying out his own undertakings, should seek to progress from decline to stable condition and from stable condition to advancement.
37. Or, if he were to think, 'I shall promote my own undertakings by peace on one side and ruin the enemy's undertakings by war on the other side,' he should secure advancement through a dual policy.
38. Situated in the circle of constituent elements, he should, in this manner, with these six measures of policy, seek to progress from decline to stable condition and from stable condition to advancement in his own undertakings.

CHAPTER TWO

SECTION 100: CONDUCT WHEN SEEKING SHELTER

1. If there is equal advancement in peace or war, he should resort to peace.
2. For, in war there are losses, expenses, marches away from home and hindrances.
3. By that is explained preference for staying quiet, as between staying quiet marching.
4. As between dual policy and seeking shelter, he should resort to dual policy.
5. For, he who resorts to the dual policy, giving prominence to his own undertakings, serves only his own interests, while he who takes shelter with another serves the interests of the other, not his own.
6. He should seek shelter with one whose strength is superior to the strength of the neighbouring enemy.

7. In the absence of one superior in strength to him, he should seek shelter with the enemy himself and, remaining out of sight, should try to serve him with any one of the three: treasury, army and territory.
8. For, union with one superior in strength is a great danger to kings, except when he is at war with an enemy.
9. If this be impossible, he should behave like one submitting with troops.
10. And when he sees that the enemy is afflicted by a fatal disease or is facing an internal revolt or a growth in power of his enemy or a calamity of his ally and sees thereby his own advancement, he should go away under a plausible pretext of illness or the performance of a religious duty.
11. Or, if he is in his own territory, he should not go to him.
12. Or, if near him, he should strike in his weak points.
13. Or, if situated between two stronger kings, he should seek shelter with one capable of protecting him, or with one whose intervening weak neighbour he may be, or with both.
14. He should resort to the potsherd-treaty, declaring one to the other as plotting to seize his patrimony.
15. Or, he should employ dissension between the two by falsely implicating one against the other, and use silent punishment when they are in discord.
16. Or, if situated at the side of two strong kings, he should take steps against immediate danger.
17. Or, taking shelter in a fort, he should resort to the dual policy.
18. Or, he should act on motives for resorting to peace or war.
19. He should give support to the treasonable officers, the enemies and forest chiefs of both.
20. Going over to one of these two, he should strike in the other's calamity with these same treasonable officers, etc.
21. Or, if pressed by both, he should resort to the circle of kings for shelter, or find shelter with the middle or the neutral king.
22. Together with him, he should support one and exterminate the other, or exterminate both.
23. Or, if exterminated by both, he should find shelter with the justly behaved from among the middle king, the neutral king or kings belonging to their parties.
24. From among those equally just, he should resort to that king whose constituents would give him happiness or by staying with whom he

would be able to raise himself or where his ancestors may have been accustomed to go or he may have close connections or where there may be many or very powerful friends.

25. He to whom he may be dear or he who may be dear to him, which one among these two should he approach for shelter? He should go to him to whom he may be dear. This is the best course for seeking shelter.

CHAPTER THREE

SECTION 101: ADHERENCE TO POLICIES BY THE EQUAL, THE WEAKER AND THE STRONGER KINGS

SECTION 102: PEACE-TREATIES BY THE WEAKER KING

1. The conqueror should employ the six measures of policy with due regard to his power.
2. He should make peace with the equal and the stronger; he should make war with the weaker.
3. For, going to war with the stronger, he engages as it were in a fight on foot with an elephant.
4. And at war with the equal, he brings about loss on both sides, like an unbaked jar struck by an unbaked jar.
5. At war with the weaker, he attains absolute success, like a stone with an earthen vessel.
6. If the stronger were not to desire peace, he should resort to the conduct of one submitting with troops or measures recommended for the weaker king.
7. If the equal were not to desire peace, he should do harm to him in return to the extent that he may have done to him.
8. For, heat is the means of joining together.
9. Metal that is not heated does not become joined with metal.
10. If the weaker were to remain submissive in all respects, he should make peace with him.
11. For, heroism born of grief and resentment makes one fight bravely like a forest fire.
12. And he becomes the object of favour of the circle of kings.
13. If, when at peace, he were to see, 'The enemy's subjects, who are greedy or impoverished or rebellious, do not come over to me through fear of being seized again by the enemy,' even the weaker should make war.
14. If, when at war, he were to see, 'The enemy's subjects, greedy, impoverished or rebellious, do not come over, being frightened of

war,' even the stronger should make peace, or should allay the fear of war.

15. Even in case of simultaneity of calamities, if he were to see,'I am in a greater calamity; the enemy in a lighter calamity, will easily overcome his own calamity and attack me,' even the stronger should make peace.
16. If by resorting to peace or war, he were not to see the weakening of the enemy or increase in his own strength, then even the stronger should stay quiet.
17. If he were to see the enemy's calamity to be irremediable, then even the weaker should march against him.
18. Even the stronger, whose immediate calamity is irremediable, should seek shelter.
19. If he were to see success in his work by peace in one place and war in another, then even the stronger should resort to the dual policy.
20. Similar is the use of six measures by the equal.
21. With regard to that, however, the special points are:
22. A weak king, overrun by a strong king who has set his armies in motion, should quickly submit, seeking peace with the offer of his treasury, army, himself or territory.
23. That he himself has to wait upon the enemy with a stipulated number of troops or according to the strength of the army, this treaty is known as 'one with himself as prey'.
24. That the commander-in-chief or the crown prince has to wait upon the enemy, this would be 'the treaty through another person,' not through himself, hence one in which he himself is saved.
25. Either himself or the army has to go elsewhere alone; this treaty is 'with persons unseen', in which the army chiefs and he himself are saved.
26. In the first two treaties, he should bring about a marriage alliance of the chiefs; in the last, however, he should secretly get rid of the enemy. These are treaties with troops submitted.

27-28. The release of the rest of the constituents by handing over the treasury would become the treaty 'purchase.' And the same, when it is to be delivered in parts many times, at one's convenience, should be known as the treaty 'support'; the tribute restricted as to time and place, would be support.

29. Tolerable because of payment of a bearable amount in future, even because of a marriage alliance, it would be the 'golden treaty', bringing about union through mutual confidence.

30. The reverse would be the 'potsherd' treaty, so called because of excessive payments received. In the first two treaties, he should deliver forest produce, or elephants and horses that are poisoned.
31. In the third, he should pay the amount; in the fourth, he should tarry telling him of the decline of undertakings. These are treaties with treasury submitted.
32. The saving of the rest of the constituents by the surrender of a part of his territory is the 'directed' treaty, desirable in the case where one wishes to injure through secret agents and robbers.
33. The surrender of lands from which all riches have been removed, with the exception of his base, is the 'exterminated' treaty, desirable in the case where one hopes for a calamity for the enemy.
34. The saving of lands by the surrender of the produce is the 'hire' treaty.
35. He should resort to waiting in the first two, in the last two, however to 'practices of the weaker king', taking the produce himself. These are treaties with territory surrendered.
36. These three types of treaties by the weaker king recommended for use at the proper place and time in accordance with one's own undertakings, should be entered into as 'practices of the weaker king.'

CHAPTER FOUR

SECTION 103: STAYING QUIET AFTER MAKING WAR

SECTION 104: STAYING QUIET AFTER MAKING PEACE

SECTION 105: MARCHING AFTER MAKING WAR

SECTION 106: MARCHING AFTER MAKING PEACE

SECTION 107: MARCHING TOGETHER WITH OTHER KINGS

1. Staying quiet and marching in peace and war now explained.
2. Remaining still, staying quiet and remaining indifferent are synonyms of staying quiet.
3. The distinction, however, is: when there is only a part of the excellences present, it is remaining still; staying quiet is for attaining one's own advancement; non-employment of the means is remaining indifferent.
4. When the enemy and the conqueror, desirous of overreaching each other, are unable to injure each other, staying quiet after making war or after making peace is recommended.

5. Or, when he were to see,'With my own troops or the ally's troops or forest troops, I can weaken the equal or stronger king,' then he should make war and stay quiet after taking precautions in the outer regions and in the interior.
6. Or, when he were to see, 'My constituents, full of energy, united and thriving, will carry out their works unhindered or will destroy the works of the enemy,' then he should make war and stay quiet.
7. Or, when he were to see, 'The enemy's subjects, rebellious, impoverished, greedy, or harassed by the enemy's own troops, robbers or foresters, will come to me of their own accord or through instigations; sources of livelihood in my state are flourishing, those of the enemy ruined, hence his subjects stricken by famine will come to me; sources of livelihood in my state are ruined, those of the enemy flourishing, my subjects will not go over to him only if there is war, and after making war I shall plunder his grains, cattle and cash; or, I shall keep out the enemy's goods that are harmful to my own goods, or highly valuable goods will come to me from the enemy's trade route, when he is at war, and will not go to the other; or, when at war, he will not suppress his traitors, enemies or forest-tribes, or will be involved in war with these same; marching against my ally having the nature of a true ally, he will obtain abundant wealth in a short time, with small losses and expenses or excellent land which can be easily seized; or, wishing to march with all troops mobilised in disregard of me, he must not somehow be allowed to march,' then in order to hinder the advancement of the enemy and to affirm his valour, he should make war and stay quiet.
8. 'Turning back, he might swallow him up,' say the teachers.
9. 'No,' says Kautilya.
10. He would only cause a weakening of the conqueror, if he is not in a calamity, but when augmented by the acquisition of the enemy's prosperity, he would cause extermination.
11. If he acts thus, the vulnerable foe of the enemy would render help to him, being not destroyed.
12. Therefore, he should make war on one acting with all troops mobilised, and stay quiet.
13. In cases the reverse of the motives for staying quiet after making war, he should make peace and stay quiet.
14. When grown in power on the occasions for staying quiet after making war, he should make war and march, except when the enemy has mobilised all his troops.

15. Or, when he were to see, 'The enemy is in a calamity or, a calamity of his constituent cannot be remedied by the remaining constituents; or, his subjects, harassed by his own army, or disaffected with him, are easy to entice, being weakened, without energy or divided among themselves; the enemy has his drought-animals, men, stores and fortifications reduced in consequence of fire, floods, disease, epidemic or famine,' then he should make war and march.
16. Or, when he were to see, 'My ally in front and my rear ally have brave, prosperous and devoted subjects, the enemy, the rear enemy and the rear enemy's ally have subjects the reverse of this, I shall therefore be able to march after engaging the enemy's ally in a fight with my ally or my rear enemy in a fight with my rear ally,' then he should make war and march.
17. Or, when he were to see that the fruit can be attained by a single person within a short time, then he should make war on the rear enemy and his ally and march.
18. In the reverse cases, he should make peace and march.
19. Or, when he were to see,'It is not possible to march along, but it is necessary to march,' then joining forces with confederates, equal, weaker or stronger than himself, he should march, for a stipulated share if in one place, for an unstipulated share if in more than one place.
20. In case there is no confederacy with them, he should request for troops from one of them in return for a fixed share.
21. Or, the troops should be hired by a promise of marching together with them, with a fixed share when the gain is certain, with a portion of the gain when it is uncertain.
22. A share in conformity with troops is of the first type, in conformity with efforts is best; or plunder, as obtained by each, should be the share, or a share in conformity with the amount lent.

CHAPTER FIVE

SECTION 108: CONSIDERATIONS REGARDING AN ATTACK ON A VULNERABLE KING AND THE NATURAL ENEMY

SECTION 109: CAUSES LEADING TO DECLINE, GREED AND DISAFFECTION AMONG THE SUBJECTS

SECTION 110: REFLECTION ON CONFEDERATED ALLIES

1. In case the calamities of two neighbouring princes are alike, should one march against the vulnerable king or the enemy? In such a

case, he should march against the enemy; after subduing him, against the vulnerable king.

2. For, the vulnerable king might give him help in subduing the enemy, not the enemy in subduing the vulnerable king.
3. Should one march against a vulnerable king in a serious calamity or the enemy in a light calamity? 'He should march against the one in a serious calamity, because of ease in subjugating,' say the teachers.
4. 'No,' says Kautilya.
5. He should march against the enemy with a light calamity.
6. Even a light calamity becomes dangerous to him when attacked.
7. True, even a serious calamity becomes more serious in that case.
8. But the enemy with a light calamity, if not attacked, might easily overcome his calamity and go to the rescue of the vulnerable king, or might attack in the rear.
9. In case there are many vulnerable kings at the same time, when the choice is between one in a serious calamity but justly behaved and one in a light calamity but unjustly behaved or with disaffected subjects.
10. The subjects help the king who is justly behaved but suffering from a serious calamity, when he is attacked; remain indifferent to one unjustly behaved, suffering from a light calamity; but if disaffected, exterminate even a strong king.
11. Therefore, he should march only against one with disaffected subjects.
12. When the choice is between one with impoverished and greedy subjects and one with rebellious subjects, 'He should march against the one with impoverished and greedy subjects; for, impoverished and greedy subjects easily yield themselves to instigations or harassment, not the rebellious who can be overcome by the suppression of their leaders,' say the teachers.
13. 'No,' says Kautilya.
14. For, impoverished and greedy subjects, when devoted to their master, remain steadfast in what is beneficial to the master or make the instigations futile, on the principle, 'Where there is love, all qualities are present.'
15. Hence, he should march only against one with rebellious subjects.
16. When the choice is between a strong king unjustly behaved and a weak king justly behaved, he should march against the strong king unjustly behaved.

17. The subjects do not help the strong unjust king when he is attacked, they drive him out or resort to his enemy.
18. But the subjects support in every way the weak but just king when he is attacked or follow him if he has to flee.
19-26. For, by discarding the good and favouring the wicked and by starting unrighteous injuries not current before, by discontinuing customary practices that are righteous, by indulgence in impiety and suppression of piety, and by doing acts that ought not to be done and by ruining rightful acts, and by not giving what ought to be given and seeming what ought not to be given to him, and by not punishing those deserving to be punished and punishing those not deserving to be punished, by seizing those who ought not to be seized, and by doing harmful things and destroying beneficial things, and by ruining human exertions, by spoiling the excellence of works done, by doing harm to principal men and by dishonouring those worthy of honour, and by opposing the elders, by partiality and falsehood, by not requiting what is done and by not carrying out what is settled, through the negligence and indolence of the king and because of the destruction of well-being,—through these causes decline, greed and disaffection are produced among the subjects.
27. Subjects, when impoverished, become greedy; when greedy they become disaffected; when disaffected they either go over to the enemy or themselves kill the master.
28. Therefore, he should not allow these causes of decline, greed and disaffection among the subjects to arise, or, if arisen, should immediately counteract them.
29. Which are worst, subjects that are impoverished or greedy or disaffected?
30. The impoverished, through fear of harassment of extermination, prefer an immediate peace or fight or flight.
31. The greedy, dissatisfied because of greed, willingly respond to the enemy's instigations.
32. The disaffected rise in revolt when there is an enemy attack.
33. Among them, the exhaustion of money and grains is destructive of everything and difficult to remedy, the diminution of drought animals and men can be remedied with money and grains.
34. Greed, restricted to a part, being confined to the principal men, can be directed to spend itself on the enemy's possessions or can be removed.

35. Disaffection can be overcome by suppression of the leader.
36. For, subjects, without leaders, become easy to rule, not susceptible to instigations by others, become, however, incapable of putting up with troubles.
37. But those divided into many groups by the favouring of the leaders of the subjects, become protected and able to put up with troubles.
38. Even among confederated allies, he should consider the grounds for making peace or war and march after joining forces with those possessed of power and uprightness.
39. For, the powerful king is capable of attacking in the rear or rendering help in the expedition, the upright one carries out what is settled, in success as well as in failure.
40. Among them, as between marching after joining forces with one stronger king or two equals, it is better to march with two who are equals.
41. For, with a stronger, he moves overpowered by him; with two equals with a greater possibility of overreaching.
42. For, they are easy to divide from each other, and if one of them becomes treacherous, he is easy to restrain for the two or to seize through dissensions.
43. As between one equal and two weaker kings, it is better to march with two weaker kings.
44. For, they carry out two tasks and remain under control.
45. However, when the undertaking has succeeded, he should secretly go away under some pretext from the stronger who has achieved his object, if he is not upright; in the case of the upright, however, he should wait till he is sent away.
46. Or, from a dangerous situation he should move away with effort, after removing his women-folk. For, even from the equal who has achieved his object there might be danger to the trusting one.
47. And even the equal who has achieved his object tends to be stronger, and when augmented in power, untrustworthy; prosperity tends to change the mind.
48. Even if he received a small share or even no share from a superior, he should go away with a contented face; then striking at him when in his power, he should recover double.
49. But the leader, when he has himself achieved his object, should send away the confederated allies; he should, if need be forgo his dues, not score over them. Thereby he would be liked by the circle of kings.

CHAPTER SIX

SECTION 111: CONCERNING THE MARCH OF TWO KINGS WHO HAVE ENTERED INTO A TREATY OF ALLIANCE

SECTION 112: TREATIES WITH STIPULATIONS, WITHOUT STIPULATIONS AND WITH DESERTERS

1. The conqueror should overreach the second member of the circle of kings in this manner.
2. He should induce the neighbouring king to march after entering into a treaty, 'you march in this direction, I shall march in that; the gains shall be equal.'
3. In case the gains are equal, there should be peace, if unequal, fight.
4. A treaty is with stipulations or without stipulations.
5. 'You march to this region, I shall march to this,' this is treaty with stipulations as to place.
6. 'You operate for this length of time, I shall operate for this length of time,' this is treaty with stipulations as to time.
7. 'You carry out this much work, I shall carry out this much work,' this is treaty with stipulations as to objects to be achieved.
8. If he were to think, 'The enemy will march against a region, with a mountain-fort, a forest-fort or a river-fort, separated by a forest, with supplies of grains and men and allied troops cut off, deficient in fodder, fuel and water, unknown, far distant, or with natives hostile, or one in which land is not available for the operations of the army, and I shall march against a region the reverse of this,' in such a situation he should enter into a treaty with stipulations as to place.
9. If he were to think, 'The enemy will operate at a time when there is excessive rain, heat or cold, when there is plenty of illness, when food and other articles of use are exhausted, which is a hindrance to the operations of the army, which is too short or too long for accomplishing the work and I at a time the reverse of this,' in such a situation, he should enter into a treaty with stipulations as to time.
10. If he were to think, 'The enemy will achieve an object, easily recoverable from him, causing revolt among the subjects, taking a long time, involving heavy losses and expenses, insignificant, bound up with troubles in future, unwholesome, unlawful, opposed by the middle or neutral king, or ruinous to his own ally, and I shall achieve the reverse of this,' in such a situation, he should enter into a treaty with stipulations as to objects to be achieved.

11. By the fixing, in this manner, of place and time, of time and object, of place and object, and of place, time and object, the treaty with stipulations becomes seven-fold.
12. In the case of that treaty, he should start and establish his own undertakings right in advance and attack the enemy's undertakings.
13. Wishing to overreach an enemy, who is vicious, hasty, contemptuous, slothful or ignorant, he should create confidence with a treaty, saying 'we are in alliance,' without the fixing of place, time or object, and after finding the enemy's weak point, strike at him, this is treaty without stipulations.
14. In that connection, the following occurs:
15. The wise conqueror, making one neighbouring king fight with another neighbouring king, should seize the territory of another, cutting off his party on all sides.
16. Of a treaty there are the desire to make a treaty not yet made, clinging fast to a treaty made, spoiling a treaty made and repair of what is broken.
17. Of war, there is open war, concealed war and silent war.
18. Thus, we have treaty and war.
19. The examination of a new treaty in relation to conciliation and other means with their consequences, and the fixing of equal, weaker and stronger kings according to their strength, is the desire to make a treaty not made.
20. The observance, on both sides, of a treaty made, by means of what is agreeable and beneficial, and the carrying out of conditions as agreed upon and their safeguarding by seeing that he may not be divided from the other party, is clinging fast to a treaty made.
21. Violation of the treaty after establishing that the enemy deserves to have the treaty with him broken, by cheating him through treasonable persons, is spoiling a treaty made.
22. Becoming reconciled with a servant or an ally who had deserted through some fault is repair of what is broken.
23. In that case, the deserter returning is of four kinds: one deserting and returning on good grounds, the reverse of this, one leaving on good grounds and returning without such grounds, and the reverse of this.
24. One deserting because of the master's fault and returning because of his virtue, or deserting because of the enemy's virtue and returning because of his fault, is one deserting and returning on good grounds, fit to be made peace with.

25. One deserting and returning because of his own fault ignoring the virtues of both, is one deserting and returning without ground, unfit to be made peace with, being fickle in mind.
26. One deserting because of the master's fault and returning from the enemy because of his own fault is one deserting on good grounds and returning without ground, about whom he should reflect, 'Has he come with the intention of doing harm at the enemy's instigation or through his own evil mindedness, or knowing my enemy to be an exterminator of his enemy returned through fear of reprisal, or leaving the enemy, who is planning to exterminate me, returned out of a feeling of compassion?'
27. On finding out, he should honour one with benevolent intentions, should keep away at a distance one with different intentions.
28. One deserting because of his own fault and returning because of the enemy's fault is one deserting without ground and returning on good grounds, about whom he should reflect, 'Will he make good my weak point? Is he accustomed to live here? Do his people not find pleasure at the enemy's place? Is he in alliance with my allies? Is he at war with my enemies? Is he frightened of the greedy or cruel enemy or of the enemy in alliance with his enemy?'
29. On finding out, he should keep him in accordance with his intentions.
30. 'Destruction of what one has done, diminution of power, treating learning as a commodity, despair in hopes, eagerness for seeing different lands, lack of trust, or conflict with a powerful person are the occasions for leaving the master,' say the teachers.
31. 'Fear, lack of livelihood and resentment are the main occasions,' says Kautilya.
32. Among these, one who has done harm to him should be abandoned, one who has done harm to the enemy should be made peace with, regarding one who has done harm to both, he should reflect as before.
33. In case, however, it is absolutely necessary to make peace with one unfit to make peace with, he should take precautions with regard to that wherein the other has might.
34. In repairing what is broken, he should station one who belongs to the enemy's party, if on coming to him he has conferred benefits, away from himself, guarded till the end of his life.
35. Or, he should make him fight against his master, or, if completely secured, make him a leader of the army against the enemy or forest tribes or station him on one side on the frontier.

36. Or, if not seemed, he should sell him as a commodity, or sell even a secured one concealed by that one, blaming him with the fault of that other one himself, for the sake of making peace with the enemy.
37. Or, he should do away with him silently for the sake of the future; and finding that the deserter who has returned is desirous of killing him in future, he should slay him.
38. One who has come from the enemy is a danger, caused by his staying with the enemy; being of the nature of staying with a serpent, it suffers from the defect of constant fear.
39. He becomes a cause of constant fear and dangerous even afterwards like danger to a *salmali* tree from a pigeon feeding on *plaksa* seeds.

40-41. Open war is fighting at the place and time indicated; creating fright, sudden assault, striking when there is error or a calamity, giving way and striking in one place, are types of concealed warfare; that which concerns secret practices and instigations through secret agents is the mark of silent war.

CHAPTER SEVEN

SECTION 113: PEACE AND WAR CONNECTED WITH THE DUAL POLICY

1. The conqueror should accept as ally the second member of the circle of kings in this manner.
2. He should march against a neighbouring king after joining forces with the neighbouring enemy if he were to think. 'Thus he will not attack me in the rear, will ward off my rear enemy, will not go to the help of the king against whom I am marching, there will be double troops at my disposal, he will provide me with supplies and reinforcements, will prevent these from reaching the enemy, will crush for me the thorns on the way full of many dangers, will operate with his army against the enemy's retreats in forts or forests, will place the king I am marching against in an unbearable danger or bring him to terms of peace, or as he receives his share of the gain, will create confidence in my other enemies.'
3. Or, resorting to the dual policy, he should seek to obtain from one of the neighbouring kings troops in return for treasury or treasury in return for troops.
4. Among them, from the stronger for a larger share, from the equal for an equal share, from the weaker for a smaller share, — this is an equal pact.

5. In the reverse case, it is an unequal pact.
6. By receiving a special gain in these two, there is overreaching.
7. A weaker king may bargain with a stronger king with the offer of a gain equal to his troops, when he is in a calamity or is addicted to what is harmful or is in trouble.
8. He with whom the bargain is made should fight if capable of doing harm to him; else he should make the pact.
9. A weaker king, when in the same situation, may bargain with a stronger king with the offer of a gain greater than what is equal to the troops, for the sake of recouping his diminished powers and might or for the sake of guarding his base or rear when going after an object which it is possible to secure.
10. He with whom the bargain is made should help one with honourable intentions, else fight.
11. A weaker king, entrenched in a fort or supported by an ally, may bargain with a stronger king on whom a calamity has fallen or who has a weak point amongst his subjects or to whom troubles have come, with the offer of a gain less than what is equal to his troops, when intending to march against an enemy over a short route or when intending to secure a gain without a fight or a gain of which the attainment is certain.
12. He with whom the bargain is made should fight if capable of doing harm to him, else make the pact.
13. A stronger king, even when without a weakness or a calamity, may accept a lesser gain when intending to make a weaker king who made a bad start in his undertaking suffer greater losses and expenses, or when intending to get his own treasonable troops killed, or when intending to cause trouble to his own enemy fit to be harassed or exterminated through the weaker king, or if he, attaching importance to peace, has honourable intentions.
14. Joining forces with one who has honourable intentions, he should seek to achieve his object, else fight.
15. In the same way, an equal should overreach or help an equal.
16. An equal may bargain with a gain equal to the troops, for troops capable of fighting against the particular kind of the enemy's troops or against those of the ally or forest troops, or for troops that would serve as a guide in terrains unfavourable to the enemy or for guarding his base or rear.
17. He with whom the bargain is made should help one with honourable intentions, otherwise he should fight.

18. An equal may bargain with the offer of a gain less than equal to the troops with one on whom a calamity has fallen or who has a weak point among his subjects or who is opposed by many kings or when he himself can get help from another source.
19. He with whom the bargain is made should fight if capable of doing harm to him, else make the pact.
20. An equal, in this situation himself, should bargain with the offer of a gain greater than what is equal to the troops, if his affairs are dependent on the neighbouring king or when his strength is to be built up.
21. He with whom the bargain is made should help one with honourable intentions, otherwise fight.
22. One may ask for more gain from a stronger, a weaker or an equal, if intending to strike at him when a calamity has befallen him or his subjects show a weakness, or if intending to ruin his undertaking that may have been well started or that may be sure of success, or if intending to strike at his base or expedition, or if he is getting more from the king against whom the other is marching.
23. The one, asked for more, may give more for the sake of protecting his own troops when intending to crush another's unassailable fort or allied or forest troops by means of enemy troops, or when intending to make the enemy troops suffer losses and expenses on a distant or prolonged expedition, or when intending to exterminate the enemy himself after growing in power through his troops, or when intending to take the enemy troops himself.
24. A stronger king may bargain with a weaker king with the offer of a gain greater than what is equal to the troops, when intending to get him in his power under the pretext of the enemy to be attacked, or when intending to exterminate him after exterminating the enemy, or when, after making the bestowal, intending to recover it later.
25. He with whom the bargain is made should fight if capable of doing harm to him, otherwise make the pact.
26. Or, he should enter into an alliance with the king to be attacked by the other, or should give treasonable or alien or forest troops.
27. A stronger king, suffering from a calamity or a weak point among his subjects, may bargain with a weaker one with the offer of a gain equal to the troops.
28. He with whom the bargain is made should fight if capable of doing harm to him, otherwise make the pact.

29. A stronger king may bargain with a weaker one who is in this situation with the offer of a gain less than what is equal to the troops.
30. He with whom the bargain is made should fight if capable of doing him harm, otherwise make the pact.
31. The one to whom a pact is proposed and the one proposing the pact should first find out the motives; then after reflecting on both sides, he should follow the course wherein lies his well-being.

CHAPTER EIGHT

SECTION 114: CONDUCT PROPER FOR THE KING ABOUT TO BE ATTACKED

SECTION 115: DIFFERENT KINDS OF ALLIES FIT TO BE HELPED

1. The vulnerable king, about to be attacked, should bargain with one of the confederates with the offer of double the gain, with the intention of removing the motive of the alliance or of destroying it.
2. Proposing the bargain, he should describe to him likely losses, expenses, marches, hindrances, benefits to enemies and danger to his person.
3. If he agrees, he should bestow wealth on him.
4. Or, making him entertain enmity towards the others, he should divide him from them.
5. When intending to make one who has made a bad start in his undertaking suffer further losses and expenses, or when intending to obstruct the success of his expedition that has begun well, or when intending to strike at his base or expedition, or when intending to ask for more again after becoming allied with the king to be attacked, one may accept a small gain in the present and a large gain in the future, even when difficulties of money have arisen or he has no confidence in that other king.
6. When he sees a benefit to his ally or harm to his enemy, with a continuity of advantage to himself, or when he intends to make the king who has helped him before help him further, he should forgo a great gain in the present and seek a small gain in the future.
7. When he wants to save a king engaged in a fight with traitors or enemies or with a stronger king seeking to seize his kingdom, or when he wants to make that king render the same kind of help to himself or when he takes relationship into consideration, he should not accept a gain in the present and in the future.

8. When after making a pact he intends to violate it, or when he intends to bring about the impoverishment of the enemy's subjects or the breaking up of his alliance with his allies or foes, or when apprehensive of any attack by the enemy, he should demand a gain not received or more.
9. With respect to that, the other should consider the order of preference in the present and in the future.
10. By that are explained the earlier cases.
11. But when the enemy and the conqueror help each his respective ally, a special advantage results from an ally whose undertaking is possible or sound or productive or who is resolute in his undertakings or who has loyal subjects.
12. One with a possible undertaking starts a work capable of accomplishment, one with a productive undertaking what leads to good results.
13. One resolute in his undertakings does not stop without completing his work.
14. One with loyal subjects accomplishes his work even with a little help, since he has already good helpmates.
15. These allies, when they have achieved their objects, easily and abundantly oblige in return.
16. The reverse of these should not be helped.
17. In case the two give help to the same individual, he who helps his ally or a better ally of his overreaches the other.
18. For, from the ally he attains his own advancement, the other gets only losses, expenses, marches and beneficence to enemies.
19. And the enemy, on achieving his object, becomes hostile.
20. But when the two help the middle king, he who helps the middle king when he is his ally or a better ally, overreaches the other.
21. For, from the ally he attains his own advancement, the other gets only losses, expenses, marches and beneficence to enemies.
22. If the middle king, after being helped, turns hostile, the enemy overreaches the conqueror.
23. For, he obtains as an ally the enemy of the middle king, who had made exertions, but who has now deserted him and come to him with a common goal.
24. By that is explained help to the neutral king.
25. In the matter of giving a portion of one's troops to the middle or neutral king, he who gives troops that are brave, skilled in the use of weapons, able to put up with troubles or loyal, is overreached.
26. The opposite king overreaches.

27. Where, however, the troops, when sent, can accomplish that object as well as others, he should give any of the hereditary, hired, banded, allied or forest troops, when the place and time are known, or alien and forest troops, when the place is distant and time long.
28. But if he were to think of a king. 'On achieving his object, he will appropriate my troops, or will camp them among alien or forest troops or in an unsuitable region or season, or might render them unserviceable,' then he should not help him on the pretext that his troops are engaged elsewhere.
29. If, however, he has necessarily to be given help in this manner, he should give him troops able to put up with that occasion only.
30. And till the end of the campaign he should get them to encamp and fight in another place and guard them from the calamities of an army.
31. And when the other has achieved his object, he should, under some pretext, get them removed from his.
32. Or, he should give him treasonable, alien or forest troops.
33. Or, making a treaty with the king to be attacked, he should overreach him.
34. For, when the gain is equal there should be peace, when unequal war is considered desirable for the equal, weaker and stronger kings.

Thus, have peace and war been described.

CHAPTER NINE

SECTION 116: PACTS FOR SECURING AN ALLY, MONEY, LAND AND AN UNDERTAKING

(i) Pact for an Ally

(ii) Pact for Money

1. When marching after making a pact, of the gains of an ally, money and land, the gain of each later one is preferable to that of each earlier one.
2. For, an ally and money come from the gain of land, and an ally from the gain of money.
3. Or, that gain, which when secured helps in securing one of the remaining two is preferable.
4. 'Let us two secure an ally each,' this and the like is an equal pact.
5. 'You secure an ally, I one of the other two,' this and the like is an unequal pact.

6. By securing a special gain in these two cases, there is overreaching.
7. In an equal pact, however, he who secures an excellent ally or an ally in the ally's difficulty, overreaches.
8. For, troubles produce firmness in friendship.
9. Even in the case of an ally's difficulty, when there is a choice between one who is constant but not under control and one inconstant but under control, 'The constant, though not under control, is preferable; for he, though not helping, does not do harm,' say the teachers.
10. 'No,' says Kautilya.
11. One under control, though inconstant, is preferable.
12. As long as he helps, he becomes an ally; for the characteristic of an ally is conferring benefit.
13. Even between two allies under control, when there is a choice between one rendering abundant help but inconstant and one rendering small help but constant, 'The one rendering abundant help, though inconstant, is preferable; one rendering abundant help, though inconstant, gives great help in a short time and provides against large items of expenditure,' say the teachers.
14. 'No,' says Kautilya.
15. The constant one, though giving small help, is preferable.
16. The inconstant, though capable of great help deserts through fear of having to render help or after giving help strives to take it back.
17. The constant one, giving a small help, rendering the small help continuously, renders great help over a long period of time.
18. As between a big ally mobilising slowly and a small ally mobilising quickly, 'The big ally, mobilising slowly, gives great prestige, and when he does mobilize, he secures the object,' say the teachers.
19. 'No,' says Kautilya.
20. A small ally mobilising quickly is preferable.
21. The small ally mobilising quickly does not allow the time for action to pass, and because of his weakness becomes fit to be used at one's will, not so the other, with an extensive territory.
22. As between dispersed troops and troops not under control, 'Dispersed troops can be collected together again, being under control,' say the teachers.
23. 'No,' says Kautilya.
24. Troops not under control are better.
25. For, uncontrolled troops can be brought under control by conciliation and other means; the other kind, being engaged in their work, cannot be collected together.

26. As between an ally giving the help of men and one giving the help of money, 'The ally giving the help of men is preferable; the ally giving the help of men gives prestige and when he mobilizes, he achieves the object,' say the teachers.
27. 'No,' says Kautilya.
28. The ally giving the help of money is preferable.
29. For, the use of money is made at all times, only sometimes that of troops.
30. And with money, troops and other objects of desire are obtained.
31. As between an ally giving the help of money and one giving the help of land, 'The one giving the help of money, being possessed of mobility, enables one to meet all expenses,' say the teachers.
32. 'No,' says Kautilya.
33. That an ally and money come from the acquisition of land has been stated before.
34. Therefore, the ally giving the help of land is preferable.
35. When help in men from two allies is equal, valour, ability to put up with troubles, loyalty or the gain of all troops from the side of the ally becomes a special advantage.
36. When the help in money is equal, getting the things asked for, plentifulness, smallness of exertion and continuity become a special advantage.
37. With respect to that, the following occurs:
38. A perfect ally is said to have six qualities, namely, constant, under control, quickly mobilising, hereditary, great and not given to double-dealing.
39. One, that is protected and that protects out of love, without consideration of money, with relationship grown since old times, is called the constant ally.
40. One under control is said to be three-fold, helping with all, with various or with great resources; giving help on one side, on both sides and on all sides is another three-fold ally under control.
41. One who, whether receiving or giving help, lives by doing harm to one's enemies, and is possessed of a fort or forest as a place of retreat, is a constant ally, but not under control.
42. He who, when engaged in war with another or even when only in a light calamity, makes a pact for help, is an ally under control, but not constant.
43. Now one related by a common objective, helpful and never changing, is the ally endowed with the nature of an ally, not given to double-dealing in times of trouble.

44. The ally is permanent because of exclusive feeling of friendship, fickle because of his feelings being common to the enemy, indifferent when not interested in either, with feelings for both when interested in the two.
45. That ally, really and enemy of the conqueror, who has become a buffer between two strong kings, does not help, being not placed under obligations or being unable to help.
46. The ally who, though dear to the enemy or deserving to be protected or honoured by him or related to him, gives help, is common to the enemy.
47. The ally with an extensive territory, contented, strong and indolent becomes indifferent, also one disrespected because of a calamity.
48. One who, because of his weakness, is subservient to the prosperity of the enemy and the leader and is not treated as an enemy by either, should be known as the ally with feelings for both.
49. He, who would remain negligent about an ally who had deserted with or without reason and who has returned with or without reason, embraces death.
50. As between a small but quick gain and a large gain after a long time, 'The small but quick gain is preferable, if in consonance with the undertaking, the place and the time,' say the teachers.
51. 'No,' says Kautilya.
52. A large gain after a long time is preferable, if not liable to disappear and if of the nature of a seed; in the reverse case, the former.
53. On thus perceiving the presence of excellence in a gain or a portion of a gain, which is definite, he should march after making pacts with confederates, being intent on achieving his own object.

CHAPTER TEN

SECTION 116 (CONTINUED): PACTS FOR SECURING AN ALLY, MONEY, LAND, AND AN UNDERTAKING

(iii) Pact for Land

1. 'Let us two obtain land,' this is a pact for land.
2. Of the two, he who obtains land possessed of excellences, when need for it has arisen, overreaches.
3. In case there is an equal acquisition of excellent land, he who obtains land after attacking a strong king overreaches.
4. For, he secures acquisition of land, weakening of the enemy and prestige.

5. It is true in obtaining land from a weak king, there is case.
6. But the gain of land is poor and his neighbour, who was an ally, becomes an enemy.
7. In case the strength of kings overthrown is equal, he who obtains land after uprooting a firmly entrenched enemy, overreaches.
8. For, the acquisition of a fort brings about the protection of his own land and the repulsion of enemies and forest tribes.
9. In case of acquisition of land from a moving enemy, there is special advantage from a weak neighbour.
10. For, land with a weak neighbour has its well-being and security quickly augmented.
11. Land with a strong neighbour is the opposite of this and becomes ruinous to the treasury and the army.
12. As between excellent land with permanent enemies and one with few excellences without permanent enemies, 'The excellent land with permanent enemies is preferable; for, excellent land enables one to secure treasury and army, and these two destroy enemies,' say the teachers.
13. 'No,' says Kautilya.
14. In acquiring land with permanent enemies, there is a greater acquisition of enemies.
15. And a permanent enemy remains an enemy whether he is obliged or injured; the impermanent enemy, however, ceases to be so through obligations conferred on him or by desisting from injury to him.
16. The land, whose frontiers have many forts beyond them and are never devoid of robber-bands or Mleccha forest tribes, is one with permanent enemies; in the reverse case, it is one without permanent enemies.
17. As between a small proximate land and a big land that is distant, the small proximate land is preferable.
18. For, it is easy to obtain, to protect and to get it to rescue oneself.
19. The distant one is the opposite of this.
20. Even of two distant lands, as between land held by troops and one held by itself, the one held by itself is preferable.
21. For, it is held by the treasury and the army produced within itself.
22. That held by troops is the opposite of this, being merely a station for troops.

23. As between acquisition of land from a foolish king and from a wise king, the acquisition of land from a foolish king is preferable.
24. For, it is easy to obtain and protect and cannot be taken back.
25. That from a wise king is the opposite of this, being loyal to him.
26. As between an enemy fit to be harassed and an enemy fit to be exterminated, acquisition of land from an enemy fit to be exterminated is preferable.
27. For, the king fit to be exterminated, being without support or with a weak support, is deserted by his subjects when, on being attacked, he wishes to flee taking with him the treasury and the army, not the one fit to be harassed, entrenched in a fort or supported by an ally.
28. Even of two kings entrenched in a fort, one in a land-fort and the other in a river-fort, the acquisition of land from one in a land-fort is preferable.
29. For a land-fort is easy to besiege, to storm and to assault suddenly and does not allow the enemy to slip out.
30. A river-fort, however, causes double exertion, and water has to be drunk and it yields livelihood to the enemy.
31. As between an enemy in a river-fort and an enemy in a mountain fort, acquisition of land one in a river-fort is preferable.
32. For, a river fort can be conquered by means of elephants, bridges of wooden posts, embankment and boats, it is of varying depth and its water can be made to flow away.
33. A mountain fort, however, is easy to protect, difficult to lay siege to, difficult to climb; and even if one part is breached, the destruction of all does not follow; and there can be throwing down of rocks and trees on those doing great damage.
34. As between those who fight in water and those who fight on land the acquisition of land from those who fight in water is preferable.
35. For, those fighting in water are restricted as to the place and time of fighting; fighters on land, however, can fight in all places and in all seasons.
36. As between fighters in trenches and fighters in the open, acquisition of land from trench-fighters is preferable.
37. For, trench-fighters fight with both trenches and weapons, those fighting in the open, with weapons alone.
38. The king conversant with the science of politics, acquiring land from kings like these, secures a special advantage over confederates and enemies.

CHAPTER ELEVEN

SECTION 116 (CONTINUED): PACTS FOR SECURING ALLY, MONEY, LAND, AND AN UNDERTAKING

(iv) A Pact for Unsettled Land

1. 'Let us two settle waste land,' this is a pact for unsettled land.
2. Of the two, he who causes settlement on land possessed of excellences as mentioned, when the need for it has arisen, overreaches the other.
3. Even in that case, as between a dry tract and land abounding in water, a small land abounding in water is preferable to a large dry tract, because of the continuousness and fixity of produce.
4. Even between two dry tracts, one with plentiful earlier and later crops, with crops ripening with a little rain, with undertakings not held up, is preferable.
5. Even between two tracts abounding in water, one with sowings of grains is preferable to one not conducive to the sowing of grains.
6. In the case of the smallness or largeness of these two, a large tract, though unfavourable to crops, is preferable to a small one favourable to crops.
7. For, in a large tract, there are plants growing on land and those growing in water.
8. And undertakings like the fort and so on are carried out in plenty.
9. For, the qualities of land are such as are contrived by man.
10. As between the benefit of mines and that of grains, the benefit of mines brings the treasury into being, that of grains brings the treasury and the magazine into being.
11. For, the undertaking of works like the fort and so on is dependent on grains.
12. Or, the benefit of mines, with an extensive sale of their produce is preferable.
13. 'As between the usefulness of a material forest and an elephant forest, the use of a material forest is the source of all undertakings and able to secure plenty of stores, the reverse is the use of an elephant forest,' say the teachers.
14. 'No,' says Kautilya.
15. It is possible to plant many material forests in many tracts of land, not so an elephant forest.
16. For, the destruction of an enemy's forces is principally dependent on elephants.

17. As between the use of a water-route and that of a land-route, the use of a water-route is not constant, the use of a land-route is constant.
18. As between land with people disunited and one with people in bands, that with people disunited is preferable.
19. One with people disunited becomes easy to enjoy, not susceptible to the instigations of others, is, however, unable to bear difficulties.
20. One with people in bands is the reverse of this, full of danger when there is a revolt.
21. In the matter of settling the four *varnas* on that land one consisting mostly of lower *varnas* is preferable because of its capacity to yield all kinds of benefits, one with farmers being preferable because of plentifulness and definiteness of agriculture, one with cowherds because of its starting agriculture and other undertakings, one with rich traders because of the benefit of stores of goods and loans.
22. Of the excellences of land, affording shelter is best.
23. As between land with the support of a fort and one with the support of men, the one with the support of men is preferable.
24. For, a kingdom is that which has men.
25. Without men, like a barren cow, what could it yield?
26. But when intending to acquire land, the settlement of which would entail heavy losses and expenses, he should first make a bargain with a purchaser, who is weak, or not of royal blood, or without energy, or without a party, or unjustly behaved, or vicious, or trusting in fate, or who does whatever pleases him.
27. For, a weak king, though of royal blood, settling on land, the settlement of which entails heavy losses and expenses, perishes with his subjects bound to him by ties, because of the losses and expenses.
28. One not of royal blood though strong, is deserted by his subjects not bound by ties to him, through fear of losses and expenses.
29. One without energy, however, not using force even when possessed of troops, is broken along with his troops because of the losses and expenses.
30. One without a party, though possessed of a treasury, does not achieve anything, being deficient in conferring the benefit on the land of losses and expenses.
31. The unjustly behaved would cause even settled land to be laid waste.

32. How could he cause settlement on unsettled land?
33. By that is explained the vicious king.
34. One trusting in fate, being devoid of human endeavour, perishes, because he does not start undertakings or his undertakings have miscarried.
35. One doing whatever pleases him does not achieve anything.
36. And he is the worst of them all.
37. 'One undertaking any work whatever, may perchance find a weak point of the conqueror,' say the teachers.
38. 'As he may find a weak point, so he may meet with destruction as well,' says Kautilya.
39. In case he does not find any of these, he should settle the land as we shall explain in 'securing the enemy in the rear.'
40. This is a pact of fixing.
41. When asked by a strong king to sell land which is possessed of excellences or which can be seized by him, he should give it after making a pact.
42. This is an open pact.
43. When asked by an equal, he should give after considering grounds for doing so; 'The land is easily recoverable by me or under my control; being tied to it, the enemy will come under my control; or, through the sale of the land, I shall get an ally and money, which will strengthen my undertakings.'
44. By that is explained a weaker king purchasing land from him.
45. A king knowing the science of politics, acquiring in this manner an ally, money and land with men and without men, overreaches the confederates.

CHAPTER TWELVE

SECTION 116 (CONTINUED): PACTS FOR SECURING AN ALLY, MONEY, LAND, AND AN UNDERTAKING

(v) Pact for an Undertaking

1. 'Let us two build a fort,' is a pact for an undertaking.
2. Of the two, he who causes a fort to be built that is nature made, unassailable, and requires small expenses in making, overreaches.
3. Even among them, of a land-fort, a river-fort and a mountain-fort, each later one is preferable to each earlier one.
4. Of two water-works, one with naturally flowing water is preferable to one into which water has to be brought.

5. Even among two water-works with naturally flowing water, one with an extensive region for sowing is preferable.
6. Of two material forests, he who fells for his use a material forest, which is large, has forest land rich in materials of high value, is on the border of his territory and is watered by a river, overreaches.
7. For, that which is watered by a river has easy means of livelihood and becomes a refuge in times of trouble.
8. Of two elephant forests, he who raises an elephant forest, with many brave animals, with weak neighbours, causing endless trouble to enemies, on the border of his territory, overreaches.
9. Even in that case, 'As between one with many but dull elephants and one with few but brave, the one with few but brave elephants is preferable; for on the brave depends the fight; the few brave rout the many dull, and those routed become the destroyers of their own troops,' say the teachers.
10. 'No,' says, Kautilya.
11. The many dull are preferable; because of their use in the army, they carry out many tasks, become the refuge of their own troops in battle and unassailable and frightful to the enemies.
12. For, to the many dull, bravery can be imparted by means of training, but numerousness cannot be created at all in the few brave.
13. Of two mines, he who causes a mine to be opened, yielding plenty of valuable ores, with roads not inaccessible, and operated with small expenditure, overreaches.
14. Even in that case, as between few things of high value and plenty of things of small value, 'The few things of high value are to be preferred, for, diamonds, rubies, pearls, corals, and gold and silver ores swallow up the many objects of small value by their excessively high value,' say the teachers.
15. 'No,' says Kautilya.
16. A purchaser for an object of high value is rare and found after a long time, while there are plenty for objects of small value because of a constant demand.
17. By that is explained the trade route.
18. Even as to that, 'As between a water-route and a land-route, the water-route is preferable, involving little expenditure and exertion and yielding plenty of goods,' say the teachers.
19. 'No,' says Kautilya.
20. The water-route is restricted in movements, not usable at all times, a source of great dangers and without remedies; the land route is the opposite of this.

21. In the case of a waterway, however, as between a route along the shore and one on high sea, the route along the coast is preferable because of the large number of ports, or a river-route, because of perennial use and because the dangers in it can be withstood.
22. Even in the case of a land-route, 'The route to the Himavat is preferable to the southern route, for the commodities of elephants, horses, perfumes, ivory, skins, silver and gold are of very high value,' say the teachers.
23. 'No,' says Kautilya.
24. These with the exception of the commodities of blankets, skins, and horses, besides the commodities of conch-shells, diamonds, rubies, pearls and gold are more plentiful on the southern route.
25. Even in the case of the route to the south, the trade route with many mines, with commodities of high value, with well-secured, movements, or requiring little expenditure and exertion, is preferable, or one with commodities of small value, with an extensive scope for sale.
26. By that are explained the trade routes to the east and the west.
27. Even in that case, as between a wheel-track and a foot-path, the wheel-track is preferable, as it enables undertakings on a large scale, or the path for donkeys and camels in conformity with the place and time.
28. By these is explained the 'shoulder' path.
29. The flourishing of an enemy's undertaking is decline for the leader, advancement in the reverse case; when the course of undertakings is equal, that should be known by the conqueror as his own stable condition.
30. Smallness of profit and excess of expenditure is decline, advancement in the reverse case; equality of income and expenditure in undertakings should be known as the stable condition for himself.
31. Therefore, from among a fort and so on, he should secure an undertaking requiring little expenditure and yielding large profit and get a special advantage. Thus, have been described pacts for undertakings.

CHAPTER THIRTEEN

SECTION 117: CONSIDERATIONS REGARDING THE KING ATTACKING IN THE REAR

1. Of the conqueror and the enemy, who, joining together, intend attacking in the rear two enemies who have attacked their enemies,

he, who attacks in the rear a king rich in powers, overreaches the other.

2. For, one, rich in powers, might, after exterminating the enemy, exterminate the attacker in the rear, not the one, weak in power, who has not obtained any gain.
3. In case of equality of power, he, who attacks in the rear one with an extensive undertaking, overreaches.
4. For, one with an extensive undertaking, might, after exterminating the enemy, exterminate the attacker in the rear, not the one with a small undertaking, with his army stuck.
5. In case of equality of undertaking, he, who attacks in the rear one marching with all troops mobilised, overreaches.
6. For, with his base denuded of troops, he becomes easy to overpower for him, not the one marching with a part of the troops only, who has made provision for guarding his rear.
9. For, that king, if he is repulsed by the fort and turns round against the attacker in the rear, is checked by the entrenched enemy.
10. By that are explained the earlier kings.
11. In case of equality of the enemies, he, who attacks in the rear one attacking a righteous king, overreaches.
12. For, one attacking a righteous king is hated by his own people and by others, one attacking an unrighteous king is liked by them.
13. By that is explained the attack in the rear of one who squanders his patrimony, one living in the present and the niggardly one.
14. The same motives hold good for attacking in the rear those attacking their allies.
15. As between one attacking his ally and the other attacking his enemy, he, who attacks in the rear the one attacking his ally, overreaches.
16. For, one attacking an ally, might, after easily obtaining success, exterminate the attacker in the rear.
17. For, it is easy to make peace with an ally, not with an enemy.
18. As between one uprooting an ally and one uprooting an enemy, he who attacks in the rear one uprooting an enemy, overreaches.
19. For, one uprooting his enemy, with allies grown in strength, might exterminate the attacker in the rear, not the other, destroying his own party.
20. In case the two enemies have come away without obtaining a gain, that attacker in the rear, whose enemy is frustrated in securing a great gain or whose enemy has suffered heavy losses and expenses, overreaches.

21. In case they have come after obtaining a gain, that attacker in the rear, whose enemy is weaker in point of gain or power, over-reachers, or in whose case the enemy against whom his enemy had marched might do harm to the enemy in battle.
22. Even of two kings attacking their enemies in the rear, he who is superior in raising troops for an undertaking capable of achievement, or who is an entrenched enemy, or who is situated on the flank of the enemy, overreaches.
23. For, one situated on the flank can go to the rescue of the king to be attacked and is dangerous to the enemy's base, one situated in the rear is only dangerous to the enemy's base.
24. Three kinds of attackers in the rear should be known as impeding the activity of the enemy: the group of neighbouring kings in the rear and the two neighbours on the two flanks.
25. The weak king situated between the leader and enemy is called a buffer; he is a hindrance to the strong, if possessed of a fort or a forest as a place of retreat.
26. But when the conqueror and the enemy, intending to secure the middle king, attack the middle king in the rear, he who, when that king returns after securing the gain, divides the middle king from his ally and secures a former enemy as an ally, overreaches.
27. The enemy who helps is fit to be allied with, not the ally who has renounced his friendly feelings.
28. By that is explained the intention to secure the neutral king.
29. 'But in the case of attack in the rear and march against an enemy, prosperity results from diplomatic fight.
30. For, in a fight with military operations, there is loss of prosperity for both sides because of losses and expenses.
31. For, even after winning, a king with his army and treasury depleted becomes a loser,' say the teachers.
32. 'No,' says Kautilya.
33. Even with very great losses and expenses, the destruction of the enemy must be brought about.
34. When losses and expenses are equal, he who, after first bringing about the destruction of his own treasonable troops and becoming free from thorns, would afterwards fight with troops under control, overreaches.
35. Even of two, securing first the destruction of their treasonable troops, he, who would secure the destruction of a large number, of more powerful and extremely treacherous troops, overreaches.
36. By that is explained the destruction of alien and forest troops.

37. When the conqueror may become the attacker in the rear, the attacker in front or one marched against, then in those cases, he should carry out the following course for a leader.
38. The leader should attack in the rear the enemy attacking his ally, after first making the enemy's ally in his rear become engaged in a fight with the rescuer of the attacker in the rear *i.e.* of himself.
39. When attacking in front he should keep off the enemy in his rear by his ally in the rear, similarly keep off the ally of the enemy in the rear by the ally of his ally in the rear.
40. And in front he should make his ally engage in fight with the enemy's ally, and should keep off the ally of the enemy's ally by the ally of his own ally.
41. When attacked, he should cause the rear of the attacker to be attacked by his ally and keep off the rear ally of the attacker from the attacker in the rear by the ally of his ally.
42. In this way, the conqueror should establish in the rear and in front, a circle of kings in his own interest, with the excellences of the constituent, called the ally.
43. And in the entire circle, he should ever station envoys and secret agents, becoming a friend of the rivals, maintaining secrecy, even if achieved with particular success, undoubtedly perish, like a broken boat in the ocean.

CHAPTER FOURTEEN

SECTION 118: RECOUPMENT OF POWERS THAT HAVE BECOME WEAK

1. When attacked by confederates in this manner, the conqueror should say to the one who is the principal among them, 'With you, I would make peace; here is money and I shall be an ally, you will thus have a double advancement; it does not behave you to let your enemies, masquerading as friends, thrive at your cost; for, these, when grown powerful, will overthrow you yourself.'
2. Or, he should sow dissensions, saying 'Just as I, who had done no harm, am attacked by these kings joining together, so will they, with their forces combined, attack you also, when at ease or in a calamity; for, strength changes the mind; prevent that strength of theirs.'
3. When they are divided, he should support the principal and make him fight with the weaker confederates or giving help to the weaker make them fight with the principal, or so act as he may consider better for himself.

4. Or, making one entertain enmity towards the others, he should divide him from them.
5. Or, secretly offering a greater gain to the principal, he should get peace made through him.
6. Then agents in the pay of both, pointing to the greater gain, should poison the minds of the confederates, saying 'You have been cheated.'
7. When they have become vitiated, he should violate the treaty.
8. Then agents in the pay of both should bring about a further discord among them, saying 'This is what we had pointed out.'
9. When they are divided, he should act by supporting one of them.
10. In the absence of a principal among them, he should secure from among the confederates one who had roused them, or one persevering in his undertakings, or one with loyal subjects, or one who had joined the confederacy out of greed or fear, or one afraid of the conqueror, or one bound to his kingdom, or his ally or a moving enemy, the earlier ones in the absence of the later ones in this list, — one who had roused them by a surrender of himself, one persevering in his undertakings by bowing down with conciliation, one with loyal subjects by offering and accepting girls in marriage, the greedy one by double the share, one afraid of them by helping him with treasury and army, one afraid of himself by creating confidence by the giving of a surety, one bound to his kingdom by becoming one with him, his ally by doing what is agreeable and beneficial to both or by giving up benefits received, the moving enemy by reassuring him by desisting from doing harm and rendering help to him.
11. Or, by whichever means any of them may be separated, by that he should secure him, or by means of conciliation, gifts dissension and force, as shall be explained in the section on troubles.
12. Or, when in a hurry because of harm caused by a calamity, he should enter into a treaty with the surrender of his treasury and army, stipulating the place, the time or the work.
13. After making the treaty, he should try to remedy his weakness.
14. If weak in a party, he should create a party of kinsmen and allies, or an unassailable fort.
15. For, one entrenched in a fort or supported by allies, becomes worthy of honour by his own people and by those of others.
16. If weak in the power of counsel, he should get a large number of wise men in service or associate with elders in the sciences.
17. For, in that way, he attains immediate good.

18. If weak in might, he should endeavour to secure the welfare of his subjects.
19. The countryside is the source of all undertakings; from them comes might.
20. The abode for it and for himself, when in trouble, is the fort.
21. Water-works are the source of crops.
22. For, ever continuous is the benefit as from an excellent rainfall to sowings watered by irrigation.
23. A trade route is the means of overreaching the enemy.
24. For, along the trade route is made the carrying over of troops and secret agents into enemy territory and the purchase of weapons, armours, carriages and vehicles, as well as bringing in and taking out.
25. Mines are the source of implements of war; material forests, of fortification work and of carriages and chariots; elephant forests, of elephants; and herds, of cattle, horses, donkeys and camels.
26. In case of their non-availability obtaining them from groups of kinsmen and allies should be resorted to.
27. If weak in energy, he should secure the services, as they may be available, of heroic men from bands, robber-bands, foresters and Mleccha tribes, and of secret agents capable of doing harm to enemies.
28. Or, he should employ against the enemies 'step against an enemy-mixed trouble' or 'the conduct of the weaker king'.
29. Being thus enriched with a party, with counsel, with material resources and army, he should march out to overthrow the suppression of himself by enemies.

CHAPTER FIFTEEN

SECTION 119: REASONS FOR ENTRENCHING ONESELF IN A FORT AFTER MAKING WAR WITH A STRONG KING

SECTION 120: CONDUCT PROPER FOR THE KING SURRENDERING WITH HIS TROOPS

1. A weak king attacked by a strong king, should resort for shelter to one with strength greater than his, whom the other would not over-reach by the power of counsel.
2. Among those with an equal power of counsel, superiority comes from the excellence of men under them or from association with elders.

3. In the absence of one of greater strength, he should stay joining forces with kings equal in strength or with oligarchies equal in strength to the strong king, whom he would not overreach with powers of counsel and might.
4. Among those with equal powers of counsel and might, superiority comes from extensiveness of undertakings.
5. In the absence of those equal in strength, he should stay joining forces with kings inferior in strength who are upright, energetic and opposed to the strong king, whom he would not overreach with powers of counsel, might and energy.
6. Among those with an equal power of energy, superiority comes from the attainment of terrain suitable for one's own mode of fighting.
7. Among those with an equally suitable terrain, superiority comes from the attainment of a season suited to one's own mode of fighting.
8. Among those with equally suitable terrains and seasons, superiority comes from drought animals, weapons and armour.
9. In the absence of help-mates, he should find shelter in a fort where the enemy, even with a large army, would not cut off his food, fodder, fuel and water, and would himself meet with losses and expenses.
10. Among forts equally impregnable, superiority comes from stores and refuge.
11. 'For, one should seek a fortress with men, rich in stores and provided with refuge,' says Kautilya.
12. He should resort to that fort for these reasons: 'I shall win over the enemy in the rear or his ally or the middle king or the neutral king; or, I shall cause his kingdom to be seized or destroyed by one of these, *viz.*, his neighbouring king, a forest chief, a pretender from his family and a prince in disfavour; or, by supporting the party of likely seceders, I shall raise a revolt in his fort, country or camp; or, I shall kill him as I please, when he comes near, by the use of weapons, fire or poison or by occult means; or, I shall put him to losses and expenses on account of secret practices employed by myself; or, I shall succeed in gradually instigating against him the group of his allies or his army, when they are severely afflicted by losses, expenses and long marches; or, by destroying his supplies, reserves and foraging parties, I shall bring about the subjugation of his encamped army; or, by taking out troops, I shall create a weak point in him and strike with all troops mobilised; or, I shall secure

a treaty with him as desired when his energy is damped; or, while he is engaged in a struggle with me, insurrections will rise all round him; or, I shall cause his base, denuded of reserves, to be devastated by my ally's troops or forest troops; or staying in this fort, I shall protect the welfare of a vast territory; or, if I stay here, my own dispersed troops and those of my ally will collect in one place and be irresistible; or, my army skilled in fighting in water, in trenches or at night, being freed of the dangers of marches on the roads, will carry out operations when the enemy is near; or, coming here on a terrain and in a season adverse to him, he will himself cease to be because of losses and expenses, as this region can be approached only with heavy losses and expenses because of the abundance of forts and forests as places of refuge, is full of sickness for foreigners and without a suitable terrain for the operation of their troops, and hence he will enter it only when in trouble, and will not get out of it if he enters.'

13. 'In the absence of such reasons, or when the enemy has very great strength, he should leave the fort and go away.
14. Or, like a moth in fire, he should fall desperately on the enemy.
15. For, achievement of one thing or the other is certain for one giving up all hope of himself,' say the teachers.
16. 'No,' says Kautilya.
17. Finding out suitable conditions for peace between himself and the enemy, he should make peace.
18. In the reverse case, he should seek peace after a fight or seek escape.
19. To one with whom peace is possible, he should send an envoy.
20. Or, if one is sent by him, he should welcome him with money and honour, and say, 'These are gifts for the king, these for the queen and princes from my queen and princes; this kingdom and myself are at your disposal.'
21. After obtaining shelter, he should behave towards the suzerain as in the section on 'proper behaviour'.
22. And he should carry out undertakings like the fort and others as well as the accepting and giving of princesses in marriage, coronation of the prince, purchase of horses, catching of elephants, holding sacrificial sessions or fairs and going on pleasure trips, only when permitted.
23. Agreements with constituents remaining in his own territory or punishment of deserters,—he should carry out all, when permitted.

24. Or, if his citizens and country people have turned hostile, he should request for another land, being justly behaved.
25. Or, he should deal with them by silent punishment, as with treasonable persons.
26. He should not accept even suitable land being given to him from his ally.
27. When the suzerain cannot be seen, he should see one of these, *viz.*, his minister, chaplain, commander-in-chief and crown prince, and should confer obligations on them as far as he is able.
28. On occasions of worship of deities and recitations of blessings, he should cause blessings to be pronounced on him.
29. In every case, he should speak of his surrender as an excellent thing.
30. One surrendering to force should thus behave towards the suzerain in a steadfast manner, waiting on the strong, united with him and opposed to those suspected and so on by him.

CHAPTER SIXTEEN

SECTION 121: CONDUCT PROPER FOR THE KING SUBJUGATING OTHER KINGS BY FORCE

1. The strong king, desirous of conquering one causing harassment, though the terms of the treaty were accepted by him, should march in that direction in which there is suitable terrain, suitable season and livelihood for his own troops, in which the enemy is without the refuge of a fort and without protection in the rear and the help of an ally.
2. In the reverse case, he should march after taking protective measures.
3. He should subjugate the weak by means of conciliation and gifts, the strong by means of dissension and force.
4. And he should secure the members of the king's circle who are immediately next to him and who are separated by one intervening state, by the exclusive use, the alternative use or the combined use of the four means.
5. The protection of those dwelling in villages and forests, of cattle-herds and trade-routes, and the handing over of those who are discarded, who have deserted and who have done harm,—thus, should he practise conciliation.

6. The giving of land, money and girls, and the promise of safety,—thus, should he practise gifts.
7. Making a demand for treasury, troops, land or inheritance by supporting one of these, *viz.*, a neighbouring prince, a forest chief, a pretender from the family and a prince in disfavour,—thus, should he sow discord.
8. Subjugation of the enemy in open, concealed or silent war or through 'means for taking a fort,'—thus, should he make use of force.
9. Thus, he should place those full of energy in such a way that they are helpful to the army, those possessed of might so that they are helpful to the treasury, those endowed with intellect so that they are helpful to the land.
10. Among them, he who helps in many ways with gems, articles of high value, of low value and forest produce produced in his ports, villages and mines, or with carriages and vehicles arising from material forests, elephant forests and herds, is the ally of varied usefulness.
11. He who gives substantial help with troops or treasury is one of great usefulness.
12. He who helps with troops, treasury and land is one of all-sided usefulness.
13. He who withstands one's enemy on one side is the ally useful on one side.
14. He who withstands the enemy and the enemy's ally on the two sides is one useful on both sides.
15. He who withstands the enemy, his ally, the neighbour and the forest chief on all sides is one useful on all sides.
16. And if an enemy in the rear,—a forest chieftain, a principal officer of the enemy or the enemy himself—be found capable of being secured by a gift of land, he should win his support with the grant of land without excellences; one stationed in a fort, with land not contiguous; a forest chief, with land not yielding livelihood; a pretender from the family of the enemy, with recoverable land; a prince in disfavour of the enemy, with land snatched; one with banded troops, with land having permanent enemies; one with compact troops, with land having strong neighbouring kings; one opposing in war, with land having both these characteristics; one with energy, with land where military operations are not possible; one belonging to the enemy's party, with waste land; one enticed

away, with impoverished land, a deserter who has returned, with land the settlement of which would involve great losses and expenses; the deserter from the enemy who has come over, with land without shelter, with land that cannot be occupied by any one else, he should secure the support of its master himself.

17. He should allow to continue as before that one among them who is of great help and unchanging in loyalty.
18. He should silently do away with the contrary one.
19. He should gratify, according to his power to help, one who has helped him.
20. And in conformity with his efforts, he should bestow wealth and honour on him, and give help in calamities.
21. To those coming of their own accord, he should grant interviews as desired and make arrangements for receiving them.
22. He should not use towards them insults, injuries, contemptuous words or reproaches.
23. And after promising them safety, he should favour them like a father.
24. And if any of them were to do him harm, he should proclaim his guilt and slay him openly.
25. Or, because of fright likely among others, he should act as in 'infliction of secret punishment'.
26. And he shall not covet the land, property, sons or wives of the slain one.
27. He should place in their appropriate positions even the members of his family.
28. He should place on the throne the son of one killed in action.
29. In this way, the princes surrendering to force remain loyal to his sons and grandsons.
30. But the circle of kings, being frightened, rises to destroy one who were to kill or imprison those who have submitted and covet their land, property, sons or wives.
31. And those ministers, who are under his control in their own lands, become frightened of him and resort to the circle.
32. Or, they themselves seek to take his kingdom or life.
33. And therefore, kings, protected in their own territories by means of conciliation, because favourably disposed towards the king, remaining obedient to his sons and grandsons.

CHAPTER SEVENTEEN

SECTION 122: THE MAKING OF PEACE
SECTION 123: LIBERATION OF THE HOSTAGE

1. Peace, treaty, hostage, these are one and the same thing.
2. The creation of confidence among kings is the purpose of peace, treaty or hostage.
3. 'Plighting one's truth or taking an oath is an unstable pact, a surety or a hostage is stable,' say the teachers.
4. 'No,' says Kautilya.
5. Plighting one's truth or taking an oath is a pact stable in the next world as well as here, a surety or a hostage is of use only in this world, depending on strength.
6. 'We have made a pact,' thus kings of old, faithful to their word, made pacts by plighting their truth.
7. In case of fear of its transgression, they touched fire, a furrow in the field, a clod of earth from the rampart, the shoulder of an elephant, the back of a horse, the box of a chariot, a weapon, a gem, seeds, a fragrant substance, a liquid, gold or money, affirming with an oath, 'May these kill or abandon him who would break the oath.'
8. In case of fear of transgression of oath, the binding to suretyship of great men, ascetics or principal men constitutes surety.
9. With respect to that, he who receives sureties capable of suppressing the enemy, overreaches.
10. The opposite of this is overreached.
11. The holding of a kinsman or a principal officer, is receiving a hostage.
12. With respect to that, he who gives a treasonable minister or a treasonable child, overreaches.
13. The opposite of this is overreached.
14. For, the enemy strikes without compunction at the weak points of one who is trustful because of receiving a hostage.
15. When keeping a child as a hostage, however, as between giving a son and a daughter, he who gives a daughter overreaches.
16. For, a daughter is not an heir, and is of use to others only and cannot be harassed.
17. A son is the reverse of this.
18. Even of two sons, he who gives a son legitimately born, wise, brave, trained in the use of weapons, or an only son, is overreached.
19. The opposite of this overreaches.

20. For, it is better to hand over as a hostage an illegitimate son than a legitimate one, because of the loss of continuity of heirs in his case, an unwise son than a wise one, because of the absence of the power of energy, one not trained in the use of weapons to one trained in their use, because of the absence of the ability to strike, one not an only son than an only son, because of the absence of expectations being centred in him alone.
21. As between a legitimate son and a wise son, the attribute of sovereignty goes with one who is legitimate though unwise, the function of counsel goes with one who is wise though illegitimate.
22. Even in the matter of counsel, the legitimate overreaches the wise through association with elders.
23. As between a wise son and a brave son, the possession of acts of intelligence belongs to the wise though cowardly, the function of valour to the brave though unwise.
24. Even in the matter of valour, the wise one overreaches the brave, as the hunter does the elephant.
25. As between a king with many sons and a king with an only son, the one with many sons, handing over one and supported by the rest, can violate the pact, not the other.
28. If the pact is on condition of giving the son who is his all, advantage comes from the offspring of the son.
29. Between two, equally having offspring from a son, advantage comes from the power to procreate.
30. Even between two, possessing the power to procreate, advantage comes from the birth being close at hand.
31. But when there is a capable only son, he should hand over himself, if he has lost the power of procreation, but should not give the only son.
32. When grown in strength, he should bring about the liberation of the hostage.
33. Secret agents disguised as artisans or artists, carrying out works in the proximity of the prince, should dig up a subterranean passage at night and carry away the prince.
34. Or, actors, dancers, singers, musicians, reciters, minstrels, rope-walkers and showmen, stationed there beforehand, should wait upon the enemy.
35. They should then wait upon the prince one after the other.
36. He should fix for them entry, stay and departure without restriction as to time.

37. Then, disguised as one of them, he should leave at night.
38. By that are explained courtesans and women appearing as wives.
39. Or, he should go out carrying the box of their musical instruments of other articles.
40. Or, he should be carried out by cooks, waiters, bath-attendants, shampooers, bed-preparers, barbers, toilet-attendants or water-servers along with boxes of materials, dresses and articles, beds and seats after they have been used.
41. Or, he should go out at a time when the appearance cannot be distinguished, disguised as a servant, carrying something with him, or go out through a subterranean passage with materials for a night oblation.
42. Or, he should practise the trick of Varuna in a reservoir of water remaining submerged in water for a long time.
43. Or, secret agents disguised as traders should administer poison to guards by selling cooked food and fruits.
44. Or, on the occasion of offerings to deities or worship of manes or picnic parties he should administer food and drink mixed with a stupefying mixture or poison, and depart, or he should leave by seducing the guards.
45. Or, secret agents disguised as gallants, minstrels, physicians or vendors of cooked food should set fire at night to house of the rich or of the guards.
46. Or, those disguised as traders should set fire to the market place.
47. Or, after throwing another body inside, he should set his own residence on fire, for fear of pursuit.
48. Then he should leave through a hole in the wall, a channel or a subterranean passage.
49. Or, disguised as a carrier of loads of goods in jars suspended in slings from a pole, he should leave at night.
50. Or, entering the roving camps of ascetics with shaved heads or matted hair, he should leave at night disguised as one of them, or with the help of one of these, *viz.*, change of appearance, inducing a malady and the disguise of a forester.
51. Or, made to appear as a corpse, he should be carried out by secret agents.
52. Or, dressed as a woman, he should follow the funeral procession of some one dead.
53. And agents appearing as foresters should direct pursuers to another direction when he is going in one.

54. Then he should go in another direction.
55. Or, he should escape through groups of carts of cartmen.
56. And when pursuit is close on his heels, he should remain hidden.
57. In the absence of a hiding place, he should scatter on both sides of the road money or poisoned food-stuffs.
58. Then he should go away in another direction.
59. If caught, he should overreach the pursuers with conciliation and other means, or with poisoned food on the way.
60. Or, in the trick of Varuna and in acts of setting fire, he should place another body and accuse the enemy, 'You have killed my son.'
61. Or, taking up weapons secretly brought, and falling on the guards at night, he should escape on quick marching horses along with secret agents.

CHAPTER EIGHTEEN

SECTION 124: CONDUCT TOWARDS THE MIDDLE KING
SECTION 125: CONDUCT TOWARDS THE NEUTRAL KING
SECTION 126: CONDUCT TOWARDS THE CIRCLE OF KINGS

1. With respect to the middle king, he himself, the third and the fifth constituents are friendly elements.
2. The second, the fourth and the sixth are unfriendly elements.
3. If the middle king were to help both these, the conqueror should be favourably inclined towards the middle king.
4. If he does not help either, he should remain favourable to the friendly elements.
5. If the middle king were to desire to seize an ally of the conqueror having the feelings of a friend, he should save the ally by rousing the allies of the ally and his own allies, and dividing his allies from the middle king.
6. Or, he should incite the circle; 'This middle king, grown very powerful, has risen for the destruction of all of us; let us join together and frustrate his expedition.'
7. If the circle were to favour that, he should, by suppression of the middle king, augment himself.
8. If it were not to favour, helping the ally with treasury and army, he should win over by conciliation and gifts one—the principal or the proximate—from among the kings inimical to the middle king, who, many in number, may be helping each other, or of whom, by winning over one, many would be won over, or who, being afraid of each other, would not rise.

9. Being thus double, he should win over a second king; being three-fold, a third king.
10. Augmented in power in this way, he should suppress the middle king.
11. Or, if place and time were to lapse, he should make peace with the middle king and be helpful to the ally, or make a pact for an undertaking with the treasonable officers of the middle king.
12. If the middle king were to desire to seize an ally of his deserving to be weakened, he should sustain him, saying 'I will save you,' till he is weakened.
13. He should save him when weakened.
14. If the middle king were to desire to seize an ally of his deserving to be exterminated, he should save him when weakened through fear of the increase of the middle king's power.
15. Or, if he is exterminated, he should get him in his power by the grant of land, through fear of his going elsewhere.
16. If the allies of his ally, deserving to be weakened or exterminated, were to be helpful to the middle king, he should have peace made through another person.
17. Or, if the allies of those two were capable of suppressing the conqueror, he should make peace with the middle king.
18. If the middle king were to desire to seize his that is the conqueror's enemy, he should make peace.
19. Thus, his own ends are secured and the middle king is also pleased.
20. If the middle king were to desire to seize his own ally having friendly feelings, he should have peace made through another person.
21. Or, if he were to care for the conqueror, he should dissuade him, saying 'It does not behave you to exterminate an ally.'
22. Or, he should remain indifferent, thinking 'Let the circle be enraged with him on account of the destruction of his own party.'
23. If the middle king were to desire to seize his own enemy, he should help him with treasury and army, unseen.
24. If the middle king were to desire to seize the neutral king, he should give him aid, thinking 'Let him be divided from the neutral king.'
25. Of the middle and the neutral kings, he should resort to the one who is liked by the circle of kings.
26. By conduct towards the middle king is explained conduct towards the neutral king.
27. If the neutral king were to desire to seize the middle king, he should turn to that where he would overreach his enemy or render help to

his ally or secure the neutral king for rendering aid with troops to himself.

28. Augmenting himself in this way, he should weaken the constituent, enemy and support the constituent, ally.
29. Though there are feelings of enmity among all, the enemy in front not self-possessed and constantly doing injury, or the enemy in the rear in league with the enemy in front, one vulnerable, being in a calamity, or one attacking the leader in his calamity, these are neighbouring kings with a hostile disposition; one marching for a common objective, one marching for a separate object, one marching after joining forces, one marching after making a pact, one marching for his own object, one rising together with the leader, one purchasing or selling either treasury or troops as he resorts to a dual policy, these are with a friendly disposition; the neighbour placed in between or at the side as a hindrance to the strong king, or one in the rear of the strong king, one who has submitted to force, either submitting of his own accord or submitting because of the might, these are neighbours with a dependent's feelings.
30. By these are explained those separated by one intervening state.
31. Of these, that ally who after conquering the enemy, might grow in strength and go out of control, into conflict with the two constituents, the neighbour and the one separated by one state.
32. Or, he should cause his territory to be seized by a pretender from his family or a prince in disfavour or so act that he would remain under control in consideration of help received.
33. That ally, who being much weakened might not help or might go over to the enemy, he, well-versed in politics, should keep neither weak nor strong.
34. That unstable ally, who for the sake of his own ends makes peace with him,—he should remove the reason for his leaving, so that he would not waver.
35. That ally who remains common to the enemy and himself, he should divide that rogue from the enemy, and when divided, exterminate him, thereafter exterminate the enemy.
36. And he should get that ally, who would remain indifferent, into conflict with neighbouring kings; then when he is severely distressed by the fight, he should place him under his obligations.
37. That weak ally, who goes to the enemy and the conqueror for support he should help with troops, so that he would not turn away from him.

38. Or, removing him from that territory he should settle him in another land, after first settling another ally there because of help with troops received from him.
39. That ally who might do harm or who, though capable, would not help in times of trouble, he should certainly exterminate him, when trustingly, he comes within his reach.
40. When the enemy has risen, unrestrained, because of a calamity of the ally, he should be got overpowered by that ally himself, with his calamity removed by him.
41. That ally who, after rising because of a calamity of the enemy, becomes disaffected, is overpowered through the enemy himself, by overcoming the calamity of the enemy.
42. He, who is well-versed in the science of politics, should employ all the means viz., advancement, decline and stable condition as well as weakening and extermination.
43. He who sees the six measures of policy as being interdependent in this manner, plays, as he pleases, with kings tied by the chains of his intellect.

Herewith ends the Seventh Book of the Arthasastra of Kautilya
'THE SIX MEASURES OF FOREIGN POLICY'

22

BOOK EIGHT

Concerning the Topic of Calamities

Kautilya was very ambitious and great visionary. His ambition never concerned his personal aggrandizement, but that of the State. He very carefully studied the multi-faceted and multidimensional administrative machinery and formulated remedial measures, *inter alia*, rules to counter any evil influence, or situation as would endanger the stability and the security of the State, as also the well-being of the Subjects. Calamities, either man-made or natural were identified and made the exhaustive subjects of this Book by Kautilya. The following types of calamities have been discussed in this Book:

1. The Group of Calamities of Constituent Elements. 2. Considerations regarding Calamities of the King and Kingship, 3. The Group of the Vices of Man. 4. The Group of Afflictions, The Group of Hindrances, The Group of Stoppages of Payment to the Treasury. 5. Group of Calamities of the Army; The Group of Calamities of the Ally, these constitute the Eighth Book 'Concerning the Topic of Calamities'.

CHAPTER ONE

SECTION 127: THE GROUP OF CALAMITIES OF THE CONSTITUENT ELEMENTS

1. In case of simultaneity of calamities the question arises should one march or guard oneself because of ease, hence a consideration of calamities is necessary.
2. A calamity of a constituent, of a divine or human origin, springs from ill-luck or wrong policy.

3. Inversion of excellences, absence, a great defect, addiction, or affliction constitutes a calamity.
4. It throws out a person from his good, hence, it is called *vyasana*.
5. 'Of calamities befalling the king, the minister, the country, the fort, the treasury, the army and the ally, that of each earlier one is more serious', say the teachers.
6. 'No,' says Bharadvaja.
7. 'Of calamities befalling the king and the minister, the calamity of the minister is more serious.
8. Deliberation in counsel, securing the fruits of deliberation, carrying out undertakings, managing income and expenditure, infliction of punishment, warding off of enemies and forest tribes, protection of the kingdom, taking steps against calamities, guarding of princes and the installation of princes, are all dependent on ministers.
9. In the absence of these, those activities are lacking, and there is loss of all activity on the part of the king, as of a bird with clipped wings.
10. And in the calamities of these, secret instigations by the enemy are close at hand.
11. And if these are hostile, there is danger to the king's life, since they move near the person of the king'.
12. 'No,' says Kautilya.
13. It is the king alone who appoints the group of servants like the councillor, the chaplain and others, directs the activity of departmental heads, takes counter-measures against the calamities of constituents, whether human or material, and secures their advancement.
14. If the ministers are suffering from calamities, he appoints others who are not in calamities.
15. He remains ever diligent in honouring those worthy of honour and suppressing the treasonable.
16. And when the king is possessed of excellences.
17. What character he has, that character the constituents come to have, being dependent on him in the matter of energetic activity and remissness.
18. For, the king is in the place of their head.
19. 'Of calamities befalling the minister and the country, the calamity of the country is more serious,' says Visalaksa.
20. 'The treasury, the army, forest produce, labourers, means of transport and stores spring from the country.

21. In the absence of the country, there would be lack of these, and the disappearance of the king and the minister would follow immediately thereafter.'
22. 'No', says Kautilya.
23. All undertakings have their origin in the ministers, *viz.*, successful execution of works in the country, bringing about its wellbeing and security from one's own and from the enemy's people, taking counter-measures against calamities, settlement of new lands and their development, and bringing in the benefit of fines and taxes.
24. 'Of calamities befalling the country and the fort, the calamity of the fort is more serious,' say the followers of Parasara.
25. 'For, it is in the fort that the treasury and the army spring up and a place secured for the country people in times of trouble.
26. And city-dwellers are stronger than the country people and being steadfast in loyalty are helpful to the king in times of trouble.
27. Country people, on the other hand, are common to the enemy.'
28. 'No,' says Kautilya.
29. The undertakings of the fort, the treasury, the army, waterworks and the occupations for livelihood have their source in the country.
30. And bravery, firmness, cleverness and large numbers are found among the country people.
31. And mountain forts and island forts are not inhabited because of the absence of the country.
32. However, in a country inhabited mostly by agriculturists, the calamity of the fort is more serious, while in a country inhabited mostly by martial people, the calamity of the country is more serious.
33. 'Of calamities befalling the fort and the treasury, the calamity of the treasury is more serious,' says Pisuna.
34. 'For, dependent on the treasury are building of the fort, protection of the fort, control over the country, the allies and the enemies, incitement of those away from the land, and the use of armed forces.
35. A fort is susceptible to secret instigations by enemies with money.
36. And in a calamity, it is possible to go away with the treasury, not with the fort.'
37. 'No,' says Kautilya.
38. Dependent on the fort are the treasury, the army, silent war, restraint of one's own party, use of armed forces, receiving allied troops, and warding off enemy troops and forest tribes.

39. And in the absence of a fort, the treasury will fall into the hands of enemies,
40. For, it is seen that those with forts are not exterminated.
41. 'Of calamities befalling the treasury and the army, the calamity of the army is more serious,' says Kaunapadanta.
42. 'For, dependent on the army are restraint of allies and enemies, rousing alien troops to action, and reinforcement of one's own troops.
43. And in the absence of an army, the loss of the treasury is certain.
44. And in the absence of a treasury, it is possible to collect an army with forest produce or land or by allowing seizure of enemy's land by each for himself, and to collect a treasury, when one has an army.
45. And being in close proximity to the king, the army has the same characteristics as the minister.
46. 'No,' says Kautilya.
47. The army, indeed, is rooted in the treasury.
48. In the absence of a treasury, the army goes over to the enemy or kills the king.
49. And the treasury, ensuring the success of all endeavours, is the means of deeds of piety and sensual pleasures.
50. In conformity with the place, the time and the work, however, one of the two, treasury and army, becomes important.
51. For, the army is the means of acquiring and protecting the treasury, and the army.
52. Because it brings into being all objects, the calamity of the treasury is more serious.
53. 'Of calamities befalling the army and the ally, the calamity of the ally is more serious,' says Vatavyadhi.
54. 'The ally does the work without being paid and at a distance, repels the enemy in the rear, his ally, the enemy and the forest chief, and helps with treasury, army and territory, remaining united in conditions of calamity.'
55. 'No,' says Kautilya.
56. When one has an army, one's ally remains friendly, or even the enemy becomes friendly.
57. However, in a work that can well be performed either by the army or the ally, advantage comes from their strength and the attainment of suitable place and time for their own type of warfare.
58. But an ally is of no avail in a speedy expedition against enemies or forest chiefs and in a rising in the interior.

59. An ally looks to the securing of his own interests in the event of simultaneity of calamities and in the event of the growth of the enemy's power.
60. Thus, has been stated the determination of the seriousness of calamities befalling the constituents.
61. But in accordance with the peculiar nature of the calamity, the numerousness or loyalty or strength of parts of the constituent leads to the accomplishment of a work.
62. But when the calamity of two constituents is equal, the difference arises from a decline in qualities, if the possession of excellences by the rest of the constituents is not rendered unserviceable.
63. But where the destruction of the rest of the constituents is likely to follow from the calamity of one, that calamity would be more serious, whether of the principal or of some other constituent.

CHAPTER TWO

SECTION 128: CONSIDERATIONS REGARDING THE CALAMITIES OF THE KING AND KINGSHIP

1. The king and his rule, this is the sum-total of the constituents.
2. For the king, there is danger of revolt in the interior or in the outer regions.
3. Because of danger as from a snake, a rising in the interior is a greater evil than a rising in the outer regions, and a rising of ministers of the interior greater evil than a rising in the interior.
4. Therefore, he should keep the power of the treasury and the army in his own hands.
5. 'As between rule by two and rule without the legitimate king, rule by two is destroyed by hatred and loyalty towards each other's parties or by mutual rivalry; rule without the legitimate king, on the other hand, looking to the winning of the hearts of the hearts of the subjects, is enjoyed by the others as exists,' say the teachers.
6. 'No,' says Kautilya.
7. Rule by two, *e.g.*, by father and son or by two brothers, continues to exist, with well-being and security equally shared and with ministers held in check.
8. Rule without the legitimate king, on the other hand, snatching what belongs still living, and thinking, 'This does not belong to me,' impoverishes it, carries it off or sells it or, if still disaffected, leaves it and goes away.

9. As between a king blind and a king deviating from the science, 'The king, blind because he is without the eye of science, doing whatsoever pleases him, obstinately resolved, or led by others, ruins the kingdom with his acts of injustice; but one deviating from the science is easy of persuasion in those cases where his mind has strayed from the science,' say the teachers.
10. 'No,' says Kautilya.
11. The blind king can be made to follow any course of action through the excellence of his associates.
12. One deviating from the science, however, with his mind firmly fixed on what is contrary to the science, ruins the kingdom and himself with his injustice.
13. As between a sick and a new king, 'The sick king meets with the danger of the overthrow of his rule caused by ministers or danger to his own life caused by carrying on the rule; the new king, on the other hand, busies himself with acts like observance of his duties, showing favours, granting exemptions, bestowing gifts and conferring honour, which please and benefit the subjects,' say the teachers.
14. 'No,' says Kautilya.
15. The sick king carries on the kingly duties as they were going on before.
16. The new king, however, thinking the kingdom, won by force, to be his, behaves as he likes without restraint.
17. Or, being in the power of his associates in revolt, he tolerates the ruin of the kingdom.
18. Not being rooted among the subjects, he becomes easy to uproot.
19. With respect to the sick king, there is this distinction, one afflicted by a foul disease and one not so afflicted.
20. With respect to the new, also, the distinction is one of noble birth and one not of noble birth.
21. As between a weak king of noble birth and a strong king not of noble birth,'The subjects yield with difficulty to the overtures of the weak though nobly-born king, having regard to his weakness, but easily yield to those of the strong though low-born king, having regard to his strength,' say the teachers.
22. 'No,' says Kautilya.
23. The subjects submit of their own accord to a weak king of noble birth, as a natural capacity to rule devolves on one of noble birth.

24. And they frustrate the overtures of the strong but low-born king since in love are all virtues present.
25. The loss of the crops is a greater evil than the loss of sowings, as it involves loss of efforts, drought a greater evil than excessive rain, as it involves loss of livelihood.
26. The relative seriousness or otherwise of calamities of the constituents, taken two at a time, has been set forth in the traditional order, as the ground for marching or staying quiet.

CHAPTER THREE

SECTION 129: THE GROUP OF THE VICES OF MAN

1. Absence of training in the lores is the cause of a man's vices.
2. For, an untrained person does not see the faults in vices.
3. Kautilya set them forth.
4. A group of three vices springs from anger, a group of four springs from lust.
5. Of the two, anger is more serious.
6. For, anger acts everywhere.
7. And mostly kings under the influence of anger are known to have been killed by risings among the subjects, those under the influence of lust are known to be killed by enemies and diseases as a result of losses.
8. 'No,' says Bharadvaja.
9. 'Anger is behaviour proper for a good man, a means of requiting enmity, extirpation of insults and keeping men in dread.
10. And resort to anger is ever needed for putting down evil.
11. Lust is a means of attainment of success, conciliation, generosity of nature and being lovable.
12. And resort to lust is ever needed for the enjoyment of fruits of works done.'
13. 'No,' says Kautilya.
14. Becoming hated, making enemies, and association with pain, that is anger.
15. Humiliation, loss of wealth, and association with harmful persons like thieves, gamblers, hunters, singers and players on instruments, that is lust.
16. Of these, being hated is a greater evil than humiliation.
17. One humiliated is held in their power by his own people and by others; the hated one is exterminated.
18. Making enemies is a greater evil than loss of wealth.

19. Loss of wealth endangers the treasury, making enemies endangers life.
20. Association with pain is a greater evil than association with harmful persons.
21. Association with harmful persons can be remedied in a moment, association with pain causes prolonged distress.
22. Therefore, anger is more serious.
23. Verbal injury, violation of property and physical injury are vices springing from anger.
24. 'As between verbal injury and violation of property, verbal injury is worse,' says Visalaksa.
25. 'For, a spirited man, spoken to harshly, retaliates with energy.
26. The barb of offensive speech, embedded in the heart, inflames the spirit and afflicts the senses.'
27. 'No,' says Kautilya.
28. Honouring with money removes the dart of speech, but violation of property means loss of livelihood.
29. Not giving what belongs to the other, taking away, destroying or abandoning property is violation of property.
30. 'As between violation of property and physical injury, violation of property is worse,' say the followers of Parasara.
31. 'Spiritual good and pleasures are rooted in money.
32. And the world is tied up with money.
33. Its destruction is a greater evil.'
34. 'No,' says Kautilya.
35. Even for a very large sum of money, no one would desire the loss of his life.
36. And through physical injury a person incurs that same danger at the hands of others.
37. This is the group of three vices springing from anger.
38. The group of favourites springing from lust, however, is hunting, gambling, woman and drink.
39. Among them, 'Of hunting and gambling, hunting is worse,' says Pisuna.
40. 'For, in it, the danger of robbers, enemies, wild animals, forest fires and stumbling and loss of way as well as hunger and thirst constitute a danger to life.
41. In gambling, however, there is only winning for one expert in dice, as it was for Jayatsena and Duryodhana.'
42. 'No,' says Kautilya.

43. Of the two parties in gambling there is also loss for one, as is illustrated by Nala and Yudhisthira.
44. And the same money, won at gambling, becomes a bait and leads to formation of enmities.
45. Uncertainty as to existing wealth and obtaining non-existing wealth, loss before a thing is enjoyed and getting illness due to retention of urine, motions of the bowel, hunger and so on, are the evils of gambling.
46. But in hunting, there is exercise, getting rid of phlegm, bile, fat and a tendency to perspiration, practice in hitting the targets of moving and stationary bodies, knowledge of the minds of animals in anger, fear and condition of ease, and only occasional marching.
47. 'Of the vices of gambling and women, the vice of gambling is worse,' says Kaunapadanta.
48. 'For, continuously, at night in lamplight, and even when the mother has died, the gambler goes on playing.
49. And if questioned in difficulties, he becomes enraged.
50. But in case of indulgence in women, questioning concerning spiritual and material well-being is indeed possible on occasions of bath, toilet and meals.
51. And it is possible to employ a woman in what is beneficial to the king or to turn her away by means of silent punishment or disease or to make her go away.'
52. 'No,' says Kautilya.
53. Deliverance is possible in gambling, without deliverance is addiction to women.
54. Failure to show himself, aversion for work, absence of material good and loss of spiritual good by allowing the right time to pass, weakness in administration and addiction to drink result from addiction to women.
55. 'Of the vices of women and drink, indulgence in women is worse,' says Vatavyadhi.
56. 'For, harmfulness among women is of various kinds as explained in the section on rules for the royal residence.
57. In drink, on the other hand, there is the enjoyment of pleasures of the senses, such as sound and others, making gifts of love, honouring attendants, and the removal of fatigue caused by work.'
58. 'No,' says Kautilya.
59. In the case of indulgence in women there is begetting of an offspring and protection of oneself with wives at home, the

opposite of this with outside women, ruin of everything with women unapproachable for one.

60. Both these evils are there in the vice of drink.
61. The excellences of drink are: loss of consciousness, insane behaviour of one not insane, appearing like a corpse when not deceased, exposing private parts to view, loss of learning, intellect, strength, wealth and friends, separation from the good, association with the harmful, and attachment to skill in lute and song, destructive of wealth.
62. Of gambling and wine, gambling is worse.
63. The success or failure of one side, due to the stakes, leads to strife among the subjects by creating two factions concerning animate and inanimate objects.
64. And in particular, in the case of oligarchies and of royal families having the character of an oligarchy, there are dissensions caused by gambling and destruction caused by that; hence it is the most evil among vices, as it favours evil men, and since it leads to weakness in administration.
63. Lust means the favouring of evil persons, anger, the suppression of good persons. Because of the multitude of evils resulting from them, both are held to be a calamity without end.
66. Hence, the self-possessed king should give up anger and lust, the starting point of all calamities, the destroyers of the patrimony, by waiting upon elders and gaining control over his senses.

CHAPTER FOUR

SECTION 130: THE GROUP OF AFFLICTIONS

SECTION 131: THE GROUP OF HINDRANCES

SECTION 132: THE GROUP OF STOPPAGES OF PAYMENT TO THE TREASURY

1. Visitations from the gods are: fire, floods, disease, famine and epidemic.
2. 'Of fire and floods, the affliction of fire is irremediable and all-consuming while the affliction of floods is such that escape from it is possible and its dangers can be tided over,' say the teachers.
3. 'No,' says Kautilya.
4. Fire burns at most a village or half a village; floods, on the other hand, carry away hundreds of villages.

5. 'Of disease and famine, disease ruins undertakings by hindering the activity of workers who die or are sick or afflicted, whereas famine does not ruin undertakings and yields taxes in money and cattle,' say the teachers.
6. 'No,' says Kautilya.
7. Disease afflicts only one region and remedies can be found for it, while famine afflicts the whole country and leads to absence of livelihood for living beings.
8. By that is explained epidemic.
9. 'Of the loss of common men and that of chiefs, the loss of common men brings about insecurity of undertakings, the loss of chiefs is characterised by a hindrance to the carrying out of works,' say the teachers.
10. 'No,' says Kautilya.
11. The loss of common men can be made good because of the very large number of common men, not the loss of chiefs.
12. For, among thousands there is one chief or not even one, because of the right degree of spirit and intelligence necessary, and because of the dependence of common men on him.
13. 'Of one's own army and an enemy's army, one's own army harasses by excessive violence and levies, and cannot be warded off, whereas an enemy's army can be given a fight or can be escaped from by means of fight or by a treaty,' say the teachers.
14. 'No,' says Kautilya.
15. Harassment by one's own army can be avoided by winning over or destroying the leaders among the principal officers or it afflicts only a part of the country, whereas the enemy's army, which afflicts the whole country, ruins it by plunder, slaughter, burning, destroying and carrying people off.
16. 'Of strife among subjects and strife in the royal family, strife among subjects, creating a split among subjects, invites attack by enemies, while strife in the royal family brings about double food, wages and exemptions for the subjects,' say the teachers.
17. 'No,' says Kautilya.
18. Strife among subjects can be averted by winning over the leaders among the subjects or by removal of the cause of strife.
19. And subjects, contending among themselves, benefit the king by their mutual rivalry.
20. Strife in the royal family, on the other hand, leads to harassment and destruction of the subjects and can be overcome only with a double exertion.

21. 'Of indulgence in pleasures by the country people and that by the king, indulgence in pleasures by the country people brings about the destruction of the fruits of works for all three times, whereas indulgence in pleasures by the king confers benefit on artisans, artists, actors, reciters, prostitutes and traders,' say the teachers.
22. 'No,' says Kautilya.
23. Indulgence in pleasures by the country people consumes little for the sake of the removal of fatigue caused by work and, after consuming, leads to application to work once again, whereas indulgence by the king afflicts the subjects through seizure of what he pleases, demands, gifts and seizure of works by the king himself and by his favourites.
24. 'Of the king's beloved and the prince, the prince harasses through seizure of what he pleases, demands, gifts and seizure of works by himself and by his favourites, the king's beloved through enjoyment of pleasures,' say the teachers.
25. 'No,' says Kautilya.
26. The prince can be held in check through the minister and the chaplain, not the king's beloved, because of her foolishness and association with harmful persons.
27. 'Of a band of fighting units and a chief, the band, impossible to suppress because of large numbers, harasses, through robbery and forcible seizure, the chief through favouring and destroying undertakings,' say the teachers.
28. 'No,' says Kautilya.
29. A band is easy to restrain because of common character and vices or through the winning over of the chief or a part of the band.
30. The chief, full of hauteur, harasses by destroying the lives and property of others.
31. 'Of the Director of Stores and the Administrator, the Director of Stores harasses by finding fault with what is done and by imposing penalties, while the Administrator, supervised by a bureau, enjoys only the fruit assigned,' say the teachers.
32. 'No,' says Kautilya.
33. The Director of Stores receives as admissible in the treasury what is guaranteed by others, whereas the Administrator first secures wealth for himself, then collects revenue for the king or allows it to perish, and in the matter of receiving others' property he acts on his own authority.

34. Of the frontier officer and the trader, the frontier officer harasses a trade route by allowing the activity of robbers and charging excessive duties, whereas traders promote trade route through benefits conferred by goods brought in exchange,' say the teachers.
35. 'No,' says Kautilya.
36. The frontier officer maintains a trade route by favouring the bringing together of goods, whereas traders, joining together and raising or lowering the prices of goods, make a profit of one hundred *panas* on one *pana* or of one hundred *kumbhas* on one *kumbha*.
37. As between land seized by a person of noble birth and land occupied by herds of cattle, 'Land seized by a person of noble birth, though yielding abundant produce, is not fit to be retrieved if useful in providing soldiers, because of the fear of the danger of a calamity, while land occupied by herds of cattle, being suited for agriculture, is fit to be reclaimed.
38. For, pasture land is made to yield before fields,' say the teachers.
39. 'No,' says Kautilya.
40. Land seized by a person of noble birth, even if yielding extremely great benefit, is fit to be retrieved because of the fear of the danger of a calamity, whereas that occupied by herds of cattle, of benefit to the treasury and useful for transport is not fit to be reclaimed, except in case of obstruction to the sowing of crops.
41. 'Of highway robbers and forest tribes, highway robbers, operating at night and lying in wait, attack men's bodies, are a constant danger, rob hundreds of thousands in cash and stir up principal men, while forest tribes, operating in forests on the frontier far away, are openly known and move before the eyes of all, and harm only a part of the country,' say the teachers.
42. 'No,' says Kautilya.
43. Robbers rob only the negligent, are few in number, powerless and easy to know and capture, whereas forest tribes, living in their own territory, are many in number and brave, fight openly, seize and ruin countries, having the same characteristics as a king.
44. Of deer parks and elephant forests, deer, being plenty in number, yield the benefit of abundant meat and skins, cause little trouble about fodder and are easy to control.
45. Elephants are the reverse of this when being caught, and if rogues, they lead to the ruin of the country.
46. Of benefit conferred on one's own *sthaniya* and that conferred on an enemy's *sthaniya*, the benefit conferred on one's own *sthaniya*,

viz., the benefit of grains, cattle, money and forest produce, is capable of sustaining the lives of the country people in times of trouble.

47. The reverse is the benefit conferred on an enemy's *sthaniya*.
    Thus, ends the topic of afflictions.
48. Internal hindrance is hindrance by the chiefs, the external hindrance caused by enemies or forest tribes.
    Thus, ends the topic of hindrances.
49. Affected by those two hindrances and by the afflictions as described, appropriated by chiefs, impaired by exemptions, scattered, wrongfully collected, and carried off by neighbouring kings and forest tribes,—these are stoppages of payment to the treasury.
50. The king should strive to prevent the afflictions from arising and to overcome those that have arisen, as well as to destroy the hindrances and stoppages of payment for the sake of the country's prosperity.

CHAPTER FIVE

SECTION 133: THE GROUP OF CALAMITIES OF THE ARMY

SECTION 134: THE GROUP OF CALAMITIES OF THE ALLY

1. The calamities of the army are: the state of being unhonoured, dishonoured, unpaid, sick, newly arrived, come after a long march, exhausted, depleted, repulsed, broken in the first onslaught, caught in an unsuitable terrain, despondent of hope, deserted, with women-folk inside, with 'darts' inside, with a rebellious base, split inside, run away, widely scattered, encamped near, completely absorbed, blocked, encircled, with supplies of grains and men cut off, dispersed in one's own land, dispersed in an ally's land, infested by treasonable men, with a hostile enemy in the rear, with its base denuded of troops, not united with the master, with head broken and blind.
2. Among these, as between an unhonoured and a dishonoured army, the unhonoured would fight when honoured with money, not the dishonoured, with resentment in its heart.
3. As between an unpaid and a sick army, the unpaid would fight if given pay at once, not the sick, unfit for work.
4. As between a newly arrived army and one that has come after a long march, the newly arrived would fight after learning about the regions from others and being mixed with old troops, not the

one that has come after a long march, being troubled by the long march.

5. As between an exhausted and a depleted army, the exhausted would fight after getting refreshed with bath, food and sleep not the depleted, with its drought-animals and men reduced in a fight elsewhere.
6. As between a repulsed army and one broken in the first onslaught, the repulsed, thrown back in the first encounter, would fight, being rallied by heroic men, not the one broken in the first onslaught, with its heroic men slain in the first encounter.
7. As between an army caught in an unsuitable season and one caught on an unsuitable terrain, the one caught in an unsuitable season would fight when equipped with vehicles, weapons and armours suited to the season, not the one caught on an unsuitable terrain, with its foraging raids and operations impeded.
8. As between an army despondent of hope and deserted one, the despondent would fight when its desires are fulfilled, not the deserted one, from which its chiefs have run away.
9. As between an army with women-folk inside and one with darts inside, the one with women inside would fight after getting rid of the women, not the one with darts inside, having enemies inside it.
10. As between an army with a rebellious base and one split inside, the one with a rebellious base would fight when its resentment is overcome by conciliation and other means, not the one split inside, divided from one another.
11. As between an army run away and one widely scattered, the army that has run away, having crossed over to a single realm, would fight with diplomacy and military activity, finding shelter in fastness or an ally, not the widely scattered one, gone to more than one realm, because of there being many dangers.
12. As between an army encamped near the enemy and one completely absorbed in his forces, the one encamped near, having separate marches and halts, would fight by overreaching the enemy, not the one completely absorbed, with its halts and marches one with the enemy.
13. As between a blocked and an encircled army, the blocked one would fight the obstructer by getting out in another direction, not the encircled one, obstructed on all sides.
14. As between an army with supplies of grains cut off and one with reserves of men cut off, that with supplies of grains cut off would

fight after bringing grains from elsewhere or by subsisting on animal and vegetable food, not the one with reserves of men cut off, being without help.

15. As between an army dispersed in one's own land and one disappeared in an ally's land, that dispersed in one's own land, being disbanded in one's own territory, can be collected together in case of trouble, not the one dispersed in an ally's land, because of the distant place and time.
16. As between an army infested by treasonable men and one with a hostile enemy in the rear, that infested by treasonable men would fight when officered by trustworthy men and kept apart, not the one with a hostile enemy in the rear, being frightened of an attack in the rear.
17. As between an army with a denuded base and one not united with the master, that with a denuded base would fight with full mobilisation, after protection is secured through the citizens and the country people, not the one not united with the master, being without the king or the commander-in-chief.
18. As between an army with head broken and a blind army, the one with head broken would fight under the command of another commandant not the blind one, being without a guide.
19. Removal of defects, insertion of fresh troops, overreaching by remaining in a strong place, and peace with a superior party, are the means of overcoming the calamities of an army.
20. Being ever active, he should protect his own army, in its calamity, from the enemies; and being ever active, he should strike at the weak points of the army of the enemies.
21. The king, ever diligent, should take steps right beforehand against that cause because of which he might suffer a calamity of the constituents.

22-27. An ally against whom one has marched oneself after joining forces with others or under the influence of others, or who is deserted through weakness or greed or regard for another, or who is sold to the attacker by turning away from the battle or by planning to march against another enemy in another direction when pursuing the dual policy who after being inspired with confidence is overreached either in a separate or a joint march, or who is not rescued from a calamity through fear or disrespect or laziness, or who, being kept out of his own lands, has gone away from one's side through fear, or who is humiliated by snatching something away from him or by not giving something to him, or even by giving something away from him or by not giving something to him, or whose wealth is extorted from him by oneself or through another's agency or who, being assigned a very heavy task, is broken in the attempt and has gone over to the enemy or who, neglected because of weakness, is antagonised after making a request, such an ally can be secured with difficulty, and even when secured becomes quickly disaffected.

28-29. An ally, who has exerted himself or is worthy of honour, but is not honoured through one's folly, or is not honoured in a suitable manner, or who is prevented from gaining strength, or who is frightened because of harm done to another ally, or who is suspicious of oneself making a treaty with the enemy, or who is divided from oneself by treasonable persons, is easy to secure and remains loyal, when secured.

30. Therefore he should not allow these defects harmful to allies to arise, or, when they have arisen, he should remove them by qualities capable of removing the defects.

Herewith ends the Eighth Book of Arthasastra of Kautilya

'CONCERNING THE TOPIC OF CALAMITIES'

23

BOOK NINE

The Activity of the King About to March

Kautilya had not left any situation for the speculation of the king. In those turbulent and transient days when the kingdom was surrounded from all directions by the enemies of the State, appropriate and timely action by the king was the only imperative expedient. Kautilya had dexterously worked out all such situations and formulated elaborate plans of actions by the king to counter them. Various alternatives to achieve success with profit were worked out with all their computations and permutations, and the ultimate success ensured. Since the material wealth was the root of spiritual good and has pleasures for its fruits, the king was entrusted by the people to strive his best for that attainment. His efforts involved wars, diplomacy, sabotage of enemy's potentials and even extirpation of the foes, internal as well as external. In this Book Kautilya had dwelt upon the following co-related subjects:

1. Ascertainment of the Relative Strength or Weakness of Power, Place and Time, Seasons for Marching on an Expedition. 2. Occasions for the Employment of the Different Kinds of Troops, Merits of Equipping for War the Different Kinds of Troops, The Work of Employing Suitable Troops Against Enemy Troops. 3. Consideration of Revolts in the Rear, Counter-measures Against Rising of Constituents in the Outer Regions and in the Interior. 4. Consideration of Losses, Expenses and Gains. 5. Dangers from Officers in the Outer Regions and the Interior. 6. Danger Connected with Traitors and Enemies 7. Dangers Associated with Advantage, Disadvantage and Uncertainty, Overcoming these Dangers by the Use of the Different Means.

These constitute the Ninth Book 'The Activity of the King About to March'.

CHAPTER ONE

SECTION 135: ASCERTAINMENT OF THE RELATIVE STRENGTH OR WEAKNESS OF POWERS, PLACE AND TIME

SECTION 136: SEASONS FOR MARCHING ON AN EXPEDITION

1. After ascertaining the relative strength or weakness of powers, place, time, seasons for marching, time for raising armies, revolts in the rear, losses, expenses, gains and troubles, of himself and of the enemy, the conqueror should march if superior in strength, otherwise stay quiet.
2. 'Of the powers of energy and might, energy is superior.
3. For, the king himself, if brave, strong, healthy, trained in the use of missiles, is able to conquer a king possessed of might with the aid of the army alone.
4. And even his small army becomes capable of achieving its object because of its spirit.
5. But a king without energy, though possessed of might, perishes when overpowered by valour,' say the teachers.
6. 'No,' says Kautilya.
7. The king, possessed of might, overreaches the king possessed of energy, by his might, by inviting another king superior to him in energy, by hiring or purchasing heroic men.
8. And his army, richly endowed with abundant might, horses, elephants, chariots and equipment, moves unhindered everywhere.
9. And winning over and purchasing men of energy, those possessed of might, even women, children, lame and blind persons, have conquered the world.
10. 'Of the powers of might and counsel, might is superior.
11. For, one, though richly endowed with the power of counsel, has only barren wisdom, if without might.
12. And lack of might ruins his works decided upon after deliberation, as lack of rain ruins the grains in the womb of the earth,' say the teachers.
13. 'No,' says Kautilya.
14. The power of counsel is superior.
15. For, the king with the eyes of intelligence and science, is able to take counsel even with a small effort and to overreach enemies

possessed or energy and might, by conciliation and other means and by secret and occult practices.

16. Thus, the king, superior in each later one among the powers of energy, might and counsel, overreaches the enemy.
17. Place means the earth.
18. In that, the region of the sovereign ruler extends northwards between the Himavat and the sea, one thousand *yojanas* in extent across.
19. There the various types of land are: forest land, village land, mountainous land, marshy land, dry land, level land and uneven land.
20. In them, he should start work that would augment his own strength.
21. That in which there is terrain suitable for the operations of one's own army and unsuitable for those of the enemy, is the best region, the opposite kind is the worst, alike to both is middling.
22. Time is of the nature of cold, and rain.
23. Its various parts are: night, day, fortnight, month, season, half year, year and *yuga*.
24. In them, he should start work that would augment his own strength.
25. That in which the season is suitable for the operations of one's own army, unsuitable for those of the enemy, is the best time, the opposite kind is the worst, alike to both is middling.
26. 'Of power, place and time, however power is superior,' say the teachers.
27. For, one possessed of power is able to counteract the difficulties of marshy or dry region and those of time with cold, heat or rain.
28. 'Place is superior,' say some.
29. 'For a dog on land drags a crocodile, a crocodile in water drags a dog.'
30. 'Time is superior,' say some others.
31. 'By day a crow kills an owl, at night an owl kills a crow.'
32. 'No,' says Kautilya.
33. Power, place and time are mutually helpful.
34. Grown superior in these, keeping a third or a fourth part of army as protection in the base, in the rear, and in forests on the borders and taking with him treasury and troops capable of carrying out the undertaking, he should march against the enemy, whose old stocks of food are exhausted, who has not yet collected the new food-grains and whose fort is unrepaired, on an expedition in

Maragasirsa, with a view to destroy his monsoon crops and winter sowings.

35. He should march on an expedition in Caitra, with a view to destroy his winter crops and spring sowings.
36. He should march on an expedition in Jyestha, against the enemy, whose stores of grass, timber and water are exhausted and whose fort is unrepaired, with a view to destroy his spring crops and monsoon sowings.
37. He should march in winter against a country which is very hot or which has little fodder, fuel and water.
38. He should march in summer against a country with showers of snow or consisting mostly of deep water or with dense grass and trees.
39. He should march when it is raining against a country suited to the operations of his own army and unsuited to those of the enemy.
40. He should march on an expedition of long duration between the Maragasirsa and the Pausa foil moon days, on one of medium duration between the Caitra and the Vaisakha full moon days, on one of medium duration between the Jyestha and the Asadha full moon days, on the fourth expedition if desirous of burning up the enemy in his calamity.
41. Marching in the enemy's calamity has been explained in the section on 'marching after making war'.
42. And in general the teachers advise, 'One should march in the enemy's calamity'.
43. 'On accession of strength one should march, there being uncertainty as to calamities,' says Kautilya.
44. Or, he should march when by marching he would be able to weaken or exterminate the enemy.
45. At a time when excessive heat is over, he should march with elephant divisions for the most part.
46. For, elephants, sweating inside, become leprous.
47. And not getting a plunge in water or a drink of water, they become blind through internal secretion.
48. Hence, in a region with plenty of water and when it is raining he should march with elephant divisions for the most part.
49. In the reverse case, he should march with troops consisting mostly of donkeys, camels and horses, in a region with little rain and mud.
50. In a region mostly desert, he should march with the fourfold army when it is raining.

51. He should regulate the expedition in accordance with the evenness or unevenness of the road, the presence of water or land on it, or the shortness or length of the march.
52. Or, all expeditions should be of short duration in conformity with the lightness of the undertaking, or of long duration in conformity with the heaviness of the undertaking, and then there may be camping during rains in the foreign land.

CHAPTER TWO

SECTION 137: OCCASIONS FOR THE EMPLOYMENT OF THE DIFFERENT KINDS OF TROOPS

SECTION 138: MERITS OF EQUIPPING FOR WAR THE DIFFERENT KINDS OF TROOPS

SECTION 139: THE WORKS OF EMPLOYING SUITABLE TROOPS AGAINST ENEMY TROOPS

1. Occasions for the employment of the hereditary, the hired, the banded, the ally's, the alien and the forest troops are:
2. When hereditary troops are in excess of what is required for the defence of the base; or, when hereditary troops, being overstrewn with treasonable men, might create trouble at the base; or the enemy has plenty or loyal hereditary troops or a strong army, hence, it is necessary to fight with military operations; or because on a long march or on one of long duration; hereditary troops can bear losses and expenses; or when plenty of loyal troops being got together, no trust can be placed in other troops, hired and other, through fear of secret instigations by the enemy against whom one is marching; or when the strength of all other troops is depleted; these are occasions for the use of hereditary troops.
3. When he thinks, 'I have a large hired army and only a small hereditary army; or, the enemy has a small or disaffected hereditary army or a hired army consisting mostly of weak troops or without strong troops; or, it is to be a fight with diplomacy with slight military operations; or, the distance is short or duration brief, involving few losses and expenses; or, my army is with few treasonable men in it, with secret enemy instigations frustrated, and trustworthy; a small raid of the enemy is to be repelled;' these are occasions for the use of hired troops.
4. When he thinks, 'I have a large army of warrior bands, capable of being used at the base and in the expedition; the distance is short,

the enemy, having mostly an army of warrior bands, intends to fight with diplomacy and military operations; use of armed forces is to be made;' these are occasions for the use of an army consisting of bands.

5. When he thinks, 'I have a large allied army that can be used at the base and in the expedition; the distance is small and war with military operations is to be more extensive than diplomatic war; or, having first engaged in fight the forest troops or the allied troops, I shall then engage them in fight with my own troops; or, my undertaking is shared in common with the ally; or, the success of my undertaking is dependent on the ally, or, my ally is close to me, deserving to be favoured; or I shall destroy the excess of traitors in his troops for him,' these are occasions for the use of an ally's troops.
6. When he thinks, 'I have a large alien army, with alien troops I shall fight at the site of the enemy's capital or against his forest troops, in that case I shall again in either eventuality, as does the Candala in a fight between a dog and a boar; or, I shall make these the means of crushing the thorns among allied or forest troops; or, when they have grown excessively large, he should always station alien troops in close proximity to himself for fear of a revolt, except in case of fear of a rising in the interior; and when the time for one's own fighting is later than that for the enemy's fighting; theses are occasions for the use of alien troops.
7. By that are explained occasions for the use of forest troops.
8. When useful for showing the way; when suited for the terrain of the enemy; when capable of counteracting the enemy's mode of fighting; or when the enemy has mostly forest troops, on the principle 'let the Bilva-fruit be destroyed by the Bilva-fruit': when a small raid is to be repelled;—these are further occasions for the use of forest troops.
9. An army not one unit, coming from many regions, which, whether asked or unasked, gets ready with the object of getting plunder is the volunteer army, not given food and wages, carrying out plunder, doing labour and heroic deeds, liable to be divided if consisting mostly of person from the same region, caste or profession, united and large in number. These are occasions for the use of various kinds of troops.
10. Of these, he should remunerate alien and forest troops with forest produce or with booty.

11. Or, when an occasion has arisen for the enemy, to raise troops, he should keep alien troops in his control, or send them elsewhere, or render them ineffective, or keep them dispersed, or should release them when the time for them is past.
12. And he should obstruct such raising of troops by the enemy and secure that for himself.
13. And it is better to equip for war each earlier one among these than each later one.
14. Because of their having the same feelings as the king and because of constant enjoyment of his regard for them, hereditary troops are better than hired troops.
15. Being always proximate to him, quick in rising for action, and under control, hired troops are better than banded troops.
16. Being native to the country, actuated by a common purpose, and having the same rivalry, resentment, success and gain as the king, banded troops are better than allied troops.
17. Being not restricted as to place and time and because of having a common purpose, allied troops are better than alien troops.
18. Being under the command of Aryas, alien troops are better than forest troops.
19. These two have plunder as their objective.
20. When there is no plunder or when there is a calamity, there might be danger from them as from a snake.
21. 'Among Brahmin, Ksatriya, Vaisya and Sudra troops, each earlier one is better for equipping for war than each later one, on account of superiority of spirit,' say the teachers.
22. 'No,' says, Kautilya.
23. By prostration, an enemy may win over Brahmin troops.
24. A Ksatriya army, trained in the art of weapons, is better, or a Vaisya or a Sudra army, when possessed of great strength.
25. Therefore, he should raise troops keeping in mind 'The enemy has these would be counter-troops.'
26. That with elephants, machines and carts at the centre, equipped with lances, javelins, spears, reeds and arrows, is a counter-force against elephant divisions.
27. The same, equipped mostly with stones, clubs, armours, hooks and 'hair-seizures', is a counter-force against chariot divisions.
28. The same is a counter-force against cavalry, or mailed elephants or mailed horses.
29. Mailed chariots and armoured infantrymen are a counterforce against the four-fold troops.

30. Thus, he should carry out the raising of troops so as to withstand enemy troops, in conformity with the strength of his own troops, and in accordance with the various types of divisions that may be necessary.

CHAPTER THREE

SECTION 140: CONSIDERATION OF REVOLTS IN THE REAR

SECTION 141: COUNTER-MEASURES AGAINST RISINGS OF CONSTITUENTS IN THE OUTER REGIONS AND IN THE INTERIOR

1. As between a small disturbance in the rear and a large gain in front, the small disturbance in the rear is of greater importance.
2. For, when he is gone, treasonable men, enemies and foresters augment the small disturbance in the rear on all sides, or a rising of the constituents augments it.
3. And if this happens servants, allies, losses and expenses eat up the large gain in front even if obtained.
4. Therefore, the advantage from a gain in front being one in a thousand or at most one in a hundred when there is a disturbance in the rear, he should not march.
5. 'Misfortunes, indeed, have the mouth of a needle' is a saying among the people.
6. In case of revolt in the rear, he should make use of conciliation, gifts, dissension and force.
7. For the gain in front he should make the commander-in-chief of the crown prince the commandant of the troops.
8. Or, if strong and capable of suppressing the revolt in the rear, the king himself should march to secure the gain in front.
9. In case of suspicion of a revolt in the interior, he should march taking with him the suspected persons, or in case of suspicion of a revolt in the outer regions, taking with him the sons and wives of these.
10. He should march after suppressing the revolt in the interior and appointing a regent with many types of troops under more than one chief, or he may march.
11. That a revolt in the interior is a greater evil than a rising in the outer regions has been stated before.
12. A revolt by one of the following, the minister, the chaplain, the commander-in-chief and the crown prince, is a revolt in the interior.

13. He should overcome that by giving up his own faults or in accordance with the power and offence of the other.
14. In the case of the chaplain, even when his offence is great, the punishment should be confinement or exile, in the case of the crown prince, confinement or death, if there is another virtuous son.
15. He should overcome, with energy, a son, brother or another member of the family, planning to seize the kingdom; if lacking in energy, by acquiescing in what is seized and by entering into a pact with him, for fear that he might join the enemy.
16. Or, he should create confidence in him by grants of land to others like him.
17. Or, he should send against him troops superior to him, that are permitted to seize what they can, or a neighbouring vassal or a forest chieftain, and should overreach him when he is fighting with these.
18. Or, he should make use of ways for securing a prince in disfavour, or secret ways of capturing an enemy's town.
19. By this are explained the minister and the commander-in-chief.
20. A revolt by any one of the officers of the interior except the minister and others is a rising of ministers of the interior.
21. In their case, too, he should use means as deserved.
22. A revolt by one of the following: the chief of the countryside, the frontier officer, the forest chieftain and the vassal surrendering to force, is a revolt in the outer regions.
23. He should cause that to be suppressed through one another.
24. Or, if he is strongly entrenched in a fort, he should cause him to be suppressed by any one of the following, a neighbouring prince, a forest chieftain, a pretender from his family or a prince in disfavour.
25. Or, he should make his ally win him over, so that he does not go over to the enemy.
26. Or, a secret agent should divide him from the enemy, saying 'This enemy, looking upon you as a secret agent, will make you fight against the king himself, and with his object achieved, will employ you, in charge of troops, against his enemy or forest chieftain or in a difficult undertaking, or will post you at the frontier, separated from wife and sons.
27. If you fail in the fight against your king, he will sell you to the king, or making peace through you, will conciliate the king himself.
28. You should go to his best ally.'

29. If he agrees, he should honour him by, the fulfilment of his wishes.
30. If he does not agree, the agent should divide the support from him, saying, 'He is kept as a secret agent against you.'
31. And the secret agent should get him killed on the strength of letters carried by men condemned to death or through secret agents.
32. Or, he should win back warriors, who had left along with him, by granting their wishes.
33. The secret agent should then declare them as having been employed by him.
34. Thus, is success to be achieved.
35. And he should cause these revolts to arise for the enemy, and suppress those against himself.
36. Secret instigations to revolt should be made to one who is capable of starting or putting down a revolt.
37. A response to instigations to revolt should be made to one who is true of promise, capable of helping in carrying out the undertaking and securing its reward and of saving in case of failure, and about him one should form a conjecture as to whether he has honest intentions or is a rogue.
38. A roguish officer from the outer regions instigates an officer in the interior to revolt with these motives; 'If after killing the king, he will make me accepted as king, I shall make a double gain, death of the enemy and acquisition of land; or, the enemy will kill him, so that the party of kinsmen of the officer put to death and those frightened of punishment because of a like offence, will become for me a very large non-seducible party; or, the king will be suspicious even of others like him, and then I shall get his other chiefs killed one by one through letters carried by men condemned to death.'
39. Or, a roguish officer from the interior instigates an officer in the outer regions to revolt with these motives: 'I shall appropriate his treasury or I shall destroy his troops, or I shall get the wicked king killed by him; when he responds I shall make the officer from the outer regions fight against the enemy or forest chieftains with the idea, "Let his army get stuck, let his enmity be firmly fixed, then he will be in my power, then I shall conciliate the king himself or shall seize the kingdom myself"; or, after imprisoning him, I shall secure both the territory of the officer from the outer region and the territory of the king; or, inviting the officer from the outer region, when he has become hostile to the king and is full of trust in me, I shall get him killed; or, I shall seize his base when it is without him.'

40. One with honest intentions, however, instigates others to revolt in the interests of those who live with him.
41. One should make a pact with one of honest intentions; agreeing 'So let us do,' one should overreach a roguish one.
42. Understanding all this, the wise king should guard others from others, his own people from his own people, his own people from others, and others from his own people and from others.

CHAPTER FOUR

SECTION 142: CONSIDERATION OF LOSSES, EXPENSES AND GAINS

1. The diminution of drought-animals and men is loss.
2. The diminution of money and grains is expense.
3. He should march when the gains superior, because of many good points, to these two.
4. That which can be seized, which can be recovered, which is pleasing, which is rousing to anger, which requires a short time, which involves small losses, which requires small expenses, which is great, which leads to further increase, which is safe, which is lawful and which is foremost, these are the excellences of gain.
5. That which is easy to obtain and protect, and cannot be recovered by the enemies is the gain which can be seized.
6. In the reverse case, it is one that can be recovered.
7. One, seizing it or staying there, meets with destruction.
8. If, however, he were to see, 'After seizing the recoverable gain, I shall cause the enemy's treasury, army, stores and fortifications to disappear; I shall make the mines, the produce forests, the elephant forests, water-works and traderoutes denuded of all valuables; I shall impoverish his subjects, carry them away or conciliate them by suitable means, while the enemy will afterwards rouse them by contrary means; or, I shall sell this gain to his rival or make his ally or a prince in disfavour accept it; or, remaining here, I shall take steps against the harassment of my ally's or my own territory by robbers and enemies; or, I shall make his ally or support realise his deficiency, so that being disaffected with the enemy, he will accept a member of his family; or, I shall honour him and return the land to him, so that I shall have an ally bound to me and acting with me for a long time;' in such cases, he should seize even a recoverable gain.

9. Thus, the gains that can be seized and that can be recovered have been explained.
10. The gain, being obtained by a righteous king from an unrighteous one becomes pleasing to his own people and to others.
11. The reverse rouses to anger.
12. A gain, not being obtained on the advice of ministers, leads to a rising, as they think, 'He has been made to undergo losses and expenses by us.'
13. A gain, being obtained in disregard of treasonable ministers, leads to a rising, as they think, 'Having achieved his object, he will destroy us.'
14. The reverse is the gain that pleases.
15. Thus, the gains that please and that rouse have been explained.
16. Because it can be secured by merely going there, the gain is one requiring a short time.
17. Because it can be secured by diplomacy, it is one involving small losses.
18. Because there is only the expense of food, it is one requiring small expenses.
19. Because of vastness in the present, it is great.
20. Because it leads to continuity of advantage, it is one that leads to further increase.
21. Because it is free from dangers, it is one that is safe.
22. Because it is obtained in a praiseworthy manner, it is one that is lawful.
23. Because it comes without restrictions in the case of confederates, it is one that is foremost.
24. When the gain is equal from two expeditions, he should consider the place and the time, powers and means, agreeableness and disagreeableness, speed and absence of speed, nearness and distance, the present and consequences in the future, valuableness and continuousness, and abundance and richness in qualities, and seize that gain which is possessed of many good points.
25. Hindrance to gain are: passion, anger nervousness, pity, shyness, ignobleness, haughtiness, a sympathetic nature, regard for the other world, piousness, illiberality, abjectness, jealousy, contempt for what is in the hand, wickedness, lack of trust, fear, failure to counteract, inability to endure cold, heat and rain, and fondness for auspicious days and constellations.
26. The object slips away from the foolish person, who continuously consults the stars; for an object is the auspicious constellation for achieving an object; what will the stars do?

27. Men, without wealth, do not attain their objects even with hundreds of efforts; objects are secured through objects, as elephants are through elephants set to catch them.

CHAPTER FIVE

SECTION 143: DANGERS FROM OFFICERS IN THE OUTER REGIONS AND THE INTERIOR

1. The use of peace and other policies not in the prescribed manner is wrong policy.
2. From that spring dangers of conspiracy of revolt.
3. Originating in the outer region and responded to from the interior, originating in the interior and responded to from the outer region, originating in the outer region and responded to from the outer region, and originating in the interior and responded to from the interior: these are the four types of conspiracies.
4. Where those in the outer regions instigate those in the interior, or those in the interior instigate those in the outer regions, in these cases where there is association between the two types, success over the one who responded is of greater advantage.
5. For, those who respond are full of guile, not those who instigate.
6. When they are subdued, the instigators would not be able to instigate others.
7. For, those in the interior are difficult to instigate for those in the outer regions, or these for the former.
8. There is a waste of great effort for the others and a continuous advantage for oneself.
9. When those in the interior responded, he should make use of conciliation and gifts.
10. Giving a position and showing honour is conciliation.
11. Favours and exemptions or employment in works is gifts.
12. When those in the outer regions respond, he should make use of dissension and force.
13. Secret agents, posing as friends of those in the outer regions should communicate to them the following, as secret information spied out, 'This king intends to overreach you through these posing as treasonable men; beware'.
14. Or, secret agents, posing as treasonable men, employed with the treasonable men in the interior.
15. Or, assassins, insinuating themselves, should slay the treasonable men with weapon or poison.

16. Or, after inviting to the capital those from the outer regions, they should get them killed.
17. Where those in the outer regions instigate others in the outer regions or those in the interior instigate others in interior, in these cases, where there is association at one end only, success over the instigator is of greater advantage.
18. For, when the evil of treason is removed, there remain no treasonable men.
19. But when treasonable men are overcome, the evil again makes others treasonable.
20. Therefore, when those in the outer regions are instigators, he should make use of dissension and force.
21. Secret agents, posing as friends, should say, 'This king himself intends to seize you; you are at war with this king; beware.'
22. Or, assassins, insinuating themselves in the troops of the envoy of the one responding, should strike at their weak points with weapon, poison and so on.
23. Then secret agents should accuse the one responding of that crime.
24. When those in the interior instigate others in the interior, he should make use of the means as deserved.
25. He should use conciliation in the case of one discontented through showing signs of contentment, or the reverse of this.
26. Honouring under the pretext of appreciating integrity or capability or by showing consideration in a calamity or on a happy occasion, is the use of gifts.
27. Or, an agent posing as a friend, should say to them, 'In order to find out your feelings, the king will put you to test; you should disclose them to him.'
28. Or, he should divide them from each other, saying, 'So and so is thus whispering to the king about you'; thus, is dissension to be brought about.
29. And force should be used as in the infliction of secret punishment.
30. Of these four conspiracies, he should first deal with that in the interior.
31. That a rising in the interior is a greater evil than a rising in the outer regions because of danger as from a snake has been stated before.
32. Of the conspiracies, he should know each earlier one as a less serious conspiracy than each one, or that starting from strong men as more serious, the reverse as less serious.

CHAPTER SIX

SECTION 144: DANGERS CONNECTED WITH TRAITORS AND ENEMIES

1. That from the treasonable only and that from the enemies only: this is the two-fold unmixed danger.
2. In the case of unmixed danger from the treasonable, he should use against the citizens and the country people the various means, excepting force.
3. For, force cannot be used against a multitude of people.
4. Even if used, it might not achieve its object and at the same time might bring on another disaster.
5. But against the leaders among them, he should act as in the infliction of secret punishment.
6. In the case of unmixed danger from enemies, he should seek success by conciliation and other means in that place where the enemy, whether the principal or the subordinate, is.
7. Success over the principal is dependent on the king, success over dependents on ministers, and success over the principal and the dependents is dependent on both.
8. Because the treasonable and the non-treasonable have joined hands, it is mixed danger.
9. In the case of mixed danger success should be sought through the non-treasonable.
10. For, in the absence of the support, the supported do not exist.
11. Because allies and enemies have become one, it is danger mixed with the enemy.
12. In the case of enemy-mixed danger, success should be sought through allies.
13. For, peace is easy to make with an ally, not with an enemy.
14. If the ally were not to desire peace, he should constantly instigate him secretly.
15. Then dividing him from the enemy through secret agents, he should win the ally.
16. Or, he should win over the king situated on the border of the confederacy of allies.
17. When one situated on the border is won over, those situated in the centre become divided.
18. Or, he should win over one situated in the centre.
19. When one situated in the centre is won over, those situated on the border do not remain united.

20. And he should use such means as would secure the defection of the support of these confederates.
21. He should conciliate a pious king by extolling his birth, family, learning and conduct, by mention of relationship of ancestors of both or by rendering service and refraining from injury in all three times.
22. He should win over by conciliation one whose energy has left him, one weary of war, one whose efforts are frustrated, one distressed by losses and expenses and by the expedition abroad, one seeking another ally with his integrity, one afraid of another or one of honourable intentions, attaching prominence to friendship.
23. He should win over a greedy or a weakened king with gifts after first making an ascetic or a chief stand surety.
24. Gift is five-fold: relinquishing what is due, acquiescense in what is taken, return of what is received, bestowal of one's own goods not given before, and permission to seize what he can from others' goods.
25. This is making gifts.
26. He should divide one frightened because of mutual hatred or enmity or afraid of seizure of his land, through one of these causes of fear.
27. He should divide a timid king by threat of reprisals, 'After making peace, this king will take action against you; his ally has been sent to negotiate; you are not in the peace negotiations even.'
28. Or, when for any king goods from his own land or from another's land should come as presents, secret agents should spread reports, 'These have been received from the king against whom we are to march.'
29. When the report is spread wide, he should send a letter with a man condemned to death. These goods have been sent by me to you as a present; attack your confederates or desert them; then you will receive the rest of the stipulated amount.'
30. Then secret agents should make the others realise, 'This was given by the enemy.'
31. Or, an article, well-known belonging to the enemy, should go unkown, to the conqueror. Secret agents appearing as traders from him should sell it among enemy chiefs. The secret agents should make the others realise, 'This commodity was given to the enemy.' Or, after favouring with money and honour persons who have committed great crimes, he should employ them against the enemy with weapon, poison and fire.

32. Then he should make one minister seemingly desert,
33. Taking his sons and wife under protection, he should have it proclaimed, 'They were killed at night'.
34. Then the minister should disclose those criminals one by one to the enemy.
35. If they were to act as directed, he should not get them seized.
36. Or, if unable to do as told, he should get them seized,
37. Securing the position of a trusted counsellor, the minister should speak of the necessity of the enemy being on his guard against the chief confederate.
38. Then an agent in the pay of both should get an order of the enemy for the chief's destruction seized.
39. Or, he should send a letter to one possessed of the power of energy, 'Seize the kingdom of so and so; our treaty stands as before.'
40. Then secret agents should have it seized among the enemies.
41. Or, agents should destroy the camp or supplies or allied troops of one of the confederates.
42. Speaking of friendship with the others, they should suggest to him, 'You are sought to be destroyed by these.'
43. Or, if a great warrior or an elephant or a horse of someone were to die or to be killed or carried away by secret agents, other secret agents should declare him as destroyed by others.
44. Then he should send a letter to the one who is accused, 'Do more of this; then you will receive the rest of the stipulated amount.'
45. Agents in the pay of both should get that seized.
46. When they are thus divided, he should secure one of them.
47. By that are explained dissensions among commanders-in-chief, princes and commandants of armies.
48. And he should make use of dissensions as for oligarchies.
49. This is the work of creating dissensions.
50. Secret agents should dispose of a fiery or energetic enemy or one in a calamity or one entrenched in a fort, by weapon, fire, poison and so on, or one of them should do so because of ease in doing it.
51. For, an assassin, single-handed, may be able to achieve his end with weapon, poison and fire.
52. He does the work of a whole army or more.
53. This is the group of four means.
54. In that, each earlier one is lighter than each later one.
55. Conciliation is one-fold.
56. Gifts are two-fold, being preceded by conciliation.
57. Dissension is three-fold, being preceded by conciliation and gifts.

58. Force is four-fold, being preceded by conciliation, gifts and dissension.
59. Thus, has been declared what is to be done against those who attack.
60. But the same means are to be used against those in their own territories.
61. Special steps, however, are :
62. He should frequently send well-known envoy-chief with presents to one of the confederates who are in their own territories.
63. They should urge him to a treaty or to kill another confederate.
64. If he does not agree, they should announce, 'We have made a treaty.'
65. Agents in the pay of both should communicate that to the others adding. 'This king of yours is treacherous.'
66. Or, if any of them has fear of or enmity towards or hatred of another, agents should divide him from the other, suggesting, 'This king is making peace with your enemy; presently he will overreach you; make peace yourself very quickly and try to restrain him.'
67. Or, establishing relationship by accepting or giving girls in marriage, he should divide those not so related.
68. He should cause their kingdoms to be destroyed by a neighbouring prince or a forest chieftain or a pretender from his family or a prince in disfavour, or destroy their caravans, herds and forests or troops approaching to render help.
69. And guilds of castes, supported by one another, should strike at their weak points, and secret agents should strike with fire, poison and weapon.
70. And in case of enemy-mixed danger, he being deceitful, should kill the enemies by secret practice like a fowler using a clock and a bait to lure birds by creating confidence and offering bait.

CHAPTER SEVEN

SECTION 145: DANGERS ASSOCIATED WITH ADVANTAGE, DISADVANTAGE AND UNCERTAINTY

SECTION 146: OVERCOMING THESE DANGERS BY THE USE OF THE DIFFERENT MEANS

1. Immoderation, such as passion and so on, rouses one's own constituents, wrong policy rouses foreign constituents.
2. Both those amount to demoniacal conduct.
3. A change in one's people is revolt.

4. In cases that causes advancement of the enemy, there may be advantage that is dangerous, disadvantage or uncertainty.
5. That gain, which when not obtained leads to the prosperity of the enemy, or when obtained is recoverable by enemies, or when being obtained gives rise to loses and expanses, is recoverable by enemies, or when being obtained gives rise to losses and expenses, is a dangerous advantage.
6. For example, a gain which is a tempting morsel for neighbours being caused by a calamity of the neighbour, or a gain sought by the enemy obtainable by him by its very nature, or a gain in front contested by a rising in the rear or an enemy in the rear, or a gain repugnant to the circle of kings because of the extermination of an ally or the violation of an ally or the violation or the violation of a treaty, is an advantage that is dangerous.
7. The rise of danger from one's own people or from enemies is a disadvantage.
8. Concerning these two, 'Is it an advantage or no'? 'Is it a disadvantage or no?' 'Is the advantage a disadvantage?' 'Is the disadvantage an advantage?' is uncertainty.
9. Thus, stirring up an ally of the enemy is uncertainty as to whether it is an advantage or no.
10. Inviting alien troops with money and honour is uncertainty as to whether it is a disadvantage or no.
11. Seizing land with a strong neighbour is uncertainty as to whether the advantage is disadvantage.
12. Marching after joining forces with a superior king is uncertainty as to whether the disadvantage is an advantage.
13. Among these, he should act in the case of the uncertainty associated with advantage.
14. Advantage followed by advantage, advantage without a consequence, advantage followed by disadvantage, disadvantage followed by advantage, disadvantage without a consequence, disadvantage followed by disadvantage: this is the group of six consequences.
15. Seizing the enemy in the rear after uprooting the enemy in front is advantage followed by advantage.
16. Helping the neutral king with troops in return for reward is advantage without a consequence.
17. Uprooting a buffer king of the enemy is advantage followed by disadvantage.

18. Helping the enemy's neighbour at the side with treasury and troops is disadvantage followed by advantage.
19. Desisting after stirring up a weak king is disadvantage without a consequence.
20. Desisting after rousing a superior king is disadvantage followed by disadvantage.
21. Of these, each earlier one is better for attaining than each later one.
22. Thus, has been laid down the nature of enterprises.
23. The presentation of advantages simultaneously from all sides is the danger of advantages from all sides.
24. The same, when contested by the enemy in the rear, is the danger of uncertainty concerning advantages from all sides.
25. In the case of these, success should be sought by securing the support of the ally and the rear ally.
26. The appearance of danger from enemies from all sides is danger of disasters from all sides.
27. The same, when checked by the ally, is the danger of uncertainty concerning disasters from all sides.
28. In the case of these, success should be sought by securing the support of a mobile enemy and the rear ally or taking the steps recommended against enemy-mixed danger.
29. When there is gain from one side and gain from another side, that is danger of advantage from two sides.
30. In that and in the one with advantages from all sides, he should march to obtain the object possessed of the excellences of a gain.
31. If excellences of the gains are equal, he should march to secure that which is prominent or proximate or not brooking delay or in which he may be deficient.
32. When there is disaster on one side and disaster on another side, that is danger with disasters on two sides.
33. In that and in the one with disasters on all sides, he should seek success through allies.
34. In the absence of allies, he should overcome the disaster on one side with a less important constituent, the disaster from two sides with a more important constituent, the disaster from all sides with his base.
35. If that is impossible, he should leave everything and go away.
36. For, the coming back to the throne of one continuing to live observed as in the case of Suyatra and Udayana.
37. When there is gain on one side and an attack on the kingdom on the other, that is danger with advantage and disaster on the two sides.

38. In that, he should march to secure that object which would overcome the disaster.
39. Otherwise, he should ward off the attack on the kingdom.
40. By that is explained the danger with advantage and disadvantage on all sides.
41. When there is disaster on one side and uncertainty as to advantage on the other, that is danger with disaster and uncertainty as to advantage on the two sides.
42. In that, he should first overcome the disaster; when that is overcome, he should seek the uncertain gain.
43. By that is explained the danger with disaster and uncertainty as to gain on all sides.
44. When there is gain on one side and uncertainty as to disaster on the other, that is danger with gain and uncertainty as to disaster on the two sides.
45. By that is explained one with gain and uncertainty as to disaster on all sides.
46. In that, he should strive to rescue each earlier one among the constituents from the possibility of disaster in preference to each later one.
47. For, it is better that the ally remains in peril of disaster, not the army, or the army, not the treasury.
48. If the entire constituent cannot be saved, he should strive to rescue parts of the constituents.
49. Then of constituents consisting of men, he should rescue the more numerous or the loyal, excepting the sharp and the greedy, of material constituents, that of high value or of great benefit.
50. By peace or staying quiet or the dual policy, he should rescue the insignificant ones, by the opposite of these the important ones.
51. And of decline, stationary condition and advancement, he should seek to attain each later one in preference to each earlier one.
52. Or, he may see a special advantage in the future by seeking decline and other in the reverse order.
53. Thus, has been laid down place in the matter of dangers.
54. By this is explained meeting with gain, disaster and uncertainty at the start, in the middle or at the end of an expedition.
55. And because gain, disaster and uncertainty are immediately effective, it is better to obtain gain at the start of an expedition, as it becomes useful for overcoming the enemy in the rear and his ally, for reimbursing losses, expenses and marches and for guarding the base.

56. Similarly, a disaster or an uncertainty becomes bearable to one staying in his own territory.
57. By this is explained meeting with gain, disaster and uncertainty in the middle of an expedition.
58. At the end of an expedition, however, after weakening an enemy fit to be weakened or exterminating one fit to be exterminated, it is better to meet with a gain, not a disaster or uncertainty, because of the fear of danger from an enemy.
59. But for one not the leader among confederates, it is better to meet with disaster or uncertainty in the middle or at the end of an expedition, because of its affecting all without restrictions.
60. Material gain, spiritual good and pleasures: this is the triad of gain.
61. Of that, it is better to attain each earlier one in preference to each later one.
62. Material loss, spiritual evil and misery: this is the triad of disaster.
63. Of that, it is better to remedy each earlier one in preference to each later one.
64. 'Is it material gain or loss?' 'Is it spiritual good or evil?' 'Is it pleasure or pain?': this is the triad of uncertainty.
65. Of that, it is better to secure the first alternative after overcoming the second in each case.
66. Thus, has been laid down time in the matter of dangers.
    Thus, ends the topic of dangers.
67. The means of overcoming these are:
68. In the case of a son, a brother or a kinsman, overcoming dangers from them through conciliation and gifts is appropriate, in the case of leaders among citizens, country people and in the army, through gifts and dissension, in the case of neighbouring princes and forest chieftains, through dissension and force.
69. This is the natural method; in the reverse case, it is unnatural.
70. In the case of allies and enemies, success should be sought by a combination of the means.
71. For, the means help each other.
72. Conciliation used in the case of ministers under suspicion of the enemy renders unnecessary the use of the remaining means, gifts used in the case of treasonable ministers, dissension used in the case of confederates, and force used in the case of the powerful render other means unnecessary.
73. And in accordance with the seriousness or lightness of the dangers, there is restriction or option or combination in the use of means.
74. With this means only, not with another: this is restriction.

75. With this means or with another: this is option.
76. With this and with another: this is combination.
77. Of these, the use of one means at a time is four-fold, so is the use of three at a time; the use of two at a time is six-fold; the use of four at a time is single.
78. Thus, there are fifteen ways of using the means.
79. The same number of using them are there in an unnatural way.
80. Of these, success with one means is single success, with two, two-way success, with three, three-way success, with four, four-way success.
81. And since material wealth is the root of spiritual good and has pleasurc for its fruit, that attainment of material gain which continuously results in spiritual good, material gain and pleasures, is attainment of all gains.

    These are ways of overcoming dangers.
82. Caused by providence are the troubles: fire, floods, disease, epidemic, panic, famine and demoniacal creation.
83. Overcoming them is through prostration before gods and Brahmins.
84. When there is excessive rain or drought or demoniac creation, then the means of overcoming it are rites prescribed in the Atharvaveda and undertakings by holy men.

Herewith ends the Ninth Book of the Arthasastra of Kautilya

'THE ACTIVITY OF THE KING ABOUT TO MARCH'

24

BOOK TEN

Concerning War

Kautilya's versatile erudition was *par excellence* without a match. He was a celebrated and distinguished preceptor, legislator, judge, jurist, and as much the army commander as a soldier; and well-versed not only with the essentials of these sciences but also with their intricate details. His innovating and ingenious brain had master-minded the various battle arrays, stratagems and manoeuvres with all their subtleties for the deployment of the then prevailing and traditional four arms of the army—Infantry, Cavalry, Chariots and Elephants. All the army formations were thoroughly known to him, together with their merits and demerits. He was thoroughly conversant with the frontal, flank and rear-guard attacks in the bid to the total elimination of the enemy.

He was equally acqainted with all the successful methods of espionage and counter-espionage of an utilitarian army and the stratagems for ensuring victory. A separate Sappers and Miners was inducted in the army in order to hasten and secure the defeat of the enemy. The terrains of the marching army, its camp and ordnance required were tactically described and feasible methods suggested to overcome any difficulty that might likely to arise. Even, Medical Corps was required to accompany the army. In this Books Kautilya had deliberated on the following subjects:

1. Setting up of the Camp. 2. March from the Camp. Guarding Troops during the Calamities of the Army and at the Time of Attack. 3. Various Types of Covert Fighting. Encouraging one's Own Troops, Disposition of one's Troops to Counteract Enemy Troops. 4. Ground Suitable for Fighting. Functions of Infantry. The Cavalry. The Chariots and the Elephants. 5. Arrangement of Battle Arrays. Modes of Fighting of

the Infantry, the Chariots and the Elephants. 6. Arrangement of the Staff. The Snake, the Circle and the Diffuse Arrays. Arranging Counter-Arrays Against Them. These constitute the Tenth Book 'Concerning War'.

CHAPTER ONE

SECTION 147: SETTING UP OF THE CAMP

1. On a site, approved by experts in the science of building, the commandant, carpenters and astrologers should cause the camp to be set up, circular, rectangular or square or in conformity with the nature of the ground, with four gates, six roads and nine divisions, endowed with a moat, a rampart, a parapet, gates and towers, when there is danger and when the army has to halt.
2. In the ninth part to the north of the central should be erected quarters for the king, one hundred *dhanuses* in length and half that in width, with the royal residence in the western half of that.
3. The palace guards should be stationed on the borders.
4. In front should be erected the audience-hall, to the right the treasury and offices for issuing orders and carrying out works, to the left for elephants, horses and chariots intended for the king's use.
5. Beyond this at a distance of one hundred *dhanuses* from each other there should be four enclosures, with carts, stretches of thorny branches, pillars and the parapet.
6. In the first enclosure in front, the councillor and the chaplain should be encamped, to the right the magazine and the kitchen, to the left the store for forest produce and the armoury.
7. In the second, there should be quarters for hereditary and hired troops, for horses and chariots and for the commander-in-chief.
8. In the third, elephants, banded troops and the camp-superintendent should be encamped.
9. In the fourth, the labour-corps, the commandant and allied, alien and forest troops under the command of their own officers should be encamped.
10. Traders and courtesans should be encamped along the highways.
11. Outside the camp, fowlers and hunters should be stationed with drums and fire, as well as secret guards.
12. In the path of the march of enemies he should cause to be placed hidden wells, concealed hollows and barbed wires.

13. He should cause a change of guards to be made in the eighteen groups.
14. And he should cause watches to be kept even by day in order to discover spying.
15. He should prohibit disputes, drinking, festive gatherings and gambling and secure the guarding of the seal.
16. The regent shall arrest a soldier returning from the army without a written order.
17. The camp-superintendent should march ahead on the road, and should make carpenters and labourers prepare arrangements for protection and for water in the proper manner.

CHAPTER TWO

SECTION 148: MARCH FROM THE CAMP
SECTION 149: GUARDING TROOPS DURING THE CALAMITIES OF THE ARMY AND AT THE TIME OF ATTACK

1. After calculating the halts on the way in villages and in forests, in accordance with the supply of fodder, fuel and water, and calculating the time for camping, halting and marching, he should start on the expedition.
2. He should cause food and equipment to be transported in double the quantity required to meet the case.
3. Or, if unable to do so, he should assign it to the troops, or should store them at intervals on the route.
4. In front shall march the commandant, in the centre women-folk and the king, on the flanks horses as repellers with arms, at the end elephants for extensive raids, in the rear the commander-in-chief shall march and encamp.
5. Getting supplies from forest on all sides is a raid.
6. The flow of equipment and men from one's own country is supplies.
7. An ally's army is help.
8. The place where the women-folk are kept is a place of retreat.
9. In case of an attack in front he should march in the crocodile array, in the rear, in the cart array, on the two flanks, in the thunderbolt array, on all sides, in the 'excellent-on-all-sides' array, in a region where march in a single file alone is possible in the needle array.
10. In case of two alternate routes, he should march in a region suitable to himself.

11. March on terrain suitable to himself
12. For, those on terrain suitable to themselves effectively resist those on unsuitable terrain.
13. One *yojana* is the slowest rate of marching, one and a half middling, two *yojanas* fastest, or, the rate of march may be as possible for him.
14. When steps have to be taken against an enemy in the rear, his ally, the middle or the neutral king, who may give shelter to the enemy and destroy one's rich lands; when a difficult path has to be cleared; when the treasury, the army, allied, alien or forest troops, labourers or a suitable season has to be awaited; when he thinks 'There will come about a deterioration in the fortifications made by the enemy, in his stores and in his precautions for protection, a feeling of despondency in his purchased troops and feeling of despondency in his ally's troops; or, the instigators are not very quick; or, the enemy will fulfil my desires;' then he should march slowly, in the reverse case, quickly.
15. He should make the army cross waters with the help of elephants, pillar-bridges, embankments, boats, rafts of wood and bamboos and by means of gourds, leather baskets, skins, canoes, tree-stems and ropes.
16. In case the fort is seized by the enemy, he should get the army across at another place at night with the help of elephants and horses and lie in ambush.
17. And in a waterless region, he should make carts and animals carry water according to their capacity, in conformity with the length of the route.
18. He should guard his own army when on a long march in a wilderness, when without water, when lacking in fodder, fuel and water, when marching on a difficult road, when broken by an attack, when exhausted by hunger, thirst or a long march, when engaged in crossing rivers deep in mud and water or climbing up and down valleys and mountains, when crowded on a road where march in a single file alone is possible or in a region uneven with mountains or in a narrow place, when without equipment whether in the camp or on the march, when engaged in meals, when tired after a long march, when sleeping, when troubled by diseases, epidemics or famine, when infantrymen, horses and elephants are ill, when not on terrain suitable to it, or when any of the calamities of an army has befallen it; and he should strike at the enemy's troops when they are in these predicaments.

19. Ascertainment of the strength of the enemy's army is made by counting the number of troops marching out along a route allowing a march in a single file only, their fodder, foodstuffs, beds spread out, cooking fires laid out, banners and weapons.
20. He should conceal all that in his own case.
21. After securing a mountain fort or a forest fort in the rear, with means of retreat and reserves, he should fight and encamp on land suitable to himself.

CHAPTER THREE

SECTION 150: VARIOUS TYPES OF COVERT FIGHTING

SECTION 151: ENCOURAGING ONE'S OWN TROOPS

SECTION 152: DISPOSITION OF ONE'S TROOPS TO COUNTERACT ENEMY TROOPS

1. When he is superior in troops, when secret instigations are made in the enemy's camp, when precautions are taken about the season, and when he is on land suitable to himself, he should engage in open fight.
2. In the reverse case, he should resort to concealed fighting.
3. He should strike at the enemy on the occasions of the calamities of his troops and on occasions for assault, or when he is on unsuitable terrain, being himself on suitable terrain, or even one on suitable terrain, if he himself is possessed of the support of constituents.
4. Or, feigning a rout with treasonable, alien and forest troops, he should strike at the pursuing enemy when he has reached unsuitable ground.
5. He should break compact ranks through elephants.
6. He should strike by turning round at the enemy who is pursuing when a rout is first feigned and who is broken in the attempt, himself remaining unbroken.
7. Or, striking in front, he should strike in the rear with elephants and horses, when the enemy is reeling or has turned back.
8. Striking in the rear, he should strike in front with strong forces, when the enemy is reeling or has turned back.
9. By these are explained attacks on the flanks.
10. Or, he should strike at the point where the treasonable or weak troops of the enemy may be stationed.
11. If the ground in front is uneven, he should strike in the rear.

12. If uneven in the enemy's rear he should strike in front.
13. If uneven on one flank, he should strike at the other flank.
14. Or, after first engaging the enemy in fight with treasonable, alien and forest troops, he should strike at him when he is exhausted, himself remaining fresh.
15. Or, making a show of a rout himself through treasonable troops, he should strike at the enemy, who is confident that he has won, by resorting to ambuscade, being himself on his guard.
16. Remaining ever vigilant he should strike at the enemy negligent when engaged in plundering a caravan, a herd of cattle, an encampment or transport.
17. Or, with strong troops concealed by weak troops, he should enter the ranks of enemy warriors and slay them.
18. Or, luring enemy warriors with prospects of cattle seizure or hunting wild animals, he should, conceal in an ambush, strike at them.
19. After keeping enemy troops awake at night by a sudden assault, he should slay them by day when they are overpowered by sleep or are asleep.
20. Or, he should make an attack on those asleep at night with elephants having leather-cases on their feet.
21. He should strike in the latter part of the day at troops exhausted by keeping fighting equipment on for the day.
22. Or, he should strike at the enemy, whose elephants and horses are made ineffective through herds of cattle, buffaloes and camels carrying sacks of dry skins containing round pebbles and taking fright, who is broken and has turned back in fight; remaining unbroken himself.
23. Or, he should strike at all kinds of troops when they are facing the sun or the wind.
24. A desert, a forest, a strait path, a muddy place, a mountain, a marshy place, uneven ground, a boat, cattle, a cart array, mist and night; these are places for ambush.
25. And the occasions for assault mentioned before are also occasions for concealed fighting.
26. Open warfare, however, in which the place and time for the fighting are indicated, is most righteous.
27. Collecting the troops together, he should address them, 'I receive a wage like you; this kingdom is to be enjoyed together with you; the enemy should be attacked by you at my request'.

28. Even in the Vedas, on the occasions of the concluding baths of sacrifices in which fees have been fully received, it is declared,'That will be your condition after death, which is obtained by the brave fallen on the field.'
29. Moreover, there are two stanzas in this connection:
30. "Brave men giving up their lives in good battles, reach in one moment even beyond those worlds, which Brahmins, desirous of heaven, reach by a large number of sacrifices, by penance and by many gifts to worthy persons."
31. "A new vessel, filled with water, properly consecrated, with a mantle of *darbha* grass—may this not be the share of him and may he go to hell, who would not fight for the sake of the lump of food received from the master".
32. He should make the minister and the chaplain encourage the warriors by pointing out the excellences of the array.
33. And the group of his astrologers and others should fill his own side with enthusiasm, by proclaiming his omniscience and association with divine agencies, and should fill the enemy's side with terror.
34. When 'tomorrow is the fight', he should observe a fast and sleep beside his weapons and vehicles.
35. He should offer oblations in the fire with *Atharva*-mantras.
36. He should make Brahmins recite blessings invoking and securing heaven.
37. And he should consign himself to the care of Brahmins.
38. He should make troops that are possessed of bravery, skill, nobility of birth and loyalty and that are not cheated in the matter of money and honour, the centre of the ranks.
39. A bare army, without standards, consisting of warriors related as fathers, sons and brothers, should be the place for the king.
40. An elephant or a chariot should be the vehicle for the king, guarded by cavalry.
41. He should mount that vehicle, of which the army mostly consists or in which he may be trained.
42. One appearing as the king should be stationed at the head of array.
43. Bards and panegyrists should describe the attainment of heaven by the brave and the absence of heaven for cowards, and sing praises of the caste, corporation, family, deeds and conduct of the warriors.
44. Assistants of the chaplain should speak of the use of sorcery and black magic, mechanics, carpenters and astrologers should speak of success in their own works and failure in those of the enemy.
45. The Commander-in-Chief should address the ranks after they are carefully made well-disposed with money and honour, 'One

hundred thousand shall be the prize for killing the enemy king, fifty thousand for killing the Commander-in-Chief or a prince, ten thousand for killing a foremost warrior, five thousand for killing an elephant or chariot warrior, one thousand for killing a horseman, one hundred for killing a chief of infantrymen, twenty per head of infantrymen killed, beside double the wage and whatever one seizes.'

46. Heads of groups of ten should ascertain that about them.
47. Physicians, with surgical instruments, apparatus, medicines, oils and bandages, and women in charge of food and drink and capable of filling men with enthusiasm, should be stationed in the rear.
48. He should arrange his ranks in a battle-array on ground suitable to himself in such a way that it does not face the south, has the sun at the back and the wind favourable.
49. And in a battle-array on land suitable to the enemy, they should set the horses moving.
50. Where a firm stand and speed in movements of the array have no favourable terrain, there he would be conquered in either case, whether standing firm or moving quickly.
51. In the reverse case, he wins in either case by standing firm or moving quickly.
52. Ground being level, uneven or mixed, its nature in front, on the flanks and in the rear should be ascertained.
53. On level ground there should be the staff and circle arrays, on uneven the snake and diffuse arrays, or mixed arrays.
54. After breaking an enemy superior in strength he should ask for peace.
55. If sued for peace by one equal in strength, he should make peace.
56. He should continue to strike at one inferior in strength, but not at all at one who has reached his own land or is ready to sacrifice himself.
57. The vehemence of one returning again to the fight and despairing of his life becomes irresistible; therefore, he should not harass a broken enemy.

CHAPTER FOUR

SECTION 154: FUNCTIONS OF THE INFANTRY, THE CAVALRY, THE CHARIOTS AND THE ELEPHANTS

1. Suitable ground is desirable for infantrymen, horses, chariots and elephants, for fighting and for camping.

2. Battle-fields and seasons for men fighting in deserts, forests, water or dry lands and for those fighting in trenches, on open ground, by day or by night, and for elephants from rivers, mountains, marshes and lakes, and for horses are desirable for each as suited to him.
3. Level, firm, clear, not causing jolting, not causing wheels or hooves to get stuck, not obstructing axles, not broken with trees, thickets, creepers, tree-stems, fields under water, pits, ant-hills, sand and mud, and free from clefts, this is ground for chariots, beneficial also to elephants and horses as well as men, for fighting and for camping, in normal and in difficult situations.
4. That with small stones and trees, with small pits that can be jumped over, and with the blemish of small clefts is the ground for horses.
5. That with big tree-stems, stones, trees, creepers, ant-hills and thickets is the ground for infantrymen.
6. That with traversable mountains, water and uneven places, with trees that can be uprooted and creepers that can be cut, broken with mud and free from clefts is the ground for elephants.
7. Without thorns, not very uneven, with room for retreat, this is excellence of ground for infantrymen.
8. With double the room for retreat, free from mud, water and bogs and devoid of pebbles is excellence for horses.
9. With dust, mud, water, reeds and growth of rushes, free from 'dog's teeth,' and free from obstruction by big branches of trees, is excellence for elephants.
10. Possessed of water-reservoirs and shelters, not causing jolting, without fields under water, and enabling a turn round, is excellence for chariots.
11. Ground suitable for all has been declared.
12. By this camping and fighting of all kinds of troops become explained.
13. Investigation of the ground, the halting place and forests, securing land without unevenness, water, ford, wind and sun's rays, destruction of supplies and reserves or their protection, cleansing and steadying the army, extension of raids, repelling as with arms, making the first attack, penetration, breaking through, comforting, capturing, setting free, causing a change in the path of pursuit, carrying off the treasury of the prince, assault on the rear and tips, pursuit of the weak, accompanying, and the work of rallying, these are the functions of cavalry.

14. Marching in the van, making new roads, halting places and fords, repelling as with arms, crossing and descending in water, remaining steadfast, marching forward and descending, entering difficult and crowded places, setting fire and extinguishing it, securing victory single-handed, reuniting broken ranks, breaking up unbroken ranks, protecting in a calamity, assault, frightening, causing terror, showing magnificence, capturing, setting free, breaking ramparts, gates and towers, bringing in and carrying away treasury, these are the functions of elephants.
15. Guarding one's own troops, repelling the four-fold army in battle, capturing, setting free, reuniting broken ranks, breaking up unbroken ranks, causing terror, showing magnificence, and making a frightful din, these are the functions of chariots.
16. Bearing arms in all places and seasons, and military activity are the functions of infantrymen.
17. The work of clearing camps, roads, water-works, wells and roads, carrying machines, weapons, armours, implements and food, and removing from the battle-field weapons, armours and wounded men are the functions of labourers.
18. A king, with few horses, should yoke bullocks and horses to chariots; similarly, one with few elephants, should make the centre consist of carts driven by donkeys and camels.

CHAPTER FIVE

SECTION 155: ARRANGEMENT OF BATTLE-ARRAYS IN WINGS, FLANKS AND FRONT IN ACCORDANCE WITH THE STRENGTH OF TROOPS

SECTION 156: DISTRIBUTION OF STRONG AND WEAK TROOPS

SECTION 157: MODES OF FIGHTING OF THE INFANTRY, THE CAVALRY, THE CHARIOTS AND THE ELEPHANTS

1. He should engage in fight after establishing a fortified place at a distance of five hundred *dhanuses*, or in accordance with the nature of the ground.
2. The Commander-in-Chief and the commandant should arrange the army in a battle-array, with chiefs assigned different positions, after detaching it out of sight of the enemy.
3. He should place a foot-soldier at a distance of one *sama* from the next, a horseman at a distance of three *samas*, a chariot or an elephant at a distance of five *samas*.

4. Or, he should arrange with double or treble the distance.
5. Thus, one should fight in comfort, without being crowded.
6. A *dhanus* is five *aratnis*.
7. At that distance from the next he should place an archer, at a distance of three *dhanuses*, a horseman, at a distance of five *dhanuses*, a chariot or an elephant.
8. Five *dhanuses* should be the juncture of the divisions of wings, flanks and centre.
9. For a horse, there are three soldiers as fighters in front.
10. There are fifteen for a chariot or an elephant, as well as five horses.
11. The same number of foot-guards should be arranged for horses, chariots and elephants.
12. He should place at the centre a division of three rows of three chariot-units, a flank and a wing of the same size on either side.
13. There are thus fortyfive chariots in a chariot division, two hundred and twentyfive horses, six hundred and seventyfive soldiers as fighters in front and the same number as foot-guards.
14. This is the uniform array.
15. It may increase in size by two chariot units at a time up to twentyone chariot units.
16. Thus, the odd numbers become the ten bases of the uniform array.
17. In case of an unequal number in the wings, the flanks and the centre as compared to one another, there is uneven array.
18. It may also increase in size by two chariot units at a time up to twentyone chariot units.
19. Thus, the odd numbers become the ten bases of the uneven array.
20. Troops left over after this array should be made an insertion.
21. He should insert two-thirds of the chariots in the outer parts, the rest he should place at the centre.
22. Thus, an insertion, of chariots less by one-third should be made.
23. By that is explained the insertion of elephants and horses.
24. The insertion should be so made that it does not cause crowding in the fighting of horses, chariots and elephants.
25. Excess of troops is insertion.
26. Excess of infantry is counterinsertion.
27. Excess of one arm is side-insertion of the enemy. Excess of reasonable troops is overinsertion.
28. By the chariot-array is explained the elephant-array. Excess of reasonable troops is over insertion.

29. Or, the array may be mixed, of elephants, chariots and horses—elephants at the ends of the army, horses on the flanks, chariots in the centre.
30. A centre of elephants, flanks of chariots and wings of horses—this is an array breaking with the centre.
31. The reverse is one breaking with the ends.
32. But the unmixed array of elephants is—war elephants at the centre, riding elephants in the rear, vicious elephants at the tips.
33. An unmixed horse-array is—a centre of armoured horses, flanks and wings of unarmoured.
34. An unmixed infantry-array is—armoured soldiers in front, archers behind.
35. Thus, the unmixed arrays.
36. Foot-soldiers should be in the wings, horses on the flanks, elephants in the rear, chariots in front, or a reversal of this may be made in accordance with enemy's array.
37. This is disposition of troops with two arms.
38. By that is explained disposition of troops with three arms.
39. In the case of men, the excellences of an army constitute the best troops.
40. In the case of elephants and horses, special excellences are: pedigree, breed, mettle, youthfulness, vigour, height, speed, spiritedness, training, firmness, loftiness, obedience and possession of auspicious marks and good conduct.
41. He should place one-third of the best among foot-soldiers, horses, chariots and elephants as the centre, two-third as flanks and wings on the two sides, behind them the second best, against the order the third best, weak troops against the order.
42. Thus, he should make use of all.
43. By placing weak troops at the ends, he becomes able to overpower the enemy with his vehemence.
44. Placing the best troops in front he should place the next best at the ends, the third best in the rear, and weak troops in the centre.
45. Thus, it becomes capable of resisting.
46. After arranging the battle-array, however, he should strike with one or two out of the wings, flanks and centre; with the remaining he should support the attack.
47. He should attack plenty of best troops that army of the enemy which is weak, lacking in elephants and horses, with treasonable officers in it or seduced by secret instigations.

48. Or, when the enemy's army is most strong, he should attack it with double that number of best troops.
49. He should reinforce that arm of his which has few best troops with a large number of them.
50. He should arrange the troops near the place where the enemy has suffered a loss, or whence there may be danger.
51. Rushing forth, rushing about, rushing beyond, rushing back, holding together after pounding, encircling, moving zigzag, encircling, scattering, turning back after fleeing, guarding broken ranks along the lines, in front, on the flanks and in the rear, pursuing broken ranks—these are modes of fighting for horses.
52. These same with the exception of scattering, destruction of the four arms whether combined or separate, smashing of wings, flanks and centre, making a sudden assault, and attacking those asleep—these are modes of fighting for elephants.
53. These same with the exception of holding together after pounding, and marching forth, marching away, fighting in a stationary position on land suitable to them—these are modes of fighting for chariots.
54. Striking in all places and at all times, and silent punishment are the modes of fighting for foot-soldiers.
55. In this manner he should arrange battle-arrays, odd and even, in such a way that the strength of the four arms becomes suitably used.
56. Retiring to a distance of two hundred *dhanuses*, the king should remain in the rear; from that comes the rallying of broken ranks; he should not fight without reserves in the rear.

CHAPTER SIX

SECTION 158: ARRANGING THE STAFF, THE SNAKE, THE CIRCLE AND THE DIFFUSE ARRAYS

SECTION 159: ARRANGING COUNTER-ARRAYS AGAINST THEM

1. Two wings, a centre and reserves—this is the arrangement of a battle-array according to Usanas.
2. Two wings, two flanks, a centre and reserves—this is according to Brhaspati.
3. According to both, arrays with wings, flanks and centre are the basic arrays, the staff, the snake, the circle and the diffuse.
4. Among them, that with crosswise operations is the staff array.
5. Operation of all one after the other is the snake array.

6. Operation on all sides of advancing is the circle array.
7. The separate operation of divisions as stationed is the diffuse array.
8. That operating evenly with wings, flanks and centre is the staff array.
9. That, marching beyond with the flanks is the 'splitter'.
10. The same falling back with wings and flanks is the 'strengthener'.
11. The same, marching out with the wings is the 'unbearable'.
12. Marching out with the centre keeping the wings stationary is the 'falcon'.
13. In the reverse case, these four become the 'bow' the 'bow-flank', the 'established' and the 'well-established' respectively.
14. That with wings of bows is the 'conqueror'.
15. The same, marching out with the centre, is the 'victory'.
16. That with wings like big ears is the 'pillar-eared'.
17. That with double pillars in the wings is the 'extensive-victory'.
18. That with wings augmented three-fold is the 'army-face'.
19. In the reverse case, it is the 'fish-mouth'.
20. The staff, in a straight line, is the 'needle'.
21. Two staffs is the 'bracelet'.
22. Four staffs is the 'invincible'.
23. These are staff arrays.
24. That operating unevenly with wings, flanks and centre is the snake array.
25. It is 'moving-like-a-serpent' or 'cow's-urination'.
26. That with two divisions at the centre and staffs in the wings is the 'cart'.
27. In the reverse case, it is the 'crocodile'.
28. The cart, inter-mixed with elephants, horses and chariots is the 'flying-about'.
29. These are snake arrays.
30. When the wings, flanks and centre become one, it is the circle array.
31. That with faces on all sides is the 'good-on-all-sides'.
32. That with eight divisions or faces is the 'invincible'.
33. These are circle arrays.
34. Because of the disjoined nature of the wings, flanks and centre it is the diffuse array.
35. By the formation of the figure with five divisions, it is the 'thunder-bolt' or the 'lizard'.
36. With four divisions, it is the 'hearth' or the 'crow-feet'.
37. With three, it is the 'half-moon' or the 'crab-horned'.

38. These are diffuse arrays.
39. One with chariots at the centre, elephants on the flanks and horses in the rear is the 'unharmed' array.
40. Foot-soldiers, horses, chariots and elephants, one behind the other is the 'immovable' array.
41. Elephants, horses, chariots, and foot-soldiers, one behind the other is the 'unrepulsed'.
42. Among these, he should counteract the 'splitter' with the 'strengthener', the 'strengthener' with the 'unbearable', the 'falcon' with the 'bow', the 'established' with the 'well-established', the 'conqueror' with the 'victory', the 'pillar-eared' with the 'extensive-victory', the 'flying-about' with the 'good-on-all-sides'.
43. With the 'invincible', he should counter-arrange against all other arrays.
44. Of foot-soldiers, horses, chariots and elephants, he should strike at each earlier one with each later one and an inferior arm with a superior arm.
45. The one commander of ten single units is the lieutenant, the one commander of ten lieutenants is the general, the one commander of these is the commandant.
46. With drum-beats, flags and banners, he should establish signals for the divisions of the array, for dividing themselves into sections, for joining together, for halting, for marching, for turning back and for attacking.
47. In case the opposite arrays are equally matched, success comes from the possession of suitable place, time and strength.

48-50. He should strike terror in the enemy with machines, by the employment of occult practices, through assassins slaying those engaged in something else, by magical arts, by a show of association with divinities, through carts, by frightening with elephants, by rousing the treasonable, through herds of cattle, by setting fire to camps, by attacks on the tips and in the rear, by creating dissensions through agents appearing as messengers saying, 'Your fort has been burnt down or captured; a revolt by a member of your family has broken out; or, your enemy or a forest chieftain has risen against you.'

51. An arrow, discharged by an archer, may kill one person or may not kill even one; but intellect operated by a wise man would kill even children in the womb.

Herewith ends the Tenth Book of the Arthasastra of Kautilya

'CONCERNING WAR'

25

BOOK ELEVEN

Policy Towards Oligarchies

When Chandragupta Maurya ascended the throne of Magadha with the help and the contrivances of Kautilya, in Hindustan there was no other kingdom capable and strong enough than the Magadha Empire (329 B.C.). At that time the entire country was not formulated into an integrated nation—HINDUSTAN. On the contrary it was a conglomeration of various independent states or principalities and their respective rulers independently administered their territories. Most of the states or principalities were either conquered, annexed or made the tributaries of the expanding Magadha Empire with the natural consequence of bitterness, jealousy and estranged relationship with the Emperor. It was as imperative as beneficial for Chandragupta Maurya to keep under close surveillance all the confederating units and take timely and effective measures in order to check, thwart and nip in the bud any attempt of treachery, or treason against the Emperor. Kautilya was the chief advisor of Chandragupta Maurya and through his usual foresight and acumen, he framed for the guidance and action of the latter various directive principles to control the federated rulers of the Maurya Empire. These measures have been elaborated in this Book; and they are on the following subjects: (1) Ways of Resorting to the Policy of Sowing Dissensions, and (2) Forms of Silent Punishment.

CHAPTER ONE

SECTION 160: WAYS OF RESORTING TO THE POLICY OF SOWING DISSENSIONS

SECTION 161: FORMS OF SILENT PUNISHMENT

1. The gain of an oligarchy is best among gains of an army and an ally.
2. For, oligarchies being closely knit are unassailable for enemies.

3. He should win over those of them who are friendly with conciliation and gifts, those hostile through dissensions and force.
4. The Kambojas, the Surastras, the Ksatriyas, the Srenis and others live by an economic vocation and the profession of arms.
5. The Licchivikas, the Vrjikas, the Mallakas, the Madrakas, the Kukuras, the Kurus, the Pancalas and others make use of the title of kings.
6. In the case of all, secret agents close to them should find out one another's defects, and occasions for mutual hatred, enmity or strife among members of the oligarchy, and should sow discord in one who is gradually brought round to believe them saying, 'So and so is slandering you.'
7. When resentment is thus built up on both sides, agents serving as teachers should start quarrels among pupils concerning learning, skill, gambling and pleasure sports.
8. Or, assassins should start quarrels among the followers of the chiefs in the oligarchy by praising the opponents in brothels and taverns, or by supporting seducible parties.
9. They should stir up princelings enjoying low comforts with a longing for superior comforts.
10. And they should prevent inter-dining or inter-marriage of the superior with the inferior.
11. Or, they should urge inferiors to inter-dining or inter-marrying with superiors.
12. Or, they should urge the very low ones to obtain a position of equality in the matter of family, valour or change of status.
13. Or, they should nullify a transaction that is settled by establishing its opposite.
14. Or, in cases of legal dispute, assassins should start quarrels by injuring objects, cattle or men at night.
15. And in all cases of strife, the king should support the weak party with treasury and troops and urge them to kill the rival party.
16. Or, he should carry away those that have been divided.
17. And he should settle groups of five families or ten families of them on land suitable for agriculture.
18. For, if stationed in one place, they might be capable of bearing arms.
19. And he should fix a penalty if they come together.
20. He should appoint as crown prince a nobly born member of the ruling families, who is in disfavour or has been discarded by those using the title of king.

21. And the group of his astrologers and others should declare among members of the oligarchy the possession of marks of royalty by him.
22. And he should instigate the pious chiefs of the oligarchy, saying 'Observe your duties towards the son or brother of such and such a king.'
23. When they have agreed, he should send money and troops for supporting the seducible party.
24. At the time of fighting, agents appearing as vintners should offer, in hundreds, jars of wine mixed with a stupefying liquid, as libation to the deceased, under the pretext of the death of a son or wife.
25. And secret agents should point out the depositing of an object after an agreement, such as sealed bags with money and vessels containing money, at the gates of sanctuaries or temples and near fortified places.
26. When members of the oligarchy are seen approaching, they should declare, 'These belong to the king.'
27. Then he should make an attack.
28. Or, borrowing for temporary use vehicles or money from members of the oligarchy, he should give a well-known article to a chief of the oligarchy.
29. When it is demanded back by them, he should say, 'It has been given to such and such a chief.'
30. By this is explained the method of creating dissensions in the enemy's camp and among forest chieftains.
31. Or, a secret agent should make a son of a chief of the ruling council, who thinks highly of himself, come to believe, 'You are the son of such and such a king, kept here through fear of the enemy.'
32. When he agrees, the king should support him with treasury and troops and make him fight the members of the oligarchy.
33. When his object is achieved, he should get him also slain.
34. Keepers of prostitutes or acrobats, actors, dancers or showmen, employed as agents, should make chiefs of the ruling council infatuated with women possessed of great beauty and youth.
35. When passion is roused in them, they should start quarrels by creating belief about their love in one and by going to another, or by forcible abduction by the other.
36. During the quarrel, assassins should do their work, saying, 'Thus, has this passionate fellow been slain.'

37. Or, if the one frustrated puts up with his disappointment, the women should approach him and say, 'Such and such a chief is harassing me, who am in love with you; so long as he is alive, I shall not stay here,' and thus urge his murder.
38. Or, the woman, if forcibly abducted, should get the abductor murdered at night by an assassin at the edge of the park or in a pleasure house, or should herself kill him with poison.
39. Then she should proclaim, 'My lover has been killed by so and so.'
40. Or, an agent appearing as a holy man should create confidence in a chief in whom passion is roused, by means of love-winning herbs and then killing him with poison should disappear.
41. When he has gone away, secret agents declare that as the act of the other.
42. Or, female secret agents posing as rich widows or living by a secret profession, and contending for inheritance or a deposit should infatuate chiefs of the ruling council, or Aditikausika female secret agent or dancers or songstresses should do so.
43. When they have agreed and come to secret houses for the night's meeting, assassins should kill them or carry them off imprisoned.
44. Or, a secret agent should describe to a chief of the oligarchy who is fond of women, 'In such and such a village, the family of a poor man has migrated; his wife is fit for a king; seize her.'
45. When she is seized, after a fortnight, an agent appearing as a holy man should cry out in the midst of the chiefs of the treasonable oligarchy, 'That chief has violated my wife or daughter-in-law or sister or daughter.'
46. If the ruling council were to chastise him, the king should support him and make him fight against those hostile to him.
47. If he is not punished, assassins should slay at night the agent appearing as a holy man.
48. Then others appearing in the same disguise should cry out,'So and so is a Brahmin-slayer and the paramour of a Brahmin woman.'
49. Or, an agent appearing as an astrologer, should describe a maiden chosen as the bride by one chief to another, 'The daughter of so and so is destined to become the wife of a king or the mother of a king; get her by spending all you have or by force.'
50. If she cannot be obtained, he should rouse the other party.
51. If she is obtained, the strife is at once brought about.
52. Or, a female mendicant should say to a chief fond of his wife, 'Such and such a chief, conceited by reason of youth, sent me to your

wife; through fear of him I have brought a letter and ornaments from him; your wife is innocent; steps against him should be taken secretly; in the meantime I shall accept on your wife's behalf.'

53. On these and other occasions of strife, whether the strife has arisen of its own accord or has been created by assassins, the king should support the weak party with treasury and troops and make him fight against those hostile to him, or should carry him away.
54. The single monarch should deal with oligarchies in this manner.
55. The oligarchies also should thus guard themselves against these deceitful tricks by the single monarch.
56. And the head of the oligarchy should remain just in behaviour towards the members of the oligarchy, beneficial and agreeable to them, self-controlled, with devoted men, and following the wishes of all.

Herewith ends the Eleventh Book of the Arthasastra of Kautilya
'POLICY TOWARDS OLIGARCHIES'

26

BOOK TWELVE

Concerning the Weaker King

The Arthasastra was composed by Kautilya generally for the guidance of kings and particularly for Chandragupta Maurya who had considerably expanded his Empire—Magadha (317-293 B.C.). As stated earlier this Empire was surrounded from all sides by independent, annexed, or tributary states and they posed considerable danger to the stability and safety of the Mauryan Empire. In order to emasculate the power of such states, Kautilya had identified these states in this book. His intention is obvious that Chandragupta should take such necessary action against these states as would emaciate their potentials and in consequence, help Chandragupta emerge a very strong king and acquire more territories under his domain. *Prima facie*, it may appear that the various methods suggested by Kautilya are not ethical, or on occasions they tend to be immoral. Since the inherent intention of Kautilya in adopting these methods is the acquisition of more territories for the Magadha Empire and their protection, the accrued ends had justified the means. Perhaps, this is the only reason that Kautilya has been euphemistically stigmatized 'knave'.

The subjects dealt with in this Book are:

1. The Mission of the Envoy. 2. Fight with the Weapon of Diplomacy. Assassination of the Enemy's Army Chief. 3. Stirring up the Circle of Kings. 4. Secret Use of Weapons, Fire and Poison Destruction of the Enemy's Supplies, Reinforcements and Foraging Raids. 5. Overreaching the Enemy by Trickery. Overreaching the Enemy by Force. Victory of the Single King. These constitute the Twelfth Book 'Concerning the Weaker King'.

CHAPTER ONE

SECTION 162: THE MISSION OF THE ENVOY

1. 'A weak king, attacked by a stronger king, should everywhere remain submissive showing the characteristics of a reed.
2. For, he submits to Indra who submits to a stronger king,' says Bharadvaja.
3. 'He should fight with the mobilisation of all troops.
4. For, valour overcomes a calamity.
5. And this is a Ksatriya's special duty, whether there be victory or defeat in war,' says Visalaksa.
6. 'No,' says Kautilya.
7. One submissive everywhere lives despairing of life like a ram strayed from a herd.
8. And one fighting with only a small army perishes like one plunging in the ocean without a boat.
9. He should, however, act finding shelter with a king superior to him or in an unassailable fort.
10. There are three kings who attack: the righteous conqueror, the greedy conqueror and the demoniacal conqueror.
11. Of them, the righteous conqueror is satisfied with submission.
12. He should submit to him, also when there is danger from others.
13. The greedy conqueror is satisfied with the seizure of land and goods.
14. He should yield money to him.
15. The demoniacal conqueror is satisfied with the seizure of land, goods, sons, wives and life.
16. By yielding land and goods to him, he should take countersteps, remaining out of reach himself.
17. When one of these is making ready to start, he should make a counter-move through peace or diplomatic war or concealed warfare.
18. He should win over the party inimical to him with conciliation and gifts, his own party through dissension and force.
19. Secret agents should destroy his fort, country or camp with weapons, poison or fire.
20. He should cause his rear to be attacked from all sides.
21. Or, he should cause the kingdom to be destroyed through forest tribes or to be seized by a pretender from his family or a prince in disfavour.

22. And at the end of such injurious acts, he should send an envoy for peace.
23. Or, peace may be used without doing any injurious act.
24. If he marches even then, he should sue for peace with a successive increase of one-quarter of the treasury and troops or a successive increase of a day and night.
25. If he were to sue for peace with the offer of troops, he should give him dull elephants and horses, or such energetic ones as are administered poison.
26. If he were to sue for peace with men, he should give him treasonable, alien or forest troops under the command of secret agents.
27. He should so manage that the destruction of both would take place.
28. Or, he should give him troops with a fiery temper which, when insulted, would injure him, or hereditary, loyal troops that would injure him in his calamity.
29. If he were to sue for peace with treasury, he should give him articles of high value, for which he would not find a purchaser, or forest produce that is unfit for use in war.
30. If he were to sue for peace with land, he should give him land which can be easily recovered, or which has constant enemies, or which is without a shelter, or such that settlement on it would involve heavy losses and expenses.
31. Or, he should sue a stronger king for peace with the offer of all his possessions, with the exception of the capital.
32. That which the other might seize by force, he should offer through one of the means. He should preserve his body, not wealth; for, what regret can there be for wealth that is impermanent?

CHAPTER TWO

SECTION 163: FIGHT WITH THE WEAPON OF DIPLOMACY

SECTION 164: ASSASSINATION OF THE ENEMYS' ARMY CHIEFS

1. If he were not to accept a peace treaty, he should say to him, 'Such and such kings, under the influence of the group of six enemies, have perished; it does not behove you to follow in the footsteps of those who were without self-control.
2. You should pay regard to spiritual and material well-being.
3. For, those are really enemies, wearing the mask of friends, who make you undertake a rash deed, an impious act and the forgoing of material good.

4. To fight with brave men who have given up all hope of life is a rash deed, to bring about the loss of men on both sides is an impious act, to give up a good in hand and to forsake a blameless ally is forgoing of material good.
5. And that king has allies and with this object he will raise more allies, who will attack you from all sides.
6. Nor is he forsaken by the middle and neutral kings or by the circle of kings; you, however, are forsaken, by them since, while you are ready to fight, they are looking on, "Let him meet with further losses and expenses, let him be divided from his ally; then we shall easily exterminate him when he has left his kingdom."
7. It does not behove you, therefore, to listen to enemies masquerading as friends, to frighten your allies and to confer good on your enemies and to face the risk of losing your life and meet with disaster;' thus he should try to restraint him.
8. If he starts even then, he should engender a revolt among the constituents as explained in the 'policy towards oligarches' and in 'drawing out by means of stratagems'.
9. And he should employ assassins and poison givers.
10. He should employ assassins and poison-givers at those points which have been declared as fit to be guarded in 'concerning self-protection'.
11. Keepers of prostitutes should make the enemy's army chiefs infatuated with women possessed of great beauty and youth.
12. When many or two of the chiefs feel passion for one woman, assassins should create quarrels among them.
13. Agents should urge the party worsted in the strife to go away elsewhere or to render help to their master in the expedition.
14. Or, agents appearing as holy men should cause poison to be given to those among the chiefs who are under the influence of passion, along with love-winning medicines, in order to overreach them.
15. Or, an agent appearing as a trader should shower wealth on an intimate maid of the favourite queen of the enemy for the sake of love and then leave her.
16. An agent appearing as a holy man, recommended by an agent appearing as an attendant of that same trader, should give a love-winning medicine, saying, 'This should be placed on the person of the trader.'
17. When this has succeeded, he should advise this remedy also to the favourite queen, saying, 'This should be placed on the king's person.'

18. Then he should overreach with poison.
19. Or, an agent appearing as an astrologer should declare to a high officer, whose confidence has been gradually won, that he is possessed of the marks of a king.
20. A female mendicant should declare to his wife, 'You will be the wife of a king or the mother of a king.'
21. Or, a female agent who is the wife of a high officer should say to him, 'The king wants to keep me in his harem; this letter and these ornaments have been brought to your house by a female mendicant.'
22. Or, an agent appearing as a cook or a waiter should inform a chief about the king's instruction for administering to him poison and the money offered to tempt him to do so.
23. An agent appearing as a trader should corroborate that information of his, and should speak of the success of the undertaking.
24. Thus, with one or two or three means, he should incite the high officers one by one to fight or to desert him.
25. And in his fortified cities, secret agents serving in close proximity to the Regent, should declare among citizens and country people, as if out of friendship, "The Regent has said to warriors and heads of departments, 'The king is in a difficult position; he may or may not come back alive; obtain wealth by force and slay your enemies'."
26. When the rumour has spread far and wide, assassins should rob citizens at night and slay chiefs, saying at the time 'Thus are dealt with those who do not obey the Regent.'
27. And they should leave blood-stained weapons, articles and binding ropes in the quarters of the Regent.
28. Then secret agents should proclaim, 'The Regent is slaying and robbing,' the subject.
29. In the same manner, they should divide the country people from the Administrator.
30. But assassins should kill the subordinates of the Administrator in the midst of villages at night and say, 'Thus, are dealt with those who oppress the countryside unrighteously.'
31. When trouble has thus started, they should cause the Regent or the Administrator to be killed by a rising of the subjects.
32. They should get a pretender from his family or a prince in disfavour accepted as a ruler.
33. They should set fire to royal palaces and city gates, to stores of articles and grains, or should kill those officers there and, crying pitiably should declare that as done by him.

CHAPTER THREE

SECTION 164: FIGHT WITH DIPLOMACY (CONCLUDED)

SECTION 165: STIRRING UP THE CIRCLE OF KINGS

1. Secret agents working in close proximity to the enemy king and the king's favourites should inform those in the position of friends to chiefs of infantry, cavalry, chariots and elephants that the king is enraged with these, by showing confidence as in a friend.
2. When the rumours have become thick, assassins, after taking precautions against dangers arising from moving at night time, should go to their houses and say, 'At the king's order, come with us.
3. They should slay them even as they come out and say to those near, 'This is the king's message.'
4. And to those who have not been slain, secret agents should say, 'This is what we had told you; he who wants to remain alive should go away.'
5. And to those whom the king does not give something when asked for it, secret agents should say, "The Regent was told by the king, 'Such and such persons are asking me for something that ought not to be asked for; refused by me, they have joined the enemy; strive to exterminate them.' "
6. Then he should act as before.
7. And to those to whom the king gives something when asked for it, secret agents should say, "The Regent was told by the king, "Such and such persons ask me for something that ought not to be asked for; I gave it to them to ensure trust in me; they are in league with the enemy; strive to exterminate them.' "
8. Then he should act as before.
9. And to those who do not ask him for something that ought to be asked for, secret agents should say, "The Regent was told by the king, 'Such and such persons do not ask me for something which ought to be asked for; what else could not be but their being apprehensive because of their own guilt? Strive to exterminate them.' "
10. Then he should act as before.
11. By this is explained the whole party of seducible persons.
12. Or, a secret agent, serving in close proximity, should give the enemy king to understand, 'Such and such a high officer is in communication with men of the enemy.'

13. When this is believed, he should show treasonable men carrying letters from him and say, 'This is it.'
14. Or, after tempting with land or money the principal officers among the chiefs of the army, he should make them fight their own people or should carry them away.
15. He should cause that son of his, who may be staying near or in a fort, to be instigated through a secret agent, 'You are a son possessed of greater personal excellences, yet you have been set aside; why then are you indifferent? Fight and seize the kingdom; the crown prince will soon destroy you.'
16. After tempting with money a pretender from his family or a prince in disfavour, he should say to him, 'Crush his troops inside the kingdom or the troops on the frontier or the frontier fort.'
17. After winning the forest chieftains with money and honour, he should cause his kingdom to be destroyed.
18. Or, he should say to the enemy in the rear of the enemy, 'This king, after exterminating me, will indeed exterminate you; attack him in the rear; if he turns round on you, I shall attack him in the rear.'
19. Or, he should say to the allies of the enemy, 'I am your dam; with me broken, this king will overwhelm all of you; let us join together and frustrate his expedition.'
20. And he should send letter, to those united with him and to those not united, 'This king, after uprooting me, will indeed take action against you; beware; it is better for you to help me.'
21. He should send appeals to the middle king or again to the neutral king, according as the one or the other may be near, making a surrender to him of all possessions, in order to be saved.

CHAPTER FOUR

SECTION 166: SECRET USE OF WEAPONS, FIRE AND POISON

SECTION 167: DESTRUCTION OF THE ENEMY'S SUPPLIES, REINFORCEMENTS AND FORAGING RAIDS

1. And those agents who are living disguised as traders in the fortified towns of the enemy, disguised as householders in his villages, disguised as cow-herds and ascetics in the frontier posts of the country, should send, along with presents word to a neighbouring prince, a forest chief, a pretender from his family or a prince in disfavour, 'This region can be seized.'
2. And when secret agents of these have come to the fortified town, they should welcome them with money and honour and show them the weak points of the constituents.

3. They should strike at those weak points along with them.
4. Or, an agent appearing as a vintner in his camp, showing a person condemned to death as his son and killing him by poison at the time of an attack should offer, in hundreds, jars of wine as libation in honour of the dead.
5. He should give on the first day unadulterated wine or wine with one quarter (poison), on the next, (wine) mixed with poison.
6. Or, giving unadulterated wine to the army chiefs, he should give them (wine) mixed with poison when they are in a state of intoxication.
7. Or, an agent, serving as a chief in the army, should show a condemned person as a son and so on, as before.
8. Or, agents disguised as dealers in cooked meat or cooked rice or vintners or dealers in cakes, should advertise their special goods and, in mutual rivalry, call the enemies, proclaiming 'This is given on credit, this is very cheap,' and mix their goods with poison.
9. Or, women and children, purchasing wine, milk, curds, butter or oil from dealers in these commodities, should pour them in their own vessels containing poison.
10. Saying 'Give us at this price, or give us of better quality again,' they should pour that in the same place.
11. Agents appearing as traders or those who bring goods for sale to the camp, should sell these same articles after mixing them with poison.
12. Those near should mix poison with the fodder and grass for elephants and horses.
13. Or, agents appearing as workmen should sell grass or water mixed with poison.
14. Or, cattle traders, long associated with the camp should let loose herds of cattle or of sheep and goats on the occasion of an attack, in places likely to cause confusion among the enemies, also should let loose the vicious among horses, donkeys, camels, buffaloes and other animals.
15. Or, agents appearing as above should loose animals whose eyes have been smeared with the blood of musk-rats.
16. Or, those appearing as hunters should let loose wild animals from their cages, or snake charmers, serpents with deadly poison, or those living by elephants, elephants.
17. Or, those living by fire should set fire to things.
18. Or, secret agents should kill the chiefs of infantry, cavalry, chariots or elephants when they have turned back, or should set fire to the quarters of the chiefs.

19. Those appearing as treasonable or alien or forest troops, being employed with the enemy, should make an attack on the rear or give support to the weak king's attack.
20. Or, those concealed in forests should lure out troops on the frontier and slay them, or should destroy the supplies, the reinforcements and foraging raids on a path where march in a single file alone is possible.
21. Or, on the occasion of a night-battle, they should strike many drums, fixed beforehand as a signal, and announce,'We have entered it, the kingdom is won.'
22. Or, entering the king's quarters, they should kill the king in the tumult.
23. Or, if he is trying to escape, leaders of Mleccha and forest troops, on all sides, should kill him, taking cover in places of ambush or taking cover behind hedges of tree-stems.
24. Or, agents appearing as hunters should, in the tumult of an attack, strike at him on occasions fit for secret fight.
25. Or, they should strike at him when he is on a path where march in a single file alone is possible or on a mountain, or behind a hedge of tree-stems or in a marshy place or inside water, in accordance with the favourableness of the terrain to themselves.
26. Or, they should drown him through a rush of water by breaking dams in rivers, lakes and tanks.
27. Or, if he is in a desert fort, a forest fort or a water fort, they should destroy him with poisonous fire and smoke.
28. Assassins should do away with him by fire when he is in a narrow place, by smoke when he is in a desert, by poison if he is in his residence, by frightful crocodiles or persons moving in water if he has taken a plunge in water, or kill him as he is coming out of his quarters set on fire.
29. He should overreach the enemy, clinging to the places mentioned, by forcing him out through trickery and by secret practices or by using one of the secret tricks.

CHAPTER FIVE

SECTION 168: OVERREACHING THE ENEMY BY TRICKERY
SECTION 169: OVERREACHING THE ENEMY BY FORCE
SECTION 170: VICTORY OF THE SINGLE KING

1. On the occasion of a festival in honour of a deity, there may be many places for the enemy's coming to worship because of his devotion.

2. In those places, he should practice secret tricks on him.
3. When he has entered the temple, he should cause a concealed wall or a huge stone to fall on him by the release of a mechanism.
4. Or, he should cause to be dropped down on him a shower of stones and weapons from an upper chamber, or a door panel thrown down or a door-bar placed in a wall and fixed at one end.
5. Or, he should cause the image, the banner and the weapon of the deity to fall upon him.
6. Or, in the places where he stays, sits or moves about, he should cause poison to be used along with the cow-dung smearing or with the scented water used for sprinkling on the floor, or with the offering of flowers and fragrant powder.
7. Or, he should carry over to him, poisonous smoke concealed by perfume.
8. Or, he should make him drop down, by the release of a pin, into a well with spikes or a pit, underneath the bed or seat, where the floor is fixed by a mechanism.
9. Or, when the enemy has come near, he should carry over into the fort persons capable of withstanding a siege from the countryside.
10. And from the fort he should remove those incapable of withstanding a siege or send them to the enemy's territory which is easily recoverable.
11. And he should place the country people in one place in a mountain fort, a forest fort or a river fort, or in regions separated by forests, in charge of a son or a brother.
12. Reasons for entrenching oneself in a fort have been explained in 'the conduct of one surrendering with troops'.
13. He should cause grass and wood to be burnt up to one *yojana* all round the fort.
14. And he should cause waters to be spoiled and to flow away.
15. And he should place wells, concealed pits and barbed wires outside.
16. Making an underground passage with many openings up to the enemy's camp, he should cause the chiefs of stores to be carried away, or the enemy himself.
17. Or, if an underground passage is made by the enemy, he should cause the moat to be dug deeper till its water reaches the passage, or a well-shed along the rampart.
18. In suspected places, he should cause to be placed jars of water or bell-metal vessels, in order to find out any digging done there.
19. When the underground passage is known, he should cause a counter-passage to be dug.

20. Breaking it in the middle, he should let in smoke or water.
21. Or, making arrangements for the defence of the fort, and appointing a kinsman as regent in the base, he should go in the direction opposite to that of the enemy, or where he might be united with allies, kinsmen or forest chiefs or with great enemies and traitors of the enemy, or whereby going there, he might be able to separate him from his allies or to attack him in the rear or cause his kingdom to be seized or to prevent his supplies, reinforcements and foraging raids, or from where he might be able to strike at him with a foul throw like a gambler, or from where his kingdom may be protected or he might be able to secure desirable peace. Or, he should go there where he might be able to secure desirable peace.
22. Or, those who have left the fort with him should send word to the enemy, 'This enemy of yours has fallen in our hands; on the pretext of the purchase of a commodity or of doing injury, send money and a strong force, to which we should hand him over, bound or killed.'
23. When he agrees, he should appropriate the money and the strong force.
24. Or, the commander of a frontier fort, by offering the surrender of the fort, should get a part of the enemy's troops and destroy them when full of trust.
25. Or, the regent should invite a division of the enemy's army to destroy the country people stationed in one place.
26. Taking it to the enclosed region, he should destroy it when full of trust.
27. Or, an agent posing as a friend should send word to the besieger, 'In this fort, grains, fats, sugar or salt is exhausted; new stocks of it will come in at this place any time; seize it.'
28. Then treasonable, alien or forest troops should bring in poisoned grains, fats, sugar or salt, or others condemned to death should bring it in.
29. By that is explained the seizure of all goods and supplies.
30. Or, making peace, he should give him a part of the tribute money, the rest after a long delay.
31. Then he should cause his fortifications to be weakened.
32. Or, he should strike with fire, poison or weapon.
33. Or, he should favour those of his favourites who come to receive the money.
34. Or, if quite exhausted, he should surrender the fort to him and depart.

35. He should go out by an underground passage or an opening in the rampart, breaking through the side.
36. Making a sudden assault at night, he should remain if successful; if not successful he should go out by some stratagem.
37. In the disguise of a heretical monk, he should go out with a small retinue.
38. Or, he should be carried out decked as a corpse by secret agents.
39. Or, wearing a woman's garb, he should follow a funeral procession.
40. Or, he should go away leaving behind poisoned food and drink on occasions of offerings to gods, obsequious rites or festivals.
41. After making secret instigations, he should come out with apparently treasonable troops and strike with the concealed army.
42. Or, if his fort is thus seized, he should, after setting up a sanctuary with plenty of food to eat, remain concealed in a hollow inside the image of the deity or in a hollow wall or in an underground chamber endowed with the image of a deity.
43. When things are forgotten, he should enter the king's chamber at night by an underground passage and kill the sleeping enemy.
44. Or, loosening something that can be loosened by a mechanism, he should make it fall down on him.
45. Or, as the enemy is sleeping in a house smeared with a poisonous fire-mixture or in a lac-house, he should set it on fire.
46. Or, when the enemy is careless in a place of recreation in a pleasure park or other recreation grounds, assassins, entering through underground chambers or tunnels or hollow walls, should slay him, or those employed in secret service should do so by poison.
47. Or, when he is sleeping in a secluded place, female secret agents should drop on him serpents or poisonous fire and smoke.
48. Or, when an occasion arises, he should, moving about secretly, use everything that may be possible against the enemy staying in the palace.
49. Then he should go away in a secret manner, and give signals to his own men.
50. Calling by signals of drums door-keepers, eunuchs and others secretly employed with the enemy, he should get rest of the enemies killed.

Herewith ends the Twelfth Book of the Arthasastra of Kautilya

'CONCERNING THE WEAKER KING'

27

BOOK THIRTEEN

Means of Taking Forts

During the times of Kautilya the army of a powerful king had four wings, *viz.*, 1. Infantry, 2. Cavalry 3. Chariots, and 4. Elephants. As acquisition of territories and their protection were the primary aims and consideration of an Emperor, according to the Arthasastra, the Emperor was supposed to construct new forts and conquer those belonging to the enemy with the ulterior object of speeding the total subjugation of the enemy together with the treasury. In those days forts were considered to be very useful in protecting one's kingdom as they were used to be constructed on such a terrain and in such a manner as would make them command a large area around them. They were made impregnable and invincible by sufficiently providing with troops, the ordnance, food, water etc., Forts were also able to sustain a war of attrition, on its imposition on the enemy. As Aeroplanes were not inducted in those days in the army, only the elephants, supported by infantry were capable to besiege and conquer them with great difficulty. Kautilya was fully conversant with these tactical problems, and therefore, advocated the employment of various subterfuges to achieve the objective of conquering forts. All these stratagems have been elaborated under the following subjects.

1. Instigation to Sedition. 2. Drawing out the Enemy by Means of Stratagems. 3. Employment of Secret Agents. 4. The Work of Laying Siege to a Fort. Storming a Fort. 5. Pacification of the Conquered Territory. These constitute the Thirteenth Book 'Means of Securing a Fort.'

CHAPTER ONE

SECTION 171: INSTIGATION TO SEDITION

1. The conqueror, desirous of capturing the enemy's fortified town, should fill his own side with enthusiasm and fill the enemy's

side with terror, by getting his omniscience and association with divinities proclaimed.

2. The proclamation of omniscience, however, is to be made thus; after ascertaining secret information from their houses, communicating it to the chiefs; after finding out through spies used in suppression of criminals, bringing to light traitors to the king; announcing a request or a present about of association; showing knowledge of news from foreign lands on the same day through a domestic pigeon carrying a sealed communication.
3. The proclamation of association with divinities, however, should be arranged thus: conversing with and worshipping agents appearing as deities in fire-sanctuaries, who have entered the hollow images of deities in fire-sanctuaries by an underground passage; or, conversing with and worshipping agents appearing as Nagas or Varuna risen from the water; showing a row of fire at night inside water by placing a container with sea-sand; standing on a boat held down by slings containing stones; application to the nose of oil boiled a hundred times with the entrails of a spotted deer or the fats of crabs, crocodiles, dolphins and others, to a person whose head without the nose is covered with water-bladder or an embryo-covering.
4. With that, the group of natural creatures moves about.
5. These are ways of moving in water.
6. Through them there is use of speech by Varuna or by Nagas maidens and conversation with them, and the emitting of fire and smoke from the mouth on occasions of anger.
7. Soothsayers, interpreters of omens, astrologers, reciters of Puranas, seers, and secret agents, those who have helped and those who have witnessed it, should broadcast that power of the king in his own territory.
8. In the enemy's territory, they should speak about his meeting with divinities and the acquisition of a treasury and army from a divine source.
9. And when interpreting questions to deities, omens, crow's fight, the science of the body, dreams and utterances of animals and birds, they could predict victory for him, the reverse of it for the enemy.
10. And they should point to a meteor in the enemy's constellation with a beat of drum.
11. Agents working as envoys, speaking to the chiefs of the enemy out of friendship, should tell them of the king's high regard for them,

of the strengthening of his own party and the deterioration of the enemy's party.

12. They should tell ministers and soldiers of the same well-being and security as before.
13. He should show consideration for them in calamities and on festive occasions, and honour their children.
14. In that way he should stir up the enemy's party against him as explained before.
15. And we shall explain further.
16. He should stir up the diligent by speaking of the ordinary donkey; the leaders of the army, by the stick and the striking of the branch; those frightened, by the ram strayed from the herd; those insulted, by a shower of thunder-bolts; those with hopes frustrated, by the cane bearing no fruit, balls of rice to crows and the cloud created by magic; those receiving the reward of honour, by decoration of a disliked wife by one who hates; those who constantly oblige, by the eating of the *pilu-fruit*, the hail, the female camel and churning of the she-donkey's milk.
17. Those who agrees to desert, he should endow with money and honour.
18. And in their difficulties regarding goods and food, he should favour them with gifts of goods and food.
19. In the case of those not accepting these, they should bring ornaments to their women and children.
20. And on occasions of famine, or troubles by robbers or forest tribes, secret agents, stirring up the citizens and the country people, should say, 'Let us ask the king for help; if we do not get help, let us go elsewhere'.
21. When, saving 'All right', they agree, help should be given to them by the grant of goods and grains. Thus, there is great miracle of secret instigation.

CHAPTER TWO

SECTION 172: DRAWING OUT THE ENEMY BY MEANS OF STRATAGEMS

1. An ascetic with shaven head or with matted locks, living in a mountain cave, and declaring himself to be four hundred years old, should stay in the vicinity of the city with plenty of disciples with matted locks.

2. And his disciples, approaching with roots and fruits, should induce the ministers and the king to pay a visit to the holy master.
3. And, visited by the king, he should speak of identification marks of former kings and their countries, adding, 'When every one hundred years of my life are completed, I enter fire and become a child again; so here in your presence, I shall enter fire for the fourth time; you have necessarily to be honoured by me; choose three boons.'
4. When he agrees, he should say, 'You should stay here with sons and wife for seven nights, after arranging a festival with shows.'
5. He should attack him while he is staying there.
6. Or, an agent appearing as a seer of underground objects, with shaven head or with matted hair, having plenty of disciples with matted hair, should place in an ant-hill a bamboo-strip smeared with goat's blood, after smearing it with gold powder, in order that ants may follow it, or place there a hollow tube of gold.
7. Then a secret agent should tell the king, 'That holy man knows a flowering treasure-trove.'
8. Questioned by the king, he should say, 'Yes', and point out that proof, or after placing more money in the earth.
9. And he should say to him, 'This treasure-trove, guarded by a cobra, can be obtained through worship.'
10. When he agrees, for seven nights he should be attacked.
11. Or, as an agent appearing as a seer of underground objects, with his body enveloped in a burning fire at night, is staying in a solitary place, secret agents should say to the king after making him gradually entertain faith in him, 'That holy man is able to secure prosperity.'
12. Promising to ensure what object the king were to ask for, the seer should say, 'for seven nights' and so on as before.
13. Or, an agent appearing as a holy man should tempt the king with magical lores.
14. What object the king and so on as before.
15. Or, an agent appearing as a holy man, finding shelter in the temple of an honoured deity of the country, should, by frequent festivities, win over the chiefs among the constituents and gradually overreach the king.
16. Or, as an agent appearing as an ascetic with matted locks, all white, is staying in water, with means of getting away to an underground tunnel or chamber under the bank, secret agents should tell the

king, after gradually making him believe, that he is Varuna or the King of Nagas.

17. 'What object the king' and so on as before.
18. Or, an agent appearing as a holy man, living on the border of the country, should induce the king to have a sight of the enemy.
19. When he agrees, he should make an effigy and invoke the enemy, and should kill the king, in a secluded spot.
20. Agents appearing as traders, coming with horses for sale, should invite the king to purchase or receive horses as a gift, and kill him while engrosses in inspecting the goods or when mingled with horses and should strike with the horses.
21. Or, assassins, climbing a sacred tree near the city at night-time and blowing into jars through stalks or reeds, should say indistinctly, 'We shall eat the flesh of the king or the chiefs; let worship be offered to us.'
22. Agents appearing as interpreters of omens and astrologers should make that utterance of their known.
23. Or, agents appearing as Nagas, with their bodies smeared with burning oil, should, at night-time, pound together iron clubs and pestles in a holy lake or in the middle of a tank and utter in the same way.
24. Or, agents robed in the skins of bears, giving out fire and smoke from the mouths, and having the appearance of Raksasas, should go three times left-wise round the city and utter in the same way, in the intervals between the cries of dogs and jackals.
25. Or, making the image of a deity in a sanctuary burn at night with burning oil or with fire covered by a layer of mice, agents should utter in the same way.
26. Others should make that known.
27. Or, with blood of animals they should cause an excessive flow of blood from honoured images of deities.
28. Then others should declare defeat in battle in consequence of the flow of the blood of the deity.
29. Or, on the nights of the month's junctures, they should point out a sanctuary in a prominent part of the cemetery as with men eaten standing.
30. Thereafter an agent appearing as a Raksasa should demand the offering of a human being.
31. And whoever, calling himself brave or someone else, were to come there to see, others should kill him with iron pestles, so that it would be known that he was killed by the Raksasas.

32. Those who have witnessed it and secret agents should report that miracle to the king.
33. Then agents appearing as interpreters of omens and astrologers should prescribe pacificatory and expiatory rites adding, 'Otherwise a great disaster will befall the king and the country.'
34. When he has agreed, they should say, 'In these manifestations, for seven nights the king himself should make offerings of oblations with mantras on each single day.'
35. Then as before.
36. Or, showing these tricks practised on himself, he should overcome them, in order to convince the enemies.
37. Then he should employ the tricks against them.
38. Or, by overcoming occult manifestations, he should replenish the treasury.
39. Keepers of elephant forests should tempt the enemy fond of elephants with an elephant possessed of auspicious marks.
40. When he agrees, they should take him to a dense forest or a path allowing only one person to march at a time, and kill him, or carry him off imprisoned.
41. By that is explained the enemy fond of hunting.
42. Or, secret agents should tempt the enemy greedy of money or women with rich widows or women possessed of great beauty and youth, taken to him for the sake of inheritance or deposit.
43. When he agrees, they should, concealed in ambush, kill him with weapon or poison at the time of the meeting.
44. Or, on the occasions of his frequent visits to holy men, mendicants, images of deities in sanctuaries and *stupas*, assassins, concealed in underground chambers or passages or inside hollow walls, should strike at the enemy.
45. In those places, in which the king himself is witnessing a dramatic show, or is enjoying himself in a festival or where he is sporting in water.
46. On all occasions of speaking words of reproof and so on, during sacrifices and festive parties, during birth rites, funeral rites and illness, on occasions of love, sorrow or fear.
47. Or, when at a festival of his own people he, being full of trust, becomes careless, or when he moves about without a guard, on a rainy day or in crowds.

48-49. When he has strayed from the route, or when there is a fire or when he has entered a place without any men in it, assassins, entering with packages of clothes, ornaments and flowers, with beds and seats, or with vessels containing wine and food or with musical instruments, should strike at the enemy along with those employed there beforehand.

50. And in the same way as they may have entered on the occasions for an ambush of the enemy, they should depart. Thus, has been described the drawing out of the enemy by stratagems.

CHAPTER THREE

SECTION 173: EMPLOYMENT OF SECRET AGENTS

1. He should make a trustworthy chief of a band ostensibly desert him.
2. Finding shelter with the enemy, he should bring over helpmates and associates from his own country on the pretext of their being his own party.
3. Or, bringing about an influx of secret agents, he should, after securing the enemy's consent, destroy a treasonable town of his master, or an army devoid of elephants and horses with treasonable officers, or a treasonable ally in the rear of his master, and should send word to the enemy.
4. Or, he should resort to a part of the country or a band or forest chiefs for obtaining help.
5. Winning the enemy's confidence he should send word to his master.
6. Then the master, pretending an expedition for catching elephants or destruction of forest tribes, should attack secretly.
7. By this are explained ministers and forest chiefs.
8. After making friends with the enemy, he should dismiss some ministers.
9. They should send a request to his enemy, 'Propitiate the master for us'.
10. He should upbraid the messenger whom he might send with such a request. 'Your master is dividing me from the ministers; you should not come here again.
11. Then he should make one minister desert him.
12. Finding shelter with the enemy, he should bring to the notice of the enemy treacherous spies, the disaffected and the treasonable, who are weak, or robbers and forest chiefs who harass both kingdoms.
13. Winning thus a position of trust, he should bring to his notice the offence of brave men of the enemy, such as a frontier officer or a forest chief or a leader of the army, saying, 'So and so is surely in league with your enemy'.

14. Then afterwards he should get them killed through letters carried by men condemned to death.
15. Or, he should get him destroyed by rousing the enemy with the use of armed forces.
16. Or, by supporting the seducible party, he should make the king who is the enemy's enemy do injury to himself and then should attack him.
17. Then he should send word to the enemy, 'This enemy of yours is doing injury to me; come, let us join forces and destroy him; you will have a share in his land or money.'
18. If he agrees and comes after honouring these words, he should get him killed by the enemy in a sudden assault or in open battle.
19. Or, under the pretext of giving land or crowning his son or giving protection, in order to create confidence, he should get him seized.
20. Or, if he is unassailable, he should get him killed by silent punishment.
21. If he were to lend a force and not come himself, he should get it destroyed by his enemy.
22. Or, if he were to desire to march with troops, but not with the conqueror, even then he should get him destroyed by a squeezing from both sides.
23. Or, if full of distrust, he were to wish to march, each separately, or were desirous of seizing a part of the territory of the king against whom they are marching, even then he should get him killed by the enemy or by mobilising all his troops.
24. Or, when he is engaged in a fight with the enemy, he should get his base seized from another direction by sending troops there.
25. Or, he should bargain with the ally with the offer of the enemy's land or with the enemy with the offer of the ally's land.
26. Then making the ally do injury to himself when seeking to seize the enemy's land, he should attack him and so on, all the tricks exactly as before.
27. Or, he should help with troops the enemy, who has agreed, when he is seeking to seize the ally's land.
28. Then he should overreach him, as he marches against the ally.
29. Or, after taking remedial measures, he should show a calamity for himself, and rousing the enemy through the ally, should get him to attack himself.
30. Then he should destroy him by squeezing or, catching him alive, make an exchange of the kingdom for his life.

31. If, sheltered by the ally, the enemy were to wish to remain out of reach, he should get his base seized by a neighbouring prince and so on.
32. Or, if he were to seek to protect it with troops, he should cause those to be destroyed.
33. If the two were not to become estranged, he should quite openly bargain with each other's land.
34. Then agents posing as friends or those in the pay of both should send messengers to one or the other, 'This king wants to seize your land, being in league with the enemy'.
35. If none of them is filled with apprehension or anger, he should act as before.
36. Or, he should banish chiefs of the fort or the country or the army, after proclaiming the grounds for their being the seducible party.
37. They should overreach the enemy in a battle or a sudden assault or a siege or a calamity.
38. Or, they should bring about his estrangement from his own groups.
39. They should get corroboration through letters carried by men condemned to death.
40. Or, secret agents appearing as hunters, remaining at the gates for the sale of meat, and given shelter by gate-keepers, should win the enemy's confidence by informing him of the approach of dacoits two or three times, then getting their master's army stationed in two places, one for destroying a town and the other for a sudden assault, should say to the enemies, 'A band of robbers is close by; there is a great din; let a large force come'.
41. Handing that over to the troops of their master meant for destroying the town and taking the other troops to the gates of the fort at night, they should say, 'The band of robbers is killed; the troops, successful in the expedition, have come back; open the gate'.
42. Or, those secretly employed there beforehand should open the gates.
43. Along with them they should strike.
44. Or, he should station in the enemy's fort soldiers disguised as artisans, artists, heretical monks, actors and traders.
45. Agents appearing as householders should bring to them weapons and armours in carts carrying wood, grass, grains and other goods, or in flags and images of gods.
46. Then those disguised like them should carry out the slaughter of the unwary, the supporting of sudden assault, or a strike in the

rear, or should announce by the sound of conches and drums, 'The army of the enemy has come in'.

47. They should open rampart-gates and towers, divide the enemy's divisions or destroy them.
48. The carrying over of troops into the enemy's fort is to be along with those moving in caravans or groups, with escorts, with those accompanying brides, with dealers in horses, with carriers of implements, with sellers or purchasers of grains, with those bearing the marks of monks and with envoys; peace is to be made during the period for creating confidence.
49. These are secret agents for outwitting the king.
50. These same are agents for forest tribes, also those mentioned in 'the suppression of criminals'.
51. Secret agents should cause a herd of cattle or a caravan in the vicinity of a forest to be destroyed by robbers.
52. And making the food and drink placed there, in accordance with an agreement, mixed with a stupefying liquid, they should go away.
53. Then cowherds and traders should cause the robbers carrying loads of stolen goods to be attacked when the stupefying liquid is having its effect.
54. Or, an agent appearing as an ascetic with shaven head or with matted locks and posing as a devotee of god Samkarsana, should overreach the forest robbers by using a stupefying liquid after holding a festival.
55. Then he should make an attack.
56. Or, an agent appearing as a vintner should overreach foresters by using a stupefying liquid on the occasion of the sale or presentation of wine during festivities in honour of gods or funeral rites or festive gatherings.
57. Then he should make an attack.
58. Or, after scattering in many groups the forest tribes that have come for plundering the worn, he should destroy them. Thus, secret agents for robbers have been described.

CHAPTER FOUR

SECTION 174: THE WORK OF LAYING SIEGE TO A FORT

SECTION 175: STORMING A FORT

1. The work of laying siege to a fort should be preceded by weakening the enemy.

2. He should grant safety to the countryside as it may have been settled.
3. He should induce those, who have risen, to settle down through favour and exemptions, excepting those who go away.
4. He should settle them on land away from the battlefield or make them stay in one region.
5. For, there is no country without people and no kingdom without a country, says Kautilya.
6. He should destroy the sowings or crops of one entrenched in an inaccessible fort, also his supplies and foraging raids.
7. By cutting off foraging raids and supplies, also by destroying sowings and crops, by removing from their place and by secret murder, a deterioration of the constituents takes place.
8. When he thinks, 'My troops are fully supplied with abundant and excellent grains, forest produce, machines, weapons, armours, labourers and ropes; the season is favourable to me, unfavourable to the enemy; he is suffering from a deterioration of his stores and fortifications through diseases and famine, there is weariness among his purchased troops and weariness among the ally's troops;' then he should lay siege.
9. After securing the protection of the camp, of supplies and reinforcements and of the roads, he should encircle the fort along the moat and the rampart, defile the water, empty the moats or fill them, and cause the parapet and the rampart to be taken by means of an underground passage and storming by troops, and the breach by means of elephant armours.
10. He should fill hollows with piles of earth.
11. He should destroy with machines what is guarded with many troops.
12. Dragging out soldiers from the runway exit, they should strike with horses.
13. And in the intervals between fighting, he should seek success by the exclusive, alternate or combined use of the four means.
14. Getting hawks, crows, pheasants, kites, parrots, *sarikas*, owls and pigeons, with nests in the fort, caught, he should release them in the enemy's fort with fire-mixtures tied to the tails.
15. Or, from the camp stationed at a distance from the fort he should set fire to the enemy's fort with human fire, being guarded by bows with flags raised a loft.

16. And secret agents, serving as guards inside the fort, should place fire-mixture in the tails of ichneumons, monkeys, cats and dogs, and let them loose in stores of reeds, fortifications and houses.
17. Placing fire in the interior of dried fish or in dried meat, they should have it carried in through birds by offering it to crows.
18. Balls of *sarala*, *devaddru*, 'stinking-grass', bedellium, pine-resin, *sala* resin and lac and the dung of donkeys, camels, goats and sheep, are good retainers of fire.
19. The power of *priyala*, the soot of *avalguja*, wax and the dung of horses, donkeys, camels and bullocks make a fire-mixture which can be thrown into the fort.
20. Or, the powder of all metals, of the colour of fire, or the powder of *kumbhi*, lead and tin, mixed with the flowers of *paribhadraka* and *palasa*, the soot of *kesa*, oil, wax and pine resin makes a fire-mixture, one that kills the trusting.
21. An arrow smeared with it and covered with hemp and the bark of *trapusa*, is a means of setting on fire.
22. However, when fighting is possible, he should not at all make use of fire.
23. For, fire is unreliable and is a divine calamity, the destroyer of innumerable creatures, grains, animals, money, forest produce and goods.
24. And a kingdom, with stores exhausted, even if obtained, leads only to loss.

    Thus, ends the topic of laying siege to a fort.
25. When he thinks, 'I am fully provided with equipments and labourers for the undertaking; the enemy is ill, has the constituents estranged because of secret tests, or has made no fortifications or stores; being without reinforcements or with reinforcements, he will soon make peace with allies;' that is the time for storming the fort.
26. When a fire is accidentally caused or is produced by agents, when there is a festival, when troops are engaged in witnessing a show, during quarrels caused by drink, when troops are tired by constant fighting, when his men are wounded or killed in many battles, when people, tired of keeping awake, are asleep, when it is raining or the river is flooded or there is a thick fog, he should storm the fort.
27. Or, abandoning the camp, and hiding in a forest, he should kill the enemy as he sallies out.

28. Or, one posing as the chief ally or helpmate should make friendship with besieged and send a man condemned to death as a messenger, saying, 'This is your weak point; these men are treasonable;' or 'This is the weak point of the besieger; this is the seducible party for you'.
29. As he comes out with a return messenger, the conqueror should seize him and proclaiming his offence, slay him and go away.
30. Then the one posing as an ally or a helpmate should say to the besieged, 'Come out to save me', or 'Kill the besieger along with me'.
31. When he agrees, he should destroy him by squeezing from both sides, or, catching him alive, make an exchange of the kingdom for his life.
32. Or, he should demolish his capital city.
33. Or, forcing out his best troops he should strike.
34. By that are explained the king surrendering with troops and forest chieftains.
35. One of the two, a king surrendering with troops or a forest chieftain, should send word to the besieged, 'This besieger is ill, or he is attacked by an enemy in the rear, or another weak point has appeared, or he wants to go to another land'.
36. When he has agreed, the besieger should set fire to the camp and go away.
37. Then he should act as before.
38. Or, making a collection of merchandise, he should overreach him with goods mixed with poison.
39. Or, one posing as a helpmate should send a messenger to the besieged, 'Come out to attack the enemy outside, already attacked by me'.
40. When he agrees, he should act as before.
41. Entering the fort under the pretext of seeing a friend or a kinsman, with sealed passes in the hand, secret agents should get it seized by the besieger.
42. Or, one posing as a helpmate should send word to the besieged, 'At such and such a place and at such and such a time, I shall strike at the camp; you also must fight then'.
43. When he agrees, he should show the tumult of an attack as mentioned and destroy him as he sallies out of the fort at night.
44. Or, he should invite an ally or a forest chieftain and incite him, 'Fight against the besieged and seize his land.'

45. When he fights, he should get him slain through the subjects or by supporting his treasonable chiefs, or kill him himself with poison, achieving his object of implicating the enemy 'He is the slayer of his ally'.
46. Or, one posing as a friend should inform the enemy about the ally etc. wanting to attack.
47. Securing a position of trust, he should get his brave warriors slain.
48. Or, making peace with him, he should induce him to settle the country.
49. When settled, he should, unknown, destroy his country.
50. Or, after causing an injury to be done and getting part of the enemy's troops led against treasonable or forest troops, he should capture the fort by a sudden assault.
51. Treasonable, alien and forest troops, hostile men and deserters from the enemy who have come over, being given money and honour and supplied with signals and signs, should attack the enemy fort.
52. When attacking the enemy's fort or camp, they should grant safety to those fallen down, those turning back, those surrendering, those with loose hair, those without weapons, those disfigured by terror and to those not fighting.
53. After obtaining the enemy's fort, he should enter it after it is cleared of the enemy's party and after precautions against silent punishment are taken inside and outside.
54. After obtaining the enemy's territory, the conqueror should seek to seize the middle king, after succeeding over him, neutral king.
55. This is the first method of conquering the world.
56. In the absence of the middle and neutral kings, he should overcome the enemy constituents by superiority of policy, then the other constituents.
57. This is the second method.
58. In the absence of the circle he should overcome by squeezing from both sides the ally through the enemy or the enemy through the ally.
59. This is the third method.
60. He should first overcome a weak or a single neighbouring prince; becoming doubly powerful through him a second prince; three times powerful, a third,
61. This is the fourth method of conquering the world.

62. And after conquering the world he should enjoy it divided into *varnas* and *asramas* in accordance with his own duty.
63. Secret instigation, secret agents, drawing out of the fort, laying siege and storming, these are the five means of taking a fort.

CHAPTER FIVE

SECTION 176: PACIFICATION OF THE CONQUERED TERRITORY

1. The object of the conqueror's activity is two-fold: forests and so on, and a single city and so on.
2. Its acquisition is of three kinds: new, formerly possessed and inherited.
3. After gaining new territory, he should cover the enemy's faults with his own virtues, his virtues with double virtues.
4. He should carry out what is agreeable and beneficial to the subjects by doing his own duty as laid down, granting favour, giving exemptions, making gifts and showing honour.
5. And he should cause the enemy seducible party to be favoured as promised and more if they had exerted themselves.
6. For, he who does not keep his promise becomes unworthy of trust for his own and other people, also he whose behaviour is contrary to that of the subjects.
7. Hence, he should adopt a similar character, dress, language and behaviour as the subjects.
8. And he should show the same devotion in festivals in honour of deities of the country, festive gathering and sportive amusements.
9. Secret agents should frequently point out the enemy's misconduct to chiefs in the country, towns castes and corporations, the master's great good fortune and love for them, and the master's great regard for them.
10. And he should make use of them by looking after their customary rights, exemptions and protection.
11. And he should cause the honouring of all deities and hermitages, and make grants of land, money and exemptions to men distinguished in learning, speech and piety, order the release of all prisoners and render help to the distressed, the helpless and the diseased.
12. He should order the stopping of slaughter for half a month in every four month, in every four months, for four nights and days on the occasions of full moon nights, for one night and day on the days of the constellations of the king and the country.

13. He should prohibit the killing of females and young ones and the destruction of a male's virility.
14. And discontinuing whatever custom he might regard as harmful to the treasury and the army, or as unrighteous, he should establish a righteous course of conduct.
15. And he should cause a change of residence, not in one place, of those in the habit of robbing and of Mleccha communities, and of chiefs of forts, country and army.
16. And he should cause ministers, chaplains and others favoured by the enemy, to reside on the enemy's frontiers, not in one place.
17. He should put down by silent punishment those capable of injuring or those brooding on the master's destruction.
18. In the places of those removed, he should establish men from his own country or those in disfavour with the enemy.
19. And if any pretender from the enemy's family be capable of seizing easily recoverable territory, or a nobleman staying in a frontier forest be capable of troubling him, he should give him worthless land or a fourth part of valuable land, after fixing a tribute in treasury and army, such that while paying it he would rouse the citizens and country people to revolt.
20. He should get him killed through these, when they are roused.
21. He should remove one denounced by the subjects or station him in a dangerous region.
22. In the case of territory formerly possessed and reconquered, he should cover up that defect of the constituents because of which he had to leave and should strengthen that quality on the strength of which he has returned.
23. In the case of inherited territory, he should cover up the father's defects and display his virtues.
24. He should institute a righteous custom, not initiated before and continue one initiated by others; and he should not institute an unrighteous custom, and should stop any initiated by others.

Herewith ends the Thirteenth Book of the Arthasastra of Kautilya

'MEANS OF TAKING A FORT'

28

BOOK FOURTEEN

Concerning Secret Practices

Protection of the four *Varnas* was the most important duty of the king, who was made the trustee by the subjects for the purpose of preservation of spiritual good, material well-being and pleasures, and the destruction of evil, material loss and hatred. Kautilya had expounded various devices for using secret practices only against the unrighteous and the enemy. This science was specially composed by him, who in resentment, quickly regenerated the science and the weapon and the earth that was under the control of Nanda kings, and helped Candragupta Maurya in establishing a powerful empire in Hindustan after driving away, lock, stock and barrel the Greeks from this country. It were their efforts that the confederacies of free tribes came out from their self-imposed isolation from other political systems and aggregated into a strong union and succeeded in the total rout of the Greeks from India where Hellenism could not be established as the Greeks did in the contemporay Iran, Syria, Asia Minor and Egypt.

In this Book Chemical Warfare along with Alchemy, have been described various secret methods of destruction of enemy, remedies and occult practices, including recipes intended to kill, maim or disfigure a person.

These ingredients cannot often be identified; in fact many times it is not clear if a name stands for a plant or a creature or a substance. The efficacy of these recipes cannot, of course, be tested.

The subjects espoused are:

1. Secret Practices for the Destruction of Enemy Troops. 2-3. Deceiving by Means of Occult Practices. 4. Counter-measures against

Injuries to One's Own Troops. These constitute the Fourteenth Book Concerning Secret Practices.

CHAPTER ONE

SECTION 177: SECRET PRACTICES FOR THE DESTRUCTION OF ENEMY TROOPS

1. For the sake of protecting the four *varnas*, he should use secret practices against the unrighteous.
2. The group of poisons, *kalakuta* and others, should be introduced into articles used on his person by the enemy, by approved men and women of the Mleecha communities, disguised as humpbacks dwarfs, Kiratas, dumb or deaf persons, idiots, or blind persons, in an appearance credible as to country, dress, profession, language and birth.
3. Secret agents should introduce weapons in the articles for the enemy king's sports and in objects from the stores used by him, and agents following a secret activity, moving about at night, and those living by fire, should put fire in those objects.
4. The powder of speckled frog, the insects *kaundinyaka* and *krkana*, the *pancakustha* and the centipede, the powder of *uccidinga*, *kambali*, *satakanda*, *idhma* and the lizard, the powder of the house lizard, the 'blind reptile', the *krakantaka*, the 'stink-insect', and the *gomarika*, mixed with the sap of *bhallataka* and *avalguja*, causes instantaneous death, or the smoke of these cause it.
5. Or, any one of the insects, boiled along with the black serpent and *priyangu*-one should dry up this mixture; this mixture is believed to cause instantaneous death.
6. The root of *dhamdrgava* and *yatudhana*, mixed with the powder of *bhollutaka* flowers is a preparation for bringing on death in a fortnight.
7. The root of *uyaghataka*, mixed with the powder of *bhallataka* flowers and a mixture of insects, brings on death in a month.
8. Only a minute portion is the dose for men, double for donkeys and horses, four for elephants and camels.
9. The smoke of *satakardama*, *uccidinga*, *karavira*, the bitter gourd and fish, with the stalks of *madana* and *kodrava* or with the stalks of *hastikarna* and *palasa*, when carried forth in a breeze blowing forward, kills everything to which it blows.
10. The powder of the 'stink insect', fish gourd, *satakardama*, *idhama* and the *indragopa* insect, or the powder of the 'stink-insect', *ksudra*,

arata, *hema* and *vidari*, mixed with the powder of the horns and hooves of a goat, makes a smoke that blinds one.

11. The leaves of *putikaranja*, yellow orpiment, red arsenic, *gunja* seeds and stalks of red cotton plant, made into a dough with the sap of *asphota*, *kaca* and cow-dung, make a blinding smoke.
12. The slough of a serpent, the dung of the cow and the horse and the head of a 'blind reptile', make a blinding smoke.
13. The urine and dung of pigeons, frogs and carnivorous animals and of elephants, men and boars, green sulphate of iron, asafoetida, the husk and broken and whole grains of barley, the seeds of cotton, *kutaja* and *kosataki*, the roots of *gomatrika* and *bhandi*, bits of *nimba*, *sigru*, *phanirjaka*, *aksiva* and *piluka*, the skin of a serpent and a female *saphara* and the powder of the nails and tusk of an elephant—the smoke of this produced with the stalks of *madana* and *kodrava* or with the stalks of *hastikarna* and *pilasa*, kills each singly, wherever it moves.
14. The roots of *kali, kustha, nada*, and *satavari*, or the powder of the serpent, *pracalaka, krkana* and *pancakustha*—this smoke produced in the manner mentioned before or with half-wet, half dry stalks, and directed to the enemy's coming on the battlefield or crowding in a sudden assault, by men who have taken precautions for their own eyes with 'washing water', destroys the sight of all creatures.
15. The dung of the *sarika*, the pigeon, the heron and the crane, kneaded with the milk of *arka, aksi, piluka* and *snuhi* plants is a blinding eye-slave and a polluter of water.
16. A mixture of the roots of barley and *sali*-rice, the fruit of *madana*, nutmeg leaves and man's urine, mixed with the roots of *plaksa* and *vidari*, and mixed with a decoction of *hastikarna* and *palasa*, is a stupefying preparation.
17. A mixture of *srngi*, the *gautama*-tree, *kantakara* and *mayurapadi*, a mixture of *gunja*, *tangali*, *visamulika* and *ingudi*, a mixture of *karavira*, *aksi*, *piluka*, *arka* and *mrgamarani*, mixed with a decoction of *madana* and *kodrava*, or mixed with a decoction of *hastikarna* and *palasa* is a stupefying preparation.
18. Or, all these are polluters of fodders, fuel and water.
19. The smoke of *krtakandala*, the lizard, the house lizard and the 'blind reptile' cause loss of eyesight and madness.
20. A mixture of the lizard and the house-lizard causes leprosy.
21. The same, mixed with the entrails of the speckled frog and honey brings on a disease of the bladder; mixed with human blood, it causes consumption.

22. The poison *dusivisa* and the powder of *madana* and *kodrava* is a preparation for bringing on paralysis of the tongue.
23. A mixture of *matrvahaka*, *anjalikara*, *pracalaka*, the frog, *aksi* and *piluka*, causes cholera.
24. A mixture of *pancakustha*, *kaundinyaka*, the flowers of *rajavrksa* and honey, causes fever.
25. A mixture of the flesh of *bhasa* and *nakula* and the plants *jihva* and *granthika*, kneaded with the milk of a female donkey, makes one dump and deaf, in a month or half a month.
26. Only a minute portion for men and so on as before.
27. The administration of a decoction of bits in the case of plants, powder in the case of creatures, or the administration of a decoction in all cases, thus, it becomes more potent.
28. These are the excellences of mixtures.
29. The man, whom an arrow, prepared with seeds of *salmali* and *vidari*, joined with *mula* and *vatsanabha* and smeared with the blood of muskrat, hits, bites, when wounded, by it, other ten persons, and those bitten bite other ten persons each.
30. The decoction of *elaka*, *aksi*, *gugulu*, *and hatahala*, together with the flowers of *bhallataka*, *yatudhana*, *avanu*, *dhamargava* and *bana*, mixed with the blood of a goat and man, is a preparation causing biting.
31. A measure of one-half *dharana* of this preparation, introduced in water with barley meal and oil-cake, poisons a reservoir of water, one hundred *dhanuses* in extent.
32. For, a shoal fish bitten or touched by this, becomes poisonous, also whoever drinks this water or touches it.
33. An iguana, placed along with red and white mustard seeds in a camel-shaped vessel buried in the ground for three fortnights, and taken out by a man condemned to death, kills wherever it casts its glance, or a black serpent does so.
34. A charcoal burnt by lightning or a flame caused by it, caught and fed with wood burnt by lightning—this fire, with offerings made into it under the *Krttikas* or the *Bharanis* in a rite in honour of Rudra, burns, when directed towards an enemy, without there being any remedy for it.
35. Bringing fire from a blacksmith, he should offer honey in it separately, wine in the fire from the vintner, and ghee in the fire from the roads.
36. And, he should offer garland-flowers in the fire from a woman devoted to her husband, mustard seeds in the fire from a harlot,

curds in the fire from a woman in confinement and rice-grains in the fire from one who has kept the sacrificial fires.

37. Meat in the fire from a Candala, human flesh in the fire from a funeral pyre, the fat of a goat and human *dhruva* in all these together.
38. He should offer the wood of *rajavrksa* with *mantras* in honour of Agni. This is a fire against which there is no remedy, which confounds the eyes of enemies.
39. Aditi, a salutation of thee; O Anumati, a salutation to thee; O Sarasvati, a salutation to thee; O God Savitr, a salutation to thee.
40. To Agni, hail! To Soma, hail, Earth hail! Atmosphere hail!

CHAPTER TWO

SECTION 178: DECEIVING BY MEANS OF OCCULT PRACTICES

(i) Working of Miracles

1. The powder of *sirisa*, *udumbara* and *sami*, mixed with clarified butter, is a recipe against hunger, effective for half a month.
2. That, prepared out of *kaseruka*, the bulbous root of the lotus, the root of sugar-cane, lotus fibres, *durva* grass, milk, ghee and cream, is effective for one month.
3. Drinking, with milk and ghee, the powder of *masa*-beans, barley, *kulattha* and the roots of *darbha* grass, or valli, milk and ghee boiled together in equal quantities, or the paste of the roots of *sala* and *prsniparni* along with milk, or partaking of milk boiled together with that, along with honey and ghee, one is able to fast for a month.
4. Oil, prepared from mustard seeds kept for seven nights in the urine of white goats and kept in a bitter gourd for a month and half a month, is a means of disfiguring quadrupeds and bipeds.
5. The oil of white mustard seeds, boiled with barley-grains taken from the dung of a white donkey fed on butter-milk and barley, after seven nights, is a means of disfiguration.
6. Mustard oil, boiled along with the urine and dung of either of these two, with the addition of the powder of *arka*, *tula* and *patanga*, is a means of making a person white.
7. A mixture of the dung of a white cock and a boa constrictor, is a means of making white.
8. White mustard seeds, kept in the urine of a white goat for seven nights, butter milk, the milk of *arka*, salt and grains—the mixture kept for a fortnight is a means of making white.

9. The flour of white mustard seeds, kept for half a month in a bitter gourd while still on the creeper, is a means of making hair white.
10. The insect that is known as *alojuna* and the white house-lizard—hair smeared with this paste would become as white as a conch-shell.
11. One, with his body nibbed with cow-dung or with the pulp of *tinduka* and *arista*, and smeared with the sap of *bhallataka*, gets leprosy within a month.
12. *Gunja*-seeds kept for seven nights in the mouth of a black serpent or in the mouth of a house lizard is a means of causing leprosy.
13. Application all over the body of the bile and the liquid of the egg of a parrot is a means of causing leprosy.
14. A decoction of the pulp of *priyala* is a remedy for leprosy.
15. One, eating food containing the roots of *kukuta*, *kosataki* and *satavari*, becomes fair-complexioned in a month.
16. One, bathing in a decoction of *vata* and smeared with the pulp of *sahacara*, becomes black.
17. Yellow orpiment and red arsenic, mixed with the oil of *sakuna* and *kangu*, are a means of making dark.
18. The powder of the fire-fly, mixed with mustard oil, burns at night.
19. The powder of the fire-fly and the insect *gandupada*, or the powder of the flowers of *samudra-jantus, bhrngakapalas, khadira* and *karnikara*, mixed with the oil of *sakuna* and *kangu*, is a powder that makes an object glow.
20. The soot of the bark of *paribhadraka*, mixed with the fat of a frog, is a means of making limbs burn with fire.
21. The body, smeared with the pulp of the bark of the *paribhadraka* and *sesamum* seeds burns with fire.
22. A lump, consisting of the soot of the bark of *pilu*, burns in the hand.
23. Smeared with the fat of a frog, it burns with fire.
24. The body, smeared with that, or, sprinkled with the oil of the *kusamra* fruit and mixed with the powder of a female sea-frog, sea-foam and *sarja*-exudation, burns.
25. Oil, boiled with equal quantities of the fat of the frog, crab and so on, causes the blazing of limbs with fire all over.
26. The body, smeared with the roots of bamboo and moss and smeared with the fat of a frog, burns with fire.
27. One, with his feet smeared with oil boiled together with the fat of a frog and the pulp of the roots of *paribhadraka, pratibala, vanjula, vanjra and kadali*, walks on burning charcoal.

28-29. One should prepare oil from the pulp of these namely, *upodaka*, *pratibala*, *vanjula* and *paribhadraka*, by boiling together with the fat of a frog; after smearing one's clean feet with this oil, one may walk on a heap of burning charcoal as on a heap of flowers.

30. Lamps of reeds, tied to the tails of swans, herons and peacocks or of other big birds swimming in water, is a manifestation of meteors at night.

31. Ashes caused by lighting are a means of extinguishing fire.

32. *Masa*-beans, soaked in a woman's menstrual fluid and the root of *vrajakuli*, mixed with the fat of a frog, is a means of preventing cooking even when the oven is burning.

33. Cleansing the oven is the remedy for it.

34. A ball made of *pilu*, with fire in the interior, with a knot of the root of *suvarcala* or with a knot of thread, encircled by cotton, is a means of emitting fire and smoke from the mouth.

35. Fire, sprinkled with the oil of the *kusamra* fruit, burns in rain and in strong winds.

36. Sea-foam soaked in oil, burns floating on water.

37. Fire, kindled by churning a speckled bamboo-reed in the bones of swimming birds, is not put out by water, but burns with water.

38. Where a fire kindled by churning a speckled bamboo-reed in the ribs from the left side of a man slain with a weapon or impaled on the stake, or a fire kindled by churning the rib of a human being in the bones of a woman or a man, goes round three times left-wise, there no other fire burns.

39. The musk-rat, the wag-tail and the salt-insect are ground to powder; mixed with the urine of a horse, they are a means of breaking chains.

40. Or, the load-stone, made doubly powerful by the smearing of the fats of the crab, the frog and the salt-insect, is a breaker of chains.

41. The foetus of a calf, ground together with the sides of the heron and the *bhasa*, lotus and water, is foot-salve for quadrupeds and bipeds.

42. Smearing sandals made of camel-hide with the fat of the owl and the vulture, covering them with leaves of the banyan tree, one walks fifty *yojanas* without being fatigued.

43. The bone-marrow or the semen of hawk, the heron, the crow, the vulture, the swan, the plover and the *viciralla* enables one to walk untired for one hundred *yojanas*, or the bone-marrow or semen of the lion, the tiger, the leopard, the crow and the owl.

44. After pressing in a camel-shaped vessel the aborted foetus of all the *varnas* or dead infants in the cemetery—the fat produced from that enables one to walk untired for one hundred *yojanas*.
45. He should cause fright to the enemy with these evil, miraculous portents; because it is for the consolidation of the kingdom, a similar blameworthy conduct is recommended when there is a revolt.

CHAPTER THREE

SECTION 178 (CONTINUED): DECEIVING BY MEANS OF OCCULT PRACTICES

(ii) The use of Medicines and Spells

1. Taking the right and the left eyes of one, two or more of the following, the cat, the camel, the wolf, the boar, the porcupine, the flying fox, the *naptr*, the crow, the owl or other creatures roaming at night, one should prepare two separate powders.
2. Then anointing the right eye with the powder of the left eye and the left with that of the right, one is able to see at night and in darkness.
3. One *amlaka*-fruit, the eye of a boar, the fire-fly, the black *sariva*-one with his eyes anointed with this preparation, sees objects at night time.
4. After fasting for three days and nights, one should prepare, on the *pusya* day, barley-seeds in earth in the skull of a man killed with a weapon or impaled on the stake, and sprinkle them with sheep's milk.
5. Then wearing a garland of the sprouts of barley, one is able to move about with one's shadow and form invisible.
6. After fasting for three days and nights, one should, on the *pusya* day, powder separately the right and the left eyes of a dog, a cat, an owl and a flying fox.
7. Then anointing the eyes with the powder of the corresponding eyes, one moves about with shadow and form invisible.
8. After fasting for three days and nights, one should prepare, on the *pusya* day, a pin and a salve-container out of the thigh bone of a murderer.
9. Then, with eyes anointed with the powder of the eyes of any one of these, one moves about with shadow and form invisible.
10. After fasting for three days and nights, one should prepare, on the *pusya* day, an iron salve-container and a pin.

11. Then, filling the skull of any one of the night roaming creatures with an eye-salve, one should insert it in the vagina of a dead woman and cause it to be burnt.
12. Taking out that salve on the *pusya* day, one should keep it in that salve-container.
13. With eyes anointed with that, one moves about with shadow and form invisible.
14. Where one sees a Brahmin, who has maintained the sacred fires, cremated or burning on the pyre, thereafter fasting for three days and nights, one should, on the pusya day, make a bag out of the garment of a man who has died naturally and fill it with the ashes of the funeral pyre; wearing that bag, one moves about with shadow and form invisible.
15. The skin of a serpent, filled with the powder of the bones and marrow of that bull which is slaughtered in the funeral rites of a Brahmin, is a means of making animals invisible.
16. The skin of a *pracalaka*, filled with the ashes of one bitten by a serpent, is a means of making deer invisible.
17. The skin of a serpent, filled with the powder of the tail, the dung and the knee-bones of an owl and a flying fox, is a means of making birds invisible.
18. These are the eight recipes for making invisible.
19. 'I bow to Bali, the son of Virocana and to Sambara of the hundred guiles, to Bhandirapaka, to Naraka, to Nikumbha, as well as to Kumbha.'
20. 'I bow to Devala and to Narada; I bow to Savarni Galava. According to the prescription of these this great sleep has been brought on you.'
21. 'As the boa constrictors sleep, as also the *camukhalas* sleep, so may men sleep, also those who, in the village, are curious.'
22. 'With a thousand vessels and with a hundred fellies of chariots, I shall enter this house; let the vessels remain silent.'

23-24. 'Bowing to Manu and tying the dog-kennels, and bowing to those who are gods in the worlds of the gods and are Brahmins among men, to holy men who have completed their study and to ascetics on the *kailasa*-mountain, bowing to all these holy men, this great sleep has been brought on you.'

25. 'As I go beyond, may all together go away.
26. O Alita, O Valita, hail to Manu!'
27. The method of using this is:

28. After fasting for three days and nights, one should, on the fourteenth of the dark of a month with the moon in conjunction with the *pusya*-constellation, purchase from a Svapaka woman the scrapings made by *bilakhas*.
29. Placing them with *masa*-beans in a basket, one should bury it in an uncrowded cremation-ground.
30. Taking it out on the fourteenth of the next fortnight and getting it pounded by a maiden, one should make pills out of it.
31. Then wherever one throws one pill after reciting this *mantra* over it, there one sends all to sleep.
32. In this same manner, one should bury the quill of a porcupine with three black and three white lines in a uncrowded cremation-ground.
33. Taking it out on the fourteenth of the next-fortnight, wherever one throws it along with ashes from the burning ground, reciting this *mantra* over it, one sends all there to sleep.
34. 'I bow to Brahmins with the golden flowers and to Brahman with the flag of *kusa*-grass and to all the deities; and I bow to all the ascetics.
35. May Brahmins come under my control, and may the Ksatriyas who protect the earth; may the Vaisyas and the Sudras be ever under my control.
36. Hail! O Amila, O Kimila, O Vayucara, O Prayoga, O Phakka, O Vayuhva, O Vihala, O Dantakataka, hail!
37. May the dogs sleep happily, and those who, in the village, are curious, and this quill of the porcupine, white in three places, is created by Brahman.
38. For, all successful men are asleep; this sleep has been brought on you, up to where the end of the boundary of the village is and till the rising of the sun.
39. 'Hail!'
40. The use of this mantra is as follows :
41. The quills of a porcupine with three white lines should be taken; after fasting for seven days and nights, one should, on the fourteenth of the dark fortnight, offer into the fire sticks of *khadira* accumulating them to one hundred and eight, along with honey and ghee, reciting this *mantra*.
42. Then whereat the village-gate or the door of a house, one of these is buried, with the recitation of this *mantra*, one sends all there to sleep.

43. 'I bow to Bali, the son of Virocana and to Sambara of the hundred guiles, to Nikumbha, to Naraka, to Kumbha, to Tantukaccha, the great Asura;
44. I bow to Armalava, to Pramila, to Mandolika, to Ghatodbala, and to the service of Krsna and Kamsa, and to Paulomi, the successful.
45. Consecrating with *mantras*, I take the dead *sarika* for the sake of success; may it succeed, and it does succeed; salutation to quill beings, Hail!
46. May the dog sleep happily, and those who, in the village, are curious. May those who have achieved their object—the object which we seek—sleep happily till the rising of the sun after its setting, till the objects is mine as the fruit.
47. Hail!'
48. The use of this *mantra* is as follows:
49. One who has fasted for four meals should make an offering in an uncrowded cremation ground on the fourteenth of the dark fortnight, and taking, with this *mantra*, a dead *sarika* should tie it in a bag made of a hog's snout.
50. Piercing it in the middle with the quill of a porcupine, where it is buried with this *mantra*, one sends all there to sleep.
51. 'I seek refuge with Agni and the deities, the ten quarters; and may all go away, may they be ever under my control.
52. Hail!'
53. The use of this *mantra* is as follows:
54. After fasting for three days and nights, one should, on the *pusya* day, make an aggregate of twenty-one pebble stones and offer oblations of honey and ghee in the fire.
55. Then, worshipping them with incense and flowers, one should bury them.
56. Taking them out on the next *pusya* day, one should consecrate one pebble with this *mantra* and strike a door panel with it.
57. Within four pebbles, the door is opened.
58. After fasting for four meals, one should, on the fourteenth of the dark fortnight, make a bull out of the bone of a broken man, and should consecrate it with this *mantra*.
59. A bullock cart with two bullocks yoked is brought to him.
60. Thereafter, he moves about in the sky.
61. Becoming skin to the sun, he penetrates everything beyond the gate-bar.
62. 'Thou art possessed of the bitter strength of the pitcher-gourd of a Candala woman, and possessed of a woman's organ: hail!'

63. This is a means of opening locks and sending all to sleep.
64. After fasting for three days and nights, one should, on the *pusya* day, sow *tuvari* seeds in earth in the skull of a man killed with a weapon or impaled on the stake, and sprinkle them with water.
65. When grown, he should take them on the *pusya* day itself and twist them into a rope.
66. Then, the cutting of it in front of bows and machines fitted with strings causes the snapping of those strings.
67. One should fill the skin of a water snake with the earth into which a woman or a man has breathed; this is a means of blocking the nostrils and choking the mouth.
68. Filling the skin of a boar with breathed in earth, one should tie it with a monkey's tendons; this is a means of causing suppression of urine and stools.
69. On the fourteenth of the dark fortnight, one should anoint the eyes of an effigy of the enemy made out of *rajavrksa* wood with the bile of a tawny-coloured cow killed with a weapon; this is a means of making him blind.
70. One who has fasted for four meals should make an offering on the fourteenth of the dark fortnight and make pins out of the bones of a man impaled on the stake.
71. One of these planted in the dung or urine of an enemy causes suppression of stools and urine, planted in his footstep or seat it kills by consumption, planted in his shop, field or house, it destroys the sources of his livelihood.
72. With this same procedure are explained wedges made out of a tree burnt by lighting.

73-74. He, in whose house the *punarnava* turned downwards, the *nimba* and the *kamamadhu*, the hair of a monkey and the bone of a human being, tied up in the garment of a corpse, are buried or to whose footstep one takes it after seeing it, does not survive beyond three fortnights with his sons and wife and his wealth.

75-76. He, in whose footsteps are buried the *punarnava* turned downwards, the *nimba* the *kamamadhu*, the *svayamgupta* and the bone of a human being, at the gate of the house or army camp or village or city, does not survive beyond three fortnights with his sons and wife and his wealth.

77. One should procure the hairs of a goat and a monkey, of a cat and an ichneumon, of Brahmins and Svapakas, and of a crow and an owl; the ordure of an enemy pounded with this causes immediate destruction.

78. He, in whose footsteps are buried flowers removed from a corpse fermenting stuff, the hair of an ichneumon and the skins of a scorpion, a bee and a snake, becomes immediately impotent so long as that is not removed.
79. After fasting for three days and nights, one should, on the *pusya* day, sow *gunja* seeds in earth in the skull of a man killed with a weapon or impaled on the stake, and sprinkle them with water.
80. When they have grown, one should cause the *gunja*-creepers to be taken on the new moon night or full moon night when there is conjunction of the moon with the *pusya*-constellation, and make rings out of them.
81. Vessels with food and drink, placed on them, are never exhausted.
82. When a night show is going on, one should cut out the udders of a dead cow and burn them in the flames of a lamp.
83. When burnt, he should grind them with the urine of a bull and smear a new jar inside with it.
84. When one takes it round the village leftwise, whatever butter may have been kept there by those villagers all that comes into it.
85. On the fourteenth of the dark fortnight when there is conjunction of the moon with the *pusya*-constellation, one should insert into the vulva of a bitch in heat an iron signet ring.
86. One should pick it up when fallen of its own accord.
87. Fruits from trees come to one when called with it.
88. Practices accompanied by *mantras* and medicines and those that are caused by illusion—with them he should destroy the enemies and protect his own people.

CHAPTER FOUR

SECTION 179: COUNTER-MEASURES AGAINST INJURIES TO ONE'S OWN TROOPS

1. Counter-measures against *dusivisa* and other poisons used by the enemy against one's party should be taken as follows:
2. Washing water, mixed with a decoction of *silesmataka, kapittha, danti, dantasatha, goji, sirisa, patali, bala, syonaga, punarnava*, and *svetvarna*, and mixed with sandalwood and the blood of a female hyena, is a wash for the private parts of women to be enjoyed by the king and an antidote against the poisoning of the army.
3. The powder of *mahiraji*, mixed with bile of the speckled deer, the ichneumon, the peacock and the iguana, and the mixture of *sinduvarita, varana, vdruni, tanduliyaka*, the tips of *sataparvan* and *pinditaka*, remove the evil effects of a stupefying mixture.

4. A drink of the decoction of one or of all of the roots of the following, *srgalavinna*, *madana*, *sinduvarita*, *varana*, and *valli*, together with milk, removes the evil effects of a stupefying mixture.
5. The oil of *kaidarya*, *puti* and sesame removes madness, when used in the nostrils.
6. The mixture of *priyangu* and *naktamala* cures leprosy.
7. The mixture of *kustha* and *lodhara* cures whiteness of hair and consumption.
8. The powder of *kataphala*, *dravanti* and *vilanga*, used as snuff, removes headaches.
9. The mixture of *priyangu*, *manjisthi*, *tagara*, lac-juice, luqiorice, turmeric and honey, is a means of bringing back to consciousness those who have lost it through rope strangling, water drowning, poison, beating or fall.
10. A measure of one *aksa* is the dose for men, double for cattle and horses, four times for elephants and camels.
11. And a pill made of these, with gold inside, removes the evil effects of all poisons.
12. A pill made of *jivanti, sveta, muskaka* and *puspavandaka* and of *asvattha* growing on moist soil, removes the evil effect of all poisons.
13. The sound of drums, smeared with these, destroys poison; by looking at a flag or a banner, smeared with these, one becomes free from poison.
14. After using these remedial measures for the safety of his own troops and himself, he should use against enemies poisonous smoke and pollution of water.

Herewith ends the Fourteenth Book of the Arthasastra of Kautilya
'CONCERNING SECRET PRACTICES'

29

BOOK FIFTEEN

Method of the Science

This is the last of the Books of the Arthasastra written by Kautilya. It explains and illustrates the various stylistics devices used to elucidate a scientific subject like the Science of Politics, which is the means of the attainment and protection of the earth inhabited by men. The subject is to be understood either by implication or inference. It may be presumed, however, that the definition about a certain principle or ingredient may cover the subject matter in its entirety, which on occasions has to be understood either by application, or implication; and at times by indication or analogy, followed or preceded by enumeration or explanation. What is applicable everywhere is an invariable rule. The subject enunciated in this Book is 'THE METHOD OF THE SCIENCE' wherein are seriated devices used in the treatment of the science.

CHAPTER ONE

SECTION 180: DEVICES USED IN THE TREATMENT OF THE SCIENCE

1. The source of the livelihood of men is wealth, in other words, the earth inhabited by men.
2. The science which is the means of the attainment and protection of that earth is the Science of Politics.
3. That contains thirty-two devices of treatment: topic, statement of contents, employment of sentences, meaning of words, reason for establishing something, mention, explanation, advice, reference, application, indication, analogy, implication, doubt, similar situation, contrary corollary, completion of a sentence, agreement,

emphasising, derivation of a word, illustration, exception, one's own technical term, the *prima facie* view, the correct view, invariable rule, reference to a future statement, reference to a past statement, restriction, option, combination, and what is understood.

4. The object, with respect to which a statement is made, is the topic.
5. For instance: 'This single treatise on the Science of Politics is composed mostly by bringing the teachings of as many treatises on the Science of Polities as have been composed by the ancient teachers for the acquisition and protection of the earth.'
6. A serial enumeration of the sections of the science is statement of contents.
7. For instance: 'Enumeration of the sciences, association with elders, control over the senses, appointment of ministers,' and so on.
8. The arrangement of a sentence is employment of sentences.
9. For instance: 'The people, of the four *varnas* and in the four *asramas*'.
10. That which has its limit in the word is the meaning of the word.
11. For instance: *mulahara* is the word.
12. 'He who consumes in unjust ways the property inherited from the father and the grandfather is *mulahara*,' is the meaning.
13. A reason proving a thing is the reason for establishing a thing.
14. For instance: 'For, spiritual good and sensual pleasures depend on material well-being.'
15. A statement in brief is mention.
16. For instance: 'Control over the senses is motivated by training in the sciences.'
17. A detailed statement is explanation.
18. For instance: 'Absence of improper indulgence in the pleasures of sound, touch, colour, taste and smell by the sense of hearing, touch and sight, the tongue and the sense of smell, means control over the senses.'
19. 'One should behave in this manner,' is advice.
20. For instance: 'He should enjoy sensual pleasures without contravening his spiritual good and material well-being; he should not deprive himself of pleasures.'
21. 'So and so says this' is reference.
22. For instance: "He should appoint a council consisting of twelve ministers," say the followers of Manu. "Sixteen," say the followers of Brhaspati. "Twenty," say the followers of Usanas. "According to capacity," says Kautilya.

23. Setting forth a thing with what is already said is application.
24. For instance: 'Non-conveyance of gifts is explained by the non-payment of debts.'
25. Setting forth a thing with what is going to be said is indication.
26. For instance: 'Or, by means of conciliation, gifts, dissension and force, as well shall explain in the section on troubles.'
27. Setting forth an unknown thing with the help of the known is analogy.
28. For instance: 'He should, like a father, show favours to those whose exemptions have eased.'
29. That which, though not stated, follows as a matter of course is implication.
30. For instance: 'One conversant with the ways of the world should resort to a king endowed with personal excellences and the excellences of material constituents through such as are dear and beneficial to the king.'
31. That he should not resort through one who is not dear and beneficial follows as a matter of course.
32. A thing with reasons on both sides is doubt.
33. For instance: 'Should one march against a king with impoverished and greedy subjects or a king with rebellious subjects?'
34. A thing common to another topic is similar situation.
35. For instance: 'In a place assigned to him for agricultural work and so on, exactly as before.'
36. Setting forth a thing with the help of the opposite is contrary corollary.
37. For instance: 'The opposite, as those of one displeased.'
38. That by which a sentence is completed is completion of a sentence.
39. For instance: 'And there is loss of all activity on the part of the king, as of a bird with clipped wings.'
40. There, 'of a bird' is the completion of the sentence.
41. The statement of another, not contradicted, is agreement.
42. For instance: 'Two wings, a centre and reserves,—this is the arrangement of a battle-array according to Usanas.'
43. The description of a speciality is emphasising.
44. For instance: 'And in particular, in the case of oligarchies and of royal families having the character of an oligarchy, there are dissensions caused by gambling and destruction caused by that; hence it is the most evil among vices, as it favours evil men and leads to weakness in administration.'

45. Deriving the meaning of a word through its components derivation.
46. For instance: 'It throws out a person from his good, hence it is called *vyasana*.
47. Exemplifying by means of an example is illustration.
48. For instance: 'For, going to war with the stronger, he engages as it were in a fight on foot with an elephant.'
49. Taking away from a rule of universal application is exception.
50. For instance: 'He should always station alien troops in close proximity to himself, except in case of fear of a rising in the interior.'
51. A word, not agreed to by others, is one's own technical term.
52. For instance: 'The would-be conqueror is the first constituent; one immediately next to his territory is the second; one separated by an intervening territory is the third.'
53. A statement to be rejected is the *prima facie* view.
54. For instance: 'Of calamities befalling the king and the minister, the calamity of the minister is more serious.'
55. A statement giving the final view on that is the correct view.
56. For instance: 'Being dependent on him; for, the king is in the place of the head'.
57. What is applicable everywhere is invariable rule.
58. For instance: 'Therefore, he should himself be energetically active.'
59. 'This will be stated afterwards' is reference to a future statement.
60. For instance: 'Weights and measures we shall explain in the section on the Superintendent of Standardisation.'
61. 'This has been stated before' is reference to a past statement.
62. For instance: 'The excellences of a minister have been stated before.'
63. 'Thus, and in no other way' is restriction.
64. For instance: 'Therefore, he should instruct him in what conduces to spiritual and material good, not in what is spiritually and materially harmful.'
65. 'Either in this way or in that' is option.
66. For instance: 'Or, daughters, born in the pious marriages.'
67. 'In this way and in that' is combination.
68. For instance: 'Begotten by oneself, the son becomes the heir to his father and kinsmen.'
69. The doing of what is not expressly stated is what is understood.
70. For instance: 'And experts shall fix revocation in such a way that neither the donor nor the donee is injured.'
71. Thus, this science, expounded with these devices of a science, has been composed for the acquisition and protection of this world and of the next.

72. This science brings into being and preserves spiritual good, material well-being and pleasures, and destroys spiritual evil, material loss and hatred.
73. This science has been composed by him, who in resentment, quickly regenerated the science and the weapon and the earth that was under the control of the Nanda kings.

Herewith ends the Fifteenth Book of the Arthasastra of Kautilya

'THE METHOD OF THE SCIENCE'

Seeing the manifold errors of the writers of commentaries on scientific treatises, Visnugupta himself composed the sutra as well as the bhasya.

HEREWITH ENDS THE ARTHASASTRA OF KAUTILYA.

30

Conclusion

Foreign authors and critics compare Arthasastra with political philosophy propounded by Plato, Aristotle, Machiavelli, Bismarck, Hobbes, Marx, Engel and others, and often comment that it is a very misplaced patriotism which asks others to admire Arthasastra as representing the fine flower of the Indian political thought. A fundamental difference between Arthasastra and the Greek and European writings on politics is in regard to the purpose for which they were written. The aim of the Arthasastra is thoroughly practical, to show how a state should be ruled. Greek writers scarcely concern themselves with this. Plato and Aristotle are rather concerned with the problem of the realisation of the highest good of man, how best this can be achieved through the state, and that is what they sought to investigate. Here they tried to visualise the perfect state. Plato's *Republic* is such a search for the ideal state, where justice, regarded as the highest good of man, could be perfectly assured. Justice, Plato thought, was hindered by ignorance and selfishness. His remedy for the former is the specialisation of the social functions of the state, society being divided into three classes as rulers or guardians, fighters and farmers (men of gold, of silver, and of iron and brass respectively). His remedy for selfishness was communism of a sort, involving the abolition not only of property, but also of the family. It is obvious that Plato's *Republic* is an ideal that can never be realised in the realm of practical politics as can be seen from Aristotle's criticism of it.

It should be remembered that Plato offered other solutions too. In the politics, he advocated absolute monarchy, where the ruler is unfettered by public opinion and unhampered by law. This is an extreme solution, which presupposes a monarch who must be all wise, much more practical to follow in the laws; where Plato abandons communism, recognizes the need of a patriarchial family and recommends a mixed constitution, a mixture of monarchy, oligarchy and democracy. The high idealism that permeated Plato's writings, particularly the *Republic* has inspired political thinking in the Western World all through the centuries; and also set the tone for later political thinkers. Since Plato's day, politics had been a branch of philosophy and significantly, the change has now been made from political philosophy to political science. There is little in common between Plato and Arthasastra. The latter does not look upon politics as a branch of philosophy. It has its own ideas of the highest good of man, but it does not regard the state as formed for the realisation of that good. It, therefore, keeps personal morality distinct from public good, and its practical realism is in sharp contrast with Plato's idealism.

Aristotle was a senior contemporary of Kautilya. He died in 322 B.C. about the time when the latter was plotting to overthrow the Nanda and help ascend Candragupta Maurya on the throne of Magadha. It is evident that Aristotle's pupil, Alexander's conquest could not be influenced by Aristotle's teaching, which is centred on the conception of the city state, a conception that ceased to have any meaning as a result of that very conquest. In like manner, Kautilya shows no awareness in his work of Candragupta's conquest, contenting himself mainly with the politics and policies of a moderate-sized state. 'Politics' of Aristotle is not written with the practical aim of showing how government should run. It is a theoretical investigation of political problems in terms of their basis in human association and of ends obtainable through such association. Like Plato, Aristotle, too, thinks in terms of the perfect state and analyses methods of various forms of state's constitution, monarchy, aristocracy, etc. with a view to find out which is best suited for the attainment of the highest good. He would tolerate monarchy only when there is one who is 'pre-eminent in virtue'. Aristotle defines a citizen as one who has the power to take part in the daliberative or judicial administration of state, and he limited the number to as less as possible, as he believed that, too large a number impairs the pursuits of a life of virtue, and also makes direct participation in the exercise of sovereignty by all citizens difficult. For participation, befitting education of citizens was emphasized; and in citizens, he excluded slaves. The cleavage between citizen and non-citizen was intended to be permanent by Greek philosopher, and Aristotle defended slavery as natural. At that time in the city state of Athens the number of citizens was 50,000 as against 100,000 slaves, whose labour sustained practically its entire economy and prosperity, and as human-beings they had no independence. Their status was much more worse than that of *sudras* in India, who were an inalienable portion of the Indian subjects, as per the history of that period. It proves the basic fact that no political philosophy can be detached from history, and it has to be formed and moulded according to the exigencies.

In contemporary India there were also inequalities as exhibited in the four *varnas* system, which Arthasastra fully endorses. Although the rights and privileges of the *sudras* were limited, they were not slaves. Greek political thought was part of a complete philosophy of man, who had to be idealistic, ethical, to be realised by himself, here, on this earth, in his life; and the state was intended to make the realisation of these ideals possible. The Arthasastra is not concerned with the problems of the highest good of man. That is left to philosophy of religion and spiritual edicts enumerated by *Dharmasastra*, which was not the domain of the state and, therefore, Kautilya kept it beyond the pale of his treatise. Nevertheless, the state was duty bound to protect these spiritual edicts and suitably punish the violators. According to ancient Indian tradition, ruler was not supposed to modify, amend or annul any spiritual edict of *Dharmasastra*. Therefore, Kautilya concentrated all his attention on the practical aspects of government. When one thinks of the long line of political thinkers in the West from Plato down to Marx and Engel, who made significant and original contributions to the subject of political science, the comparative barrenness of Indian thought in this field can scarcely be denied. The Arthasastra of Kautilya has practically said about all the multidimensional parameters of the subject. In the concluding verses, Kautilya asserted that the science propounded in the Arthasastra brings into being and preserves spiritual good, material well-being and pleasures, and destroys evil, material loss and hatred; and the science has been composed and expounded for the acquisition and protection of this world and the next. Kautilya was the grand-master of this science, and what he did not know was no knowledge.

The science has known no growth in India as the independence of the country was usurped for a greater period by foreign invaders over the last two thousand years. No political philosophy can be detached from its environment of history; and the conquerors had their own pattern of administration up to 1947; when India became Independent and chose to be governed as a secular democratic state through the institutions of Parliament, comprising of peoples' representatives. In consequence, Arthasastra has lost much of its relevance, *albeit* the successive alien governments made use of it only to achieve their objective of permanent subjugation of this sub-continent together with its population. It was used by them more for the protection of the rulers, rather than for the benefit of the subjects. Whenever there was a struggle for independence by the native kings, to free any territory of the country from foreign subjugation or bondage, the rulers of the freed territory were abided by the principles propounded in the Arthasastra and protected their state and the subjects according to the guidelines contained in this sastra.

The Arthasastra of Kautilya is essentially a treatise on the art of government by a monarch in that era of 330 B.C. when regal power was the rule throughout the world. In both respects—internal administration and foreign relations—the comprehensiveness of its treatment is till date unmatched and unparalleled. It rouses interest due to the antiquity to which it is ascribed, and the all pervading instructions given by Kautilya for the guidance of all kings and is meant to be useful everywhere and at all times in order to ensure and secure efficient administration for the prosperity and the well-being of the subjects. There is little doubt that most of his teachings were derived from earlier authorities and he updated them *mutatis mutandis*.

Foreign authors and commentators compared Kautilya with Bismarck, Machiavelli and Hobbes, but Kautilya and his Arthasastra emerged much more greater than them, although all of them deliberated on the following points: (1) Man is governed more by passion than by reason necessitating the control over him by the state through some suitable punishments. (2) Nations are always hostile, hence the need to get rid of the enemy by any means, including fraud or force and ends justifying the means. (3) Reasons of state must prevail over religious sentiments. (4) There are no limits to absolute sovereignty. The standpoint of these authors is that of 'Real politics' and hence according to them the statesman has to be dishonest, unorthodox, impious and egotistical, although at the same time he must be self-restrained and active with relentless candour and sobriety and eschew fatalism.

Today the administrative machinery is largely different. A number of departments visualised in Arthasastra has no place in the present set up. On the other hand, a number of departments has come into being of which the Arthasastra had little conception at that period of time. Nonetheless, what it has to say on some matters, is not without relevance even in the present day conditions. Its views, about the state servants, their qualifications and appointments, their abhorable corruptibility and ways of keeping them in check, are not quite irrelevant when scandalous scams like sugar, telecommunication, allotment of houses, animal husbandry, urea imports, and several others, big or small, by high Government officials, Governors, Chief Ministers etc., made the country suffer unprecedented and fabulous losses running into several thousand cores of rupees. On the top of it, these leaders had indulged in the fabrication of evidence to defend themselves. The Central Bureau of Investigation (CBI) tried to bale out some of them. The High Court and the Supreme Court were compelled to monitor the investigations of the aberrant police officers. Corruptions escalated to new height when some of the Members of Parliament were purchased by the head of the Congress Party in order to manoeuvre the majority in the Parliament. For all such acts of treason, the Arthasastra has prescribed the ultimate punishment of death with torture.

Its recommendations about the secret service for keeping watch and counter-watch over state employees or over political activities or for purposes of criminal investigation, espionage and counter-espionage positively have a bearing even today. The law which it embodies is the same law, which coming down through the *smritis* has been in force through all these centuries and is only now being replaced or modified by a code applicable to the whole of India. The very liberal views expressed in this treatise on many matters could well be of interest even to modern legislature.

The strict control of economic life by the state that is visualised in this text is something not dissimilar to what is being actually practised all over the modern states. Even those, that are not totalitarian cannot but afford to follow a policy of *laissez faire*. Moreover, the disintegration of various Communist states in Europe in the recent past has shown the general aversion of the people to this totalitarian form of government. The reservation of certain spheres for the public sector and the regulation of private enterprise are features characteristic of the economic policy being followed at present in India. In essence, the Arthasastra recommends a similar vibrant policy and there lies Kautilya's comprehensive visionary capabilities before over two thousand years, when the concept of socialistic pattern of government *vis-a-vis* society was not even dreamt of, as monarchy was the order of the day throughout the world and supported by spiritual edicts. Its modest aim was the welfare of the subjects together with the advancement of the state, and it is cognate in today's administrative set up, although in the sphere of foreign policy the *sastra* has lost much of its validity. Even then, what it had enumerated about foreign policy is still largely true, when we have the same distrust of one nation by another, the same pursuit of its own interest by every nation tempered only by consideration of expediency, the same efforts to secure alliance with the same cynical disregard of them in self-interest, the same kind of intelligence service maintained by one nation in the territory of another, which we find referred to in the Arthasastra. The present day cold war tactics are not essentially different from what the text recommends to *vijigisu* when placed in similar situation.

Now with the unlimited devastative powers of atomic weaponry, the danger arising from fanaticism or insensate hatred has become so great that an abhorable race to acquire more and more nuclear strength has started in various countries of the world, and in consequence, the essential wherewithals meant for the benefit of the subjects are being diverted for the purchase of these weapons. They cumulatively threaten the very existence of humanity. Our relations with Pakistan and China for the last 50 years should be taken into consideration in this respect.

However, the advent of the nuclear age installed the United Nations Organization (UNO), which failed to strengthen its hold on its constituents and maintain peace and tranquility among the belligerent states. Even the UNO could not check the rising tide of genocide currently taking place in various countries of the world. The big powers (so-called 'vijigisu') have made the UNO impotent and infructuous. Such type of *vijigisu*, who fails to ameliorate the living condition of the millions of people was never contemplated by Kautilya in his Arthasastra, but contrarily he prescribed severe punishment to such enemies of human race.

Although, a new factor—'World Opinion', has emerged in recent times as a check on blatantly selfish policies, it is difficult to see how rivalry and the struggle for supremacy between the nations can be avoided, and the teachings of the *sastra* which are based on these very realities, rendered altogether superfluous until some sort of one world government, or an effective supranational authority is established. But until that happens, which is the remotest possibility, the preachings of Arthasastra could in actual practice be followed by nations of the world though they may be unknown to them, or they may be openly criticized or condemned by those who know them. And this immemorability has crowned perennial and sublime glory on ARTHASASTRA AND ITS PROGINATOR KAUTILYA THE GREAT.

Appendix 'A'

LOCALITIES AND PEOPLES

Sr. No.	Name used in Arthasastra	Present Identification
1	2	3
1.	Ahichchhatraka	Capital of north Pancala. Modern Ramnager in Bareilly District
2.	Alakanda	Laccadiva Islands
3.	Anga	East Bihar
4.	Angaras	Between Vidisa, the Narmada, Brahmabardhan and the Pariyatra Mts.
5.	Antaravati	In Kamrup (Modern Assam)
6.	Apranta	North Kokana
7.	Aratta	Vahika near the Vipasa
8.	Aroha	In the Himalayas
9.	Asmakas	The Central Godavari Region near Pratishana (Modern Paithan)
10.	Asokagramika	In Kamrup (Modern Assam)
11.	Bahlava	Bactria
12.	Bahlika	Bactria (Modern Balkh)
13.	Cedi	Cedi Karusaka-vana lies between Mekala, Tripuri, Dasarna, Ganga and Himvat
14.	Cina	Cina
15.	*Das'-arnas*	Das'arna-vana lies between the Das'arna, Mahagiri, Vindhys, and Vetravati

1	2	3
16.	Devasabha	Devasaila—Devabhadra near the Bhadra tributary of the Tunga river
17.	Donga	In Kamrup (Modern Assam)
18.	Dvadasa grama	Near Badrinath
19.	Gauda	Kamrupa Region (Modern Assam)
20.	Gosirsa	Unidentified
21.	Grameru	Unidentified
22.	Hari	Unidentified
23.	Hataka	Unidentified
24.	Indravana	Kalinga/Kalindi (Bihar and Orissa region)
25.	Indravanaka	Kalinga
26.	Jongaka and Tampa Japa, Jonga, Turup	In Kamrup (Modern Assam)
27.	Kalinga	In the region of Bhubaneshwar
28.	Kamboja	Ancient Kingdom, north of Gandhara
29.	Kasi	Country around Varanasi
30.	Kastira rastra	Kasmir
31.	Kukuras	In Punjab
32.	Kurus	In Meerut Dist. and Delhi Region
33.	Licchivikas	In Vasali on the left bank of river Gandak.
34.	Madhyamarastraka	In Kosala
35.	Madhura	Madhura (in the north) and Madhura (in the south)
36.	Madrakas	In N.E. part of Punjab or adjoining region
37.	Magadha	Patna and Gaya districts
38.	Mahisa	Mahismati, Mahisamandal (Northern part of Mysore State in the 5th cent.), Mahisas
39.	Mallakas	Malloi on both banks of the Hydraotes (Old channel of the Jhelum river in Punjab)

1	2	3
40.	Mala	Part of Malaya
41.	Nepala	Nepal
42.	Odra	Orissa
43.	Pancalas	In North Pancala: Rohilkhand division of U.P. South Pancala: Farrukhabad district of the Ganga Basin
44.	Pancanadas	Between Kuruksetra, Kalika kanan, the Sindhu and Himvat
45.	Panchajana	Pancanadas Preferred.
46.	Pandyakavata	Mt. Malayakoti Negapatam/Ramnad, the port of embarkation for Sri Lanka (Ceylon)
47.	Papeya	Uncertain
48.	Parasmadraka	Island of Simhala
49.	Pundras	Western and Northern Bengal Varendri lying in Gauda
50.	Purnakadvipa	In Kamrup (Modern Assam)
51.	Sabha-rastra	Vidarbha
52.	Sakala	Sialkot: Madra District around Sialkot, Capital of the Madras (Jartikas and Bahikas) now in Pakistan
53.	Saurastras	Kathiawad Gujrat State
54.	Sauvira	East of the Lower Indus included Multan in the north
55.	Sitodaka	Uncertain
56.	Sindhu	West of the Lower (Country and Indus People)
57.	Srotasi	In the sea off the coast of Barbara or Parpara
58.	Surastras	The Saurastraka-vana lies between Avanti, the Narmada, Dvarja and Arbuda
59.	Survacala	could not be identified

1	2	3
60.	Survarna-Kudya	In Kamrup (Modren Assam)
61.	Svarnabhumi	Burma
62.	Tajjamarastra	Bhogavalli in the Kalingas
63.	Taitala	Titala in Orissa
64.	Vaivarnaka Vivarna	The Ocean near the island of Yavanas
65.	Vanayu	Arabia Persia
66.	Vanga Vangas	East Bengal
67.	Vatsas	Kosaumbi
68.	Vivarna	See No. 64
69.	Vrijikas	North of Patna

MOUNTAINS AND MOUNTAIN RANGES

1.	Cakarvala	Mythical Mountain could not be identified
2.	Himavat	Himalaya
3.	Kailasa	Kailasa
4.	Kala	In Malaya Region
5.	Kambu	Unidentified
6.	Kosagara	*Ibid.*
7.	Koti	Between Malaya and the sea
8.	Kuta	As above
9.	Mahendra	The Eastern Ghats
10.	Manimanta	In the Uttarpath
11.	Mala	Part of Malaya
12.	Muleya (Mata)	Unindentified
13.	Naga	In Malaya Region
14.	Parasumdrakah	Mt. Rohana in Sri Lanka
15.	Satakumba	Unidentified
16.	Satana	Unidentified
17.	Srikantak	Unidentified
18.	Trnasa	From the mountain on the bank of the river Trnasa (Trsrnga)
19.	Tuttha	Could not be identified

1	2	3
20.	Vedokata	Unidentified
21.	Venu	Probably close to the source of the Venumati river near Panna.

RIVERS AND OTHER WATER-BODIES

1.	Curna Curni	Near Muraci in Kerala (the Caurneya)
2.	Ganga	Ganga, Ganges
3.	Hadra	Lake Srighanta in the sea of coast Barbara/in the sea Parpara.
4.	Jambu	Near Mt. Meru
5.	Kardama	In Parasika
		In Conidesa in the Uttarapatha
6.	Kasi	Same as for Mahendra Parvata river of the same name
7.	Kula	Near Mayurgrama in Sri Lanka
8.	Lauhitya	Brahmaputra
9.	Pasika/ Pasikan country	The Pasika in Pandya
10.	Sitodaka	A river in Malaya Region
11.	Srotasi	On the shore of Barbara/Papara
12.	Tamraparni	Tamraparni (in the extreme south of India) most probably Tamil Nadu
13.	Tapi	Tapi

Bibliography

ENGLISH

A Concise Encyclopaedia of a Indian History, M.B. Chande, 1995, Delhi.

The Police in India, M.B. Chande, 1996, Delhi.

Arthasastra of Kautilya, R. Shama Sastri, (Mysore, 1924).

The Arthasastra of Kautilya (New Edition) J. Jolly and R. Schmidt, Vol. I, Text Vol. II, Notes with the Commentary, Lahore, 1923.

The Kautilya Arthasastra, R.P. Kangle (Three Volumes, Bombay, 1969).

The *Arthasastra of Kautilya*, Shamasastry, R., Bangalore, 1960.

HINDI

Kautilya Arthasastra, with Hindi commentary, Ramteja Sastri Pandeya (Kashi, 1959).

Kautilya Arthasastra, Mimonsa, G.D. Tamaskar, 1920, Allahabad.

Kautaliya Arthasastra, Vidyalankar Prannath, Lahore, 1923.

Kautaliya Arthasastra, Sastri Udayvira, Lahore, 1925.

Kautaliya Arthasastra, Shastri Gangaprasadji, Delhi, 1940.

Kautaliya Arthasastra, Sastri Devadatta, Allahabad, 1957.

MARATHI

Kautaliya Arthasastra, H.A. Bhave, Pune.

Kautaliya Arthasastra, Mr. and Mrs. Hardas, Nagpur.

Kautaliya Arthasastra, Karandikar, J.S. and Hivargaonkar, Karjat, 1927-1928.

Kautaliya Arthasastra, Pradipa, Tipnis, G.G., Bombay.

OTHER WORKS IN ENGLISH

Hindu Culture in Greater India, Swami Sadanand, 1949.

Early History of India, Smith, V. A.

The Gupta Empire, Mookerji, R.K.

Political History of Ancient India, Raye Chaudhari, H.C.

Ancient India as described by Megasthenes and Arrian, McCrindle & Basham, A.L. Delhi, 1983.

A Cultural History of India, Oxford University Press, Basham, A.L., Delhi, 1983.

Imperial History of India, Jayswal, K.P.

Cambridge History of India, Burn Richard and Haig and Burn.

Ancient History of India, Mahajan, V.D.

Public Administration in Ancient India, Banerjea, P.N.

The State in Ancient India, Beni Prasad, Allahabad, 1928.

Some Aspects of Ancient Hindu Polity, Bhandarkar, D.R., Benares, 1929.

Candragupta Maurya and His Times, Mookerji, R.K., Mardas, 1943.

A Study of the Economic Conditions of Ancient India, Pran Nath, London, 1929.

Sovereignty in Ancient Indian Polity, Sinha, H.N., London, 1938.

The Kautaliya Arthasastra on Forms of Government, Deb, H.K.

Kautilya Studies, Our Heritage, Hazra, R.C. (Calcutta, 1962).

The Geography of Kautilya, Trivedi, H.V.

Mahabharata.

Bhagwad Geeta.

Plato's *Republic*.

Various books on Political Science and Criminology.

Index of Principal Topics

How to read *e.g.*, Accounts, checking of, 2.7.16-40. It means 2 is Book number. 7 is the chapter number. 16-40. Serial numbers in that chapter. Please also see pages 68 to 76.